OUTRIDER *of* EMPIRE

THE LIFE AND ADVENTURES
OF ROGER POCOCK
(1865–1941)

Gerald Hudson, portrait of *Captain Roger Pocock*.

[Scanned, with permission from the Legion of Frontiersmen
(Countess Mountbatten's Own), from a print owned by the author.]

OUTRIDER of EMPIRE

The Life & Adventures of

1865 1941 ROGER POCOCK

GEOFFREY A. POCOCK

THE UNIVERSITY
of ALBERTA PRESS

Published by
The University of Alberta Press
Ring House 2
Edmonton, Alberta, Canada T6G 2E1
Copyright © 2007 Geoffrey A. Pocock

LIBRARY AND ARCHIVES CANADA
CATALOGUING IN PUBLICATION
Pocock, Geoffrey A., 1938–
Outrider of empire : the life and adventures
of Roger Pocock / Geoffrey A. Pocock ;
foreword by Merrill Distad.

Includes bibliographical references
and index.

ISBN 978-0-88864-448-0

1. Pocock, Roger, 1865–1941.
2. Adventure and adventurers—Great
   Britain—Biography.
3. Travelers—Great Britain—Biography.
4. Legion of Frontiersmen—Biography.
5. Authors, English—19th century—
   Biography.
6. Authors, English—20th century—
   Biography.
7. North West Mounted Police (Canada)—
   Biography.
I. Title.

DA69.3.P63P63 2007 941.081092
C2007-903767-4

Copyediting by Brendan Wild and Linda Distad
Indexing by Judy Dunlop
Book design by Jason Dewinetz

Every effort has been made to provide
proper acknowledgement for photographs
that appear in this book. If any information
is incorrect, please contact the press and we
will update the information in subsequent
editons.

The University of Alberta Press is committed to protecting our natural environment.
As part of our efforts, this book is printed
on Enviro Paper: it contains 100% post-
consumer recycled fibres and is acid- and
chlorine-free.

The University of Alberta Press gratefully
acknowledges the support received for
its publishing program from The Canada
Council for the Arts. The University of
Alberta Press also gratefully acknowledges
the financial support of the Government of
Canada through the Book Publishing Industry Development Program (BPIDP) and
from the Alberta Foundation for the Arts for
its publishing activities.

Canada   Canada Council   Conseil des Arts
for the Arts   du Canada

CONTENTS

FOREWORD

THE BRITISH EMPIRE REACHED ITS GREATEST extent and prosperity during the late-Victorian and Edwardian eras, between 1870 and 1914. It also engendered a vast literature that ranges from history and biography to fiction, both popular and literary. The advent of motion pictures created a further medium for dramatic portrayals of imperial themes.

The literature and cinema of empire once existed largely to celebrate and promote the virtues and glory of a vast empire upon which, proverbially, the sun never set. Over the course of the last century, however, the devolution of that empire, clearer assessments of its malign effects upon aboriginal people, assertion of unique national identities among Britain's former colonies and self-governing dominions, and shifting social values have all but extinguished the triumphalism that formerly characterized both the popular and scholarly portrayals of British imperial history. Indeed, the post-colonial era brought forth an abundance of books and films that catalogued and condemned the iniquities of imperialism. These, in turn, have elicited books reasserting the more positive aspects of empire. Such value judgements will continue to shift over time, but are quite extraneous to the primary task confronting historians and biographers, which is to describe, analyze, and explain both the events of the past and the lives of its men and women.

The biographical literature of the Empire is replete with studies of many prominent empire builders, especially the colonial proconsuls, governors, and administrators who maintained Britain's imperial authority over a quarter of the globe and its inhabitants. Nor is there any shortage of accounts written by, or biographies of, those whose many contributions to the Empire were more mundane, for the British Empire was a collective enterprise that depended upon the contributions of explorers, prospectors, sailors, and merchants who extended its boundaries and exploited its resources and markets; of soldiers and lawmen who established and maintained peace and order; of settlers and missionaries who transplanted

their own culture; and of journalists and writers who recorded and celebrated its development and progress.

Roger Pocock was an outstanding example of the men and women
who built and sustained the Empire, because he played so many of those
roles at one time or another during a lengthy career that included service
in three wars on as many continents. Working by turns as a NorthWest
Mounted Policeman, peddler, journalist, missionary, sailor, prospector,
soldier, amateur spy, novelist, and artist, Roger struggled to make his mark,
and a living, in any way he could. While his failures were many and often
self-inflicted, he never lost faith, including an earnest faith and belief in
the righteousness of the British Empire, of which he was a true son, born
in Wales, and raised in England and Canada (his "second native land").

As a writer, Roger celebrated and idolized Canada and his beloved
Mounted Police, yet, with a characteristic candour that often landed him
in trouble, he sharply criticized its government for its often shameful treatment of First Nations people. His brief service in the NWMP during the
North-West Rebellion of 1885 provided him with a wealth of inspiration
for his writing and for his most significant contribution to the Empire,
the founding of the Legion of Frontiersmen.

This engaging biography, based upon original sources and two decades
of research, recounts a life filled with both adventure and mishap. Roger,
the author notes, "lived a life that many an adventurous boy of the time
might have desired." It was, indeed, a life reminiscent of stories in *Boy's
Own* or *Chums*. In a sense, Roger Pocock embodied the highest hopes
and aspirations of the British imperial ideal, which throughout his life he
promoted and defended.

MERRILL DISTAD
University of Alberta

ACKNOWLEDGEMENTS

THIS BOOK HAS BEEN MANY LONG YEARS in the writing and also re-writing as the paper chase that Roger Pocock left around the world has slowly given up its treasures. Over these many years countless people and organizations have been asked for and freely given their help and advice. Sadly, many of those individuals who supported the project with enthusiasm from the early years are no longer with us. It would take many pages of this book to list all the good people who have helped in one way or another, so I must ask them to accept that their support has been greatly appreciated and without it the story of Roger Pocock would never have been told. Some forty years ago, the naval historian, Tom Pocock, another member of the Pocock "clan," considered writing Roger Pocock's biography and did some early research work. He kindly handed those results to me and always gave me encouragement, although his death in the early summer of 2007 has meant that he will not see the written story that always interested him greatly. Of others who have died during this period I will only mention one, the late Capt Charles Dudley, nephew of Harwood Steele and grandson of Sam Steele. Charles Dudley died suddenly and unacceptably young. He had always been most generous in allowing me access to the Roger Pocock papers he owned and supportive of my work. He would have been delighted to know that this biography has now been published. Roger Pocock's nephew, Kennedy (Ken) Pocock, was always unstinting with his help and advice. Since his death, his daughter, Mrs. Laurie Leonard, and all her family have continued that support.

Since the University of Alberta Press offered to publish this biography, several individuals at the University of Alberta have supported this project, and have given unstintingly of their time: Ernie Ingles, Vice-Provost and Chief Librarian, Merrill Distad, Associate Director of Libraries, and Jeff Papineau at the Bruce Peel Special Collections Library. Linda Distad has been a careful guide, ensuring that I kept to the trail and did not get lost in the wilderness of tracks leading off our main path of research. I would also like to thank the staff of the University of Alberta Press for their help: Linda Cameron, Michael Luski, Cathie Crooks, Alan Brownoff, Jeff Carpenter and Peter Midgley all contributed their expertise. The University of Alberta Press would also like to thank Brendan Wild for his copyediting and proofreading and Judy Dunlop for indexing.

I have also been fortunate to be able to call on the advice of some true friends who have shared my fascination with the exceptional organization that Roger Pocock founded, the Legion of Frontiersmen. From the time of my earliest researches, Graham Bunting of New Zealand urged me on. B.W. "Will" Shandro of Edmonton and Dean Bruckshaw of Surrey, B.C., Bruce Fuller in New Zealand, and Brian Tarpey in Malta have always been there for me with words of wisdom. Many a long-distance telephone conversation with Will Shandro has successfully cleared my mind of problems. I have also been able to enjoy the support of countless other members of today's Legion of Frontiersmen under their Patron, the Countess Mountbatten of Burma.

My wonderful wife of 50 years and my family have kept my feet firmly on the ground. My son, whose naming as Roger first led me onto the trail of the original Roger Pocock, has also carefully read my writings and pointed out grammatical errors in need of correction. Any that remain are mine and not his.

Heather Lane at the Scott Polar Research Institute provided valuable assistance, as did Doug Cass at the Glenbow Museum in Calgary, Carmen Harry at the RCMP Museum in Regina, Graham Bradshaw of the University of Toronto Library, and Jennifer Toews at the Thomas Fisher Rare Book Library, University of Toronto. Kenneth Tingley of Edmonton contributed to the legwork at the National Library and Archives Canada in Ottawa. The Secretary and Archivist of Charterhouse kindly supplied me with photocopies of the correspondence regarding Roger's application for leave and gave permission for this material to be reproduced. The staff at the National Archives at Kew have always been most friendly and helpful and this also applies to the many libraries and archives, both small and large, that I have consulted. I can only apologize that there were too many to mention individually.

To those many friends, acquaintances and correspondents whom I am unable to mention, please accept my grateful thanks. The publication of the story of this extraordinary man, Roger Pocock, shows that all the work has been worthwhile.

Lavant, Chichester, England
June 2007

OUTRIDER *of* EMPIRE

THE LIFE AND ADVENTURES OF ROGER POCOCK (1865–1941)

Roger Pocock, Founder of The Legion of Frontiersmen.

INTRODUCTION

Civilisation is a poor thing to one who has lived the
spacious life of the West, for no splendour of cities or rural
comfort can make amends for that. It is all very well for a
tame man...to be contented with quite limited matters —
he knows nothing about it; but one who has been a citizen
of the enchanted land cries to ride again with the vanguard
of mankind, to fight at the front clearing a road for the
world, to live the generous life, to die the fearless death,
and be forgotten as becomes a frontiersman.[1]

ONE LATE SUMMER DAY IN 1899, a solitary unarmed Englishman,
leading two packhorses, rode up to the main log cabin at what came to
be known as Robbers' Roost in Utah. Followers of Wild West yarns and
western films might next expect to read that The Wild Bunch greeted him
with a hail of bullets. On the contrary, Roger Pocock, for this was the name
of the brave (or some might say foolhardy) fellow, was welcomed peacefully
into this outlaw haven, for news of his arrival had surely preceded him
along the bush telegraph that alerted people living in lonely settlements
to strangers in the area. The residents of Robbers' Roost quickly realized
that this representative from *Lloyd's Weekly Newspaper,* one of the most
popular English newspapers of its time, was no more than an eager collector of tales and was no threat to them. Roger treated the outlaws with
unusual respect and without appearing judgemental. He loved listening
to the stories of those he met on his travels, including the outlaws of The
Wild Bunch, ranchers, lawmen, sailors, and soldiers, for they provided
him with material for his prolific output of journalism and fiction that was
eagerly consumed by all classes of readers.

Roger Pocock was himself no stranger to adventure. Before his twentieth birthday, as a green recruit in Canada's North-West Mounted Police
(NWMP), he served in the campaign that crushed the North-West Rebellion

of 1885. In the decade following his service in the N W M P, he roamed the Canadian and American West as an itinerant peddler, salesman, prospector, sailor, sealer, missionary, and—most successfully—as a journalist and writer. In 1898, succumbing to the twin lures of adventure and profit, he organized and led an expedition bound for the Klondike gold fields, one that not only failed to reach its goal, but, partly due to his shortcomings as a leader, led to the death of one of its members, Sir Arthur Curtis. Stung by criticism of his role in this fiasco, and by whispered accusations that he had robbed and murdered Curtis, Roger left London in 1899 and sought to repair his reputation through a spectacular feat of horsemanship. Riding from Fort Macleod in Canada's North-West Territories to Mexico City, through a wilderness of mountains and deserts, and along the so-called Outlaw Trail, he set a record for long-distance rides. Throughout this remarkable journey, Roger provided thrilling accounts of his adventures for countless readers of *Lloyd's Weekly Newspaper*.

The success of Roger's great ride could not dull for long his thirst for adventure, however, and the prolonged war in South Africa proved an irresistible attraction. Setting out to report on the war as a freelance journalist, he was soon serving in the field in an irregular unit of National Scouts, a reprise of the military life he had so much enjoyed before leaving the North-West Mounted Police. Once back in London, he devoted himself to writing, completed the first volume of his memoirs for publication, and accompanied a Danish expedition to Greenland. Late in 1904 he received a commission from the *Illustrated Mail* to visit Russia and report on conditions in that country, which was then at war in the Far East with Japan. In addition to providing articles and photographs, Roger indulged in some amateur espionage on behalf of the British Admiralty. This adventure coincided with the beginning of an important new phase in his colourful career, as the founder of the Legion of Frontiersmen.

Inspired by his military service in Canada and South Africa, and still more wide-ranging adventures abroad, in December 1904 Roger issued a call in the press for volunteers, preferably men familiar with guns and horses, but at least with experience of "real frontier work," who would serve the British Empire in peacetime as sentinels on its borders, while training to serve as irregular mounted riflemen in time of war. For the next several years Roger devoted most of his time, energy, and limited financial resources to organizing, promoting, and sustaining the Legion of Frontiersmen. Initial recruits included many of his own friends, former soldiers, mounted policemen, war correspondents, and other writers. Enlisting Admiral Prince Louis of Battenberg to serve on the Legion's Council and Hugh Lowther, 5th Earl of Lonsdale, as its chairman pro-

vided a social cachet denied to one of Roger's background. He also recruited more than sixty contributors to *The Frontiersman's Pocket-Book*
(1909), the Legion's field training and survival manual, including such
prominent figures as Sir Francis Galton, Sir Frederick Lugard, Ernest
Thompson Seton, Colonel Sam Steele, and Edgar Wallace. Later the
Legion secured some qualified acknowledgement from R.B. Haldane at
the War Office.

By the outbreak of war in 1914, Frontiersmen commands had been
established in nearly every corner of the Empire, and more than 10,000
men enrolled and trained. The British War Office and its imperial coun-
terparts overseas nonetheless deemed many of the Legion's officers too
independent of spirit and largely too old for service, and refused to em-
ploy the Legion formations as individual military units. Members were
urged instead to enlist in existing regiments. Undeterred, the Legion's
Manchester Troop secured their own transport to cross the Channel to
Belgium, where, as the "British Colonial Horse," they joined the Belgian
army's 3rd Lancers, and were the first British unit to engage the enemy.
Back in England, other Frontiersmen were belatedly mustered as the 25th
(Service) Bn. Royal Fusiliers (Frontiersmen), under the command of the
Legion's own Commandant, Lieut-Colonel Daniel Patrick Driscoll, and
served with great distinction in the East African campaign.

Frontiersmen throughout the Empire flocked to the colours. In
Canada, the Legion had established units in Montreal, Toronto, Hamilton,
Winnipeg, Saskatoon, Regina, Moose Jaw, Calgary, Edmonton, Nelson,
Vernon, Vancouver, and Victoria. Frustrated in their desire to serve as
independent units, Frontiersmen enlisted en masse in the newly formed
Princess Patricia's Canadian Light Infantry regiment (PPCLI). Large
numbers of Frontiersmen also served in the 19th Alberta Dragoons (for-
merly known as the Alberta Mounted Rifles), which was designated the
1st Divisional Cavalry Squadron, in the 49th (Edmonton) Battalion (later
known as the Loyal Edmonton Regiment), and in the 210th (Moose Jaw)
Battalion. "In Edmonton the Legion of Frontiersmen were first to go.
They had mobilized in their regalia (bushranger hats, khaki shirts and
neckerchiefs).... Thus began Edmonton's long association with Princess
Patricia's Canadian Light Infantry."[2]

Frontiersmen in the neighbouring province of Saskatchewan showed
no less enthusiasm and determination to enlist in the PPCLI:

> A group of them in Moose Jaw, hearing that the PPCLI
> contingent from Calgary would be passing through Regina,
> wired [Major Hamilton] Gault for authority to join the train,

though it was obvious he could not reply in time. They persuaded an American C.P.R. employee...to place two coaches in a siding close to its junction with the main line. When the train from the West arrived, they bluffed the night operator at the Regina station that official arrangements had been made to hitch their carriage to it.[3]

The train's conductor was reluctant to help them, but a drawn pistol changed his mind. Although the Frontiersmen were absorbed into regular military formations, they established for themselves a proud war record of heroism and sacrifice.

Despite his age, Roger Pocock also served in His Majesty's Forces during the Great War, but, ironically, he was no longer a Frontiersman. A series of personality clashes and power struggles had driven him from his post at Legion headquarters in 1909, and in response he chose to withdraw from the organization. In September 1914 he succeeded in enlisting as a corporal in the County of London (Royal Irish) Defence Corps, went on to earn a War Service commission, rose to the temporary rank of Captain, and saw service in several branches, including Military Intelligence and, lastly, the Royal Air Force.

Roger returned to civilian life in 1919 and resumed his writing career, but he still occasionally answered the siren call to adventure by signing on as a ship's crewman, including the 1921 Oxford University expedition to Spitsbergen. Fascinated by the possibilities of air travel since his service with the Royal Air Force, Roger helped organize a round-the-world flight attempt in 1923, which led to a temporary reconciliation with the Frontiersmen, from whom he sought support. After securing a vessel and crew, he set sail from England charged with the task of caching fuel and other supplies along the pilots' route. Like too many of his other ventures, this one ended in failure, but a failure of farcical proportions. Stranded in Los Angeles when the SY *Frontiersman* was seized by the local sheriff for unpaid debts, Roger made the best of a bad situation by briefly turning his hand to filmmaking in Hollywood.

Although the last years of Roger's life were largely spent in retirement, one further adventure beckoned. The Legion of Frontiersmen, their numbers much diminished after the carnage of the Great War, sought a reconciliation with Roger, whom they belatedly chose to acknowledge, even lionize. Despite some initial reluctance, Roger agreed to undertake a world tour on behalf of the Legion.

In May 1935, he set forth from London, and over the next six months visited Legion commands in South Africa, New Zealand, Australia, Hong

Kong, Japan and across Canada. Honoured with banquets and ceremonies, Roger's triumphal tour gave him immense satisfaction. It did much to heal rifts between rival Legion factions and succeeded in promoting recruitment. While in Canada, Roger also helped promote the brief affiliation of the Legion with the Royal Canadian Mounted Police; for many years Frontiersmen served as an auxiliary police force in several Canadian cities and provinces.

The Legion's acknowledgement and celebration of Roger's role in its creation, while belated, stands in stark contrast to Lord Baden-Powell's failure to acknowledge his debt to Roger and the Legion as a model for his "Legion of Boy Scouts," as they were first labelled. Baden-Powell's manual, *Scouting for Boys*, although lacking a chapter on "Demolitions," bore a slight resemblance to *The Frontiersman's Pocket-Book*, which Baden-Powell even urged his young readers to study.[4] The widespread search for peace in the wake of the Great War led Baden-Powell's Boy Scout movement to emphasize character building, while denying and downplaying anything that suggested militaristic indoctrination. Thus, the international Boy Scout movement grew and flourished, turning its founder into something of a folk hero, while the Legion of Frontiersmen was increasingly hard-pressed to recruit new members, and was forced to seek renewed relevance by forging new peacetime roles for itself.

Roger Pocock loyally answered the Legion's call, and in the 1930s accepted the role of "Our Founder," one in which the surviving remnants of the Legion celebrate him to this day. In addition to his 1935 world tour, he often attended Frontiersmen's reviews, parades, training camps, reunions, and dinners, until prevented by his increasing age and infirmity. Certainly, the role suited him, for he was happiest experiencing life in the open, with male friends and younger companions, around a camp fire, reminiscing, telling tales, and, as ever, "spinning yarns."

A dreamer of dreams, an adventurer, and a man of many ideas, Roger Pocock was an inveterate, world-ranging traveller. But Canada was always the land he loved best after his native Britain. Although his service in the NWMP proved brief and undistinguished, the experience launched his career as a writer, and provided a major source of inspiration, both for his stories and in the creation of his greatest and longest-lived achievement, the Legion of Frontiersmen. Frontiersmen were men of action, rather than words, and few of them wrote of their experiences, so we are left with almost no formal written accounts. Roger did write about his own life, but his two autobiographies fail to tell the whole truth. This is scarcely surprising, for he made numerous mistakes in his life and many were serious ones, though any degree of culpability in the death of Sir Arthur Curtis fell well short of murder. Both Roger and the society that shaped him are long gone. But his life of adventure, with its many failures and a few outstanding successes, is well worth recording for what it reveals about both the man and his social milieu. For, truly, Roger Pocock lived the life that many an adventurous boy of the time might have desired.

PUPPYHOOD

ROGER POCOCK'S LIFE OF TRAVEL and adventure was rather different from that of his ancestors. Most southern English Pococks can trace their ancestry back to sheep farmers on the Berkshire and Wiltshire Downs. Roger was of the opinion that some of his ancestors had gained some notoriety as sheep stealers and were eventually hanged for this crime.[1] Yet the wealth of the Innes Pococks, from whom Roger was descended, was started in storybook fashion when one Nicholas Pocock left the Berkshire village of Chievely about 1720 to seek his fortune in Bristol. These Pococks amassed considerable wealth, it is believed, through the slave trade. Marriage into the Innes family brought a connection to the Dukes of Roxburgh and the Earls of Innes. The children who survived were successful, and there were many descendants, the most notable of whom was the marine landscape painter, Nicholas Pocock (1740–1821).[2] The sixth son of this Nicholas Pocock was George (1789–1820), a solicitor at Lincoln's Inn, who married Frances Ashwell (1795–1829), from a family of "West Indian planters."[3] George and Frances had three sons and two daughters. Roger's father, Charles Ashwell Boteler Pocock (1829–1899), was the third son.

According to Roger, Charles Pocock was gazetted midshipman in the Royal Navy at the age of 12. Perhaps foreshadowing some of his future misadventures, as a midshipman he achieved some small notoriety when, with another young officer, he attempted to ride a pony up the Mediterranean stairs at Gibraltar for a wager.[4] Charles served in the suppression of the slave trade, which was somewhat ironic, considering the presumed origin of the fortune of the earlier Pococks. He also served on the Brazil coast and the North Pacific Station based at Esquimault, British Columbia. During the Second Burma War (1852–1853), Charles received a musket ball in the throat during an attack near Pegue. He must have inherited some of his grandfather's artistic ability, for one or two of his sketches of that campaign still survive. Charles's main claim to fame, however, was that he had a mountain on the B.C. coast named after him.[5]

Charles probably met Sarah Margaret Stevens (1830–1887) through his naval officer friends. At the time, Charles was 28 and Sarah, a tall and slender girl with an expressive face who came from a great seafaring family in Cornwall, was only 17.[6] They were married on 20 June 1854 in St Paul's Church, Southsea, near Portsmouth, Hampshire. All through her life, Sarah had a deep love of flowers and she claimed that she could not live unless surrounded by them. She had experienced a very simple upbringing and, according to Roger's sister Lena, had never seen a mirror until the day that Charles took her, suitably chaperoned, for her first visit to the theatre, where she was surprised to see her reflection in a large mirror.[7] Both families should have been well satisfied with the match, for Charles was reasonably secure financially and Sarah was beautiful. Nonetheless, the senior branch of the Pocock family, which owned much land between Cookham and Maidenhead in Berkshire, never looked very kindly on the lives and activities of Charles and his children. It was a marriage in which Charles and Sarah had their share of happiness but also saw many troubles, including Sarah's tragically early death. A major cloud soon appeared over the marriage when Charles's eyesight began to deteriorate and he became so short-sighted that he was forced to wear spectacles virtually the whole time, a disability that forced him to retire from the Navy at half-pay with the rank of Commander.[8]

Through the influence of Sarah's family, Charles obtained employment in charge of the Overland Mail from Bombay to Cairo. This meant Charles travelled so much that Sarah was alone in a bungalow on Malabar Hill on the northern outskirts of Bombay throughout the Indian Mutiny of 1857. Charles subsequently took charge of the Royal Mail on the Spanish Main and also across the Panama railway and elsewhere in Central America. Since Charles could never settle at anything for long after he left the Navy, he next decided to take up a naval land grant at Motueka, in the Nelson district of South Island, New Zealand. By this time they had their first child, a son named Francis Agnew (1858–1948).[9] Two daughters, Rosalie

Ellis (1861–1941) and Mary Lilian (1862–1863), were born in Motueka, but the harsh pioneer life and childbearing were beginning to affect Sarah's health. In addition, Charles was not good at managing his finances (a trait that Roger inherited) and some unwise investments caused him to lose much of his money. Since Sarah was expecting again and the restless Charles had tired of sheep farming by this time, they sold up and sailed for England, and in 1865 the family took up lodgings at Tenby, in Pembrokeshire, South Wales, where Charles worked as a visitor and reader among poor parishioners. There, on 9 November, a second son was born and christened Henry Roger Ashwell Pocock.[10] Roger concealed the socially embarrassing fact that his birthplace was humble lodgings in Tenby from all but family members. He preferred the entry in *Who's Who*, where he claimed his birthplace was the senior family home at Cookham. Two years later, Georgiana Ethel (1867–1924) was born at Gravel Hill, Stanton Lacy, Shropshire.[11]

Charles was then fortunate to be given the command of the Training Ship *Wellesley* on the River Tyne in northeast England. The *Wellesley* was a wooden-walled battleship that had originally seen action against the French as the *Boscawen*. Two more girls, Lena Margaret (known as Daisy, 1869–1957) and Hilda Frances (1871–1964), were born on board the *Wellesley*.[12] An elderly ship on the rather dirty Tyne was not the healthiest place to bring up young children and Ethel damaged her hip in a fall. She suffered from the attentions of doctors, who seem to have made her condition worse. The girls were probably better respected by the boys on the ship, and this certainly appealed to Lena. According to her, the ship had "been through many stirring adventures before being turned into a home for boys 'unconvicted of crime' but under suspicion."[13] Roger was uncertain of this description when, in his 60s, he told Harry Leigh-Pink, "The brochures stated the ship was a training school for boys unconvicted of crime. When Christmas brought snow, the ice-balls rammed down my neck made me doubt this."[14] However, as the captain's son, the rather self-important Roger often expected more respect than he was shown.

According to Lena, her brother Roger was a "strange little being with an inexhaustible desire for personal knowledge; it was never enough to say that a fact was a fact because people said it was. He had to find out for himself."[15] From a very early age he had a particular passion for geology and, to Lena's apparent disgust, he was much more interested in finding fossils when he took her on an outing than in what attracted her attention.[16] It came as a shock to Roger's opinion of his own importance when he was sent away, with other sons of Navy and Army officers, to Ludlow

Grammar School.[17] His experience of this English boarding school was not one that he remembered with pleasure, and the school was pleased to forget him. Roger might then have wished to follow his father into the Navy, but the family could not afford to send him to the Royal Naval Academy at Portsmouth. Thus at the time of the 1881 British Isles census he was a student at the School of Submarine Telegraphy in Penge, Surrey. This may be where he learned the Morse code that he used later in his diaries for material he considered sensitive.

Also in 1881, Charles decided to see if he could improve his lot by moving to Canada.[18] A deeply religious man, he also wanted to take Holy Orders. Officials at the Admiralty told him that this would end his retirement half-pay because he could not draw pay from two departments of state. However, they eventually agreed with his contention that the Church was not a department of state and, besides, he would not be paid for helping the clergy of Ontario.[19] Charles believed that his half-pay could support the family in Canada and that the climate there would be better for his health than life on the polluted Tyne. Charles sailed first, to find a home for the family near the town of Brockville, Ontario. The rest of the family then sailed on the SS *Peruvian* to Quebec. The *Peruvian* weighed less than 3,000 tons, but there were nearly 1,000 people on board. Roger, who was seldom seasick in any conditions, shared a cabin with a man who was ill all the time, for it was rather early in the year for the northward course the ship took. His account of the trip gives a sense of the adverse conditions they encountered on the journey:

> As we entered the Gulf of St. Lawrence a huge piece of ice fouled the stern of the ship, shearing off the propeller as clean as one might cut cheese with a knife.
>
> There was no wireless in those days, of course, and for one terrible week we drifted helpless among the ice-pack.
>
> Luckily for us our plight was seen by the watchful light-keepers on Cape Breton and they sent news to the world.
>
> On the eighth day of the drift a full gale drove the ship broadside on with the weight of 36 miles of ice crushing our sides.
>
> We could feel the plates slowly bending beneath our feet, and all hope seemed gone.
>
> The majority of the passengers, gathered in kneeling circles, prayed for deliverance, and I know that mother, with her six children around her, felt that she had reached the end of her travels.

We learned later that father, back at Point Levis, Quebec, was making frantic efforts to obtain permission to board the tug *Progress,* one of the vessels detailed to come to our rescue.

His request was refused.

At 3 A.M. the following morning, and at the very moment when we were rescued from certain death, the unfortunate tug *Progress* caught fire and every soul between decks was burned to death.

Thus did Canada welcome the Pocock family.[20]

The house Charles had found for his family was "perched on the granite cliff in the middle of a forty-two acre pinewood.... Here there was great beauty; but also greater discomfort. No water laid on in the house, no drainage, no gas nor electric light, no modern conveniences whatever. Here were no boys to wait at table...."[21] The two hard years spent there as settlers appealed to Lena more than to her sisters. Charles sent Roger to work on a farm until the farmer, in a letter of protest, asked that Roger be removed, saying "he found himself ruled by an elderly gentleman with a mania for imparting information, and a distaste for cleaning the stables."[22] Charles nonetheless maintained that Roger was best suited to an agricultural career, so he sent him to Guelph Agricultural College. Roger, however, had no patience for conventional education; because he was convinced that he knew better than everyone else, that placement also failed. He was then found a job working for the Canada Life Assurance Company, but his own life became more financially comfortable when he received a legacy of £5 from Ashwell Currey, a distant relative. He recorded his circumstances as follows in his diary:

> Working in the office of the Canada Life Assurance Company and lodging in the house of a widow with an ugly maiden sister. Also at the lodgings was Mrs. Caldwell, a well-known singer, her husband and 2 little boys. Salary $10, board $10 so I got on famously. Got the sack for idleness after 5 months so I lost my magnificent salary. I also lost Mrs. Caldwell, for the hideous maiden sister of the widow raised a scandal.[23]

Roger also said that he "worked hard at boating, bathing, and musical evenings."[24]

With that inheritance spent and the job lost, Roger returned to his furious father in September 1883. A friend described Roger to his father as "a proper knight errant," but there was no call for knights and there were no dragons to slay in Canada. Roger's elder sister, Rosalie, had married a widower, Samuel Keefer, some years older than she, who was reasonably well off.[25] Mr. Keefer arranged a new job for Roger on the far side of Lake Superior, where Mr. Keefer's relative, Mr. Middleton, was in charge of hewing out the roadbed for the Canadian Pacific Railway. As Roger later put it, "having failed at every job they put me to, in my teens I groped my way across Ontario to the forest frontier, and joined the natives who were then building the Canadian Pacific Railway."[26] Middleton was not overly impressed by Roger, a rather puny youth who did not even bring his own blankets. Roger described his first experience of real frontier Canada this way:

> To reach my objective I travelled by train across Ontario, and by steamer through Lake Huron and Lake Superior.
> At the end of a further journey in a dug-out canoe, I came to my first camp on the great Frontier....
> The campfire was a stack of dead trees, and red-hot logs sent up a column of hissing flame that seemed to reach the sky.
> A circle of tired men huddled in the heat, behind them glimmered lighted tents, and walls of black forest towered gaunt above.[27]

The next morning he was sent along the coast to work under the surveyor at Gravel Bay, where "The problems were avalanches and rock-slides, and, after the rains, cataracts which crashed and thundered down from the sky-line. Life was indeed full and interesting and most variable."

Roger's job was to mark out the ground with numbered stakes, paint guide signs on rocks, and generally help with the fetching and carrying. Roger thought there were much more interesting things to do, and thus spent most of his time hunting for amethysts and otherwise indulging his passion for geology while climbing precarious crags. The surveyor had Roger sleep in his own tent at night, where he could keep an eye on him. Here Roger's one use was his artistic ability, since he was very good at drawing pretty girls for the men. Life was even more exciting when dynamite was around, and Roger had to be kept well away from it. Meanwhile his collection of geological specimens outside the tent grew larger, and the surveyor was not a man to hold his temper when he fell over this sharp and spiky collection at night. Sunday was a day of much needed rest for most of the men, but as young Roger had not worked overly hard during the week, he would go off exploring. He often became lost, and a grumbling, hard-swearing expedition would have to rescue him. At the end of the month, when Mr. Middleton came to inspect the camp, he was told, in no uncertain terms, what to do with Mr. Keefer's protégé, so Roger left with Mr. Middleton, who took him by steam launch to Fort Nipigon, a former trading post of the Hudson's Bay Company, then paid Roger off and left him there.[28]

Outside Fort Nipigon was a construction camp of the worst sort, "with a street of shacks and tents devoted to the Seven Deadly Sins."[29] There was a tent brothel where some very unsavoury women plied their trade for the rough, tough construction gangs. There was a flea-ridden hotel, where those who failed to pay their bills were treated to a bullet as a parting gift. Roger was not keen on spending any of the small sum of money he had, so, although he booked in at the hotel, he spent the days at the bay, hoping for a steamer to arrive that would enable him to make a quick exit without being shot for non-payment. He became anxious as winter was drawing on, for soon the ice would prevent any boat from arriving or leaving. Eventually a steamer did arrive and deposited 375 men, but it left in such a hurry that no one could board. A dishonest contractor in Toronto had taken large sums of money from these men, promising them well-paid employment at Camp Nipigon. However, there was no work for them, or even food to spare, since no more food would come before spring, so Roger earned some gratitude from the Camp by getting there ahead of this angry crowd with a warning. Work was found for the first twelve men, but the rest were forced at gun point to stay outside the Camp. They could not survive the winter there, so they began to disperse.[30]

Roger knew that he had insufficient money to last through the winter, so he decided to head for Port Arthur, Ontario, which he thought was a boom town. He met a group of Swedish navvies hitching a ride on a gravel train. The bitter cold became more intense, and he wrote that only the sparks from the wood-burning engine, which constantly made their clothes smoulder, stopped them falling into a sleep from which it was unlikely they would otherwise awake. Each of the Swedes paid two shillings for the ride, but Roger was cunning enough to escape paying when the train reached the end of the line. Then there were still many miles to walk on the made-up embankment, which did not yet have rails. At nightfall he and the navvies found a ruined wayside hut with a stove, and before dawn they had burned all the furniture and everything else they could strip from the hut, but the stove was still getting cold. Roger decided not to risk falling asleep, so he set off alone along the snowy track through the woods. All around him were sounds like gunshots, as the sap in the trees froze and the branches snapped with loud cracks. By noon,

Roger, nursing a strained muscle, limped into a wayside camp, where he was allowed to buy much needed food and a bottle of horse liniment for his sore leg. Roger appreciated his own good fortune, for "In the last few weeks no less than twenty-three men had been taken out from that camp and laid on the dump of the railway, with the next load of gravel by way of burial. Daily, the engines [of the Canadian Pacific Railway] go roaring down that curve swinging their tails of sumptuous carriages, singing their song of triumph over dead men's bones."[31] A gravel train took him the last few miles to Port Arthur, which was bursting at the seams with people. At last he found warmth, though he slept uncomfortably on a makeshift bed on a hotel's billiard table.

Roger found Port Arthur a fascinating town, and for a week or so he just enjoyed the scene, drinking it in, picking out experiences to be stored for possible use in future writing. The idea that he might one day earn his living as a writer gradually began to take shape,[32] but he soon realized that he had to find work and bolster his dwindling reserves of cash, so he started on a succession of odd jobs. He undertook a fortnight's book work for a lawyer, during which time he sorted out a milkman's accounts, who then told him to sue for his wages. Work as a general labourer on a small farm looked as if it would be a steady job. He shared the tasks with a young boy, whom the farmer and his wife appeared to have unofficially adopted. Christmas was coming and the larder seemed to be very well stocked, so Roger was looking forward to enjoying the kind of family Christmas that he had been used to in his own family's home. His hopes were dashed when the farmer and his wife loaded the sled on Christmas Eve, leaving Roger and the boy with just some bread and bacon. The family did keep the Christmas spirit long enough, however, to refrain from throwing Roger out until New Year's Eve. So it was that New Year's Day, 1884, found him homeless on the streets of Port Arthur, "enjoying a bracing wind at forty degrees below zero."[33] He then found a job in a rough hotel, where he had such entertaining tasks as cleaning out the spittoons and chopping through thick ice in the water hole for the forty buckets of water that were needed every day. On the regular occasions that the hotel caught fire, another forty buckets would be needed. The last straw for Roger came when he was told by the proprietor to exchange beds with a guest who complained that there were too many bedbugs in his bed. Good fortune arrived with a present of £5 from his father, who was having one of his rare prosperous spells. However, Roger was tricked out of this by his next landlady, who, when she thought his cash was all gone, attacked him with a knife.[34] Thus he was forced to seek other accommodation. By now, Roger's body had filled out and his muscles were sufficiently strong for him to secure a job as a labourer on the Canadian Pacific Railway (CPR). On the strength of this, and his equally short but more useless spell with the surveyor at Gravel Bay, Roger later felt able to write enthusiastically about the CPR and his personal involvement:

> For me the route had a special interest, because from the windows of a comfortable Pullman car I could look out upon the road where once I worked with pick and shovel as a navvy; or again, as the train thundered past the Lake Superior cliffs, I was able to mark the places once familiar to me in the days when I helped to build the Canadian Pacific railway.... Those were stirring times; but now, after all the spending of lives and money, the Canadian Pacific is an accomplished fact. There have been many great things achieved by the sterling pluck, patience, and manly work of the Canadians, but, surely nothing finer than this greatest of railroads, which bound the Dominion with steel bands, and welded the scattered settlements into a nation.[35]

Subsequently, Roger found a job working for an itinerant photographer selling views of the Port Arthur area. It started promisingly, but, as the photographer became more alcohol-soaked, so did his photographs, and that venture failed. It did have the effect, though, of launching Roger's interest in photography, which was useful later. Roger then became the local agent for a book by Queen Victoria, *Journal of a Life in the Highlands*.[36] The book failed to make his fortune, however, since he lacked the necessary capital for the project. By now, with the coming of spring, the whole population turned out to cheer the first boat to get through the ice. The warmer weather also permitted Roger to camp outside the town in a tent for the whole of the summer. Always ready to talk to anyone, he began to study and respect the First Nations people and pick up their lore. He also began to hear tales of the North-West Mounted Police (NWMP), which made him determined to see if he could enlist. He managed to save a little money to start on the journey to Winnipeg, the central recruiting point for the Mounted Police, so he took a steamer to Duluth, on Lake Superior, where "A kind old man, a labor agent at Duluth, took him in, fed him entirely on hot buttered toast, let him sleep by the warm stove, saved his life. Then in November came a letter from his father, with amazing news—'There is a regiment in Western Canada called the Mounted Police. Here is the railway fare.'"[37] Charles, very distressed by the wild life his son had adopted, believed that a good dose of military discipline would be very beneficial, but still cater to Roger's taste for adventure. So, on 2 November 1884,[38] seven days before he turned nineteen, Roger arrived in Winnipeg to enlist in the NWMP. Thanks to his father's help, "an adventurer had found his kind, the breed of man who live in the outdoors and follow the lure of dim trails, and what he did and what he learned in the Royal Canadian Northwest Mounted [*sic*] was to color his thought, speech, and actions to the end of his life."[39]

THE BUCK CONSTABLE
LOSES HIS TOES
at the
RIEL REBELLION

ROGER'S DESCRIPTION OF THE SCENE at Fort Osborne in Winnipeg on 3 November 1884 shows that fifty years later he still had not forgotten the excitement of this occasion and the effect it had on his romantic spirit:

> I heard the clip-clop of iron hoofs on stone, the jangle of stirrup and accoutrement, and presently a troop of twenty horsemen filed majestically between the iron gates of Fort Osborne, the recruiting depot of the North-West Mounted Police.
>
> "Troop—Tro-o-t!"
>
> They swung past me, each man with a carbine across the horn of his stock saddle, the sunlight glittering on many a point of steel.
>
> Hard-featured, weather-beaten, great big men, with clear, far-searching eyes, pride of bearing, swaggering gallantry, and wild grace in the saddle.
>
> The sentry on duty, who claimed to be a German baron, was a large man, made to look even larger by his scarlet tunic and white helmet. He directed Roger to the barracks.

Constable Roger Pocock, North-West Mounted Police, *c.*1885.
[Glenbow Archives, NA943-2]

Then I was stripped and before the doctor. For months I had starved and had no great hold on life. As the cold steel of the stethoscope touched my flesh I cringed.

Oh, they never would take me!

They must have been hard up for recruits. The German baron said so afterwards when he came off duty, and the sergeant in charge of the detachment gave me one contemptuous glance and remarked that the outfit had sure gone to the devil.[1]

Roger then went by train to Regina, where he was issued an excellent kit. Regulations stipulated each trooper receive three pairs of riding breeches annually. Every five years, they were allowed seven pairs of riding boots and moccasins, as well as three pairs of ankle boots. The kit list was so extensive it even included a red woollen nightcap.[2] The food was plain but the quantities were good and rations were increased by half while the men were out on the prairie on active service. The ready supply of food had such an effect on Roger that "when after a fortnight I tried to put on my old civilian waistcoat, it would not button either above or below."[3] Roger quickly became fairly comfortable with life in the Mounted Police:

> There is stirring music in the bugle calls. I have genial comrades, excellent quarters, perfect light, warmth, & ventilation, an active life, perfect health, and plenty of amusement and leisure. My outfit of conveniences is one of the best in the barracks[,] nearly a fourth of my associates are my equals by birth and breeding, and my bread & meat are such as I have not often seen. This with a prospect of settled residence until spring is not a life that need be lamented even when my earlier hopes and aspirations are recalled. This life indeed reminds me of the happy indifference to the future and keen appreciation of the present that I enjoyed in my last terms at Ludlow, in the months in London, on the Cornish moors[,] at Guelph & Hamilton and at Gravel Bay. I have no longer the worn anxious mein [sic] that deformed me during the long terrible trial at Port Arthur.[4]

A month later Roger was still happy to describe how he spent his time:

> Life here is curiously varied[,] as a record of the past few days will show. Friday last I was at the stables from 6:30 am

to 6 pm working cutting hay[,] carting manure[,] cleaning stables &ce, and sewed rents in my buffalo coat in the evening Saturday. Three hours at stables as usual & an hour's riding exercise. In the evening drawing & reading the Iliad. Sunday[.] Stables and cleaning myself all day. Too cold for church. Monday. Escorting prisoners for 7½ hours while they cleaned the parade ground, picked potatoes, & moved a piano all in a blizzard. Evening[.] Dined with the Bishop. Today washing dishes four hours & grooming horses three hours & Reading [*sic*] Dante's "Inferno."[5]

Five days later Roger added a note on a money matter, which was often a concern for both father and son. He had to decide whether he should pay the $22.50 he owed, so he could redeem a trunk containing, among other things, his diaries, or send the money to his father. "Tell me quickly," he requested, "whether I better help you or pay this due.… Your decision shall of course be final. But if your necessity of money be not pressing I am bound in honor to pay up."[6]

There were four other new recruits, or men with only limited service, in Roger's barracks room. He described the majority of the men favourably, although "Most of the fellows have assumed names I believe." He also conveyed the diverse backgrounds of his "comrades in No[.] 8 room":

> Winnipeg sewer hand—Jamaica plantation clerk—an ex-Constable rejoined—an old soldier—a law clerk—an Ontario Farmers [*sic*] son—an English parsons [*sic*] son—A silk designer—A Western "Tough"—a medical student—an Anglo-Indian—A brakesman—another "Tough" Irish—A Bank Clerk of Paris—a French Canadian—another farmers [*sic*] son—Charlie Sinclair—Bossange (my Austrian chum)—a barber—a bar tender,—& me. Dont [*sic*] you think we are a queer crowd? Yet we are all very good friends indeed and never quarrel.[7]

He recorded the stories these men told of their past lives, as well as many of his own activities, in his diaries and letters. He also began developing an ability to capture qualities of speech.[8] It is not clear how aware these men were that he was keeping detailed records, but Roger later featured some of them, not always with altered names, in his novels and stories. Although he sometimes modified their adventures, the roots of the tales he had recorded were clear. For example, perhaps the biggest influence on Roger's writing was the teamster, a large man known as Mutiny. He took Roger under his wing and Roger thought Mutiny saved his life when his feet became frostbitten in March 1885. Mutiny gradually told Roger the story of his life, which Roger used in several books.[9] His was not the only dramatic story, though, for Roger later claimed that "In the community of the North-West Mounted Police, when I first joined the force, every life was a vivid romance in the making; every man in the barrack-room was hero, fool, or villain—generally all three—in some ghastly tragedy or quaint comedy."[10] Most of these men's lives had been touched by violence, and a number came to a violent end. For example, Corporal Dutchy Koerner admitted to being a horse thief and outlaw wanted in the United States, but he found at least temporary refuge in the NWMP.[11] Roger described some who, like Koerner, spent part of their lives on the wrong side of the law, but "Not all were like him. I kept a records [sic] later of what happened to the strange assortment of men I served with. Some made fortunes or failed in the Klondike, some were frozen to death on duty, or died by their own hand, [or] perished in battle[,] while one won the Victoria Cross—all gallant, valiant men!"[12] There was always some special reason that led these men to join the NWMP, but in Roger's case it was at least partially the joy of regular meals after such a long struggle to find sufficient food.

He had already been noting events in his life and keeping diaries, but he nonetheless wrote: "Thursday January 1st 1885. Pay day recieved [sic] $15.50[.] Temperature -58°. Commenced a record of my life." He also recorded mundane drills and duties, purchases, and an early effort at writing: "Sent my recent 'Regimental Song' to Ethel to be put to music."[13] Another effort was a newspaper for the Troop:

My newspaper has come out at last and its history must be told. I tried to chromograph the manuscript and thought I should succeed. And in my confidence I took 17 orders from my room mates alone and so said I would print 100 copies for the Troop and sell them at 10c each for the benefit of the Mess. Then the Chromograph collapsed and I could only produce one copy. This I shewed [sic] to the Sergt Major and asked him if I might post it up. He read it all through and smiled sadly and said "There's only one thing wrong here[.] You make fun of the Arms of the Force detracting from its dignity, so no civilian must see it. You may show it to your friends if you like[.] I guess that will do no harm." So

> I gummed my precious manuscript on a high bench in the
> Wash House being forbidden to post it up. But someone tore
> it up being offended. He was the "Clerk of the Vaccillation
> [*sic*] office" alluded to[.][14]

Roger was keen, but he was not always the most docile recruit. "About the 2d of March I got into a row with Nicholls in the Recreation room and was for the first time put under arrest[.] Next day at the Orderly room I was admonished by the Adjutant Deane and sentenced to replace the torn newspaper."[15] Nonetheless, what Roger later called "a real soldier's training" seemed to appeal to him.[16] He even became so caught up in it that he wrote to his mother about the prospect of war: "There are lots of rumours about Govt preparations, and I am trying to toughen myself for one…. Next time there is powder in the air I intend to have my share of the entertainment." A few weeks later he told her he had "volunteered for the Egyptian war last week but I dont [*sic*] suppose anything will come of it."[17] Yet within a few weeks Roger was plunged into the North-West Rebellion, one of the most discussed events of the 1880s in Canada, and one that had a long-term effect on the N W M P and Roger. He was only on the periphery, but he eagerly recorded what he saw and heard.

The Rebellion was led by Louis "David" Riel (1844–1885), who returned from exile in the United States at the invitation of his Métis people. Successive petitions for recognition of their land claims had been ignored by the government in Ottawa, whose further failure to deliver promised food aid to the First Nations peoples compounded the grievances and discontent brewing in the North-West Territories. Warnings from both the Mounted Police and civil authorities about impending trouble in the Territories finally prompted action by the federal government, but it came too late to prevent an open rebellion.[18] As has often been the case, the men in the barrack rooms were more aware than the senior officers of what was likely to happen. Betting on anything and everything was also common among the men. Roger recorded Mutiny, holding forth on the subject of forthcoming trouble, for "we 'Ring-Tailed Snorters' of less than two years service were not allowed to speak":

> "Mutiny," the teamster, a huge fellow with a chest as big as
> a hogshead, generally provoked an argument with some
> random wager.
>   "Say, you fellahs, I'se got fifteen dollars that says there'll be
> war within the month."
>   That would rouse the corporal in charge.

"Bah! Don't talk punk! Where's the grass for their ponies? Can they live on ice? The nitchies can't start trouble before June."

"Ahm thinking," a Scotch voice purred, "that ye're no calculatin' on this Louis Riel, corporal—forbye his veesions...."

"Visions be damned!" interrupted "Mutiny," "Riel is a practical man, with his tail waving high, 'Jock.' Look what he done on Red River in 'Seventy!"

"Ran like a coyote!" the corporal snorted. "Him and his hull bloomin' outfit, when they seen Wolsesey's [sic] column. You ask 'Jock,' 'Mistah Mutiny,' he was right thar."

"Ahm thinkin'" began the old Black Watch veteran. But "Mutiny" planked his fifteen dollars on the table and fiercely challenged the corporal to cover it.

"War, within the month, Corp.," he snapped. "Plank down your iron dollars. I'll stake you even money that our scalps 'ull be hangin' outside Crowfoot's tepee within the month."

There were five "Ring-tailed Snorters," including myself, in that barrack-room, and our beds were arrayed side by side.

So deadly incisive was "Mutiny"—and there was no man who knew more of the country and of Indian warfare than he—that I remember we recruits sat up in our beds with a jerk, watching the teamster intently, and waiting, with bated breath, for the development to his challenge.

As this discussion proceeded,
"Mutiny" waved his arms in the directions of our five beds.
"Just look at 'em grinning in them five beds there—one grin to each bed. 'Old Crowfoot' 'ull take that grin off your dials. Wait till you hear the Sioux war-whoop, you wolf-mouthed, red-eyed, buck-hero toughs of the Wild Plains!"[19]

The centre of the Rebellion was at Batoche, southwest of Prince Albert, where the majority of the inhabitants were Métis or French-speaking settlers. Riel went to work inflaming Métis grievances and promising untold wealth to them. He also sent representatives to the local First Nations to stir up discontent there. Two of the chiefs were willing to take part: Big Bear and Poundmaker. By March 1885 Riel had formed a Council of State and a provisional government. By this time, however, he had lost any prospect of support from the English-speaking settlers, whose lives became increasingly perilous. In spite of the intervention of the local priest, Riel summoned supporters to Batoche. On 16 March he spoke to those assembled with considerable eloquence. Riel knew that almanacs stated there would be a partial eclipse of the sun the next day, so he said that "in order to sanctify his words to them, the Great Spirit would throw a darkness over the sun."[20] Although the eclipse left a glowing rim, this helped to prove that Riel was the prophet he claimed to be. Prince Albert was thought to be at risk, so Colonel Acheson Gosford Irvine, one of Roger's NWMP heroes, gathered together what men he could in Regina to begin a forced march to bring aid. Irvine managed to gather ninety-two other men, including volunteers and some less-than-fully-trained recruits, one of them Roger.

Roger wrote a careful account of his impressions:

> On March 15th a report was circulated that disturbances were
> taking place in the Sascatchewan [sic] country. Preparations
> were made for an expedition. 25 men arrived from Calgary
> and a few from Fort Osborne. On the 17th we were paid up to
> date & I was told off for infantry party. On the 18th Reveillé
> sounded at 4 A.M. and at 5.45 a party of 94 were drawn
> up on the parade ground. The order was given to march.
> The Guard turned out and we defiled out of the barracks.
> A vedette party rode first and the long train of sleighs was
> guarded at front & rear by a mounted party.
> Col Irvine was in command.[21]

The approximately 300-mile journey would be in uncertain weather through territory mainly controlled by the rebels. While it was still bitterly cold, there could be sudden thaws, and it had actually rained at Prince Albert on 15 March. On 18 March, however, "It was a cold[,] brilliant day and our trail lay accross [sic] an open field of snow for many miles. Towards noon This [sic] gave place to scrub beautifully frosted. We made our noon halt at Pie-a-pot's reserve and deeply impressed that celebrated chief with the amount of provisions disposed of." Roger then recorded the following:

> 21st Brought us over the Touchwood district of rolling prairie
> with scrub & half way accross [sic] the Salt Plain to the
> Station of the same name. We carried carbines that day and
> fortified the Camp at night.

22d My boots were very wet that night and solid ice
covered them next morning. They took fifteen minutes to
drag on, and I could get no moccassins [*sic*], mine being
in an inaccessible Kit bag. So for 20 miles accross [*sic*]
the remaining half of the desert from 3.30 am until noon
my feet froze steadily. The day was a pleasant one and
not more than 20° below zero, but running hurt me and I
was cut very deeply into the flesh from the chafing of my
boots. I had enjoyed the trip so far; but now commenced an
experience very far from pleasant. My feet were indeed very
dangerously frozen and 8 hours in ice & water was needed
to thaw them. I became entirely snowblind [*sic*]. That night
the officers [*sic*] tent was placed at the disposal of the sick
for snowblindness[*sic*] was becoming common. We were at
Humboldt.[22]

That is how Roger described this incident for his own use. In October
1886, at the request of Dr. Jukes, he described what happened a little differently:

On the morning of the 18th March 1885 I was one of a party
of 90 men, and left Regina for the north under Lt Colonel
Irvine. The weather being mild and winter apparently
ended[,] boots were worn by most of the Command.
    On the 21st inst our boots were all very wet on account of
a partial thaw. At Reveillé on the 22d inst we were in camp
at Salt Plain Station and the thermometer had fallen during
the night to about 20° to 25° below zero. Most of us had left
our moccassins [*sic*] in the kit bags, and they being 90 in
number, and exactly alike, and bound upon the sleighs, were
not readily accessible. In the haste of a forced march[,] it
was not possible to take the usual precautions against cold,
and I was obliged to wear my frozen boots for the day....
Others being as badly off as myself I did not mention that
I was cold but ran about to restore circulation, and tried to
warm my feet at the camp fire, until we started. I was posted
to the sleigh of a civilian freighter, and ran alongside, in spite
of the sloping of the bare ice making the matter very difficult.
Later in the morning I suffered so severely from a pain I
attributed to cramp, that I had to desist from running. We
halted at noon on the edge of the plain, having travelled about

18 or 20 miles. I reported at once to Staff Sergt Braithwaite
he being Hospital Steward, and he found that both my feet
were badly frozen. He placed them in ice water, in which they
remained until we reached Humboldt, nearly 8 hours. For the
remainder of the journey I suffered from exposure, sickness
of the stomach, and snow blindness greatly aggravating my
illness. Accross [*sic*] the base of the toes of the right foot a
groove formed by the pulling off of tissues already frozen
causing a bone to become visible and leaving one sinew
standing out accross [*sic*] the hollow. This groove could only
have been caused by the chafing of a wrinkle in the boot in
the action of running. I desire to urge the importance of this
fact as showing that I was not to blame in the matter....[23]

His later accounts were worded to elicit sympathy, rather than condem-
nation, for his foolishness, showing the lack of judgement that appeared
all too often in his life:

When we marched I thought it was cramp which gripped
me from the knees to the heels, and though it was difficult
to move I trotted beside a sleigh, wondering dazedly what
caused so much pain....
  The hospital sergeant soon discovered the trouble. The
chafing of the frozen leather as I ran had almost severed the
half of my right foot, and both my legs were solidly frozen up
to the calves.
  Chafing with snow would have rubbed away the tissues,
and heat would have resulted in death by gangrene; so for
seven hours of the afternoon march I was on a sleigh box
with my feet in a bucket of water kept cool with snow.[24]

What Roger should have worn were the moccasins that were issued for
just such conditions. John G. Donkin, who had been sent to Prince Albert
with an earlier detachment, gave a good description of this footwear:

We protected our feet from the dangerous attacks of the frost
by first covering them with two pairs of woollen socks. Over
these we drew a long pair of woollen stockings which covered
our riding pants to the knee. Then we adorned our feet
with moccasins. These are soft, pliable brogues of dressed
deerskin (moose), of a light yellow colour, and only reach

above the ankles. They are pliant as a glove, and thus there is liberty given to the foot, so that the circulation remains unimpeded.[25]

Roger was aware of the dangers, since he was not a greenhorn straight from England. Perhaps as a result of his experience with extreme cold before he joined the Mounted Police, in three letters Roger commented on the low temperatures with some smugness:

> Meanwhile the thermometre [*sic*] keeps steadily at -30° with an occasional blizzard. Oddly enough I am perfectly happy. And discharge all my duties with a light heart.
>
> The temperatures have been very low lately. The highest last week was 7° below zero & a gale with Snow [*sic*]. The lowest 48 below zero & calm. I was out of doors both times and was more troubled by the former than the latter. This week we turned out for parade at 56° below zero one morning and this 12° below & calm is the warmest thing we have had for two weeks.
>
> Frank ought not to freeze with warm English blood in him. His health must be bad. When in perfect health I have patrolled for an hour at 60° below zero and kept warm. When I have had colic I would be usually frozen at 10° below in walking across the parade ground.[26]

Roger was already fairly well versed in First Nations lore, and would have had a good idea of what was required for survival in such extreme temperatures. He would also have had strict warnings from the old hands. So when Roger was carried into Prince Albert with his feet a black mass as a result of frostbite, Donkin, a hospital orderly, had no sympathy for him: "He had persisted in remaining in the sleigh, and wearing boots, probably too lazy to run alongside, and he was now paying the penalty of his own folly."[27] Many years later, Braithwaite was also inclined to blame Roger:

> "It had been hot all day and the men were wearing boots," said Dr. Braithwaite. "It was March and the weather suddenly turned cold, so I told the men to change to their moccasins.
>
> "Pocock was riding in the back of a sleigh, reading a book of Greek, and didn't change his footwear. Finally, he couldn't get his boots off and we had to cut them off.

His legs were frozen from the knees down. I treated him and we saved all but his toes. Afterward, he used to say I saved his life."[28]

Charles Adamson, who went to the Klondike with Roger in 1898, was also unsympathetic: "According to Mr. Adamson[,] who heard the story from a chum of Pocock's[,] the ex-journalist refused to walk and got into one of the freight sleighs, saying that he would sooner die riding on a sleigh like a gentleman than live like a tramp, plodding through the snow."[29]

In Roger's account of the conclusion of the journey, he provided more details:

> 23d Reached Hoodoo where the night camp was kept ready for removal at a moment's notice and sentries were quadrupled at every point. News had arrived that an ambush of 300 men was lying on the road to Ft Carleton [*sic*]. I lay in a crowded hut and was very feverish & in great pain.

> 24th Reveillé at midnight and a start under the starlight. We travelled rapidly & with cautious silence. At 6 pm we crossed the South Sascatchewan [*sic*] on the ice and arrived at Prince Albert at 9 pm after a drive of 60 miles.... I was placed in [the] charge of Const Donkin at the Goschen barrac[ks] and remained there two days.

> 25th I recovered my sight. Dr. Bain commenced to treat my feet. Braithwaite had earned perpetua[l] gratitude during the awful journey of 140 miles since I fell sick.

> 27th 2 am. A Scout rode in with news that war had broken out.[30]

Roger, as well as several men who were completely snow-blind, were left at Prince Albert while, after just one day of rest, the others marched to the relief of Fort Carlton.

Roger described the journey to Prince Albert to his mother, and, with a conscious view to his future as a writer, instructed her that "if my narrative be a clear record of this adventure keep it for me." After his account of what preceded the freezing of his feet, he said he would "not describe what followed":

Seasickness[,] blindness[,] fever & incessant torture. They dared not leave a govt servant in a tract infested with the Govts enemies. Nor could any comforts beyond camp diet be found for me. During the long forced march for two days & a half we were in constant danger & but for a timely ruse would certainly have been cut off to a man. My whole mind gave way and in lassitude [I] was in great danger of freezing to death on the sleighs.

Two days after we reached Prince Albert things bettered a little. And I followed the stirring news report by report, while I enjoyed my own part in the drama despite the pain. A vedette rode in in the dead of night and roused the whole town to arms. He told how the rebels had fired from under their flag of truce and how after a splendid action & despite surpassing courage our men had even left their dead upon the field. The citizens gathered & clergy & volunteers [&] merchants & laborers & farmers[—]all the men in the place went to work in the darkness [&] before 2 P.M. that day a fort had been constructed large enough to shelter the population [by] enclosing the Presbyterian church & manse with a rampart of cordwood 10 ft high & 4 ft thick. In course of the day, Saturday, I was moved into the church and laid in a corner on the dias [*sic*]. On the way into the Fort the sentry "presented arms" to me thinking I was one of the wounded, to my intense delight. There were 40 women & children lying about the church and 50 or sixty of the Volunteer corps raised on this emergency. And the time was sunset. There was a stir outside like a breath of wind among trees. Then someone stood in the doorway & yelled "To Arms! To Arms!" Then followed a disgraceful panic. I sent a little boy to steal a revolver for me. When the terror came my heart had given two great throbs and then I felt rather amused at the ludicrous scene that was being enacted. The volunteers were squabbling over the rifles, yelling instructions, shouting "To the ramparts they are down on us" "Where's my bayonet" &ce.

There was not a man in the church who did not order the community to do something or other. There would certainly have been a general massacre had the half breeds really attacked us. The women poured in by hundreds half dressed & hysterical. I busied myself with comforting some of them as they crouched down near me. I talked religion & heroics[,] chaffed, jeered, laughed with them & prayed with them. I had two women & a baby on my bed & 8 women & 7 children on the little space set apart for me in the crowded church, all warm[,] comfortable & cheerful before we knew that the panic was only a false alarm.

During that long awful night I had to tell wives that their lost husbands had not been taken by the enemy & comfort the amiable daughters with promises that their lost fathers should be restored to them. The cause of the trouble was that two horsemen had been seen 18 miles off & the result was cramp that made me wish every one elsewhere & tell them how glad I was to have them by me. A red coat & a complete disregard for truth is an excellent reciepe [*sic*] for pastoral work among frightened women.

Our entire forces numbering 200 men or so had the day before arrived from Carleton [*sic*] and so Palm Sunday was spent listening to the stories my chums told of the campaign. They were all terribly exhausted and all the polish & neatness that used to become them so well in time of peace was gone. Buttons were rusty, badges awry, and boots unspeakably filthy. But there was a better sound in every voice for they had suffered too much to grumble. I was deeply impressed with the story of burning Carleton [*sic*]. It was a little fort lying in a little hollow in the woods and its interior was commanded by rifles from every tree on the surrounding hills. Col[.] Irvine saw this and prepared to evacuate the death trap and fall back on Prince Albert. While preparations were going forward about midnight[,] the Hospital was found to be in flames & the wounded were dragged hastily from the burning rooms. Had the insurgents been less cowardly an attack on the retreating party as they climbed laboriously up a three[-]mile slope through heavy timber would have been completely successful[,] for not a white man would have lived to tell the story. Experience has now shown that the government is dealing with a band of brigands rather than of patriots[,] who want plunder & not political independence.[31]

When Irvine and his men, the men of the Fort Carlton garrison, and the Prince Albert volunteers who had accompanied Irvine entered Prince

Albert, their first duty was to look after their horses and see that the wounded received care. Irvine instructed the local residents to return to their homes, but to reassemble at the stockade if the church bell sounded. Too excited to think about his damaged feet, Roger buttonholed every man, woman and child who came near. He was constantly seeking information and opinions about what was going to happen, what was happening, what had happened, and particularly about events at Duck Lake and Fort Carlton, so he could record these in his diary and letters. It proved very helpful later when he was writing his *Blackguard* books. If Roger wanted anything, he had only to grab a couple of the youngsters and send them scurrying off on his errands. He "met two of those same boys in 1901 as veteran troopers returned from the South African War, and they told [him] that the earliest memory of their lives was that fort of refuge."[32]

Roger later told a tale of the bishop of the district, John McLean, known as Saskatchewan Jack, who found himself deserted by his staff at Emmanuel College. The bishop had

> loaded his treasure, a case marked "Bibles," on the episcopal sleigh, and travelled to seek refuge with the rest.
>
> Someone stole that case marked "Bibles," and well I remember his lordship swinging his short legs on the corner of a table and eating a hard-tack biscuit, while he chanted the iniquities of the Mounted Police.
>
> "One would think," he blared, "that in a time of general peril these profane troopers might shrink at least from open robbery."
>
> "Why, what have you lost, your lordship?" a feminine voice demanded.
>
> "A case of Bibles!" declared Jack, somewhat viciously, I thought.
>
> A ripple of laughter followed.
>
> Imagine the "Mounted" filching Bibles!
>
> I may mention now that our boys of the Prince Albert detachment found something more than spiritual consolation within the case marked "Bibles," and were fattening on the luxuries of the episcopal larder while his lordship did a little slimming in church.[33]

After this excitement at Prince Albert, Roger received surgical treatment for his feet: "On April 10th...Dr. Miller Regtl Surgeon removed five toes from my right foot. I was under influence of ether and was dosed five times unsuccessfully." The high dose of anaesthetic had such a disturbing effect on him that he recorded, in Morse code, "See supplement concerning dream."[34] Under the effect of chloroform he experienced what he considered religious visions. These puzzled and worried him. He later wrote down what he recalled, and attempted to get some sort of explanation from his father:

> I had several repetitions of a dream of supreme horror. For two or three hours afterwards I remembered all about it but when my head cleared to its normal state I remembered only the vague horror of it. It threw me into a state of nervous excitement that lasted several days[,] and once when a friend coughed in a queer way he saw me start & turn pale. For somehow it had had a part in the dream[.]
>
> My vague consciousness of what had passed in the sleep caused a train of what was at first morbid thought. But this was replaced by logical[,] healthy[,] intellectual recearch [sic] into the state of mind left by the dream[,] and there arose in me a fabric of thought that seemed entirely new & original and well worth committing to paper.
>
> But there is in my mind a conception which to any one [sic] possessing it would give absolute proof that the "Void" is a fact, but I am convinced that nothing in the English language would express what no composition could describe.
>
> To me the Knowledge given by the forgotten dream more than compensates for the injury that has maimed me for life[.] And with the paper I send you in my hands I thank God for the pain that purchased it.[35]

Nonetheless, Roger would not risk the use of chloroform for a second operation: "May 4th left off using opiates. 6th Sessamied [sic] bone removed and ends of first and second metatarsal bones by sawing. Refused chloriform [sic] and used whiskey....9th Very bad night....26th sent copy of dream to Father." It took him a month to recuperate sufficiently to go outdoors, so it was not until 3 June that he could write that he "got out in the sun for first time."[36] In July Roger said of Dr. Miller that "He has saved me from being hopelessly lame by consummate surgical skill and I am deeply grateful."[37] The effect of the trauma he suffered, and his need to deal with, or sometimes evade, the knowledge that it was his own foolhardiness that caused the injury, is evident in some of his stories, including "The Blackguard's Brother" in his book *The Arctic Night*.[38]

As days turned into weeks, the tension gradually eased. For nearly eight monotonous weeks, virtually nothing happened to break the routine of those confined to Prince Albert. The main topic of conversation was why Irvine's force did not move against the rebels. However, Major-General Middleton, Commander of the Canadian militia and all other forces in the field (including the NWMP), had rejected Irvine's proposal that they lead coordinated attacks upon Batoche from north and south, ordering him instead "not to attack but to look out for flying half-breeds."[39] Thereafter, Middleton kept Irvine completely in the dark. Without any help from Irvine and the Mounted Police, Middleton's troops fought at Fish Creek and Batoche; then, on 20 May, Middleton's column marched into Prince Albert. In his honour, Irvine paraded his men in their best uniforms. The sight of the NWMP's bright scarlet uniforms, contrasted with his own men's faded and battle-worn uniforms, incensed Middleton, who later foolishly ignored Irvine's offer of 175 Mounted Police to join in the pursuit of Big Bear.[40] As a result of their inactivity during the final defeat of the rebels, enforced though it was, Middleton's contempt for the NWMP became general among government officials in Ottawa and was spread by an unsympathetic press to the Canadian public at large. Yet Irvine's men remained his loyal supporters, and Roger would tolerate no word spoken against him. Irvine publicly defended his conduct and thus indirectly commented on Middleton's flawed strategy:

> I can and do state positively, that the presence of the police force saved Prince Albert from falling into the hands of the rebels. Had such a catastrophe come about, the rebellion would have assumed proportions of much greater magnitude. Unless I am utterly at fault in this, and I cannot think I am, Prince Albert was the key of the whole position, and had it fallen into the hands of the rebels the result would have been disastrous to the Dominion, and involved great loss in lives and property.[41]

Immediately after the Rebellion, medals were struck and land grants given to troops and militia who had taken part in the suppression of the Rebellion, while members of the NWMP, who were also under fire, were not honoured until some years later. The following year, with some bitterness, Roger recorded that

> Sir John A McDonald [*sic*] inspected F Troop at Regina and was pleased all to pieces.... The premier [*sic*] made a little

speech and a definite promise that we should all have medals who served during the Rebellion. It is said that only those *under fire* will get these medals, but I dont [*sic*] think that the corps will be insulted in that manner. Little mention is made of Land Grants, although they are now awarded to all the other corps.... Battalions stationed at Winnipeg & Regina having a military picnic were awarded a medal & 360 acres of good land. My comrades who perchance were 20 minutes under fire were given medals. I maimed for life got neither of them. Such things make a loyal citizen hostile.[42]

Roger's brief service in the NWMP coincided with the one period in its history when it declined in public esteem. Nonetheless, Roger's great pride in the service was unshaken by public opinion and remained with him until his death.

In Roger's summary of the campaign, he strongly praised the NWMP as he led up to his description of the capture of Big Bear:

Then General Middleton sent a dispatch conferring the honour of finishing the work on Colonel Irvine. [In] the remote forests Colonel Irvine asked his men if they would do the work that had turned back the brigade. He asked them to traverse impassable jungles, lakes, and swamps, with neither food nor forage, and they readily consented. So they drove the rebels down to the Saskatchewan, men and horses alike weak with privation. Such hardships as they encountered were never recorded in the stories of the campaign; no chronicle at all was kept of the finest episodes of the whole revolt.

Roger concluded with this assessment of Canada:

The revolt was not very big, but it enhanced in its suppression the self-respect of a young nation. Canada was a little bit pleased, and a little bit garrulous about it. But the nation has shown all the elements of greatness. The strength of an untried power has been put forth, and the great Dominion has proved worthy of her mother. Let the dead past bury its dead, even should another rebellion attend the funeral.[43]

After frostbite in March, and surgery in April and May 1885, Roger went through a long convalescence. He passed his time writing "bad verses, worse fiction, and sold incredibly vile sketches in water-colour, helped in the spelling and grammar of local journalism, and traded in cigars, giving credit, much to the amusement of the troop."[44] However he also spent many hours writing to his family, especially his mother, to whom he sometimes showed more confidence in the quality of his writings and drawings. He was able to pour his thoughts out to her and receive a sympathetic response, whereas he seemed wary of his father, who often appeared to be ready to criticize:

> Father is mistaken in this passage of one of his letters:—
> "I suppose your account of yourself is good but it is a
> mighty long time to get over a frost bite."
> It is time that I told you that my injury is much worse
> than you have supposed, and that very grave fears have been
> entertained concerning me. I came near death, far nearer than
> I told you; and only lately no one would believe that I could
> ever walk straight again. There was a man in Prince Albert
> last year who had had an open wound for six years and his
> case was less serious than mine. The danger of frost bite was
> agrivated [sic] by a long forced march, the hardship in the
> Stockades, camp diet, and neglect, by snow blindness and
> fever.[45]

Roger was also carrying on correspondence with men he had met in Port Arthur before he joined the NWMP, as well as two women, Mary Powell and Ada Wright, who seemed to be at least friends of the family. In July 1886 he seemed rather pleased with one of her letters: "Ada Wright thinks I am a young person of brilliant and varied talent[;] you know she used to imagine me as a being of surpassing beauty!"[46] After he had his photograph taken professionally, he sent copies to his family and to Mary Powell in September 1885. In February 1886 he confessed to his mother that he had received "a jolly letter from Mary Powell.... [S]he does not like my photograph because she thinks that I look 'wicked[.]' Otherwise she is pleased with it and promises photographs of all the family."[47]

Roger was also looking to his future as a writer. In November 1885 he reported his first contact with the Montreal *Witness,* a newspaper that provided him with an outlet for his journalism and some income over the next several years:

I have by good fortune obtained a letter of introduction to one of the chief men on the "Witness" staff of Montreal. My letter is also in the enclosure forwarding three of my best pieces.... I want the man to recieve [*sic*] three pieces of different character that he may be able to judge of my whole work as represented by them.

In the same letter, he gave an idea how his writing plans were taking shape:

On my return home I shall get half a ream of foolscap and reconstruct my diaries in the form of autobiography up to January 1885.... I shall get the account of the Peruvian in the Montreal papers and fish up all the drawings[,] photos &ce I can lay hands on to illustrate the work.... It would be unwise to lose all the valuable record permanently for I should regret it in after years.

He finished that letter with the command: "Dont [*sic*] let there be any delay about the letter to Mr. Forrest[;] it is only necessary to pick out three manuscripts and post the letter as it is."[48]

By February 1886 he was pleased to report he was walking. "During the last week I have got on splendidly in walking and can now get about with a walking stick & a bad limp."[49] That February he also told his mother of the adventurous lives of two of his comrades, Beeby and Williamson. This letter is important, for it is probably the first expression of Roger's belief that even rough men from the frontiers could be of service to the British Empire. Nineteen years later this idea had germinated and he set out to gather together just such men in the Legion of Frontiersmen. He wrote:

They are children of nature, when vexed they swear and blaspheme with enthusiasm, they chew tobacco constantly, they always speak what they think and spit on the floor. They are generous and sensual, happiest when drunk, and always natural and unaffected. Such are the men you call ruffians and blackguards. They have built the Empire as they have hurried in advance of civilization with axe and shovel. They have made our fleets and armies and filled our gaols. Let such be taken to the forests and frontiers of the Empire and they will extend the Imperial domains where man has never been

before; and there will be no customers for the gaols. For even
dirt is only "matter out of place."

I dont [*sic*] think that you understand the true nature of
my companions even now, but you will fear their influence
upon me much less as you know them better. Men cannot be
judged "good" or "bad" by any one who searches for Truth.
I believe that there is nothing so subtle as the distinction
between right and wrong in a mans [*sic*] conduct. *A hasty
judgement is nearly always a proof of ignorance,* for even
instinctive knowledge can only date from *one* standpoint.[50]

Even while Roger was in the N W M P , worry about debt and lack of money,
which recurred throughout his life, caused him concern. He earned a
little money by selling some of his paintings and drawings, and then in
February 1886 he had the idea that he might improve matters by a little
local trading. Via his mother, he asked for the family's help:

To-morrow is pay day but it is not of much use to me. My
debts and obligations amount to $18.00 while my cheque is
only for $15.40....

It has just occurred to me that I can help my-self to a
certain extent by a little trading. Cigars are sold at 10c each
or [$]8.00 the hundred here. Will you ask Frank to tell
some leading retailer to send his prices to my address.... I
dont [*sic*] smoke myself but if I can lower the prices here a
little it will be greatly to my own advantage and that of the
Troop....[51]

By May he was able to write to his mother to tell her of his success:

I have ordered cigars to the value of $53.00 on which I hope
to realise $40.00 clear profit.

Of course this will all be absorbed in future investments.

I have invested this week in $5.00 worth of Seaside Library
books; but, since it is on borrowed capital, I cannot get more
than 10 per cent on that investment. By rigid economy I hope
to get enough capital to start a general trading enterprise.
The business flourishes far beyond my expectations, and my
custom is growing steadily. I have now about half of the cigar-
smoking members of the troop as regular customers. Capt

Perry gives me all encouragement and runs a small account with me himself.[52]

Early in July Roger exuberantly told her that he had received a letter from a new cigar supplier at Belleville: "The new man is cheap, and his goods are better than my Brockville man's. So I will order 1000 from him at once. I ordered another 1000 from my Brockville man, because he is so innocent, and would be so unhappy if I didnt [sic], and he writes such funny letters every time he sends a box."[53] However, Roger's enterprises never achieved more than short-term success, and this one was no exception. His comrades soon discovered that he was willing to supply them on credit, and his trading faltered when his creditors were unwilling or unable to pay him. So later that July he declared, "I have lost $16.00 more this month by giving credit, I have now stopped credit altogether. I could not pay tithe or mess bill this month & am much annoyed about it."[54]

Roger was not just involved in marketing cigars. He was delighted to report on some of his literary activities in April 1886:

> Monday [12 April] writing three [sic] stories, founded on facts, of Lake Superior viz "Fred," "The Amethyst," & "The Ice Cortége" [sic] [&] "A Useless Man[.]" My essay on the Rebellion was published in the York Herald (England) and reprinted thence.[55]

He was convinced that what he had seen and experienced in his time in the NWMP, brief though it was, would provide him with a large stock of stories to serve as a foundation for successful writing:

> The life in the force is almost unequalled for picturesqueness and interest. It is a vast field for the research of novelists and artists and one that can never be explored by outsiders. I have seen the life of railway construction and of rough hotels[,] which are both almost unknown to the general public. But both of them lack the brilliancy and variety of this one. Surely such a subject would interest the world as other like subjects have. Brigandage, pirate life, army life, life at sea. These have all been talked to death. Beyond a few references to it by the Canadian press, the matter has never been even [sic] spoken of. This is mainly due to difficulty of access, because it is entirely alien to that of the colony. But I have no doubt that

it will be taken up and worried to death at a distance, like the Hudsons Bay Co life was.[56]

In his letters Roger frequently mentioned one aspect of life among the Mounted Police—the problems alcohol caused. The effects of alcohol even worried Roger sufficiently for him to write a solemn pledge: "I hereby promise before God, and on my word of honor, to touch or taste no intoxicating liquor for six months, that is until noon of the 4th Day of October 1886, except by order of a doctor."[57] Prohibition was in force in the North-West Territories but, unsurprisingly, the men found a number of ways to evade the law. Roger first recorded this in a letter in 1885:

> Cider does not seem to come under the prohibition act. And the Hudsons Bay Company imported 16 barrels. There was considerable tasting of this cider. It was delicious. The sampling continued until three barrels were emptied. The result was curious. Pandemonium lasted in the camp until dawn and there were several fights....
> Next day there was a general head ache and the officers concluded that cider was an intoxicant. A seizure followed pending investigation. Meanwhile a mixture of red ink, spruce beer, pain killer (a medicine)[,] eau-de-cologne & essence of lemon became the popular beverage!

Later in that letter, Roger expressed some sympathy for drunkards:

> Men are often urged by bitter trouble into bad ways....
> It is very wrong to despise a drunkard, because misfortune taken without submission is the subtlest of the Devil's agencies. And this was the ruin of most of the drunkards that I have met.
> The topic is profoundly interesting.[58]

However, he could also be a little cruel: "It is absurd to suppose that there is no fun connected with drinking. In watching a drunken crowd there are wonderful facilities for studying human nature and the grotesque. There are other aspects beside the moral ones."[59] A month later Roger detailed the extraordinary and dangerous lengths to which some men would go to experience some form of intoxication: "When on Picquet the other night a man was brought to the guard room drunk and partly

insane from drinking 'cider' (Sulphate of Copper & Tartaric Acid &ce)."
Roger went on to say,

> This horrible compound is doing deadly work in Prince
> Albert, and already neglected wives lack food, and children
> run wild & uncared for. Several attempts have been made
> to suppress the traffic, but it has never hitherto been proved
> that the stuff is intoxicating. Every body [sic] knows that it
> is so, but it is found that all the evidence taken, denies the
> undoubted fact.[60]

In April 1886 he noted in his diary, and in a letter to his mother, that his
foot had improved sufficiently to allow him to wear boots, walk several
miles, and perform more than just a few light duties. So when Battleford
suffered an outbreak of typhoid that summer, and a detachment of thirty
men left Prince Albert on 25 August to relieve the district, Roger was allowed to join the detachment:

> The distance is only 180 miles but I shall be greatly cheered
> by the change. The trail passes the ruins of Fort Carlton,
> the scene of the "Poundmaker Racket" & of the action of
> Cut Knife Hill [&] also the well known Eagle Creek & the
> destination Fort Battleford is one of the most interesting
> spots in the Territories. It was of old one of the wildest &
> most remote of all the forts in Ruperts [sic] Land [&] a well
> known stopping place & depot for voyageurs and the scene
> of innumerable battles with the tribes. I shall meet many old
> friends there including the mountain fever which is making a
> grand harvest in the post. Dr Miller is dangerously ill with it
> and about 40 men are said to be sick.[61]

When he reached Battleford on 29 August, he wrote in his diary, "Dr.
Miller, Joe Howe & 70 men sick with Mountain fever. In cases where it
developed into Typhoid[,] Rummerfield & Sturge died. The citizens are
sick too & the whole population are white like ghosts."[62] Roger's detachment was commanded by Inspector Bégin, whose service in the Mounted
Police is highly praised in histories of the NWMP. Yet Roger held him in
low regard in comparison to his commanding officer at Prince Albert,
Superintendent A. Bowen Perry. Thus, of his ride to Battleford, Roger
told his mother, "I am cooking for the officer in charge[,] a frenchman
[sic] of low pretension, but so thorough is my contempt for his greed[,]

meanness & selfishness that I shall be rude to him if I dont [sic] leave him."[63] Roger had a far worse opinion of the officer who took over command at Battleford, Alexander Roderick Macdonell. Roger always referred to him by the nickname Paper Collar Johnny (or Johnnie), or just Paper Collar.[64] Roger was quite disgusted when Macdonell ordered his troop to enter the infected barracks at Battleford and carry out duties, but praised Bégin who "bucked against the Officer Commanding here in obedience to Supt Perrys [sic] orders & refused to let his men do any duty about the barracks or even to enter them."[65] In October he had an even more scandalous tale about the officers, and Macdonell in particular. At Battleford, Roger wrote:

> filled up my postcard with local news. Among other things
> I stated that the officers had been having a prolonged
> "drunk" on "Hospital Comforts" (Liquor) which was strictly
> true. I also stated that "Paper Collar Johnnie" (the Officer
> Commanding) had had the last consignment taken to his
> bed room [sic] for "security." Now it so happened that when
> I posted my letters Old paperCollar [sic] was in the Post
> Office and I believe he picked up my post card from the pile
> and read it. I was secretly warned to expect trouble, and
> was despatched to Prince Albert to await the decision of
> the Commissioner to whom the card appears to have been
> given. Had I been charged with it I should certainly have got
> three months hard labour for giving cheek; for I should have
> stated that 'paper Collar' [sic] had exceeded his authority
> in tampering with Her Majesty's mail (*he stole my card*) &
> moreover that he was *no gentleman* in that he read my private
> missive[.]
>
> And let me protest to you as I did to Harry Keenan that the
> liquor provided for the sick in every post and the alcohol for
> sick horses is *generally* stolen and drunk, either by the officers
> or by those in charge of it.[66]

These two men for whom Roger had so little respect probably influenced his writing, for it seems fairly certain that the villainous Inspector Sarde in Roger's *Blackguard* books was mainly based on the worst aspects of the characters of Macdonell and Bégin.

Throughout his life Roger believed that the best cure for any ailment was to take a tent and live the outdoor life, so the time spent outside Battleford was mainly a delight to Roger, although events in typhoid-ridden Battleford were deeply upsetting. From a distance they watched the funeral processions and grieved the loss of NWMP brothers. Even Dr. Miller, the heroic and much loved doctor, seems to have found affairs too much to take and committed suicide. After a while, the survivors of "D" Troop from Battleford were sent away to recover, "C" Troop came from Fort Macleod to take over, and Roger's "F" Troop was sent back across the plains to Prince Albert. Roger's description of camp that summer is one of his best pieces of descriptive writing:

> Presently a mounted man came out upon the edge of the
> ravine, the sun glowing chestnut upon his horse, flame upon
> the scarlet of his coat, star specks on bright accoutrements.
> Then in half sections came our twenty riders, each man with
> a carbine poised across the horn of the stock saddle, and
> many a point of glittering light upon his harness. At a word of
> command the riders dismounted to lead, while behind them
> appeared five waggons [sic], each with driver and off man, and
> a pair of troopers, our rearguard, waiting for the dust to abate
> before they followed down the breakneck hill. Our fellows
> were dressed in suits of brown canvas, or fringed deerskin,
> or grey flannel shirts with a silk kerchief round the neck, or
> an old red jacket, just as we pleased, long boots, sombrero
> hats, belts glittering with a line of brass cartridges, and big
> revolvers at the right hand ready. Ours were hard-featured,
> weather-beaten, dusty, great big men, with such clear, far-
> searching eyes, such pride of bearing, swaggering gallantry,
> and wild grace in the saddle that one despairs of ever, with
> words or colors, making a picture worthy of the theme.[67]

Several years earlier Roger had described the uniform and horses with affection and his characteristic humour:

> A scarlet regiment—that was to impress the Red Indians—we
> were technically mounted infantry. The uniform was like that
> of the Dragoon Guards, with a white canvas helmet instead
> of the "tin hat," a Winchester carbine, a belt of flaming-bright
> brass cartridges, and a foot-long service revolver instead
> of the cavalry sabre. The horse was a half-broken broncho
> raised under the shadow of the Rockies, a humorous beast,
> standing, say, fifteen hands, with all the vices and an artistic
> thoroughness in bucking. The saddle weighed forty pounds,

A page from Roger Pocock's 1885 Diary.

and was of the Mexican type, high in horn and cantle, with broad-webbed cinchas instead of the English girth.

As for winter, "The uniform then was a black fur cap, a short buffalo-coat—now changed to bearskin because the bison is gone the way of all flesh—long stockings, deerskin shoes, called moccasins, and mittens or fingerless gloves."[68]

A page from Roger Pocock's 1886 Diary.

[Courtesy of the Bruce Peel Special Collections Library, University of Alberta.]

Roger was so pleased with the way his writing was going that he declared in a letter: "Do you know that since I got into print I have been convincing myself that I am a Genius! Its [*sic*] so cheap. Seriously I am beginning to believe myself talented in two or three matters and respect myself much more than I did."[69] It is likely his father would not have approved of such a statement. Perhaps Roger's far less boastful comment the next week would have been better received:

> Such as I am I am creative; It [*sic*] is impossible for me
> to acquire deep knowledge, but provided that my brain
> is nourished with desultory reading & given chances to
> *observe*[,] I can create with no little versitility [*sic*]. I cannot
> teach the world but I can do the humble service of setting
> them to thinking. That is the use of Originality[,] the
> redeeming point of a comparitively [*sic*] low talent. I can never
> aspire to the mountains of learning[,] the prodigious research,
> the concentrated & incessant thoughts of the great writers.

His father was less enthusiastic about his son's talent, but Roger went on to tell his mother he craved the adventures that would provide him with material for his writing:

> Father says that he thinks that I "have written myself out":
> the truth is that I have been stopped at the commencement
> by the deadly monotony of my life. My failing is neither due
> to want of information[,] for study would crush the very life
> out of me, or to want of mental fertility. It is necessary that I
> should *live* in order that my topics may be from life. A varied
> life, a life of adventure & travel, of hardship[,] privation &
> constant reading can alone provide material for such writing
> as I can interest the public with.[70]

Six weeks later he wrote with conviction: "I know that my writings are crude—How could they be otherwise? I am only a child in literature. But I say this—that unless God kill me, my words shall ring in every corner of the known world before I am old."[71]

While a career as a writer showed promise as he considered the possibility of being invalided out of the NWMP, he needed to find some other, and possibly speedier, way of making money. Roger had known for some time that the NWMP might invalid him out because his foot still limited the duties he could perform. As early as April 1885, he raised the idea in a letter:

> In case of any permanent lameness resulting I shall endeavour
> to obtain compensation from Govt. But the Government will

be hard up after this trouble and I have not much chance I think. If I am really lamed for life they will try and invalid me to get rid of me. I wont [sic] go. The authorities would rather pay heavily in that case than have anything brought before the public to deter recruits from joining. This is as the matter might stand from a business point of view.[72]

Thinking about what he would do with his life if he had to leave the NWMP, as ever, he put his thoughts in his regular letters to his mother. In one he made it clear that his family could not expect him to return to the family home to lead a quiet and mundane life:

I dont [sic] think I could ever live in a big town, it would be so cramped and monotonous[.] If the place got burned down once a week it might be bearable but not otherwise. You know I am not a good young man of "domestic habits" but rather a depraved "freak of nature" as you call me. As to my living by the pen in Toronto I could not do it. I breathe in all my ideas from the clouds & auroras & sunsets, from the wild men around me, from the strange picturesque life I lead among these armed children of nature, among the queer[,] beautiful plains & forests so gentle yet so terrible in their anger. I have the holy memories of wild desolate Algoma, made sacred by distance, already depicted before my mind, & ready to be adapted in threads of narrative. When I leave this prairie I shall have its memories to be remembered under new & strange conditions akin to my nature. I dont [sic] think I could live at home. I dread the restraints of civilized life so full of needless accessories—beds that make one lazy, chairs that promote sleep [by] being too comfortable, saucers to break and stoves with abominable decorations in nickel *that excite ill feeling.* Above all I should have to come under the dominion of Mrs. Grundy and wear a coat all the time.

How vile is the tyranny of Mrs. Grundy in this matter!… Why cannot men forego the heat and discomfort of coat, waistcoat, & stiff collar within the house, and reap the advantage of not requiring a supplementary over coat [sic] (like a bale of thin brown paper with spots of whitewash) when he goes out?[73]

In August, Roger returned to the subject of his plans for the future:

> There is little doubt that within a few weeks I shall be under
> efficient treatment at Regina....
> After that I must find a climate where my foot will not be
> endangered in Winter[,] that is[,] in Alberta or B.C., and be
> prepared to start in life at the place where I settle.
> Should I get no compensation I must fight my way as a
> laborer and trust in God.
> Should I get *cash* compensation[,] say $2000[,] I am
> inclined to try the following scheme modified according to
> circumstances:
> Order a stock of cigars and perhaps other merchandise
> and a camping outfit & provisions wholesale according
> to my means to be sent by freight to Vancouver or some
> other rapidly growing town—Buy a pony & saddle ($100)
> and strengthen myself by riding from such place as I may
> be discharged at, to Vancouver, & await my stock—Buy a
> town lot—camp on it & open a tent store as is usual in such
> places—Secure a substantial wholesale cigar trade with the
> saloons[,] grocers &ce and fill up time with retail work—
> When real estate reaches highest safe price sell out.[74]

When he began this letter, though, his thoughts were not fully formed,
for he struck through many other lines. Roger's fear of being discharged
was confirmed when Perry called him in after the Troop had returned to
Prince Albert from Battleford. It had been decided that there was no hope
he would be able to return to full duties:

> "Is it wise, Pocock," he asked me kindly, "to serve on with an
> open wound draining away your strength?"
> I did not care, so long as I might serve.
> "Is it quite honest," he suggested gently, "to take full pay
> for half service?"
> To that I had no reply.[75]

Roger clearly knew this was coming, for one of his father's letters said that
Roger had written to him from Battleford and said he was "to be sent to
Regina to be invalided having been reported by Commissioner Dr. Jukes
unfit for Service."[76]

The Canadian government treated Roger well, given his short service in the NWMP. However, it took some correspondence to achieve compensation for his injuries, including a letter his father wrote:

> The object of my letter is to ask you to use what influence
> you may have in our favour.
> The claim is clear enough.
> In March/85[,] when on Col. Irvine's forced march to Fort
> Carlton[,] he was very badly frozen. Although he made light
> of it, I believe he was pretty nearly gone. The toes on his right
> foot had to be amputated, and the wound has never healed.
> All last winter he was employed as clerk at the M.P. barracks
> at Prince Albert. And now Dr. Jukes gives it as his opinion
> that the wound shall take years to heal....
> There could scarcely be a more righteous claim for
> Compensation or Pension. My circumstances are such that I
> could not even support him at home. And somehow or other
> he must earn his own money. To do this he will have to get
> to some climate where his foot will not be endangered by
> frost, and obtain first rate medical advice. He is developing
> considerable talent as a writer, but there is not a living to be
> got out of that for years. What he will do I don't know.[77]

Samuel Keefer, Roger's brother-in-law, also wrote in support of his claim for compensation and made a suggestion:

> I may add for your information that young Pocock has given
> evidence of remarkable and original literarie [*sic*] ability....
> In view of this, I might be permitted to suggest that perhaps
> this early promise might be turned to good account in some
> department of the public service and thereby lessen the
> amount of compensation to which he would otherwise be
> entitled.[78]

On 13 November, 1886 the Discharge Board of the NWMP met at Regina and the process by which Roger returned the official kit was underway. His discharge was made official on 19 November 1886. At discharge his conduct was recorded as "very good."[79] On 13 November Roger also was sworn in as a "Special Constable at the rate of 60¢ per diem" with "permission to proceed to the East on leave of absence in consideration of the injuries sustained by him in the execution of his duty with the understanding that such pay shall continue until his case is disposed of by the Department."[80] (In the event, he was assigned to the Mounted Police office in Ottawa.) On 7 June 1888 he was awarded a pension of 23 cents a day for life, retroactive to 1 June 1888.[81] This success did not end Roger's efforts, for although his discharge certificate stated "This Discharge does not entitle the person named therein to a Free Grant of Land," and although he had signed a document upon his discharge stating, "I have no claim for further pay, clothing or compensation in connection with my service in the N. W. Mounted Police," on 10 November 1931 he wrote a letter asking to receive "the generous grant by the Dominion Parliament of $300 to Pensioners of the North-west [sic] Mounted Police who served in the Rebellion Campaign of 1885."[82] This was to be in lieu of scrip. At a meeting on 8 June 1932, Roger was one of twenty-nine to be approved. On 17 June 1932 the cheque was sent to him, and on 30 June 1932 Roger signed a receipt for the cheque.[83]

He had spent only two years with the NWMP in the West, but Roger never forgot that period, which had considerable bearing on the organization he formed, the Legion of Frontiersmen, and also gave him much material for his writing career. Some of that material he used immediately. He was pleased that "A Night-Halt," "A Useless Man," and "The Ice Cortege" were published so quickly, although he was displeased by the editing of "The Ice Cortege" because it was "rashly & profusely punctuated by the Editor & some of my passages thrown on their beam ends by superfluous *ands* and *thes*."[84] In his diary he mentioned, in November 1886, that he received "two guineas from Chambers Journal for the Night Halt," and on 7 December 1886 he noted that he had written "to Forrest of the 'Witness.' Sent a description of the Force to Chambers Journal and lately had an interview with the Editor of The Week who tells me my 'style is telling' and [he] is not averse to more contributions. Have completed the 2d book of the Spirit of the Plains." On 24 December 1886 he recorded his further efforts to become a writer, in a style that fortunately did not mirror his usual writing:

> I have taken all my essays and stories to a firm of type
> writers [sic] who undertake for orders of two hundred folios
> to do the copying at 3c [cents] per folio or 100 words. A
> letter to Editors I have copied by cyclograph[,] and send
> [these] stamped and addressed contributions in good
> type together[,] each with a printed letter[,] to the various
> publications of which I have taken the addresses of a large
> number at the public library. I am having 4 copies made of

the *three* complete books of the Spirit of the Plains, received a lengthy and valuable letter from Forrest of the Witness, and made enquiries concerning Copy Right, Critiques, and Publishers.

The next day he noted he had "commenced 4th Book of the Spirit of the Plains." On New Year's Day, in Brockville, Roger proudly reflected on his activities:

> During the past year [1886] I have tried shopkeeping [*sic*], being an artist in watercolor, and to learn shooting, ended my military service and demanded compensation for my injuries. Travelled 2600 miles by rail, stage, and transport, besides much riding & driving short distances. Studied a little and commenced life as a writer, nearly completing my first work & gaining publication in "Chambers" and the "Week" and favorable criticism from several persons. And ended the year in capacity of Esquire at Toronto and Brockville[.][85]

MISSIONARY, WRITER,
WANDERER,
and the
"YOKOHAMA PIRATES"

ROGER WAS GIVEN A PERIOD of leave before he had to start his new job in Ottawa as Special Constable in the office of Frederick White, comptroller of the Mounted Police, so first he travelled from Regina to Toronto, to stay with members of his immediate family. Rosalie, the exception, was still enjoying a comfortable life in Brockville. Not surprisingly, Roger had an eventful journey:

> On the 12th November I was notified that I should be discharged. I was not allowed out of Hospital. 10 am of the 13th I was let out and turned in my Kit Keeping my Buffalo Coat & a pair of Blankets[.] Bought a coat for $2.00[.] Had supper at Simpson's house and obtained my transport Requisition, sustenance, and pay, Simpson drove me into town in Evening. 14th Sold clothes, repaired buffalo coat[,] said goodbye to all the "boys" & to Dr. Jukes[.] Left the post on foot at Last Post. Heard Lights Out sounding in the distance. Reported at Detachment and waited for the train until 2 am. Monday 15th Novr Took ticket to Toronto 4 am breakfast at Broadview. Dinner at Carberry[,] which place was burned the next day. Arrived at Winnipeg at about 6 pm and hunted up Col[.] McDonald. Went to Opera

house…bed at 2 am. Tuesday 16th Novr Rose 11 am and had breakfast, in afternoon walked out to Fort Osborne and saw Roberts at the M[oun]t[e]d Infantry school[.] Missed my train to Port Arthur. bed at 1 am Wednesday 17th Explored the city and had a bath and got photographed and bought a number of views…. Took train in the evening and saw Rat Portage by starlight. 18th 11 am arr Port Arthur…. Stayed at Ottawa House [in the evening had a disgraceful drunk] 19th Friday [very sick all day.] Yesterday was Thanksgiving Day and a general holiday. Saw Frank Keefer, Walpole Roland and many others. 20th Saturday Left Port Arthur at noon. I got robbed of all I had at the Ottawa house & owed my solvency to Roland on leaving…. 6 am Monday 22d Novr arr Toronto. Went to a hotel and washed[,] arriving at Fathers [*sic*] at about 8 am. dressed in Tam-o-Shanter, a two dollar sack coat[,] flannel shirt[,] riding breeches and long boots. In course of the day I found myself stared at in the streets and was treated everywhere as a wild animal. Ordered clothes & boots[,] bought a hat[,] met Frank and had dinner with him. Went to lodgings to sleep but am to live at home. Next day I wrote to Fred White and reported[;] accepted Mr. Keefers [*sic*] offer of a $50 loan & telegraphed to Rose of my arrival[.][1]

Roger began to achieve some success as a writer during this time in Toronto. His first book, *Tales of Western Life, Lake Superior and the Canadian Prairie,* a mixture of short stories and poetry, was accepted for publication.[2] However, his pleasure in its publication was short-lived, for as early as 1903 he described this work as "a scandalously bad volume of stories and lyrics."[3] Nonetheless, he saved a newspaper clipping that praised his ability to write verse: "The Montreal *Witness* estimates the number of Canadians who have written good English verse and gives 125 or so as especially worthy of high rank. Among the latter are…H.R.A. Pocock…."[4] Gilbert Parker took the time to comment favourably on both the subject matter and the execution:

I do not know what has been said of these tales, good or bad. I hope with all my heart, much good, for here as elsewhere I shall speak and write as I feel about this strong, faithful and dramatic work. Every one of the prose tales and essays in the book is true to the life, true and full of character. I do not know the life of the mountains and plains of Canada well, but I know the great wild lands of other countries, and no man who has lived the life of the open air, in saddle and in camp, can fail to detect when the tale rings true. This is a book that Canadians should value. It is a series of pictures possessing in many points dramatic strength and always having a delightful element of suggestion. I will not say that Mr. Pocock's art is always to be praised. He sometimes lacks proportion and here and there a story finishes, as witness "D'Auguera," [*sic*] having all its power in the middle. But "A Useless Man," "The Ice Cortege" and "Buck Stanton" are as full of dramatic grip as they are of cleverness. Reducing such tales as "The Lean Man" and "Eric" to half their present length, Mr. Pocock would find his art had gained. But this being said one stands upon a broad area of excellent work, hoping at the same time that more and better tales of the kind will come from the pen of this writer, who has an eager eye for character and nature, and whose work is always human and always reverent. He is a worker in a new field. This western country should watch him as he toils, and have sympathetic regard for the results of his labors. I am glad to pay my tribute to "Tales of Western Life."[5]

Roger dedicated *Tales of Western Life* "To the 'Riders of the Plains,' the Gallant North-West Mounted Police." Some of the poems in it appealed to Victorian tastes, while a rather poignant story, "The Lean Man," shows his already deep understanding of First Nations thinking and character.[6] In that story Roger also showed his great admiration for the NWMP, and for the outdoor life they represented,[7] but he was not afraid to point out the harm they caused, as he did, for example, when he had the "Lean Man" describe the NWMP as "these robbers of his people's heritage, who had driven away the buffalo, and sent disease among the tribes, to slowly blight his kindred until they were all dead."[8] In several other stories, Roger's praise for the Mounted Police was less mediated by concern for First Nations. This was the case, for example, when he wrote, "As pioneers preparing for the advance of civilization, the Mounted Police undertake to suffer discomfort and to perform duties of unexampled difficulty, without the performance of which the new provinces of the western plains must be, as they were before the white men came—a howling wilderness."[9] While Roger indicated that "The scenes, incidents, and characters of these sketches are nearly all taken directly from life, but combined for the purposes of fiction,"[10] perhaps his most directly autobiographical story is "A Useless Man," in which his experience in the survey crew on the shore of Lake Superior is told from the point of view of the District Engineer.

Roger's focus may have been on writing, but he managed to remain at work in Ottawa for most of 1887. He also kept up a regular flow of letters to the family telling them all his news. To his sister Lena he was faintly teasing, as she was becoming an attractive young lady with a beautifully expressive face. She was still in school in Toronto, and while he teased her he tried to find out more about a young lady who interested him:

> What a jolly time you girls must be having on the river, and with the Langtons. Does the boy tease you very much? I should put it BOY or ("BOY") lest Mrs. Langton see this, and be wrath.
> I hope you will write to me and tell me some news, anything provided that it be news, for I need it sorely. I won't write to Rose until I have somewhat to say. Remember me to Mrs. Longley next time you see her, and don't remember me to Kate MacDonald less [sic] Mrs. Langton should find out—In truth I have some misgivings lest this fatal error should have been committed already by some ill[-]advised person.[11]

While Roger was working in Ottawa, his father was busy as a deacon, assisting country vicars. He had also formed the Society of the Treasury of God, which was designed to persuade Christians to be as generous as Jews and to return to the principle of paying tithes to the Church of England. Lena reported that when she was young, "Although his clothes were threadbare and his expenses limited to bare necessities, Father would give nothing less than gold at the church offertory."[12] Tragedy struck the family early in 1887, when Roger's sister Hilda was taken ill with diphtheria, and within days his mother, Sarah, was diagnosed with erysipelas. Roger was in Ottawa and his sister Ethel was not physically able to do any nursing, so his father, Charles, and his sister, Lena, divided the house in two to avoid the risk of contagion: Charles nursed Hilda in the back of the house, while Lena nursed Sarah in the front. Both Hilda and Sarah recovered. The family then decided it would be a good idea for Sarah to convalese at her daughter Rosalie's house in Brockville, where servants could attend to her and provide much greater comfort. Sarah travelled to Brockville where she rapidly gained in strength. Rosalie and Sarah received an invitation to a local wedding, and given Sarah's recovery, the two decided on 23 May to drive into Brockville to buy some new ribbons to start their preparations. On the way into town something frightened the horse; it bolted, and both women were thrown from the carriage. Rosalie got up with barely a scratch, but Sarah, only fifty-seven at the time, was killed instantly.

Roger travelled to Brockville for the funeral two days later. Unfortunately, Lena was unable to attend, so Roger wrote her a comforting and uplifting account:

> Father bravely read the lesson and read it well. At the cemetery the place selected was of great beauty, such as a nook as she loved, and on the edges near the gully that runs down to the river.... Now we are back at the house and Rose is sitting up in her little room. After dinner, father and I are going out on the river and I shall go back to Ottawa at midnight. You must not grieve about this matter because that is selfish. Mother rests and that should comfort us....[13]

In the Victorian manner, a last photograph was taken of Sarah with her head resting among the lilies in her coffin. Charles never recovered from this terrible shock, and little more than a year later felt the need to escape from the sadness of his loss and from Canada altogether. He travelled to Switzerland with Lena, Ethel, and Hilda, where the girls spent a short time at school.[14] From Switzerland they moved to London, where Lena was accepted by the Royal Academy of Music, where she studied singing and piano. Charles returned to Canada only once, after Rosalie's husband died in 1891, so that he could help her settle her affairs.

After about a year in Ottawa, Roger's damaged foot healed sufficiently to enable him to contemplate the freedom of the frontier again after the restrictions of city life. When his wanderlust became too strong to resist, he resigned his position as Special Constable.

The death of his mother would also have affected Roger emotionally. It is evident from his letters that she had been loving and supportive. Roger had been very open in his letters to his mother, although he had not told her about his problems with alcohol, which he encoded in his diary. Roger's letters also make it clear that his father was the epitome of a stern, Victorian, God-fearing father. Charles had travelled the world and seen life in the raw, both aboard ship and on land. He would certainly have lectured his son on the perils of the flesh and warned him of hell fire and damnation if he gave in to any sexual or alcoholic temptation. Roger's emotional distance from his father and the sudden death of his mother severed his strongest emotional tie to his home; now his much-loved younger sisters were to go to Switzerland to complete their education, so little remained to prevent him from seeking his fortune on the other side of Canada.

The "vague idea of riding along the Rocky Mountains from Canada to the City of Mexico" was on his mind,[15] but Roger had very little money and he reckoned on being able to earn money along the way by turning his hand to odd jobs. He took the train to Kamloops, British Columbia, where he used some of his small savings to set himself up as a peddler. Although Roger considered himself a good judge of horseflesh since he had learned to ride in the NWMP, his lack of knowledge soon became apparent. He "traded with an Indian for a horse. In the innocence of my young heart I paid a Winchester rifle, a suit of clothes, and ten dollars, getting in exchange a beautiful buckskin gelding, famous…as a man-slayer."[16] He should have realized the horse was dangerous, because it made a couple of half-hearted attacks on him before they even left Kamloops. However, the horse waited until they were sixteen miles from town, up in the mountains, before it really became nasty. Roger dismounted to have a look at the girth, whereupon the horse reared up. It seems that the horse was notorious for its ability to hold in wind. "I had regirthed at the top of a mountain pass, and was mounting, when he suddenly let out all his wind and bolted over rock heaps." Roger, with his great fondness for horses, felt that "This is the only case I have known of unprovoked, carefully planned, and deliberate crime [by a horse], as distinguished from self-defence."[17] As he remounted, the horse set off at full gallop, bucked, and threw Roger so that he smashed his right elbow, which became another noticeable injury he carried to his grave. The horse, however, did not get very far: it got tangled up with the ropes and the wares. When Roger regained consciousness, he tried to sort out the mess. He "cut the rope, cleared the horse, and made fast again to the neck-loop" of the now placid animal and tried to make the best of things.[18] The horse had other ideas, however, and set off at great speed, narrowly failing to loop a rope round Roger's legs. The horse did succeed in escaping at such a speed that Roger, now effectively one-armed, could not hold it, and the rope lacerated his left hand. That was the last he saw of either the horse or his wares, which were strewn across the countryside.

Leaving a trail of blood, Roger staggered along the path. He grew delirious due to loss of blood, but fortunately he came across the tent of a road repairer who guided him to a lonely farm. The farmers gave him first aid and took him to the hospital in Kamloops, where he spent the next two months, although he but remembered little of the first week or so. His elbow had been so badly smashed that it could not be properly set.[19] When he was close to recovery, he heard of a minor uprising on the Skeena River. Although neither the hospital's doctor nor anyone else he asked had ever heard of the Skeena River, Roger's interest was undeterred: "The moment I heard the news I got a friend to write out a telegram offering my services to the *Montreal Witness* as a war correspondent 'at the front.' 'All right,' replied the *Witness,* laconically; 'expenses limited twenty pounds.'"[20] Roger probably owed such a positive response from Forrest, the editor at the *Witness,* to their acquaintance of several years, during which Roger had proven he could write appealing material. As he was again almost penniless, and therefore forced to shelve the idea of his ride to Mexico, this Skeena River assignment gave him a new objective. A map he found in an atlas showed the Skeena River "away up north near Alaska, in a part of the map scrawled over 'un explored.' The distance was one thousand miles."[21] Roger was about to embark on the adventure that enabled him to claim the "Skeena Indian War" among his list of life experiences.

First, however, he had to find a way to get there, so Roger took a "train to the Pacific Coast, and at Victoria found a steamer going northward. She was called the Cariboo Fly, and there never was a dirtier, grimier little tramp."[22] By the time the "war correspondent" had completed his arrangements to head north, the "war" was all but over: the British Columbia Provincial Police (BCPP) had stepped in, and the single casualty had been a First Nations man, Kamalmuk, who was shot in the back by Provincial Constable Franklin Green.[23] Superintendent H.B. Roycraft of the BCPP was not satisfied with the legality of the shooting and so put Green on trial.[24] At about the time Green was pleading not guilty, Roger boarded the *Cariboo Fly.* Roger's distance from the conflict did not deter him from writing a long article on the legal and military activities connected with these events.[25]

Measles, one constituent of the origin of the "war," was one of the diseases white settlers brought with them and it had consistently killed members of the First Nations. According to Roger, a fatal outbreak of measles among the Gitksan in late 1887 was believed to have been introduced by the Hudson's Bay Company and its local storekeeper, Charlie Clifford.[26] Thus, when Kamalmuk took his wife and two children to a tribal gathering at Forks of the Skeena (now known as Hazelton), where his children contracted measles and died, he blamed Clifford. His wife, for her own reasons, blamed the family medicine man, Neetuh.[27] Kamalmuk acted on his wife's opinion and shot Neetuh. Because Kamalmuk's wife was Neetuh's heir, they inherited his possessions, which they shared among their friends and relations, according to Gitksan custom.[28] Everyone seemed happy, except for the few local white residents who informed the BCPP. Kamalmuk felt threatened by the Provincial Police and turned his house into a fortress until he received a letter:

> The letter was from Mr. Todd, Indian agent, advising Jim
> [Kamalmuk] to surrender and take his trial. Jim, being unable
> to read, was hugely pleased at receiving a "strong paper,"
> and concluded that it was to protect him from the police. No
> longer afraid of arrest he left his wife and went for a holiday,
> travelling down from Gaetwinlthgul to the river. When
> a policeman came and arrested him at Gaetwangak[29] for
> murder, naturally Jim thought there must be some mistake.
> He bolted, and the white man shot him dead.[30]

The Gitksan were infuriated by this, and 600 armed men headed towards the white settlement at the Forks.[31] A gunboat and a military Battery were sent to demonstrate government power, but the local magistrate, Captain Napoleon Fitzstubbs, went to talk to the Gitksan alone and persuaded them to return to their villages. The chiefs agreed, but they said they required revenge and would kill the first white man to visit Gitwangak. The local missionary was away at the time on honeymoon and flatly refused to return to the village, so he was moved to another on the coast. This left the Anglican Church looking for a missionary who would be both reliable and willing to take the risky position for a stipend of £10 a month. Roger declared he was "grabbed by the despairing synod as the only possible candidate for the vacant post...."[32]

Before he assumed the post, Roger, who was having a pleasant time in the region (apart from the constant odours of a local fish cannery) had made friends with the military Battery and gone exploring in a steam launch. Back in Montreal, his editor was becoming irritated at not receiving reports about the "war," so he suggested that Roger, since he was in the neighbourhood, "might just as well report on the Behring [sic] Sea Question." Roger points out, "I was no more bothered than he by trifling points of geography. Behring Sea was only two thousand miles distant, and I still had fifty bright dollars, enough for a gorgeous autumn on lines of the strictest economy. I set out by canoe for Alaska."[33] Thanks to a letter he wrote to Frederick White and the date lines on the articles he wrote for the *Witness,* paired with comments in the articles themselves, we know he travelled to Metlakahtla by the Anglican mission steamer *Evangeline,* where he stayed from at least 15 August to 20 August before leaving for Fort Simpson by canoe. By 22 August he was in Fort Tongass;

he then travelled by canoe to Port Chester, where he arrived on 24 or 25 August. Because Mr. Duncan made him unwelcome there, he reached Tongass Narrows by 27 August. On 1 September he left on an American steamer to travel to Juneau, Alaska. By 8 September he was in Juneau; by the 15th he was in Sitka; and by the 22nd he was aboard the *Ancon*. Roger reached Metlakahtla again by the 28th and was in Hazelton by 10 October. This travel enabled Roger to describe for *Witness* readers the effect European incursions had had on the behaviour of First Nations peoples—particularly Mr. Duncan's practices, the work and quarrels of missionaries, gold mining in Juneau, the Muir glacier, and the sealing monopoly of the Alaska Commercial Company.[34] In one article Roger praised the Presbyterian "industrial school with 100 boys and 60 girls.... the place turns out Christian men and women to bless their fellow citizens and help to check the wholesale corruption of the native villages," yet he also described "the graves of 30,000 Indians who lie in the darkness, spirited thither by vooka [*sic*] (Russian spirits), small-pox, gunpowder, and social and sexual perdition—which it is only true, deplorably true, we great whites always bring with our Bibles and our bath-tubs."[35]

Penniless again, but greatly refreshed by all these adventures, Roger reported to the Diocesan Synod of New Caledonia and was told that before he could take on his position as missionary he must first preach a sermon in the cathedral. He maintained that was the most frightening event of his life, but "I remembered," he wrote, "that I had been a trooper."[36]

Earlier, while he was still on his northern travels, he had had the foresight to write a letter to Charles Todd, in which he asked for specific medical supplies "for the Indians at Kitwingar during [the] next winter," including a gallon of castor oil, "200 Cathartic Pills," a bottle of quinine, linseed meal, and "Toothache Mixture."[37] Five Christian First Nations men then took him on the nerve-racking, ten-day journey up the Skeena River through its many rapids. Roger was terrified all the time, but dared not show it for risk of losing respect. Instead, he vented his feelings by berating his crew for splashing him at every tricky rapid. They went thirty miles past the mission at Gitwangak to the Hudson's Bay post and military station at Forks of the Skeena, where Roger kitted himself out for winter. He considered staying there, but went back to Gitwangak to take up his post, where "Every morning I tramped to the village to visit the sick, then rounded up my congregation either for church or school. Every day, too, the medicine-man sat on his roof to curse me as I passed and lavish imprecations on the children, and no evening went by without a fresh rumour as to my impending death."[38] In the middle of that winter, other tribe members came down from the hills to kill Roger, as the resident white man. Roger declared to the assembly that "The Indian law is a life for a life, the white man's law is a tribe for a life, the village wrecked and burned, the people driven away into the hills, slaughtered, starved, given to the eagles and the wolves." The chief nonetheless wanted Roger killed, so Roger went to stand in front of the schoolhouse:

> At least I would not have my weak knees betray me even though I am such a coward; so, rather to cover my fright than with any better motive, I ordered those who were to fire that they should come nearer. "You cannot shoot straight," I said, "because you are frightened."
>
> So they came within ten yards, kneeling with levelled rifles, and all the people gathered behind them waiting.
>
> Then with some strange fancy moving within me, I lifted my arms, until both hands were level, touching the same beam of the log wall. I looked steadily at the chief, then at the men who were to fire, one by one in the face....
>
> "Now," I said. "Fire!"
>
> Not a man stirred.
>
> "Fire!"
>
> The silence was like the silence of death, and it seemed to me that I had already passed beyond the boundaries of life to meet my Master. My Master died like that, with His arms stretched out as though to draw all men unto Him.
>
> Then I heard a little sigh out of the silence, and looking down saw that the muzzles of all those rifles were lowered upon the ground, while the men remained kneeling.
>
> For many years the missionaries had laboured, it seemed, in vain among these people, but now because I had unthinkingly, perhaps irreverently, made the sign of the Cross, they all knelt down. The majesty of the British peace had failed me, the strength of the British law had not saved me, but the people who dared to defy the white man's power knelt down to the sign of the Cross.[39]

Despite such nervous moments, Roger's winter as a missionary passed without bloodshed, and he claimed that his simple frontier-style Christianity resulted in the conversion of the chief. Roger also claimed that he was "Teaching hygiene and making Indians dig latrines to save their lives, before I could preach a word to them.... Sanitation went before salvation, up there!"[40]

Roger had at least one visitor that winter. He reported that Fitzstubbs, the magistrate, came to Gitwangak to proclaim "that the Indian law was dead, and that the white man's law had taken its place." At that meeting on the outlawing of potlatch were 250 men, "all armed, but with their weapons hidden." Fitzstubbs sat in a chair at a table and an upturned soapbox was placed at his right for Roger. According to Roger, the local chief was contemptuous of Fitzstubbs' presentation: "The Indian law was very good, he said, and had lasted as long as the mountains whose great white spires went up above our heads. The white man's law was new, feeble as a baby, too weak to govern even the little children. Let the white man go back to the salt water, and take his law with him, for fear of its getting hurt." Fitzstubbs had such a powerful personality, however, that he stood up to threats, including one man who rushed at him with a knife. "We walked out of the house, where we had been so near, so very near, to death.... And so ended the trouble on the Skeena—ended by the matchless nerve of the old magistrate."[41]

While Roger remained in Gitwangak, though, he was not as impressed with Fitzstubbs. He went as far as to write to an official in Ottawa expressing his doubt that Fitzstubbs would actually enforce the potlatch law. When Fitzstubbs was told about this letter, he asked Roger to describe the experience they shared. In that description Roger praised both his own activities and the way Fitzstubbs handled himself:

> After the troubles of 1888, I undertook to reorganize the
> Mission of Kitwangak of the Church Missionary Society, that
> village having been the center of the disturbance. Shortly after
> my arrival you came to the village, while visiting the several
> tribes to prohibit the Potlatch.
>
> On 7th November a Council was held at Lott's house at
> which you were the only white man present.
>
> You addressed the Indians, telling them that they must desist
> from the "Potlatching." They replied, that the law was a weak
> baby, and in several speeches defied you, and the Government.
> One man also threatened your life. For over two hours I
> expected an attack, but your courage and good humor surprised
> and awed the people, and we left the house unmolested.
>
> I was told afterwards that most of those who were present
> thought you would be killed.[42]

This may not have been the "war" that Roger claimed it was later, but it cannot be denied that he showed great bravery in working among these people on his own for a winter. Roger claimed that, thanks to his perseverance, the "Diocesan Synod gave me a suit of clothes, seventy-five dollars, and the offer of further training for Holy Orders."[43] This was far from being the truth, though, for "An old timer once told me that Pocock's indiscretions with some of the Indian maidens caused the church to quickly wash their hands of him."[44] Perhaps the condition of some of those maidens also made the village reluctant to have him killed. One is led to wonder whether Roger's descendants might be found somewhere on the Skeena River today.

With his $75 and new suit of clothes, Roger decided to settle in Victoria for a while to see how successful he could be as a writer and to explore Vancouver Island. When Roger arrived in 1889, apart from the presence of its Chinatown, Victoria was little different from an English country town with a temperate climate and pleasant scenery. At least in terms of newspapers, as potential markets for his work, this was a wise move, for Victoria, with a population of about 7,000, was well equipped with newspapers: *British Colonist* (a daily, circulation 900), *Weekly Colonist* (circulation 600), *Standard* (a daily, circulation 500), *Weekly Standard* (circulation 1,000), *Star* (on Sundays), and the *Times* (daily circulation 1,200; Friday circulation 1,500).[45] One of these, the *Times,* published quite a bit of his writing. For example, "The Rocky Mountain Club," a work of fiction, was published as a serial; he appears to have earned a regular $2.50 a week from that paper. Among his articles was one in which he gave advice on developing a tourism industry in British Columbia, rather than leaving the rewards of tourism to Alaska:

> I have an extensive acquaintance with almost all parts of
> the Great Archipelago, have tasted its charms of fishing and
> hunting, have seen its most picturesque industries, have lived
> and travelled among its savages, and have travelled thousands
> of miles by sailboat and canoe, steam launch, or passenger
> vessel, and I am convinced that our province has only to
> bid for tourists, to advertise well, and accommodate them
> liberally, to make the seaboard known to the ends of the earth
> as one of its most delightful pleasure grounds.[46]

He also wrote a three-part series on the background of the people among whom he had lived as a missionary, the coming of trade to the region with Major Downie, Thomas Hankin, and A.C. Youmans, and the building of the telegraph. Then, after describing some tragedies, he ended on an unusually cheerful note: "There are now six canning establishments on the inlet and eight missions in the upper and lower valleys, and all are prospering greatly."[47] Roger was also able to write with a more historical focus on the *Beaver* and his admiration for George Vancouver.[48]

Roger needed to earn money with his writing. Nonetheless, he was quite prepared to upset the local dignitaries and federal authorities with some of his contributions. Based on his travels up the British Columbia coast, he had deduced the following about the First Nations:

> [They] were getting a jug-handled deal from the whites in general and the federal Indian department in particular.
> When he put his advanced ideas in print he got in bad with everyone, especially the Indian department.[49]

In 1888 he had criticized the Federal government for not paying sufficient attention to the First Nations in the Upper Skeena,[50] but a prime example of his willingness to criticize was his series of four articles entitled "The Coast Indians." He wrote of the "gigantic neglect of the Indian department's duty," and continued:

> There is nothing in the reports about Bella Coola, Kitamaht, Kit-kahtla, and many other of the middle coast villages; there is nothing about the Hydahs, Nishgars, or Giatkshians, no work being done for them, nothing but the misspelling of some of their tribal names and a grand masterly omission of any good done thereabout with the appropriations of public money, of which such a handsome balance can be shown on hand.[51]

As if this were not enough, he described "the Indian Office" as mildly humane, well mannered, expensive, hopeful, and utterly useless. Roger suggested that "while the public is indifferent, and the department hates to be disturbed in its ancient slumbers, the employers of Indian labour are careful that the people shall be blind to the real state of the Indians, lest their natural prey be rescued."

Roger then argued that people purveying alcohol should be removed from the region and that prostitution of First Nations women should be eliminated. He thought the prostitution was largely caused by the need to "find money to squander in the feasts." Roger explained what he saw as the many iniquities of these potlatches, and declared they should be "really prohibited, as it now is in theory." He also addressed epidemics:

Smallpox was especially frightful when some twenty-five
years ago half the nation perished. Vaccination is very
difficult here because the people are so scrofulous that it
often amounts to a serious illness. Yet it ought to be strongly
insisted upon. Measles, too, is not the trivial complaint that
we know, but a terrible disease, slaying old and young alike,
not by its own virulence, but by neglect of the sick and
exposure during convalescence.[52]

Less publicly, Roger wrote to Grant Powell, Under Secretary of State, in
Ottawa:

At this time engaged in studying the life, industries, &
advancement of Western Canada for the "Witness" of
Montreal, I have discovered a poor nation of Cannibal
heathen, dying with frightful rapidity here on the North West
Coast. I want to save them, and so appeal to you to help me
get something done for them by Government.[53]

In this letter Roger referred to articles he had written "on the Kwa-gutl"—
that is, "The Coast Indians" series he had written for the *Victoria Daily
Times*. Roger believed so strongly in his cause that he sent a note to Powell,
to accompany copies of two articles from the series, and asked Powell "to
help me by drawing attention to them in the proper quarters. Letters on
Cannibalism & proposed remedy will follow shortly."[54] These were forwarded to the Superintendent General of Indian Affairs.

These articles, however, don't seem to have elicited as much reaction as
material he wrote for the *Ottawa Free Press*. The editor of the *Ottawa Free
Press* referred to Roger being "among the aborigines of British Columbia"
and having written "a most harrowing account of their condition, which
will be found elsewhere in this paper." The editor went on to write:

Mr. Pocock charges that the Indians are being systematically
corrupted and decimated; that the policy of "cruel
and callous neglect[,]" which drove the Indians of the
Saskatchewan to desperation and insurrection, is being
pursued in the Pacific province, and that the department
is either unwilling or unable to do its duty.... Perhaps Mr.
Pocock's expose [*sic*] may arouse public sentiment in Canada
to such an extent that even Mr. Dewdney may feel impelled to

do his duty in protecting from decimation the superior race of Indians inhabiting British Columbia.[55]

Indeed, in his article for the *Ottawa Free Press,* Roger was not subtle:

> There seems to be a common impression that the Indians are not worth saving, and that work or money spent on them is wasted. It is probable that a more contemptible idea never entered a human head.
>
> They once owned this country; a capable race, of good physique, with large skulls showing reflective and executive capacity, a thing rare among savages. They were accomplished craftsmen in wood, possessed textile arts, wrought in copper and had tribal government.
>
> We came among them as gods; we, with our civilized life and its under stratum of moral and physical filth—sexual infamy, drunkenness, small pox [*sic*], and the like, and the Indians are smothered and drowned in it…. and we don't stretch out a hand to save them. It is murder to withhold aid from a drowning man—what is it to withhold aid from a drowning race?[56]

Roger went on to supply numbers and to castigate prostitution among First Nations women.

The editorial and Roger's article were both sent from the Department of Indian Affairs in Ottawa to Hamilton Moffatt, Chief Clerk in the Indian Office, Victoria, "for your information and report."[57] Eleven days later Moffatt wrote a five-page report:

> In reply I have to state that in Mr. Pocock's article there is a certain amount of truth, but so much exaggerated that it would appear to a reader versed in the history of this Province that the communication describes the condition of Indian Affairs some twenty-five or thirty years ago instead of at the present time.

Moffatt, who had lengthy personal experience in the region, then criticized the numbers Roger had cited, particularly for the smallpox epidemics of 1862 and 1866, which "of course happened before Confederation and were not caused by the neglect of the Dominion Government as the context of Mr. Pocock's article would seem to insinuate." Moffatt's assessment continued:

> In regard to the prostitution as mentioned by Mr. Pocock's article there is no doubt that in years past large numbers of the Northern Indian women came to Victoria and other cities in the Province for that purpose but at present the traffic is greatly reduced and comparatively few are to be found following this degrading business.
>
> Mr. Pocock seems to think that the evil complained of can easily be stopped by the Department, but I would remind him that for ages the Social Evil has been studied in all its phases by the most powerful Christian Governments in the World and as yet no remedy has been found and at any rate it would require some special legislation.
>
> The statement made that the "poor weak Indian Office" was reduced to snubbing the Agent at Alert Bay for endeavoring [sic] to stop women from coming to this City for the purpose of prostitution is somewhat overdrawn....

On the matter of the potlatch, Moffatt claimed that

> Until last fall this Department was powerless to stop the Potlach [sic] as the Provincial Government refused us the use of its Jails and constables—but since that time arrangements have been entered into between the two Governments by which all offenders against the Indian Act can be imprisoned in the Provincial Jails and Mr. Agent Pidcak[?] has taken advantage of the new regulation by arresting and sentencing to...imprisonment an Indian notorious for potlaching [sic] and setting the law at defiance.
>
> With regard to the neglect of the Indian Dept in not having published in its report matter relating to the Bella Coola, Kitamaht, Kitkahtla, Hydah and some other Bands, I may state for your information that the Indian Agent for the North West Coast had then but lately been approved and had not visited the whole of the Agency and was not consequently in a position to give statistics relating to the above Bands.
>
> The writer's sarcasm in regard to "Medicine for old women" is of rather a curious nature, as in this Office is to be found a letter from him making application for some drugs

for the Indians of the Upper Skeena, and signed by him as a *Missionary* of the *Church Missionary Society,* a copy of which is herewith enclosed.

In conclusion I beg to state that in my opinion the article above reported upon was written for pecuniary recompense for an opposition newspaper with the evident intention of injuring, if possible, in the public mind the Indian Department of the Dominion of Canada.[58]

There is no indication of any other action by anyone in government. Roger, however, continued writing, and produced a series of articles on the Haida.[59]

As well as claiming the "Skeena Indian War" among his experiences, Roger said that he had served at sea with the "Yokohama Pirates." His sense of romance may have caused him to give the impression that he had been a swashbuckler sailing under the "Jolly Roger." What he actually did was stow away on the fifty-ton *Adele,* an unlicensed sealing ship. The problem of his status as a stowaway was solved when Roger presented a bottle of rum to the captain, Gustave Hansen. Hansen was a notorious poacher who was known in Victoria as the "Flying Dutchman." When the Chinese-built, British-registered *Adele,* which was owned by a German company from Japan, put to sea, there were five national flags in her locker to suit all eventualities. After Roger suggested that the skull-and-crossbones would be more suitable, the captain called him a fool—not the last person to do so. Hansen's sealing activities were illegal because between 1886 and 1911 hunting fur seals in the North Pacific was covered by a treaty involving Japan, Russia, Britain, and the United States. The treaty dictated that seal hunting be pelagic, or off-shore. It was forbidden to land on the rookeries to take seals. There was a U.S. gunboat watching the fur seal breeding grounds, and Britain had H.M.S. *Pheasant* checking that all sealers were licensed. Yet it was those protected rookeries on the Pribilof Islands, north of the Aleutians in the Bering Sea, that Hansen raided.

In Victoria, Roger had encouraged a sense of mystery about himself and liked to be known as "Mysterious Pocock." While he did this partly to attract attention, particularly to his writing, it also had the effect of making crew members of the *Adele* very suspicious of him. That Roger had acquired one of the new Eastman Kodak cameras and had a natural ability with a camera, did nothing to allay their suspicions. These cameras were new enough to be rare outside the big towns; however, people were always vain enough to want to have their photograph taken, so Roger used this impulse to win over the crew. After the *Adele* experience, he always made sure to have a camera with him on his adventures. In spite of minor squabbles, and a half-hearted mutiny by some of the crew, the *Adele* survived the attentions of gunboats and the appalling weather, raided the rookeries, and killed enough seals to make a little money, although not as much as on her earlier trips. Hansen had also planned to lure the governor of the island of St. Paul and his small garrison on board and get them all drunk so his crew could raid the island's warehouse for its valuable store of skins, but "The elements had had the final say in the mutiny and piracy business, and three days afterwards, crippled, partly dismasted, and under jury sails, we headed back for Victoria."[60] Elsewhere, Roger described it thus:

> I have just returned from a ten weeks cruise in Alaskan waters undertaken for the purpose of studying the seal fishery. I shipped as a sailor and found enough of interest to make a book of which I hope soon to be able to send you a copy. Our adventures were of a very sensational character, including piracy, mutiny, & a very narrow escape from shipwreck.[61]

Roger did indeed gather enough material on that voyage, particularly from the stories the captain and crew told of earlier raids, when the *Adele* had been part of a group of twenty schooners engaged in raiding Russian and Japanese territories for fur seals, to write about the "Yokohama Pirates."[62] Roger, "on his return, gave his adventures full treatment in his Victoria paper, which displeased the Flying Dutchman so much that he waylaid Pocock in an alley one night and there was a lively fistic set-to."[63] Several of the stories set in the Aleutian Islands were published in Britain. At about the same time, Rudyard Kipling, Roger's literary hero, was writing about sealing and the Pribilofs.[64] When Roger interviewed Kipling in 1897, he questioned Kipling about the source:

> "Who told you the Rhyme of the Three Sealers?"
> "Mind your own business."
> "I've the right to know; had the yarn in my notebook for years before you printed it."
> "Where did you get it?"
> "From one of the Yokohama Pirates, the Flying Dutchman."
> "So you know Hans? Where?"
> "In Behring Sea."
> "Then you've the right to know. I got it from Captain Lake in Yokohama. So you're a pirate?"

"Yes, and your 'White Seal' contains an idiotic blunder. A fur seal sleeps with his fore flippers folded on his breast, not limp at the sides."[65]

After this productive time in Victoria, Roger made an arrangement with the *Victoria Daily Times* and some businessmen to go to the flourishing Kootenays to try to persuade some of the newly prosperous miners there to invest in the Victoria area. Before he left Victoria, Roger's brother Frank, by then a skilled mining engineer, wrote to him suggesting a joint mining project in the area. Roger replied, "I have spent 2 days considering your project," but decided against it because "I have made many enemies by plain speaking. The time is not far off when neither of us will care to patronise these dirty little blackleg governments."[66] Not surprisingly, Roger ran into financial trouble with his new venture:

> In May 1890 some Victoria merchants sent me to the Kootenay camps to advertise their resources in the press. When the work was half done their money ran short, so I tried to publish an advertising book and raise subscriptions— some $50 for that purpose. I counted on the Spokane men who owned the camp, but when I approached them I found that these capitalists wanted to keep the Kootenay dark while they bought claims. I was actually offered bribes to keep my mouth shut.
>
> So I went broke and have earned my living since then in other trades.[67]

When Roger arrived that May, some English prospectors looked with suspicion at their rather strange countryman, but Roger was happier anyway making friends with the rough and tough frontiersmen with whom he felt more at home. He was able to do a little prospecting on his own and added this to the list of trades he had plied. His travels in this region led him to maintain that the mines in the Kootenays had been discovered accidentally when hunters found what they took to be little blobs of lead in the ashes around their campfires. They were pleased to find what they thought was an easy source of lead for their bullets, but they had the wrong mineral. They had discovered silver ore.[68] In the summer of 1890, the *Victoria Daily Times* published his series of articles on mining in the Kootenays.[69]

Some of the Kootenay miners with small claims paid Roger a little money to go to Spokane to try to raise some capital for them. He went and did get publicity through the newspapers, but the owners of the biggest mines, who had their homes in Spokane, did not want publicity for the Kootenays, so they did what they could to silence him—probably by applying pressure on publishers to stop paying him. When this project failed, he came up with another scheme, this time to publicize Spokane and its industries through photographs for a special edition of a newspaper he called the *Scarehead*.[70] The editor gave him a "skeleton" of a horse, and enough money for a few days, so he set off into the surrounding country.

Once he was well away from urban life and was a frontiersman again, he had a fit of conscience and decided that he no longer liked Spokane. He wrote:

> [I was] ashamed among the honest farmers at their harvest.
> I had stooped to the cheap methods of cheap men, become
> part of the froth upon the mighty waves of American
> endeavour.... But my heart was crying for the mountains, for
> the wilder country, the gentler men of the camps. At noon
> of the third day I wrote from a village to my Editor, saying
> that his skeleton was feasting at the local stable, and might be
> collected on payment of the bill.[71]

With resources consisting of two half-dollar coins and his precious camera, Roger next resolved to try his fortune as a commercial photographer at Coeur d'Alene, Idaho. One of those coins bought him a meal and a ride on a construction train to Coeur d'Alene. After he alighted at 3 A.M., he trudged on beside the lake all that day and up the river beyond. Late in the evening he arrived at a collection of cabins known as the Old Mission Hotel. Back in Spokane Roger had hired a lad to take charge of all his belongings until his return. Roger put up at that hotel and sent word to the lad in Spokane to bring along the luggage, some of which Roger could pawn for some much needed cash. The lad, probably feeling that Roger had not kept to the agreement they made in Spokane, decided he would be better off ignoring the letter and keeping the luggage, but for three days Roger continued to run up a bill at the hotel, hoping that the lad would arrive with his property. Meanwhile, this was frontier country and, as usual, Roger could not resist turning his inquisitive nose in the direction of local affairs. In the process he succeeded in alienating gamblers, small-time crooks, and the hotel proprietor:

> That Indian Reservation, which I had crossed afoot, was on a
> near date to be thrown open by Congress as public land free

to all comers. On its western edge the farmers had gathered, led by a Mr. Truax, ready for a big rush and scramble to seize the ground. Coming from thence, I had blundered into an evil crowd of gamblers and desperadoes waiting on the eastern edge to drive the farmers away by force of arms, and themselves capture the Reservation as Mineral Lands. I was therefore a spy from the Truax gang, and the crowd determined to lynch me.[72]

He had surely lived long enough to realize that an Englishman should not make himself conspicuous in frontier America, particularly well over the border and far from the protection of the N W M P and the British Columbia Provincial Police, to which he had become accustomed. So he had to think quickly to extricate himself from this hazardous situation. He utilized three strokes of good fortune. First, frontier folk were always keen to have their photographs taken by the photographers who so rarely came their way. Second, the weather had been dull for some days and, just as the crowd began to look threatening, the sun started to lighten up the land and the clouds started to break. Third, a freight train was getting up steam, ready to move along the nearby track to the mines. The landlord of the hotel had wisely impounded Roger's one item of value, his camera, as security, but with inspired cheek Roger found a way out. He organized the landlord, his family, and some local toughs into a proud group under the sudden sunshine and called for his camera. Backing towards the tracks, he fussed over the arrangements until the train was close by and about to gather speed. He snapped the shutter, yelled goodbye, and was on the train before the group could appreciate his plan and recover their guns, which they had put aside for the photograph.[73]

That plan worked well, but soon Roger faced another danger. Freight train conductors were used to tramps hitching rides. They either tipped the tramps off the moving train, which could mean death, or they demanded a bribe. By now, Roger was looking desperate, so the conductor felt it was wiser to ask for a bribe of $1. Roger had only half a dollar, which he had no wish to spend, so he persuaded the conductor to strike a pose while he feigned taking a photograph and told the conductor that his charge was $1, so they were even. He got away with it, and late in the evening the train arrived at Wallace, "then a place of fifteen hundred people, jammed at the meeting of four gulches in the heart of the Bitterroot Mountains of Idaho. Just a month ago it had been totally wiped out by fire…." However, Wallace, a boom town, very quickly recovered from the fire. Roger observed that Wallace boasted "fifty-five saloons, the brothels were sufficient with eighteen houses, the gambling-hells, dance-houses, and theatres met all local requirements."[74]

There was no newspaper in town for which he could write, winter was approaching, the nights were getting frosty, and half a dollar was not going to last long in such a place. Regretfully, he had to pawn his treasured camera, which brought in enough money to live on for three days. In desperation, Roger went to the City Marshal, and, somewhat surprisingly, received sympathy and help from him. Throughout his writing career, Roger never failed to compare American ways unfavourably with Canadian practices, but this was just one of a number of occasions when he was treated very well by Americans. The Marshal even agreed to ask the Spokane police to find the lad who had Roger's baggage. His luck was in. The baggage was returned to him, together with £4 from a magazine that had published some of Roger's ballads. His timing was good, for the magazine went bankrupt shortly thereafter. Roger, on the other hand, set out to enjoy his new prosperity.

Now that he was no longer a poverty-stricken vagrant, but a man with a little capital, he needed to find some way to invest it to generate income through the coming winter. He then had an outstanding idea. Roger's ideas were not always good, and even when they did have merit, he failed many times to make the most of them. This time, however, he was able to achieve success, though the venture lasted only a few months. In this boom town swarming with people, every piece of land that fronted the single boardwalk through town was used by someone trading in goods or services. Roger observed that the boardwalk extended over the bridge across the Coeur d'Alene River to the far side of the railway. All day, many hundreds of men who chewed tobacco wandered out across the bridge to spit into the river below. The bridge was unusual, though, because it took a sharp dogleg bend halfway across. Roger thought he could run a plank across the angle formed by the dogleg and set up a business there, in the only unoccupied spot in Wallace:

> The City Marshal would not object—we consulted over a cocktail; the county was pacified, for I bought a five-dollar licence; but there remained the Committee of Public Safety, pledged to lynch bad men and to pitch out tramps like me. I called on Dan, Chairman of the Vigilance Committee.
> "Where?" he yelped.
> "The bridge," said I, very humbly.
> "You can't trade on the bridge."
> "Don't want to. Who's [sic] is the air over the river?"

"If you want to trade there, take out a licence from Heaven."

"Will you interfere?"

"No, I guess not. We never interfere outside our jurisdiction."

In his capacity as a merchant, Dan sold me a stock of cigars; and with the Vigilance Committee for a friend[,] one can commit all the crimes in the calendar.[75]

Roger's business prospered. The one plank across the angle became a platform, then two packing cases became counters, and he added walls and a roof. A door under the rail was followed with sliding glass windows above. Inside, he fitted a stove, bedding, and kitchen equipment. He ran supporting legs for his growing structure down to the river to provide more stability, but they raised unpleasant prospects such as rent and taxes so he removed them. The combined shop and dwelling perched above the river like some enormous bird's nest, swaying in the wind. Roger declared exultantly that "At the end of six weeks I was free of all debt, with plenty of credit, and one hundred and fifty dollars worth of stock in fruit, tobacco, and sweets laid by from my profits."[76] Dan, his supplier, was also very happy with the arrangement.

Roger used his artistic talents and ability to write verse to drum up more business. Among the strangest documents he saved are the actual paper advertisements he pinned up around Wallace. When he put up new ones, he would store the old. There is a drawing of a dog smoking a cigar, saying, "It makes me beastly sick—but I bought it at the Bridge and I'll smoke it or bust." A second shows a woman saying, "Yews allus smoking in ter the house. Gitalong then down to the Bridge—Yew—Git!" A third features a kitten with this advice: "Never smoke! But if you ever do, get a decent cigar at the Bridge." Probably the best ad pictures an unshaven tough announcing, "This durn'd seegar's got no strength to it—I'm just going down to the BRIDGE to get a good one."[77] Roger was also fond of composing poetry. The autobiographical "Song" he posted as an advertisement is one of the worst among his really bad efforts in verse, but he considered it worth taking down and saving with his papers:

> Here's the tedious song of a bore;
> You have heard of him doubtless before,
> For in Wallace his name
> Has a wonderful fame
> And you buy your cigars at his store.
> With cigars he's seen desperate at times,

When he roped in the nickels and dimes,
And the men died of the smoke
With a gulp and a choke,
He was sent to this town for his crimes.
He came here as freight on a train,
Beat his way in the dark and the rain,
He was hungry and cold,
But 'tis better than gold,
To be gifted with cheek and with brain.
He saw that the prospect was fair,
If he only could find him a lair,
But no place could be found
On the firm solid ground,
So he built up his house in the air.[78]

There are three more verses, as bad as or worse than these, but the advertisements seem to have been effective. He became a local talking point and used the interest to start an employment agency. A newspaper reported that "The 'Man on the Bridge' has developed another streak of enterprise and established an employment agency. Men will be furnished employers at short notice and situations secured for persons desiring work of any kind. If you want to hire a man or are looking for a job, consult the 'Man on the Bridge.'"[79] Wallace was certainly a tough place at the time, but Roger described it as

a peaceful little gold-mining township. On an average seven miners a night were clubbed in the street, or drugged and robbed in houses of ill-fame. One went abroad after dusk with a revolver in the side pocket and forefinger on the trigger.

But no one molested me. The "man on the bridge" was looked upon as a harmless lunatic, and I prospered.[80]

However, Roger's publicity became so effective that his success was noted by a man named Long Shorty. He "got a couple of pine trees stripped, squared, and thrown across the river just behind my house, the ends resting on either bank. On these timbers he began to run up a commodious wooden building, a saloon....he went to the City Council, offering at his own charges to widen the bridge up to the foot of the wall. The City consented, and I was to be effaced."[81] The landowners on each side of the river were unwilling to upset this ruffian, but the City Marshal, backed by

the Vigilance Committee, decided that there must be an end to the lawlessness, so one day prominent citizens banded together with the Marshal and
twenty-five of the leading criminals, including Long Shorty, were marched
out of town. Nonetheless, Roger's business did not last much longer. A
massive collapse of the local bank ended that particular boom in Wallace,
and it wiped out most of Roger's profits almost overnight.

So Roger moved on and spent the summer of 1891 as a tramp, more
or less: "The summer came, and by coach, by train, or afoot I wandered
for months through settlements of farmers in Idaho, Washington, and
Oregon, the three realms of the Columbia Valley."[82] He said that at about
this time friends recommended he follow his brother's example and take
American citizenship, but his writings were regularly anti-American and
fiercely pro-Canadian:

> Canada was a bigger, wilder country, where men went safe
> without a weapon, where aliens had human rights, where
> Judges were not bribed, Legislators not of the criminal
> classes, and honesty was not become effete. Canada had
> spoiled me, made me accustomed to deal with honourable
> men, healthy and clean, a sterling coinage of manhood, not
> crumpled rags.[83]

Given such comments, it is little wonder that the American edition of
his autobiography, *Following the Frontier,* caused such anger among
Americans when it was published in 1903. That anger, however, may also
have helped sales.

In his writings, Roger was strangely reticent about that summer, and,
commented only that he barely kept alive. He would colour photographs
or lecture for small sums of money, but he came across little towns where
"Nobody wanted to be lectured, nobody cared for painted photographs,
there was no employment offered."[84] It is possible that he fell in for a while
with the First Nations people, with whom he seemed to share sympathy
and understanding. It seems impossible that he could have had such intimate knowledge of the traditions and the way of life of the wandering
Blackfoot bands that he displayed in his books *The Blackguard* and *The
Wolf Trail* without actually having lived among them.[85] Even in *Horses*
he praised them: "The daily bathing, winter and summer…the freedom
from vermin, the chastity of the women, the valour of the men, the purity and spirituality of their life, their wonderful psychic development,
and hypnotic medical practice distinguished the Blackfeet even among
the glorious tribes of that region."[86] Although he could safely exhibit his

knowledge of the First Nations in his books, it would almost certainly have been unwise to tell members of his family he had, at any time, "gone native." It would certainly have made his social life in England more difficult. This may explain his reticence.

Eventually Roger's luck changed. He called in to see "Wilkins the Printer," the editor of a small local paper in a town south of Wallace. Wilkins, originally from Boston, Massachusetts, was a gentleman who greeted Roger with a courtesy he had not enjoyed for some time. It was agreed that Roger should become Wilkins' special correspondent to the outlying areas to bring back stories, win new subscribers, and chase up payments in arrears. So Roger went off into the late summer heat on an old but noble horse, climbing up into the mountains and forests. He met only friendly settlers and miners in these idyllic three weeks:

> The cowboys rode miles to show me the way, prospectors
> took offence unless I stayed over night, sheep herders were
> slighted if a leg of mutton proved too much for my supper.
> The Old Gentleman [Roger's horse] took me from the white
> crests into purple-red fiery-heated canyons, where down in
> the bases of the world the rattlesnakes lay drowsily hoping for
> incautious flies.[87]

With three weeks of joy behind him and masses of copy in hand, Roger was heading back to his employer when he saw a buggy he recognized, bearing the local banker:

> "Hello!" [the banker] cried, "well met! We've had no
> news of you for three weeks—thought the cougars had got
> you—going to send out a search party. So you're safe and
> homeward bound!"
> "Bringing my sheaves with me."
> "Why, our town's just crazy about you. All sorts of
> cablegrams for you from England, money in my bank for
> you from London—your luck's changed with a vengeance!
> Com'n-'av-a-drink!'"[88]

Roger's trip brought in many more subscriptions to the paper. Despite the good news about his finances, he worked another month in the farming districts, and Wilkins congratulated himself for his foresight in employing Roger. The money the banker mentioned was not just from Roger's local work: "it appeared that an old book published some years ago [*Tales of*

Western Life] had been approved by a mighty critic in London, that two short stories had been accepted by some Olympian editor, and that I was called home to a country where writers are not always starved. A trade at last, the glory of craftsmanship, my life's ambition realised. I should...take my discharge from the dusty ranks of the Lost Legion."[89] Roger thus felt he had achieved real writing success and that it was time for him to return to London to see his family again and to advance his writing career.

THE
THOUSAND MILE
PATROL

MUCH THOUGH ROGER WANTED TO return to London in 1891, it
was not long before he began to feel uncomfortable there and yearned
to be off travelling again. Roger described the hunger for adventure that
pervaded his life:

> The tamest and quietest of us have bad spells when the
> blood runs wild for the old freedom, when there is no peace
> by day, no sleep night after night; when one must be in the
> saddle again, or off to sea, or away to some mining rush; war,
> exploration, anywhere beyond the fences, out on the frontier.
>   One hears again the dip of the paddles, the click of the
> trigger, the roar of the surf, the thunder of horses. Is there any
> Englishman who will blame us for making empires?
>   [Was this prophetic? Mr. Pocock had disappeared, in
> the direction of Alaska it was believed, when [I] wanted to
> correct this proof.][1]

Nonetheless, Roger was determined to be noticed and commented on
as a writer. However, his habit of striding around London in western
clothing and wearing riding breeches in inappropriate places brought
attention of the wrong sort; apparently he had not learned from people's
reactions in Toronto, when his attire caused him to be "stared at in the
streets and...treated everywhere as a wild animal."[2] Even his sisters, who

wished to be accepted into society and dressed accordingly, found it difficult: "Our own relations and their friends imagined the Canada we had come from as a land inhabited by Fenimore Cooper's half-breeds and wild Redskins, and that our intimate companions had been addicted to scalping their victims on the war-path."[3] Even their mother's sister, Aunt Ellen, the very wealthy widow of a Dean, seems to have held a poor view of them all, perhaps encouraged by Roger's antics. Lena found that only when she began to achieve success on the stage did the aunts receive her "as a member of the family."[4]

Roger was more concerned with impressing the young ladies of polite society, but he was a wanderer, with a chequered past in a land known to most of the English mainly from adventure novels. He did not seem to be able to persuade either young ladies or their parents that he was a good match. Doubtless his generally precarious financial position contributed to these difficulties. So shortly after his return to England he noted, "Tried to make myself agreeable to Miss Nellie Powell,"[5] but he never mentioned her again in his diaries. Then he became interested in another lady: "Miss Annie Campbell arrived in London and I met her at Westminster Abbey and went for a walk then escorted her to a place in Norwood where she is visiting. We have been corresponding much of late and seen each other frequently."[6] This was another romance nipped in the bud, probably by anxious parents, and another instance of the restrictions of Victorian society that Roger found very frustrating.

Social acceptance for Roger and his sisters would not have been helped by the fact that the only rooms their father, Charles, could afford in London were rather shabby ones in Bayswater. Lena and Ethel shared his rooms, while Roger lived on his own. During this period Roger focussed on writing. Lena became a student at the Royal Academy of Music and then began her acting career. When Ethel's health permitted, she went to the Slade School of Fine Art and there began to produce some skilled work. She "was obliged to give up the violin, but did very distinguished decorative work, and was the inventor of the bead necklaces which became a world fassion [sic]."[7] This was a rather sweeping claim made by Roger, but he was never backward in making such claims about family and friends. His sister Hilda started training as a nurse before she was seventeen and, after finishing her training, joined the Army Nursing Service and later transferred to Queen Alexandra's Imperial Military Nursing Service. Their father's health began to deteriorate from bouts of Bright's disease (glomerulonephritis). Thus, in Roger's diary for February 1897, interspersed with social and business gatherings, he described six frantic days spent worrying about the health of his father and Ethel. Later that year, he again mentioned his father's deterioration: "Just before the Diamond Jubilee Father went away to a farm called Marks Hall, Margaret Ruding [*sic*], N Dunmow, Essex…. After a month or two in the country Father & Ethel came back to the Flat in Holborn. There his illness developed a dangerous crisis, & when I returned to town in the autumn he was at a nursing home."[8] Similarly, on 5 April 1898, while Roger was in British Columbia, he "rode down to Ashcroft, half crazy with anxiety about Father, reported dying. Found cable from Ethel announcing recovery."[9]

Roger found life in London frustrating, and as often as possible he went off to work his passage in some minor way on tramp ships and small steamers. He loved the sea, and these journeys to European and Mediterranean countries gave him more background for his stories, as well as some of the characters in his novels. His diaries contain notes such as "Sailed out of the Tyne on S.S. 'Crane,' a dirty Geordie 12,000 tons, carrying 25,000 tons of coal. Capt. Grout, Mate Griffin, Second Mate King."[10] He explained the appeal of these journeys by writing that on

> a number of tramp voyages I have been landed at unexpected ports in many delightful countries. Crossing the Western Ocean with cattle, loafing in enchanted cities along the Mediterranean, wandering in Spain, Denmark, or Turkey, dreaming away hot days in the gorgeous tropics, or fiercely pursued by the quaintest kinds of police—the crowding memories make me garrulous. The…lies told on the ship's bridge at midnight, meetings with berg and derelict, perils of storm and fog—there is choice from a hundred stories.[11]

Thus, at one point, Roger signed on as purser for the SS *Bretwalda,* built for the cattle trade. What he learned about cattle ships on the voyage, which began 3 October 1896, appeared in one of his articles.[12] The voyage was also the occasion for a number of letters to his father, in which he made a particular effort to describe all things naval in detail, but deliberately did not write about cattle, "because I intend to make of my notes an article or story, & have taken photographs for illustration."[13] He did share some of his excellent descriptions of the sea with his father:

> Tuesday. We might have been at Cardiff this morning but are only abreast of Chideock in Dorset, because a head wind has followed no wind, blowing a gale all the way from Dover. Last night we made 13 miles in 11 hours. We were about two miles off St. Catherine's point [*sic*] at 9 pm in a medium sea, & a

hail squall which set the cordage shrieking. It was so dark
that as I went along the waist, blinded by the glare from the
lighthouse I tumbled into a scow or platform which is used
for painting ship. I was very wet from rolling in, besides being
displeased & bruised, but went on to the bridge. From there
the scene was uncanny because the light from the lighthouse
was reflected on the mist to southward where a ghostly
stream of white radiance swept round & round[,] the broad
end of it a veritable rainbow. The rest of the picture was a
phosphorescent swell, blinding hail & now & again a sudden
blaze of forked lightning[.][14]

Roger was always eager to travel, but the special impetus for this voyage was
an opportunity to visit both his brother Frank in Rutledge, Pennsylvania,
and some publishers in nearby Philadelphia. Roger spent time with the
man for whom Frank was working, G.W. Kennedy, and admired his en-
trepreneurial flair.[15] As usual, Roger's Kodak camera was busy. Among
the pictures he took were some of voters in Philadelphia during the presi-
dential election. He sent these, along with an explanation written in the
spirit of his book, *Rottenness*, to an editor, probably at the *Daily Graphic*,
but there is no indication they were published.[16]

The relative quiet of the homeward voyage led him to reflect a little on
his life and writing:

I have no idea of working, & indeed no ideas of any kind. I
am inclined to reject the theory that I am the author of several
books, & listen to the current criticism with impartial good
humour. Perhaps I am grown coarse minded, perhaps old;
anyway I look back with regret to the Bering Sea voyage
when I was a common sailor full of dreams & great thoughts
now deceased. And yet I know what I did not know then
that my head which never produced me much money
before, is capable of finding me enough gold now for the
settlement of my debts, the buying of my bread, the payment
of tithes, & the contribution of the tribute money toward
the maintenance of the Empire. Once I thought a tax an
odious thing[,] especially income tax; but perhaps it was the
school of adversity that taught me better. The United States
denied me bread in my profession, almost drove me out of it;
England more liberal has given me a fair chance as an author.
So every time I have bought an ounce of tobacco these last

few months I have felt with delight that half the money went to the maintenance of The Fleet.[17]

Roger remained in contact with Captain Aikman of the *Bretwalda*. He wrote to tell him about becoming "special correspondent" for *Lloyd's Weekly Newspaper* just before he left for Canada in July 1897. When one of Roger's sisters wrote to Aikman in September 1897, after the *Bretwalda* was wrecked off Portugal, Aikman's daughter reassured Miss Pocock that all members of the crew were safe. She also indicated that her father knew Roger well and wrote, "Father says your brother would have enjoyed the voyage very much, had he been there, for he is very fond of perilous adventures."[18]

Roger early realized that he could only write stories based on either his own experiences or stories he had been told on his travels—rather like Captain Marryat, who, in his writing, "re-created the world that he himself had experienced in his books."[19] While one of Roger's N W M P friends, novelist John Mackie, "boasted that he never wrote about anything he had not experienced,"[20] it meant that in later years Roger, when he had exhausted his fund of tales, found it impossible to earn an acceptable living from his writing. In this last decade of the nineteenth century, however, when Roger had many stories to tell, there was also a good market for them. Many more members of the working class were literate, and they were particularly eager for adventure stories set in exotic, distant places. Journeyman writers such as Roger, who could cater to that need, were able to earn at least a basic income writing for the many periodicals produced for this market. Despite his best efforts, though, Roger, like many writers in this period, was soon forgotten, for only a few, such as Sir Arthur Conan Doyle, earned a lasting name for themselves. Also, many of the periodicals prospered for only a limited time. Roger did acquire a literary agent, Mr. Hogg, whom he referred to in private letters to his father as "The Pig," but even with the help of Hogg and the other agents he employed over the years, money was a constant problem for Roger. His earnings were seldom as high as his expenses, so he often had to ask his father, who himself seldom had much money, for help. So when he found himself short of funds yet again, he wrote to his father, "I think I can dun The Pig for a pound or two."[21] Charles would not have approved of either the sentiment or the nickname.

In addition to writing for periodicals, several of Roger's novels achieved some success in these years, and *Rottenness: A Study of America and England* also found a publisher, somewhat surprisingly. The earliest of the novels was *The Rules of the Game*. Roger took it round to many publishers before he found one who was willing to see it into print. The story rambled and is rather similar to his book *The Dragon-slayer,* but less exciting. Indeed, one reviewer of *Dragon-slayer* noted that in *Rules of the Game,* "Mr. Pocock showed a good deal of promise, but the book was chaotic, the characters but half grasped, the workmanship clumsy, and the rules themselves not such as the world has agreed to honour."[22] Thanks to Douglas Sladen's influence, William Le Queux personally recommended Roger to the Tower Publishing Company, which had published a number of Le Queux's books under its Tower Romance Library banner. Tower did agree to publish *The Rules of the Game,* but Roger probably made very little from the book, as Tower soon went into liquidation. While this book may not have advanced Roger's literary or financial career, it contains in a single sentence one of the best statements of Roger's core belief:. "Civilisation is a poor thing to one who has lived the spacious life of the West, for no splendour of cities or rural comfort can make amends for that."[23]

The Blackguard, another novel, was heavily based on Roger's NWMP experiences. As a testament to Roger's use of his own experience, the central character, José de la Mancha, was inspired by his trip to Spain, but he also bestowed upon the central character his own NWMP regimental number and broken arm. In this outing for the Blackguard, the protagonist is half English and, after mild and largely romantic adventures centred on a mine in British Columbia's Kootenay mountains, the story ends with him married and living on a ranch. Roger took the opportunity to praise his beloved NWMP in this novel:

> To the stature and strength of an English Life Guardsman
> add the intelligence, courage, and impudence of a Black
> Watch veteran, and you have the prescription for a constable
> of the North-West Mounted Police. There is not in all the
> Empire a more splendid corps than this widely-scattered
> regiment of irregular cavalry, in time of peace hare-brained,
> half-mutinous, almost beyond the power of human control; in
> many a time of instant danger approved for stern endurance,
> utter loyalty, and headlong courage.[24]

Here Roger also utilized his hard-won knowledge of mining, including a detailed description in chapter nine of some mining technology. Since poetry was also near to Roger's heart, he began three of the chapters with his poetry. Roger even tried to use one of his sister's designs for the book: "I have written strongly to Beeman about the cover—which will spoil the sales. He must have Ethel's. I'll never let him rest until he does."[25]

Despite his fears, *The Blackguard* was widely reviewed, and Roger's contract with a clipping bureau Romeike & Curtice yielded reviews from a number of publications. One reviewer lovingly described the Blackguard's character and then declared the book "an interesting study, cleverly drawn, and wholly captivating" (*North British Daily Mail*). Another felt "The book affords some capital reading, and the characters, especially those of the Blackguard and Violet Burrows, are well drawn" (*Liverpool Weekly Post*). Yet another reviewer described it as a "rollicking tale" and went on to describe one of Roger's virtues as a writer: "The merit of the story lies in the exceedingly bold and graphic sketches of the rough camp life of the Columbian goldfields. These are obviously drawn by one who has been there, and who has seen and experienced many of the things he describes. It is a racy, bold, and somewhat fresh bit of fiction, and will add to the reputation of its writer" (*Scotsman*). One reviewer managed both praise and criticism with the mention of one name: "The modest little book is capitally written, in a breezy, vigorous, straightforward style, that reminds one of Rudyard Kipling; nor does the resemblance end here, for towards the end Mr. Pocock drifts into the incoherence of plot that is so character-istic of Kipling's longer stories....but taken altogether, the tale is bright and interesting, with an emphatically healthy, wholesome ring about it" (*The Lady*). Another reviewer thought the story "breezy and refreshing, with just that amount of 'go' in it which a story of life in the wilderness ought to have. Mr. Pocock may be congratulated upon having successfully por-trayed in this and his former book [*The Dragon-slayer*] two very different phases of life on the American continent."[26] Perhaps even more pleasing to him, though, would have been the letter from his friend Cutcliffe-Hyne, who complained about how much pressure he was under to meet his own writing deadlines, "When up comes your blame book 'The Blackguard' wh[ich] I take up & read which though I then be hanged if I don't read it through again. It's filled up an entire afternoon, what I says, is, no man ought to write books that get hold of one like this. It just picks you up, & takes you there....Oh Lord, oh Lord! Man, but it's just ripping."[27]

As a character, the Blackguard also made an appearance in Roger's *The Arctic Night*. This book is a collection of stories in the time-honoured tra-dition of a group of isolated people trying to entertain themselves. In this work, which might be considered an apprentice piece, four men—Billy, Jim Ballantyne, the Tenderfoot (the Honourable Larry Wych-Bradwardine), and the Captain (Richard Kendrick)—are housed for the winter in a pit with a driftwood roof and oiled skin windows in "Scurvy Gulch" because they stayed too long prospecting for gold. One man, Pierre du Plessis, has already died of scurvy, and the others are weak when the Stranger

(Colonel Hiram W. Giggleswick) arrives. He not only tells them where to find cranberries to cure their scurvy, he also suggests they tell their tales. The twelve stories in *The Arctic Night* draw on Roger's knowledge of such diverse matters as mining, First Nations culture, newspapers, sealing, and cowboys. In the prologue, told by Billy, are two elements that are very closely based on Roger's experience. The first is Billy's declaration that "Many a starlight night on the Saskatchewan Plains, I walked about warm and comfortable while the Government thermometers stood at sixty-five or more degrees below zero."[28] Second is the Stranger's feet, which are frozen, although he was wearing moccasins—"fortunately we were experienced in dealing with frost-bite; so by keeping his feet in iced water for some nine hours, we managed to thaw them without pain or injury to the skin."[29] This is Roger's experience, coupled with a touch of wishful thinking, and perhaps some self-justification, since he suffered both pain and injury while wearing boots. In "The Blackguard's Brother," Constable La Mancha's brother is the one who "lost his right toes after the great blizzard." Roger continues:

> Poor Pup! Nobody ever told him how dangerous it was to
> be without moccasins during the early thaws; and when the
> weather changed, when the wet boots froze on his feet, he
> went uncomplaining until he dropped. So he was crippled
> for life, and but for Dandy Irvine, he must have perished.[30]

A longer form of the incident in this story that involves "Shifty Lane" and Irvine, in which the Blackguard (again with Roger's regimental number) stands in for his brother, is also told in *The Blackguard*. Roger used this switch again in *The Splendid Blackguard* and *The Cheerful Blackguard*.[31]

Roger saved clippings of quite a few reviews of *The Arctic Night*. Most reviewers mentioned that it was published in the series Books for Bicyclists, although there is no apparent connection to bicycles. The reviewer for the *Manchester Guardian* praised Roger's ability to tell a short story, and particularly praised "The End of the World," for "There is sombre power in the picture of the husband and son of the crazy prophetess bent before the torrent of her eschatology." The reviewer for the *Glasgow Herald* also found that story notable. The *Evening Telegraph and Star* reviewer saw the "familiar machinery of a party of imprisoned men telling stories," but "The stories they tell, for variety, colour, and picturesque plot[,] are unsurpassable," while the *Yorkshire Post* described the stories as "fresh, vigorous, and engrossing." The *Nottingham Daily*

Guardian agreed that "Vigorous and interesting the tales undoubtedly are, and they will be read by admirers of robust fiction with pleasure." The *Newcastle Daily Chronicle* reviewer found the stories to be "written in a racy American style, and full of daring impossibilities," but the *Sunday Times* was less enthusiastic: "the cyclist may safely invest in the volume with a view to relieving the tedium of a wet evening." The *Times,* too, was rather dismissive and did not seem to know that Roger was British, not American. Roger might have particularly enjoyed how the *Reynolds's Newspaper* reviewer finished his review: "Mr. Pocock ought to have a special appointment as story-teller-in-chief to Dr. [Fridtjof] Nansen's next expedition." Some reviewers compared Roger favourably to other writers such as Bret Harte and Gilbert Parker, but it was perhaps most flattering that in a review that included four other titles, one of which was H. Rider Haggard's *The Wizard,* the reviewer wrote that Roger's *The Arctic Night* "is probably much the best work of the whole."[32]

The Dragon-slayer, another of his novels published in this period, was re-issued in 1909 as *Sword and Dragon. The Dragon-slayer* seems to draw much from the behaviour of a somewhat unethical American businessmen Roger had observed in Spokane. Roger felt the typesetting was "slovenly,"[33] but should have been pleased at how widely it was reviewed. Wrote one reviewer:

> Readers who knew their New York City in the days of Irish liberators and before the Tammany gang was broken up will understand what in *The Dragon Slayer* [*sic*]...may seem to others obscure. In any case it is a curious story; it is curiously expressed, and is, besides, a quaint mixture of actuality and allegory. If it please him, the reader may set the symbolism on one side and "go" for the story itself. Even then he will think it a somewhat strange production, full of surprising people and startling events. Brand, the hero, an honest journalist (this is not a contradiction in terms, as it appears to be), represents the spirit of truth and unselfishness warring with the elements of a corrupt civilization and national dishonour manifested in the person of a great financier. Hilda, the heroine, stands for ideal humanity rescued from the perils of gigantic self-interest and unscrupulous scheming. The world's great frauds, started in high places by notable personages, are shown up, and their mysterious emissaries tracked out and unmasked by the powers of righteousness and the courage of a trio of social reformers.[34]

In the *British Review,* the reviewer felt that "One might be inclined to think that the 'parable' is an extravagant attack on the morality of New York, 'which is, perhaps, the future capital of this planet;' but even this ray of light is forbidden us since the author, who is careful to say what his novel is not, denies that it is 'a criticism of American institutions.'" Yet even if only implied, Roger's criticisms of American institutions would probably gain some support and would not be considered outdated for well over a hundred years.

Roger also carefully saved reviews of this book. While not all reviews were enthusiastic, many reviewers saw promise in the book, and one reviewer wrote to Roger directly, congratulating him on "having written a very fine book in The Dragon Slayer and on the promise it affords of another—still finer I trust—in the near future."[35] Roger also received a letter from Charles Welsh Mason (b.1866), another adventurer who became a writer; Mason lavished both criticism and praise on Roger's book, "And yet, in summing up, there may be more merit than flaw in your treatment, for the result anyhow was to hold me absorbed & eager to the end."[36] One reviewer described it as "the best bit of excitement in English literature since 'The Woman in White'" (*Sunday Times*), and another compared elements of Roger's approach to those of Jules Verne and Rider Haggard (*Glasgow Herald*); a third said, "Colonel Giggleswick in particular is a creation almost worthy of Dickens at his best" (*National Observer*). Mason mentioned his concern about Roger receiving sufficient royalties for this book, but Roger happily noted he received a "cheque £5·13·6 Dragon Slayer Royalty."[37]

Roger's consistently cynical view of capitalists features in several stories in *The Arctic Night,* particularly "The Silver Chamber," "The Cat Factory," and "A Cowboy on 'Change.'" Stories sharing two of these titles were published elsewhere, with very slight variations.[38] Some of Roger's other contributions to periodicals in these years included "The White Man's Power," "The Mutineers," and "The Filibusters."[39] Another piece mentioned the Cody Caves in the Kootenay Mountains in British Columbia, which were discovered in the early 1890s by Henry Cody while he was prospecting for silver; in Roger's story the cave's inner chambers were walled with gold ore.[40] Of course Roger also wrote about the Mounted Police.[41]

As for Roger's non-fiction, his social commentary in *Rottenness* reflected much of his personal view on life and corruption in politics, particularly American politics. Roger had received only a very basic education, but as an avid reader he educated himself to quite a good standard, and he was certainly willing to put his deeply held convictions in print. *Rottenness* had little effect in Britain, and the anti-American sentiments manifest in parts may have upset some American readers and limited its sales there, but it was widely reviewed, especially in Britain. A few brief extracts show the immediate response on both sides of the Atlantic: "For our own part we dislike all exaggeration, and therefore, we do not think it right to speak of the undoubtedly grave disorders of modern times as rottenness" (*Progressive Review*); "A note of sincerity running through the turbulent stream of rhetorical denunciation of which the original part of the book mainly consists, redeems it from the censure due to violent language used without just cause…. Glaring exaggerations and half truths…do not, however, deprive Mr. Pocock's passionate and somewhat uncultured invective of an importance not easy to overrate" (*Observer*); "There is some very powerful writing in this hard-hitting onslaught on some of the leading evils of modern civilisation as interpreted on both sides of the Atlantic" (*Morning Advertiser*); "we recognise in it, in spite of its faults of treatment, an honest and fervent enthusiasm which in this go-as-you-please age is distinctly refreshing. The book is full of promise, graphic in description, powerful in argument, and clear and vigorous in style. He should go far and do much when experience has tempered his zeal with discretion" (*Freeman's Journal and Daily Commercial Advertiser,* Dublin); and "A wild and shrieking tirade against society, British and American, and indeed against human nature itself…" (*Scotsman*).[42]

On the whole, *Rottenness* is a forgettable book, but it does highlight Roger's concerns when he was approximately thirty. He continued to be a man of ideas and a dreamer of dreams for much of his life. Some of these ideas were silly and unworkable, but others had considerable value. In *Rottenness* he began by attacking the American press for its general vulgarity and corruption, but he was not much kinder to the British press:

> The American press is always ready, in the interest of a
> Capitalist Government and a plutocratic ownership, to divert
> public attention from home troubles by inflaming the public
> mind against the Motherland, by twisting the political news
> from London into a hideous mass of lies, by suppressing
> all that is good, exaggerating all that is evil, and distorting
> past events with indiscriminate falsehood. The British
> press treats American public affairs from a standpoint of the
> narrowest parochial bigotry, and makes all American social
> events a subject of contemptuous ridicule. But for the Anglo-
> American press these two great nations would be cordial

friends. Must we for ever blind our eyes against truth and
justice by feeding our minds upon this atrocious rubbish of
journalism?[43]

Roger also accused the British press of sensationalism, for "How many newspapers revel in the unmitigated beastliness of the Oscar Wilde type of criminal trial?"[44] In his writing, Roger was one of America's bitterest critics, yet he complained that the British press regularly attacked America. With perhaps a tinge of self-interest, Roger criticized American newspapers for reprinting material without permission or credit, creating "a system of robbery by which native American writers are kept in a condition of semi-starvation" and that eliminated "the only available training-ground for local literary and journalistic talent"; he also criticized British newspapers, asking, "How many literary editors are log-rollers for some mutual admiration society?" He concluded his critique by noting that

British journalism strives most earnestly after right; but it is
not perfect.
　　Were the British press in sympathy with American
thought, had it only an enlightened understanding of
American problems, had it but a little more courtesy, a little
more liberality, there would at least be no friction between
the sundered elements of our race.... [T]he United States
can hardly be expected to receive taunts, gibes, sneers, and
the trumpery criticism of tourists in a spirit of gratitude as
coming from their brethren over seas.[45]

The British press, of course, ignored these comments.
　　In *Rottenness,* Roger then turned his attention to Christianity, using a somewhat common argument that Christian Churches were too introspective and concerned with their own matters rather than with God. He felt Christianity must return to the teaching of Christ, but "Meanwhile we worship the gods of Anglo-Saxondom, Pleasure and Respectability, devils both, and much good do they do to us!"[46] He went from the subject of Christianity to address corruption in politics, quoting examples from American newspapers. He preached about the dangers of alcohol, or drugs that were far worse, and the scandal of harsh laws and sweat shops before he turned his lance to tilt at socialism, "the despotism of a gigantic, permanent and ultimately corrupt bureaucracy—a machine incapable of holding its own in the world's trade, not readily adaptable to the needs of growth, not consistent with the further progress of civilisation, or with

the existing liberty of the citizen."[47] Roger concluded by repeating an idea that had been discussed for some years—nationalization of all land:

> Let us take the ground rents in the name of the
> Commonwealth, compensate the landlords, then let the
> land, with its minerals, soil, and economic rents, pay all
> the expenses of government. The functions of government
> would be diminished to a mere receiving and expenditure
> of ground rents, and all other taxes would be abolished for
> ever. This is no upsetting of the existing system of commerce,
> not socialistic collectivism, or philosophical anarchism,
> or revolutionary desperation. It is a plain, common-sense
> method by which the parasite will be gradually extirpated,
> by which the land and all that is therein will pay its revenues
> to the Commonwealth. It will heal the malady which has
> overthrown all former civilisations, will give to Anglo-
> Saxondom renewed strength for its slow evolution of a
> perfect society.[48]

Roger may have read Thomas Paine, and also Thomas Spence, a man of Newcastle, where Roger spent much of his boyhood. Spence advocated that all land should be held in common by each parish. Roger would probably have been familiar with Henry George's *Progress and Poverty* (1879) and his arguments for the single tax on land.

Roger also used *Rottenness* to communicate his frustration over his inability to find a young lady with whom he could build a relationship and whose family would welcome him: "Bourgeois Englishmen may not marry until they can support their wives in comfort. Before they are earning a sufficient income they reach an average age of thirty-six years. From the age of eighteen to the age of thirty-six they must be monks, or satisfy their natural desires by making or hiring harlots. The making and hiring of harlots is the price we pay for the ignorance of the prude." Roger's solution was for girls' fathers to make a substantial annual allowance to the daughters, "to soften the struggle of the first few years."[49] Obviously, he expected fathers established in the social classes to which he aspired to be so comfortable financially that they could help support their sons-in-law. This was a cry from the heart of an impecunious young man, who had been turned down very quickly, and perhaps more than once, as an unsuitable husband for the daughter of a respectable Victorian gentleman.

When Roger sailed to the United States on the SS *Bretwalda* in October 1896, he took copies of *Rottenness* with him. He was delighted to report to his father that the chief engineer and the captain read *Rottenness*. He was not quite so pleased to report his blunder "in not making arrangements with Beeman as to [the] sale of American Rights of Rottenness," but hoped to do so when he reached Philadelphia.[50] He took "Rules of The Game, Arctic Night & Rottenness to Lippincotts, & Messrs Porter & Coates the two leading Pa [Pennsylvania] publishers, but they are both too scary so I must leave the matters to Crawford & Beeman."[51] His brother Frank was a little more forthcoming about why Roger was unable to interest an American publisher in his books:

> Rottenness is too hot for any American publisher and not
> personal enough for a campaign document for any party[,]
> besides being too late to do anything in the last fight[;] then
> it is a question as to what scale he take[s] on the money
> question.
>   They do not care about short stories & the best of the lot,
> The Rules of the Game[,] is a year old and that makes a good
> excuse to get rid of him, so there was no encouragement[.]
> I am glad they are well secured in England[,] that will cheer
> him up[.][52]

The 1890s, when these books and periodical pieces were published, were exciting years for those engaged in literature and the arts. In London, Roger energetically made useful contacts within that literary world. His greatest source of important contacts was the New Vagabonds Club, which had been organized by two very sociable writers, Douglas Sladen and G.B. Burgin, as joint secretaries. There had earlier been a Vagabonds Club, which had faded away; Burgin and Sladen had different accounts of why it failed. Sladen summarized the demise in practical terms, suggesting that to remove a particularly troublesome Socialist member it would be simplest to dissolve the existing Vagabonds Club and then reform it without inviting this particular member to return.[53] Burgin's explanation for the change is more literary:

> It had long occurred to me that a common meeting-ground
> for literary workers of all dimensions would be a very
> desirable thing. There were several exclusive clubs where
> the "big guns" met and fired at one another; but, on looking
> round, I could not discover one in which the big fry and the
> small fry commingled. Ever since the death of Philip Bourke
> Marston, the Old Vagabonds had lingered on, meeting

occasionally until, their ranks depleted by death, about twenty remained. And we were getting a little out of date.... I confided my project to Sladen, and he approved of it with his usual reckless promptitude. "I'll come in with you as joint secretary," he said, "and we'll make things hum. I know everybody and can get people to join us. We'll have women members as well. It's bound to be a success because it's never been done before."[54]

Whichever account is nearer the truth, both men did "know everybody" within literary and associated social circles. Sladen, in particular, was an inveterate namedropper and a friend of both the famous and the merely ambitious. Sladen promised 200 to 300 members, and "It was not long before we had four hundred members, half of them well-known women in the Drama, Music, Art, and Literature.... At these 'Vagabond' dinners we got an attendance of anything up to six hundred when we had a guest like Lord Roberts."[55] Burgin reported that Sladen said, "We shall go down to posterity as the pioneers of a new movement for bringing together all sorts and conditions of literary folk. The big ones must meet the little ones without wanting to eat them."[56] This was the club that Roger joined with great enthusiasm, and which provided considerable help; he owed a lot to the kindness of Sladen, who introduced him to contacts in the literary world who were able to help him in his career as a writer. The world of letters, too, owes a debt to the New Vagabonds Club, and to Burgin and Sladen, for encouraging minor authors and major ones, and for support-ing the cause of British popular literature.

Roger was thrilled that the New Vagabonds Club enabled him to meet and converse with such noted authors as Jerome K. Jerome (1859–1927) and Anthony Hope (pseudonym of Sir Anthony Hope Hopkins, 1863–1933), best known for *The Prisoner of Zenda* (1894). At the Club, Roger also began a friendship with William Le Queux (1864–1927), who exerted significant influence on Roger's major project, the founding of the Legion of Frontiersmen. Le Queux, an enigmatic character, has puzzled most who have tried to unravel his life:

Since the mid-1960s historians and others have condemned Le Queux as a talentless writer, opportunist mercenary hack, scaremonger, fraud and Walter Mitty. While fragmentary, the available evidence tends to vindicate his recent critics, and suggest that Le Queux's claims of his own importance, espionage, counter-espionage and international intrigue were essentially fantasy. Nevertheless perhaps he was a genuine patriot who strove to warn and prepare his country against real danger. Moreover he was a writer who brought, though not literary excellence, at least pleasure comparable to that later brought by television, and perhaps reassurance, to many readers. Through his fiction on invasion and espionage he influenced, though unquantifiably, the attitudes and perceptions of the public on defence and war.[57]

That "fiction on invasion and espionage" certainly played a significant role in Roger's life and his founding of the Legion.

While Roger's literary career was growing, Lena's stage career was also developing. Douglas Sladen claimed some responsibility for starting her on her way: "Lena Ashwell was the actress we knew best. We knew her while she was Daisy Pocock, a girl studying at the Royal College of Music, with the hopes of getting into Opera with her magnificent voice. I introduced her to the man who gave her her first part on the stage, and she used to come and stay with us."[58] Lena's voice, however, did not develop as expected, so Ellen Terry advised her to concentrate on becoming an actress. Lena played her first role on the stage in March 1891 and was regularly in work thereafter. By December 1896 she had married the actor Arthur Wyndham Playfair (1869–1918). Lena wrote about Arthur, saying, "I met Arthur when on tour; he was amusing and a good actor.... There was no sign of his weakness as he was on the 'water wagon [*sic*],' going through a period of reform. The reformation did not last for, immediately after our marriage, I was plunged into the world of sordid horror and misery which drunkenness creates."[59] Within a few years that misery was so serious that Roger had to hurry home from Mexico to help.

Despite Roger's busy engagement in slowly building literary successes and friendships, in 1894 he set out on a tramp steamer, on which he was rated as steward to comply with Board of Trade regulations. The ship called at Sebastopol, which enabled him to indulge in a little amateur spying, in the best Le Queux tradition. Roger called on the British consul there and claimed the consul told him the following:

> After the Crimean War Russia gave us her solemn word of honour that she'd dismantle this fortress of Sevastopol [*sic*]. Now they're mounting new batteries in all directions. They know that they're doing wrong, so naturally they suppose that every British subject must be spying on them. And as

you and I are the only British subjects ashore, of course
they're going to concentrate on you. Look out![60]

Despite the warning, Roger wandered off and said that he "blundered
into a new masked battery." He was only able to allay the suspicions of a
Russian guard by acting the complete British eccentric, "intoning in the
best clerical manner that beautiful poem 'Mary had a little lamb.'" Roger
concluded, "I did not find out the calibre of the guns, but did realize that
even a humble tourist might serve the State."[61] This encounter inaugurated Roger's notion that individual Englishmen on the frontier could
be the "eyes of the empire." Less than a decade later, he had developed
the idea sufficiently that it became one of the founding principles of the
Legion of Frontiersmen. However, precisely how much truth is in Roger's
account of this adventure and how much he embellished what happened
is open to speculation. If this account were the complete truth, he would
surely have included it in *A Frontiersman* rather than wait nearly thirty
years to include it in *Chorus to Adventurers*. The explanation for the accounts appearance might be that in the intervening years Baden-Powell's
best-selling *My Adventures as a Spy* was published. There is a clear similarity between Baden-Powell's claim that he used butterfly hunting as a
cover for his spying and Roger's that he used his interest in fossils. Baden-
Powell wrote that he "went armed with [the] most effective weapons for
the purpose, which have served me well in many a similar campaign. I
took a sketch-book, in which were numerous pictures—some finished,
others only partly done—of butterflies of every degree and rank."[62] Roger
declared he invited the corporal "to inspect the treasures from my tail
pocket, explaining that flints are fragments of fossil sponges in chalk formations of the Mesozoic."[63] Baden-Powell's biographer concluded, "There
can be no doubt that he later 'improved' and amplified his accounts of
many of his intelligence-gathering journeys."[64] It is quite reasonable to
presume the same claim can be made for Roger's description of his own
first attempt at spying.

In September 1896 Roger travelled to Edinburgh. His primary purpose
was to read proofs for a book being printed there, but he took the opportunity to explore the city, which he greatly admired for its architecture,
and because, as he put it,

Nowhere else have I seen a city which made its most splendid
monuments for mere writers of books. In London most of the
statues are to fighting men, a few to politicians[,] but science,

art, philosophy, literature are not worthy of pedestals.... There are idiotic monuments here to titled nobodies & disreputable persons with crowns[,] but Scott has the hearts of the people, Burns is their national idol, & Watt sits enthroned before a superb college.[65]

On 28 February 1897, Roger travelled to St. Helier, in the Channel Islands, to talk with Gilbert Parker, who had praised his *Tales of Western Life* in 1890. Several days later he "went down into Wiltshire to interview Kipling for my Author Adventurer series intended for a London magazine which was to be produced by Harmsworth. Saw old Mr. & Mrs. Kipling & went on to Torquay. Then I walked out to Babbacombe where I spent an hour or so with Kipling."[66] Despite the early interest expressed by Harmsworth, Roger's full account of the interview appeared in *Lloyd's Weekly News* on 4 January 1903 in his Great Adventurers series. Kipling's role there was as "The Laureate of Empire." This interview was crucial to Roger's thinking and future actions, as Robert H. MacDonald points out:

> [His] article on Kipling is an interesting example of imperial discourse in a moment of adjustment, remarkable not only for the regenerative view it attempts to promote, but also for what it reveals of the process of social mythmaking, showing both the power of imperial imagery, and the depth of the response it stimulated. That a journalist like Pocock could see in Kipling just what he wanted to see, and no more, should be no surprise. His appreciation of the mythmaker and his myth is more significant. That he was afterwards to attempt to put the dream into action, and to succeed in recruiting his own paramilitary Legion of Frontiersmen, is a sufficient measure of the myth's strength.[67]

Roger certainly had a number of heroes throughout his life, and Kipling was one of the greatest:

> Mr. Rudyard Kipling...has never had any adventures or left the beaten tracks of the globe-trotters. Yet, as an old frontiersman, I make bold to speak for all my brothers, the soldiers, sailors, stockriders, prospectors, pathfinders, and pioneers of the Empire, in claiming him as our poet laureate, story teller, and friend.[68]

About this time, Roger also wrote that "It is very difficult with a mere string of words to give the actual touch and taste and feel of that jolly headlong frontier life, as it was then and as it is to-day. It is a life that only the adventurer knows, the gentleman-adventurer of Kipling's Lost Legion, who helps to build big historical empires, and does it all for fun."[69] Roger said Kipling's "poem, 'The Lost Legion,' makes him the very apostle of the adventurers."[70] So it is not surprising that Roger ensured his favourite Kipling poem became the personal hymn of members of the Legion of Frontiersmen:

> There's a legion that never was 'listed,
> That carries no colours or crest.
> But, split in a thousand detachments,
> Is breaking the road for the rest.[71]

Roger, with his strong belief in the Empire, particularly admired the power of Kipling's writing. Roger explained Kipling's writing in this way:

> [It is] helping to make Little England feel herself, as Greater
> Britain, an Imperial world-power, carrying the light of
> civilisation into the dark places of the earth; it is making our
> national life broader, deeper, stronger as we grow towards the
> full maturity of our race. In this generation we have found...
> Mr. Rudyard Kipling as Laureate to give us a better heart on the
> difficult and often bloodstained trails of marching Empire.[72]

Despite Roger's admiration, his interview with Kipling was somewhat icy:

> He did not know my name, and resented my visit, but I
> had been ten minutes with him quarrelling, when he leaned
> forward in his chair, his face half visible in tobacco smoke,
> shiny, bronzed, his eyes veiled by the glint on spectacles,
> while he stared intently, whispering suggestions.
> *I smelt the dust of a trail, heard the creak of harness, felt*
> *between my knees the heaving flanks of a horse, saw the Great*
> *Plains reaching away for ever*—and then his voice dispelled
> the vision—"Don't you wish you were back?"[73]

MacDonald observes, "This scene, taking its form and context from the vocabulary of the yarn, with its image of Kipling as the word-spinner, characterises the myth of the frontier."[74] Certainly Kipling's response made Roger even more restless. Clearly it was time for him to leave London and return to the open spaces of the frontiers.

Before he could make any travel plans, though, he was caught up in Queen Victoria's Diamond Jubilee celebrations in 1897. The NWMP had sent to London a contingent commanded by Aylesworth Bowen Perry, one of Roger's old officers. Roger was pleased to find that he knew some of the other men as well, and that he was made very welcome at their quarters in Windsor. These celebrations were notable for the Mounted Police because it was both the first time the NWMP had been officially represented in England and the first time the Stetson was worn officially. The Stetson may have owed its presence to Samuel Benfield (Sam) Steele (1849–1919), who

> brought about a number of changes in the system, among them the adoption of the Stetson hats that later became the trademark of the Mounted Police. He permitted men in his own command to purchase a standard pattern of Stetson out of their own pockets and to wear them in place of the unsuitable helmets and pillboxes. The rank and file had long since taken to wearing an assortment of cowboy hats in their day-to-day work, but this was the first time that the standard pattern, still worn today, was adopted and sanctioned in use.[75]

The distinctive hats of the Mounted Police and of the Australians in the parade attracted public attention: "Officers and men of Canadian units wore the British helmet at the Jubilee; the British press, significantly, paid them scant attention, but pictured the police and the colourful Australians instead."[76] Roger noticed this public attention, and it played a role when the Legion of Frontiersmen was deciding on a uniform. The Stetson worn by the Legion still attracts comment and interest when members wear it at public events. It can also be a highly practical form of headgear. On 10 July 2005 a very large parade to celebrate the sixtieth anniversary of the end of the war in Europe was held in front of Her Majesty Queen Elizabeth II on Horseguards Parade in London. On an extremely hot and sunny day, members of the Legion of Frontiersmen, in their Stetsons, were the only uniformed organization wearing headgear that shaded them from the hot sun.

Roger's delight at being back with the Mounted Police is evident. He told some of the story of the Diamond Jubilee in the first volume of his autobiography, *A Frontiersman,* but returned to it with enthusiasm in *Chorus to Adventurers:*

> A special train conveyed from Windsor to Paddington the
> horses and men of a contingent, which represented my old
> corps, the North-West Mounted Police, and was commanded
> by my former commandant, Superintendent A. Bowen Perry
>   He and I shared a compartment. He told me that another
> ex-constable had lent him a smart trap, which was driven
> by his batman. At Paddington I was to get into the trap, and
> come on to dine at Chelsea Barracks. And so, when the train
> pulled into the terminal…I took my seat in the trap, having
> not the slightest suspicion, even while the advance guard
> formed up ahead, the rear guard astern. Not until the Officer
> Commanding rode up on my right, and the Second-in-
> Command on my left, did I realize that this was a Sovereign's
> Escort of scarlet cavalry! Was it my fault that Edward, Prince
> of Wales was always being mistaken for me?[77]

Roger's egotism in response to this practical joke is breathtaking. Made welcome by his old comrades, in spite of the fact that many of them would have recognized the thinly-disguised Mounted Police Roger depicted in *The Blackguard,* Roger spent much time in the barracks contentedly listening to the stories and banter of the men. In a letter to his father, Roger reported: "25th Fri. The boys [Mounted Police] have been to Perry & told him to ask me to go out with the crowd to the Naval Review…. The boys were magnificent on parade."[78] In his next letter he described the experience:

> At last I have a few minutes. On Friday a deputation waited
> on Perry asking him to take me to the Review. He consented.
> I saw him & he said that in civilian clothes it was impossible.
> "What if I go in uniform?" "That I must absolutely forbid."
> He winked at me. "If I catch you there will be trouble." So I
> got my beard shaved off, bought a switch & gloves, & some
> grub, & got back to Barracks with Sergeant Clapp at 9:30
> P.M. unchallenged. We had our grub at the canteen & turned
> in at Lights Out. Meanwhile I had secured Brooke's boots
> which fitted beautifully & Davis' breeches which might have
> been made for me. Had everything cleaned [and] ready.
> Couldn't sleep for excitement until nearly 2 am. 3.30 reveillé

sounded[;] by 4.30 I had borrowed spurs[,] sombrero, stable
jacket[;] everything a beautiful fit except the hat which was
too small & hurt terribly. At 5 we paraded & marched out
of barracks the boys steering me through the evolutions[,]
the Sergeant Major taking care to have me in the middle of a
section[.]

The marching was grand, at a brisk swinging[,]
swaggering pace which belongs to the Bluejackets & to the
Force but to nobody else on earth. At Victoria we entrained
800 men in two trains. Weather looked very wet. At 8 am
we came to Portsmouth where I expected to just have to
cross a wharf to the steamer. Instead of that the Mayor &
Corporation awaited us on the steps of the New Town Hall,
with bands to conduct us, troops lining the station entrance
and the whole population cheering like mad. I was in an
awful funk. Belcher who was in command (Perry coming
by later train) recognised me in Portsmouth Station. "Well
Pocock, I see you're with us."

"Yessir."

"Parade [march]!"

Down we went to the Mayor's Parade, & the Mayor
made a speech about breakfast & Jubilee & things—nobody
heard. Then cheers for everybody, & we marched off over
a mile of cobblestones, tramlines and, to Southsea Pier.
The crowd was far louder than on Jubilee day, crazy with
excitement. Yelling in our ears. The band was out of tune,
the Canadian Cavalry ahead couldn't march, & we were in
torment marking time until have [sic] way we took our own
pace & marched independent of both. I…went along in a
dream, part of the machine, wondering if I was really me.
We were received by generals & dignitaries at the pier. Then
we embarked & joined the Canadian Cavalry in a rush for
breakfast. The food was sumptuous but without beer. The
Steamer, the famous Koh-i-noor from the Thames. So we
steamed out to the fleet & all the morning ran up & down
among the lines. Every ship we passed, not allowed to cheer,
clapped hands, & we cheered them all.

Then we exchanged cheers with the foreigners, groans
for the Germans, & three times three for the United States.
When we took up our berth all the excursion steamers[,]
liners [&] yachts by hundreds came up to cheer us, & one

big steamer stayed to give us "Rule Britannia, God Save
the Queen, the Soldiers of Our Queen, & They are Jolly
Good Fellows." The sun was out before eleven. Canada had
a concert forward, Australasia aft, & a bugle did a concert
of its own amidships[.] MacDonell our Sergeant Major led
us in a great chanson Allouette[.] Then began the saluting
miles away a tremendous sea battle down in the first division,
which wiped itself out in the smoke. The second division
fired its hundred guns per ship all round us, the third almost
out of sight on our left. The Procession was coming[.][79]

In his next letter Roger gave more detail about the naval component,
for his father's benefit, and he then described how pleased he was to be
among the NWMP again:

At 4 pm we went back to Southsea Pier, paraded, & marched
ashore, the Canadian Cavalry leading[.] Ours next. I was no
longer frightened of making mistakes, no longer embarrassed
by the crowd. And now the crowd was bigger than ever, &
the cheering more frantic than I should have thought possible
in sober England. It got into my blood & I know that I was
no longer a sham[,] no longer a possible disgrace. I had
served in the finest cavalry in the world, I was serving again;
marching as well as any man, not deficient among the boys
in girth, stature, or carriage. My hump had entirely vanished,
my stump was behaving intelligently, my eyesight was good
enough for the present, my arm not visibly dislocated.

"Pocock" said one of the boys behind me "would your
own father know you?" & they all laughed with me.

At the station we were hot, peaceful but sleepy in the
carriages mixed up with Canadian dragoons.... We were in
Victoria station in broad daylight, & as the contingent swung
into Chelsea barracks it was 8.45 pm. Belcher marched us
about the square for being, as he thought, slack in forming
up, but I had remembered all my drill by now & was as smart
as any man. So we were dismissed.

But I could not let the tail of my joy slip through my
fingers now. I could not let the boys think I was played out.
They said they were going to bed. I couldn't have slept for
weeks. I invited George[?] Davis to dinner, & the Palace
Theatre. We went, in uniform after cleaning up, dined at

the Café D'Italie, & the uniform admitted us at the Palace. Afterwards we strolled about & had a drink or two of beer. All the way back to barracks I had to answer questions from civilians about the outfit, & wonderful information they got. I was in bed by one o'clock.

Sunday [4 July]. A civilian again, up at reveillé the boys chaffing me, & I giving more than I got. After breakfast I went over to tell Perry what a good time I had at the review. He did not know me by sight, & when he did, was obviously frightened lest I should compel him to discover my breech of discipline.[80]

Roger was very proud of his ability to keep up with the visitors from Canada, but by 4 July he did admit to having paid a physical price: "I cannot understand how it is that with half the strength of these men I seem to have more endurance[.] Ever since Sunday morning my feet have been totally unfit for use. You see wearing a pair of boots which weigh 3 ½ lb for 21 ½ hours is rough on a cripple."[81] Perhaps to thank the Mounted Police for their hospitality, Roger took them to the theatre to see his sister, Lena Ashwell, perform. In 1948, Robert J. Jones, a retired Mounted Policeman, still recalled that evening with pleasure. Jones also described one incident in Roger's participation:

Everything went well to a point where we were steaming up and down the lines of war vessels, when our hero apparently forgot himself. For, putting his glasses on, he got hold of the O.C. by the sleeve and was excitingly [sic] pointing to something that had caught his attention. Then the long arm of the sergeant major reached out and dragged him from sight. It is only fair to say that our officers never referred to the incident.[82]

Even Roger never referred to it, for he wrote that "in the parades and marches of a day lasting twenty-two hours I neither limped nor blundered."[83] That Roger was allowed to participate is an example of the high regard in which the Mounted Police held Roger throughout his life.

The train back to London from Spithead, somewhat unusually, had open compartments and a corridor. Roger was struck by the easy friendship between the men of every country in the Empire, which emphasized his view that the British Empire offered the greatest future for co-operation between nations: "I seemed to see not private soldiers enjoying a quiet gossip, but nation speaking unto nation, the Dominions of our time, world-powers of the future, with one Faith, one speech, one heritage, having perfect freedom, stern self-discipline, absolute sovereignty and brotherly alliance."[84] All through his life, Roger retained his popular imperialism and faith that the Empire, led by British ideals, set the standard for the rest of the world.

Inspired by his interview with Kipling and his renewed friendships within the NWMP, Roger began pursuing publishers to sponsor his travel:

> Monday [28 June]. Saw Daily Graphic. My offer refused. Saw Alfred Harmsworth. I had him nearly off his head over my scheme, but he kept saying to himself in an undertone "I must keep my head. I must keep my head[."] He did keep his head, & having seven special correspondents out, [and] room for only a tenth part of their copy he refused my offer. I went to Pinker, & he took me to Cooke[,] editor of the Daily News, who is giving the matter his favourable consideration. I am waiting for the telegram of refusal, & have prepared a letter to be sent by Pinker to all the other papers offering my services.[85]

His first efforts were not successful:

> After failing with the Daily Graphic, Daily Mail, Daily News & Pearsons I began to feel very bad today & went to see Burgin. He cheered me up a bit & told me to see Thomas Catling[,] Editor of Lloyd's Weekly. Catling[,] a man with a long grey beard, received me kindly & after I had told my yarn confessed that he had been in the North West Territories after the World's Fair [in Chicago] four years ago. He knew all about what I was talking of & accepted me. He wants me to find out how many articles I propose, & how much it is to cost, & I have an appointment on Tuesday to settle it. Meanwhile I must run down to Aldershot to ask Perry for date of sailing & what he proposes to do for me. I dont [sic] know anything more as yet. Today I had 6d ½ left so borrowed £2.0.0 from Pinker who will get his commission & repayment of all he advances, & considers it a mere matter of business. I have to keep him rustling anyway.
> It is difficult to talk in the blankness of my present ignorance, so I must wait until I have seen Perry.[86]

Perhaps it was just after he had posted that letter that Roger received some good news:

> On Thursday [1 July] I got my engagement with Lloyds. On
> Friday I ran down to Aldershot in search for Perry. From
> Eight oclock [*sic*] to 10.30 I searched the great camp....
> However the Aldershot Review was over (Thursday) & the
> boys had left an hour ago for Windsor. So I took train &
> followed to Windsor getting there at 1230.... I was walking
> back to town when I met the Crowd, Perry ahead, coming
> along at a magnificent pace. I swung in abreast with Perry,
> told him my good news, fell out of ranks again & went up
> to wait at the station.... The boys chaffed me for going
> up in Perry's carriage, & swore they'd cut me. But I went
> with Perry & Belcher, first class, special train[,] no ticket[,]
> covered with glory. Perry promised that from the time I
> strike Regina I shall not have to pay a penny[.] He wrote to
> the Comptroller at Ottawa asking that I might be officially
> thanked for my services to the contingent. Now he will give
> me a letter to Fred. White asking him to help me through....
> Saturday I ran down to Worcester Park to lunch with
> Pinker.... Hope to sail on Thursday by the "Parisian" if all
> goes well.[87]

Lloyd's Weekly was an important venue for Roger to display his writing skills. It was aimed at a mass audience, and in February 1896, under long-time editor Thomas Catling, *Lloyd's Weekly* "won its prolonged fight for the million circulation."[88] It was popular in Britain, but copies were also sent around the Empire to many outposts on the frontier. Catling was aware of the great interest the reading public demonstrated in the North-West Mounted Police, so when Roger emphasized his strong personal links with the NWMP and suggested that he could use these contacts to get permission to ride the Thousand Mile Patrol and send back articles, Catling was susceptible. The NWMP had undertaken sporadic patrols in its early years before Lawrence William Herchmer (1840–1915) became Commissioner on April 1886. As inspector of "Indian Agencies," Herchmer had observed an increase in crime and other problems and when he became Commissioner, he was determined to combat this trend:

> He immediately instituted a system of regular patrols to cover
> the entire North-West Territories and especially the border

areas…. This system was extended year by year in an effort to cover every corner of the Territories. The results were highly satisfactory….

As the patrol system was expanded and improved in the late 1880s and early 1890s[,] other advantages became apparent and new uses for it were discovered….

At its greatest extent, in the period 1888 to 1892, the patrol system covered not only the entire North-West Territories but the border regions of southern Manitoba and the Kootenai [*sic*] district of southern British Columbia as well….

After 1892 the patrol system began to be cut back… and after 1893 it was never possible to make the patrols as inclusive as they once were.[89]

In his enthusiasm, Roger was undeterred by the fact that there had been no Thousand Mile Patrol for some years. Nonetheless, with backing from Perry, Roger travelled to Canada. He found the voyage on SS *Parisian* comfortable, unlike many of the other passengers: "The grub is passably good & I have flourished exceedingly doing 7 to 12 miles a day by way of training for the hard work to come."[90] On the train from the east he travelled with Herchmer as far as Brandon, Manitoba. Herchmer was mainly interested in asking Roger about the Diamond Jubilee. He wanted to know how the Mounted Police had acquitted themselves in the public eye, and particularly what the cavalry officers who had been watching thought:

"Why, sir, the cavalry of the whole Empire passed by their windows, and they wanted to know '*Who are those men who can ride?*'"

The Colonel drew a deep breath. "So my boys behaved themselves! Now," he flashed round savagely, "this business of yours—Special correspondent? Pah! We don't want newspaper puffs."

"The Thousand-Mile Patrol, sir; I want to ride with the Boundary Patrol."

"Can't! Given it up for want of men—well, I don't know," it seemed as though the sun came out, "sometimes I send a patrol along there. Keeps the trail open—might send one now—they have a spare horse—sometimes—no harm to ride that—detachments? Well, you know ex-Policemen and tramps are always welcome at our detachments. So my boys behaved!" He had granted me a special patrol across the Plains![91]

Herchmer not only gave permission, he also formulated a plan:

> Well, I saw the Commissioner on Friday morning [23 July], & at once he began working out a plan. He would send a man with a buckboard & team to Wood Mountain. Officer commanding there should meet me halfway & so on. I said I didn't want to be a "distinguished visitor" but would be much happier travelling light and anyway must be in the saddle to make good special correspondence. Being carted about is not to my taste, but now I am to have my saddle horse & a man with a rig for the baggage.[92]

Thus Roger was able to begin the travels for "Into the Great Dominion," a series of sixteen articles that ran in *Lloyd's Weekly* from 3 October 1897 to 16 January 1898.[93]

When Roger reached Regina, he was delighted to report to his father that "There were lots of people who knew me. And what a welcome I got when they drove me up to Barracks!.... I keep the record of names for my own future use." Conversation in barracks also stimulated his interest in the Yukon and gold: "Insp[ector] Strickland was present fresh from the Yukon & his account was the most interesting thing, I ever heard. Five of the Yukon men are here all rich. The Detachment has made huge piles of money."[94] Roger also reported on his health. He had fallen ill on the westward journey and had to spend a week in Regina recuperating. "I have been very ill, & today my big cough turned into incipient pleurisy. I went to the Doctor who promises to pull me round & get my lung right by to-morrow noon when I start on my first 200 mile ride to Wood Mountain[.] Once in the saddle I shall be all right."[95] Roger addressed this notion for his readers: "now, patched up by the ablest of doctors and excellent nursing, [I] must needs start on the long trail. After all, there is nothing like the prairie for a robust and healthy invalid; and the open-air life is a greater restorative than all the drugs on earth."[96] Indeed, throughout his writings he declared the best cure for most illnesses was to travel, prefer-ably with a horse, and to camp out in the wide-open spaces. There was some justification in his view, as any large group of people living in close proximity lacked the hygiene and sanitation of later times.

He revelled in being back in the wide-open spaces of the frontier that meant so much to him: "To the blind there is only darkness, but to a man with eyes the prairie is alive with all sorts of little people in fur[,] hair and feathers, from the absurd little owls who openly protest against passing horsemen, to the coyote wolf upon his moonlit hill bewailing the infrequency of supper."[97]

MacDonald is of the opinion that Roger's rhetoric was derived from Social Darwinism: "Civilisation is over-bred, luxuriant, its strength spent; only on the frontier will the barbarian virtues flourish. The frontiersman is man as Nature made him and needs him: the world is a jungle, and only the strongest savage survives.... Pocock's opinions were by no means singular, and can be duplicated from a wide range of popular texts."[98] One might hesitate to claim that Roger advocated "barbarian virtues," but he did feel that First Nations peoples understood nature and life itself better than men who spent their lives dwelling in cities. For example, Roger expressed his deep regard for life in the wild when he wrote, "There is no more luxurious bedroom than the scented woods, where the camp fire shines in ruddy contrast to deep, mysterious shadows among the trees, and the moon touches the foliage here and there with her tremulous pale silver."[99] He was also inclined to a rather mystical connection with the Earth:

> One could actually realize the motion of our little planet as this grass field was rolled round backwards until its visible edge shut out the sunlight: and at night one saw the slow dial of the stars marking the old Earth's movement. From that it was easy for the mind to grasp the flight of the Earth about her principal, the rush of the sun and all his family through the great spaces of outer darkness, the drift of constellations, systems, star mists. The plains make men think. There are moments when the most graceless frontiersman becomes awed by their silence, moved by the solemnity. The sunlight has found out the springs of a deep-hidden religion, and the waters of life sparkle at their discovery.[100]

The path of the original Thousand Mile Patrol, which Roger had intended to follow, officially involved only a solitary trooper, but some of the distances between houses or settlements were more than could be covered in one day. In this case a second man would be sent with either a wagon or a pack horse, for it was still possible for a lone man to meet with an accident in country that remained wild. Roger was somewhat disappointed that, because of changes, he could not set a distance record with this ride:

My first hope was to ride the Boundary patrol from Manitoba
to the Rocky Mountains—a thousand miles—at fifty miles a
day, an achievement which would have broken the world's
record, and possibly only where relays of horses could be had
throughout that distance. But when I got to Regina I found
the force so pitifully reduced in numbers that several valuable
outposts had been abandoned, and the weekly thousand-
mile patrol suspended for want of men. A special patrol
is conducting me the whole length of the hills—some six
hundred miles—to the very base of the Rocky Mountains; but
the old fifty miles a day which enabled the Mounted Police to
do the splendid work of past times is no longer possible.[101]

Roger described the geography of the journey to his father a little differently, but expressed the same regret about its parameters: "The trip
cannot begin at the Manitoba boundary because the patrol only begins
at Wood Mountain S.W. of here, but I am to go round all the patrols to
the Rockies & thence north to Edmonton on the Saskatchewan, a total
of probably 1000 miles or more. I shall be travelling at the usual 50 mile
regulation pace, but probably not without breaks. Record breaking is I
fear impossible."[102]

Still, he was happy to depart on 30 July. Of course, rumour had gone
on ahead that a "special correspondent" from a London newspaper would
be inflicting his company on the Mounted Police outposts along the route.
Roger was pleased he was repeatedly mistaken for a trooper:

when I am asked if this *Lloyd's* correspondent is coming I
can describe him vividly in advance. He is a fat, elderly man,
useless on the trail, doesn't know enough to roll his own
blankets, weighs three hundred and fifty pounds; and the
backboard [sic] is so far behind that it must have broken
down under his baggage. No, he hasn't got a drop with
him—stingier than Government, and puts on enough airs for
a viceroy. Then the team arrives, the myth explodes, I get the
welcome of an ex-policeman....[103]

Who then was Roger Pocock, who enjoyed this mischievous joke? "I was
only a buck Policeman, a man from the next Troop, on duty as the traveller's servant, living my boyhood again, taking the old delight in the old
Frontier, but now with a clearer vision, an older head, a bigger heart, and
broader sympathies."[104]

Roger Pocock photographed near Stonepile, Saskatoon, *c.*1897. At the time, Roger
was on a journalistic tour of North-west Mounted Police posts for *Lloyd's Weekly*.
[Glenbow Archives, NA 943–3]

On the journey he honed his tracking skills and learned what he could
from his comrades, the First Nations peoples they met, and the scouts who
accompanied his party. Those scouts included Louis Cobell and Green
Grass that Grows in Water. Roger complained, though, about what he
heard on the trail: "Men I met in plenty who had seen everything; but
stories are only to be had from a Westerner when you have won his confidence. To the tenderfoot he lies invariably, of the journalist he is suspicious, whereas if you play 'old hand' you are supposed to know all about
what happened. The heroes of great adventures told me what other men
did, and shrank from publicity...."[105] He also studied Blackfoot petro-
glyphs and pictographs at Writing-on-Stone, beside the Milk River, in
what is now the province of Alberta. While he was most interested in
interactions between the Mounted Police and the First Nations, he also
rhapsodized about the natural cornucopia of Cypress Hills:

> Antelope, blacktail deer, prairie chickens, hawks, ducks,
> geese, swans enlivened the country; the fruit—service berries,
> gooseberries, choke cherries, black and white currants, and

a dozen more varieties—was in ripe perfection. The Cypress hills [*sic*] are wonderful and beautiful beyond belief, with their deep coulees, their wide lakes, their splendid tree-clad slopes, and towering buttes—above all for the upland meadows, the plains on top of the hills where the hay stands ready for cutting. Here the country is strewn with the bones of mastodon, hipparion, rhinoceros, hyena, all the great fauna of the age before the buffalo: there the rocks bristle with sea-shells of the cretaceous age, contemporary with the English chalk, all pearly and iridescent; yonder the walls of some canyon are cut into fantastic shapes of beasts mingled with huge mushroom stones perched on quaint castellated towers, and hereabouts there are grey wolves, each with a bounty on his ears—very shy.... Every mile has its wonders of petrified forest, rare flowers, valuable gypsum, rubies, coal, or lovely scenery.[106]

Roger's great interest in horses shows throughout his diary. There Roger commented most days on the quality of the horse he was riding, and often mentioned their names, for example Brownie ("very rough & shied a good deal," 31 July), Guinty ("a good roper but clumsy," 8 August), Rattler ("very rough," 9 August), Dublin ("splendid roan," 12 and 13 August), and Charlie ("white 16 ½ hands...a splendid animal," 15 August). He was also proud that he rode in the wagon only very briefly, no matter the state of his health, the weather, or the trail. Thus on 3 August he wrote: "total 28 m[iles]. Rode all of it & never drove again." While he did later spend a little time riding a wagon rather than a horse, it covered only a tiny portion of the total journey. Despite his pride, manifest in his published accounts, in his diary he was willing to mention that he was bucked off or otherwise bested by a horse.[107] He made a point of devoting one of his articles for *Lloyd's Weekly* entirely to horse ride records, and concluded proudly that nowhere else had there been "quite such riding as in the North-west Mounted Police."[108] In support of his own claim to expertise, Roger carefully noted nearly every day how far he had ridden. The first day, as he was becoming comfortable on horseback, it was twenty-two miles. Thereafter the mileage was generally greater.

Geological descriptions are also a frequent occurrence in his diary. For example, on 6 August he wrote that "Stone pile [*sic*] is named from a tumulus of stones some 6 m[iles] off of uncertain origin found to contain human bones. The coulee sides are full of white clay, gypsum I think to judge by some crystals." The next day he commented on "outcrops of coal & gypsum." On 9 August he went to some trouble to visit a ruby mine:

Roger Pocock leading two horses on a trail during his tour of the NWMP posts.
[RCMP Archives 5903 9 (Unconfirmed)]

[Rode] 16 m[ile]s & call in scout Louis Cobell who
discovered & owns it, from pass. Ten m[ile]s south of Battle
Creek the Assiniboine trail crosses Middle Fork & two
m[iles] beyond I found the track of a waggon [*sic*] off on the
left[.] This answering to description I followed it carefully for
6 m[iles] across Middle Fork [&] found it following the line
of an abandoned telegraph. Then I saw tents afar off & got
[there] in time for dinner. Saw mine & rubies, prospected,
slept, & after supper rode in with Louis.[109]

While horses, mileage, and geology played major roles in his diary, perhaps
the most common element Roger noted were the names and roles of the
people he met. He took particular pleasure in meeting current or former
Mounted Police. Some of the latter had become ranchers or cowboys,
including "([Regimental Number] 1134) Tommy Nash who was with me
at Regina & on march to Carlton" (8 August). Despite being on the move
most of the day and some evenings, and enjoying the opportunity to "yarn"

with many of the people he met, Roger was apparently able to write more than just his diary, for on 22 August, at Pincher Creek, he noted that he "sent off first 3 papers to Pinker."[110] In addition to making notes in his diary, Roger took quite a few photographs with his trusty Kodak.

In his pieces for *Lloyd's Weekly*, Roger did more than just write about the places he saw and the people he met. He was very fond of telling how the Mounted Police brought law enforcement to the West, largely through force of will rather than at the end of a gun. He was also ahead of his time in his strongly stated belief that "the Canadian Government has not dealt justly with the Indians. In the seventies, when treaties were entered into by her Majesty with her Indian allies, much was promised verbally by the whites, yet never set down on paper. The Indians believed that the treaty was a writing down of all spoken promises, and certainly never consented to any interference with what they call their religion."[111] He devoted a second article to a treasured experience: "Here was evidently a round up of cattle in the neighbourhood, and I always wanted to be a cowboy ever since I was at school. I would turn cowboy now so as to be able to tell the readers of *Lloyd's Weekly* what it feels like."[112] He joined in the duties to the best of his ability and enjoyed the experience enormously, for "Like all frontiersmen, whether Mounted Police, sailors, prospectors, gold diggers, lumbermen, or voyageurs, I found the cowboys glorious company—plain-spoken, straight-eyed, manly, generous, sound of stomach, and capable with their hands."[113] He considered that he had learned fast enough to be qualified to add another profession to his growing list of abilities and experiences, that of "cowboy." In yet another article he discussed "wheat mania" and what sort of immigrants would be best suited to the region, with particular praise for the Mormons ("Canada never did a better stroke of business than when she secured these settlers," he wrote), and he voiced concern that some ethnic groups, such as the "Mennonites from Russia, Moravians, Scandinavians, Germans, Slavs, [and] Galicians," were not receiving the respect they deserved.[114]

When Roger reached Fort Macleod on 27 August, Sam Steele, one of his heroes, was in command. Roger was made very welcome as a personal guest of the family in their spare bedroom.[115] Roger made a great impression on the Steele children—Gertrude Alexandra (c.1892–post 1978), Mary Charlotte Flora MacDonald (c.1894–c.1947), and Harwood Elmes Robert (1897–1978)—with whom he had a close and warm family friendship.[116] There he also would have heard the story of Charcoal (also known as Si'k-okskitsis, Paka'panikapi, or Opee-o'wun, c.1856–1897), who was hanged at Fort Macleod.[117] After several days Roger left Fort Macleod to visit Leavings, Mosquito Creek, Okotoks, Calgary, and High River. He returned to Fort Macleod only to depart again, this time for Banff, where he arrived on 23 September. There he was resting at the detachment when he was roped in, along with every other man who could stand, to help fight one of the forest fires that can be so perilous to settlements in that part of Canada.[118] After he made his farewells to his friends in the Mounted Police, he continued on to Mount Lefroy, Glacier, and Revelstoke, mainly by freight train and often stopping to pursue geology, one of the other passions of his life. He also spent some time on the Fraser River in British Columbia, since "An account of frontier life in Western Canada would be but half written without some description of prospecting."[119] Roger took out a Free Miner's licence, and with an experienced miner named "Weary" as his partner, set off to pan for gold in the Fraser River valley. The days of easy Fraser River gold were long gone, so Roger and his partner re-washed old gravel that years earlier had relinquished fortunes to other men. The two of them found "enough here to give two shillings, there three, and yonder four, in return for a hard day's work. All day we searched, and got back to camp by moonlight, having found no gravel worth working."[120] After declaiming caustically how extremely rare it was for miners, traders, or company promoters involved in gold rushes to make any money, he nonetheless wrote that "Weary and I worked on at Chinamen's wages in that dead Eldorado of the Fraser Canyon, until both of us were heartsick. The trains rushed on for the sea, the coffin-ships departed to their doom, but neither my partner nor I had money to reach the Klondyke [*sic*]."[121] Of course, Roger wanted to join the gold rush to the Klondike, but it was not until he returned to London that he thought of a way to finance the trek.

In his last article in "Into the Great Dominion," Roger was enthusiastic about the availability of coal, for "Here is a foundation for the industries of a wealthy and powerful nation—another England. Close by has been discovered a rich supply of petroleum and bitumen…." He also spoke keenly of the silver mines and other minerals in the West, and he wrote in some detail on the geological formation of the area. He declared:

> I have tried very hard in these poor letters to convey some impression of the life lived by the trooper, the cowboy, the miner, the settler; of the pains and pleasantries of the many-sided Frontier: also of the beauty and splendour of our Western heritage….
>
> We know we [British] are not done for yet: that we are leading mankind to new and higher planes of social progress…. We are sowing the seed in countless scattered fields—the seed of our religion, of our freedom, of our justice,

our industry, and all that has been given us of manliness and learning, and the arts. We are sowing the seed—what shall the harvest be?[122]

One thing he felt quite confident would occur, though, was the destruction of his beloved prairies:

The wheatfields [*sic*] are spreading from the east, and when they cover the prairies our Great Lone Land will be a thing of history. Our outposts by the Moose Pound, and Battle Creek, and Many Berries, Pend Oreille, the Writing-on-Stone, Whoopup, Standoff, Slideout, the Leavings, will all be cities then, our Districts sovereign states, and a nation of forty million people will send their senators to represent the Plains at Westminster.[123]

It was time for Roger to return to London, where he began plans for an expedition to the Klondike that would cast a shadow over the rest of his life.

5

THE CASE
of the
VANISHING BARONET

ROGER'S LIFE IS FULL OF STRANGE TALES, and even stranger characters, for like his friends and acquaintances, he went out to meet life head on,
without regard for the consequences. That approach might be expected
to create at least one mystery. In Roger's life, it is an adventure that could
be called, "The Case of the Vanishing Baronet." It could easily have been
featured in a Victorian melodrama, or even in one of Roger's own works
of fiction, but it wounded him so deeply he could not bring himself to use
it that way. The stage was set for this adventure when Roger returned to
London in late 1897, because he was still trying to think of a way to return
to Canada to take part in the Klondike gold rush. On its own, the adventure
of the Klondike would have attracted him, but there was a second motiva-
tion. It seems that Roger, not unusually for him, was in debt, this time to his
cousin, Herbert Currey, for some furniture.[1] Meanwhile, in attire at least,
he never really left his favourite part of Canada. He insisted on wearing
his western style of dress, even in London, to demonstrate that he was one
of a select band of British adventurers who just stopped over in London,
from time to time, to swap stories with other men with similar interests.
While this attire might have reinforced his literary reputation, its effect on
his social position would have been less positive, "for middle-class society,
hidebound in its conventionality, gave cold comfort to the black sheep that
returned to embarrass it."[2] Nonetheless, the success of Roger's "Into the
Great Dominion" series meant *Lloyd's Weekly Newspaper* and other journals and papers were happy to take more of his writing.

During this period Roger shared chambers at 15 Great Ormond Street, London, with two men. One of these was Charles Welsh Mason. Roger described Mason with particular admiration. He had served in the customs service in China and become involved in a revolution there. He was captured with a shipload of arms that he had purchased with a £7,500 legacy. Fortunate to escape to England with his life and all appendages intact, in London Mason was busily writing adventure novels.[3] The other man was Herbert Philip Hilton (1873–1915), who had served in the NWMP for a brief time and had also served in the South African War, becoming a captain in the Middlesex Regiment. Among the frequent visitors was C.J. Cutcliffe-Hyne. He had himself travelled much of the world by sea, but some of the Kettle stories have hints of Roger's tales of his adventures or those he had heard about on his many sea voyages.[4] Stories would have been exchanged in the evening over pipes of tobacco. Stanley L. Wood, who drew illustrations for *Captain Kettle* and also for Roger's *Curly: A Tale of the Arizona Desert*, was another of that little group of friends. It has occasionally been suggested that Roger was the model for Wood's drawing of Captain Kettle. Although there are slight similarities, Roger said that the actual "model for the portraits of Captain Kettle was the humble potman at a pub in Hampstead."[5] Another member of the group was Phil May (1864–1903), the artist best known for his work in *Punch*.

These men seem to have been addicted to joining clubs. Later, Roger became a member of the Savage Club,[6] but he and his friends also formed their own little private clubs. For example, Roger was the main force behind the Filibusters Club, which met at members' lodgings with "a cordial welcome, a warm hearth, and certain refreshments."[7] The Club had no fees. Men just met to swap yarns and possibly even "tall tales." Roger appears to have been an enthusiastic organizer for The Nameless Club, which even produced a privately printed publication, *The Unearthly Yelp*.[8] Members included Cecil Goodenough Hayter (1871–1922), who wrote stories for boys, accompanied Cutcliffe-Hyne to Lapland, and provided the illustrations for Cutcliffe-Hyne's *Through Arctic Lapland;* Lord Mountmorres was also a member who, according to Roger, was always arranging to journey to some far-off part of the globe.[9] The lectures arranged for The Nameless Club probably would not have appealed to the returned adventurers of the Filibusters Club. The titles included "The Early Fathers of America," "Continents Adrift—Note Wegener Thesis," "The Story of the Horse," and "The Conquest of the Air."[10] Roger may have chosen the topics, for these were all his special interests, and the theory of continental drift, in particular, took up much of his time and thought in later years.

While "Fiction creates its own reality, and tempts the reader to enter an imagined world,"[11] Roger and his friends wished to experience adventures, as well as to write about them. So, often one of his friends would announce that he was off to a distant land. Some of them were wealthy enough to do this at a whim. Roger was not wealthy, but he was determined to take part in the adventure that was a core subject of discussion at the time, the Klondike gold rush. He had been to the edge of that adventure when he was in British Columbia and Alaska, and he had seen other men go off to take part in it. He had even provided detailed and somewhat derisive advice on how to prepare for the journey to the Klondike:

> We are all going to join the gold rush next spring…and most of us will be as badly fooled as was the average Californian Argonaut of 1849. I do know something, at least, about outfitting for Alaska, British Columbia, and the Territories, having travelled for years in these regions, gaining experience which may be useful to next year's crop of victims.
>
> If you are going to the Yukon do not outfit in London. A few things you may get there which will be useful:
>
> Pocket medicine case full of concentrated drugs and instruments of minor surgery.
>
> "The Ship Captain's Medical Guide."
>
> Three-cornered needles—"surgeon's," "glover's," "sailmaker's"; sheath knife, flexible with wooden handle. Patent buttons, wax end, wax, thread, &c., underclothes, and toilet gear.
>
> For salmon—a gaff head.
>
> For trout—common tackle. Western fish despise fancy flies.
>
> For meat—a rifle, '45 calibre.
>
> Weapons are not carried on the Klondike.
>
> It is in Canada, and the Mounted Police run that department.
>
> Winter clothes get in Winnipeg.[12]

Roger also specified exactly what articles of clothing were necessary, accompanied by such items as mosquito netting, blankets, waterproof sheet, and "Pacific coast or Arctic pattern" snowshoes. The gold seeker also needed to buy a camp outfit (tent, stove, and cooking gear), a mining outfit ("Canadian axe, with spare helves, long-handled shovel, pick, and steel gold pan"), boat building outfit (nails, pitch, oakum, tools, canvas, etc.), and provisions ("Under current conditions no man is allowed to enter the country without a supply for one year. Add 1lb. citric acid as a

light substitute for lime juice…and 100lb. dried fruit and vegetables").[13]
Another London-based voyager declared that

> a police edict had been issued, in which it was announced
> that no person would be permitted to cross the boundary
> unless provided with at least two years' supplies, this extreme
> measure being taken in view of the distress caused in Dawson
> last winter in consequence of the large influx of people and
> the dearth of provisions…. A prolonged visit to the extensive
> stores of the Hudson Bay Company fixed us up with
> everything that I had been advised to take….[14]

Roger carefully provided costs for all the necessities, and calculated that,
including fares, the Klondike adventurer would need to spend at least £135,
which was rather more than he had. So he needed to think of a way to find
sufficient money to enable him to be part of that great adventure.

Roger decided he should use his knowledge of the region to lead an
expedition. He worked out the costs and decided he needed just eight
paying members to cover expenses. So on 7 and 8 January 1898, his advertisement appeared in the *Times:*

> Klondyke.—Experienced Western Traveller, bound for
> Yukon, will LEAD SMALL PARTY. Applicants, physically
> sound, must furnish expenses. Good faith guaranteed.
> Address Yukon, 15, Great Ormond street. W.C.

Roger later wrote that a notice such as his on the Continent "would have
seemed like the freak of a maniac[;] in England there were sixty-three
replies."[15] These applicants might have been influenced by Roger's description of himself as an "Experienced Western Traveller," and that image
would have been reinforced by the frontier trophies displayed on the walls,
probably in a manner designed to impress the volunteers when they visited
his rooms. From these applicants who were prepared to pay £250 to go on
the expedition, Roger had to pick the right eight men, but proved, not for
the last time, that he was not the best judge of men and character.

In addition to expedition members willing and able to pay, Roger
needed a plan and a route. His plan relied on pack horses, which he knew
were in great demand for the journey to the Klondike. He calculated that
he could buy good pack horses at Ashcroft, British Columbia, for £4 each.
His expedition would then run them 1,000 miles up the old Telegraph
Trail to the Skeena River. Just after Roger left his stint as a missionary on

the Skeena, an attempt had been made to run a pack train from Ashcroft along the abandoned Telegraph Trail, but it had been plundered by the Gitksan.[16] Roger, however, thought he could renew his friendships with the Gitksan and recruit guides to take his company on from the Skeena to the Stikine River, where he thought they could sell the horses for £40 each. This would provide a good profit for every member of the expedition, or they could earn 1s 8d per pound weight if they decided to use the horses to carry cargo to the Klondike.[17] Roger, ever optimistic, declared that "From Ashcroft to Telegraph Creek on the Stickeen [*sic*] would be one thousand miles. Now it was only another seven hundred and fifty miles on from the Stickeen [*sic*] to Klondyke [*sic*]."[18] As for the route, a major factor that Roger had strangely, or foolishly, not considered was that he was not the only man aware of the old Telegraph Trail as a route to the Klondike. Indeed, he had carefully detailed this particular route for readers of *Lloyd's Weekly* after describing the Alaska routes the previous week.[19] Hamlin Garland, the American writer, described the various trails, then indicated why, in May 1898, he began his trek to the Klondike along much the same route Roger intended to use:

> I believed that I was about to see and take part in a most
> picturesque and impressive movement across the wilderness.
> I believed it to be the last great march of the kind which
> could ever come in America, so rapidly were the wild places
> being settled up. I wished, therefore, to take part in this
> tramp of the goldseekers, to be one of them, and record their
> deeds.... I was not a goldseeker, but a nature hunter, and I
> was eager to enter this, the wildest region yet remaining in
> Northern America. I willingly and with joy took the long way
> round, the hard way through.[20]

Roger would have agreed with the appeal of the wilderness, as he would have agreed that "the love of adventure had led all of us to take the telegraph route."[21]

Wisely, Roger did not try to disguise the difficulties of the journey: "To each applicant I explained that he had no earthly chance of getting rich, but would be overworked, drenched, possibly starved, as a labourer, navvy, and scullion, and for these interesting experiences must pay two hundred and fifty pounds, cash down in advance."[22] Despite this, the lure of the Klondike was so strong that he experienced no problem selecting members for his team, although it is unknown what qualities he saw in those he actually chose. He was full of his usual enthusiasm, but then it was not in Roger's character to calculate all the risks of his enterprises before he undertook them. He never had, and never would; instead, he decided to do something and simply went ahead and did it. It was always a case of his heart ruling his head. Thus, for example, he ignored completely the fact that he would not be the only one seeking to acquire horses, and that he would not even be starting from Canada. He also ignored the reality that tales of the Klondike had spread around the world and thousands wanted to take part in this gold rush. Those who did not fancy being miners thought of ways to make money trading with those who did. It was true that high prices were being asked for freight from Telegraph Creek, but "The majority could not and would not pay this awful price...."[23] As well, the horses that arrived were little more than skeletons as a result of conditions on the way—particularly the frequent lack of feed. Far from making any money on the Telegraph Trail, many a man bankrupted himself.

Roger held the final meeting of the expedition members in his rooms on 25 January 1898, where they signed a legal and proper contract. A member of the expedition who played a recurring role in Roger's life, almost until Roger's death, was Sir Arthur Colin Curtis. Curtis, a forty-year-old baronet, was married and had a twelve-year-old son. The family home was Little Gatcombe, Hilsea, north of Portsmouth. A more logical thinker than Roger would have questioned closely why a man in Curtis's position would choose to leave his wife and son to take part in such an expedition, especially under such a leader. Nonetheless, at the final meeting it was arranged that Roger and one other man, whom Roger referred to only as *H__*, would go on ahead to buy the horses. *H__* was Herbert Philip Hilton. The other members of the expedition were medical student Norman Pern (probably the man Roger referred to in his accounts as "the doctor"), Francis J.C. Jeffcock, E.T. Boddam-Whetham, G.A. Sheppard, Hubert Swinburne, and C.J. Newbery. Charles Adamson was a later addition to the expedition, which was known as the Star Outfit. According to the Memorandum of Agreement—signed by Pocock, Jeffcock, Boddam-Whetham, Sheppard, Swinburne (by Sheppard), Hilton, Newbery, and Curtis—each expedition member other than Hilton, who as official horse-wrangler was exempt from payment, contracted to pay £250 for expenses related to the expedition. Roger would be paid £200 for his services. Any profit from the expedition was to be divided equally among "all the parties hereto."[24]

In his diary for 5 February 1898, Roger recorded that he and Hilton sailed from Liverpool on the *Etruria*, accompanied by Pern, "as representative of the party to watch my expenditures, [and] Adamson because he wants to meet his brother on the Cariboo Road." The *Etruria* arrived at

New York on 12 February. Roger visited his brother Frank in Philadelphia one day, joined Hilton and Adamson in Montreal, stopped off in Ottawa, and then headed to Winnipeg. There they "did three days heavy work shopping & business mainly Hudsons [*sic*] Bay Store." Hilton went ahead to Golden, Kamloops, and Ashcroft to gather information about the price and availability of horses. Roger met Adamson and Hilton at Ashcroft on 24 February, where they began to buy horses. Early in March they were riding through heavy snow and buying still more horses, so that on 10 March he reported a total of fifty-four horses. On 15 March they began horse breaking.[25] According to Roger, the two men were "happy as schoolboys at being in the saddle once more."[26]

Roger had reason to be happy, for not only was he back in the saddle in western Canada, but others were paying for his adventure. This contrasted sharply with the evening he dreamed up the expedition, when he admitted he had "one pound by way of capital."[27] Hilton and Roger made their way up the old coach road to Cariboo Mines, site of an earlier gold rush, through deep snow and piercing cold. Along the route were a number of rest houses where they could discuss horses with other travellers. Already his bright idea was manifesting flaws, as all the best horses from the plains had been sold to the many men who were ahead of Roger's group on the route. Sometimes, he admitted, the horses he was able to buy were insufficiently hardy, yet he could also praise them as "magnificent animals of their class."[28] The horses were wild, so "When we had hired a pair of horse-breakers[,] we drove our herd down to Hat Creek, thirteen miles above Ashcroft, and there set up our first camp. Renting a pasture and corral, we set to work horse smashing, and that was a big job, lasting a month."[29] Due to the cold, Roger was forced to pay to have his workers boarded in a hotel. He returned to Ashcroft to pick up freight and provisions, and on 16 March, in spite of night temperatures hovering around -10°F, they "went into camp." Because he needed to make further trips to Ashcroft and Vancouver, on 24 March Roger "gave up the cooking, as it interfered with all my business. Put men for meals in hotel."[30] It was a mistake, and an expensive one, not to take on a man as dedicated cook, for this is one of the most important jobs on any expedition. One writer later reported that Mr. Eagleson, proprietor of the Hat Creek hotel, charged 50 cents per meal, and Roger paid "over $900[,] nearly all for meals and drinks."[31] Roger thought he could undertake the cooking, in addition to his other duties, and this proved very wrong; it also had some bearing on the later problem with Curtis, the baronet. The first hint of Roger's lack of leadership and judgement now surfaced. Pern had suffered from fluid on the knee since arriving in Canada. Roger met him at Ashcroft and rode up with him into camp. When Roger left to return to Ashcroft, he "left [Pern with] strict orders not to risk his leg by sleeping in camp. So he slept in the camp & laid himself up with rheumatic fever."[32]

Roger spent much time recording expenses to ensure that he could account for all the expedition's money. Spring was very late that year, and they were under canvas in temperatures of -10°F. Even the eternally optimistic Roger was disturbed as he watched the horses failing as a result of being fed only on hay, a judgement error that proved to be very expensive. He received a wire on 25 March that the main party was leaving Winnipeg. Two days later the "crowd turned up[:] Newbery[,] Sheppard[,] Whetham[,] Jeffcock[,] Swinburne & Curtis, train 3 days late…. Hilton arrived on 26th with the saddle horses." After two nights in a hotel, Roger "Moved all hands into camp & turned cook."[33] It was not until 19 April that they were ready to start from Hat Creek, and by then, as Roger later wrote, "the same scheme had attracted three thousand men with seven thousand horses—the route eaten bare of all save poison weeds, and tramped into a thousand-mile mud-hole…."[34] Roger was forced to stop payment on the cheque to Herbert Currey, for 15 April he wrote, "Only $300 left & horses dying for want of fresh grass. Half of them dangerously ill with distemper. I have to send my cheque drawn in favour of Herbert Currey for $767. It was to get this money I started this outfit, and now I have lost it all. Reduced the cargo to save horses." On 19 April he sounded even more distressed: "struck camp & fled with the half ruined outfit in search of the fresh grass which alone can save the horses from death." Roger later admitted to "leaving a dead horse at nearly every camp."[35] The horses were fed on hay until the sixteenth day of their trek, when they found what appeared to be a paradise of rich grass. This did not end their troubles, though, as wild stallions came to capture the mares, and the horses, now gaining strength on the good feed, began to show signs of returning to their original wild state. As late as 2 May, Roger recorded that there was still snow in patches. However, by 13 May the weather had greatly improved, and he was able to report, "Went for a ride with a very pretty quarter breed lady, & a doctor[;] trees in half leaf, marigolds & wild fruit in bloom." By 25 May there was "Very hot weather."[36] After struggling to get their horses across the Fraser River, Roger's group reached Quesnel, at the start of the Telegraph Trail, on 29 May.

Just a few days ahead of Roger's group, Norman Lee was also heading north. He had decided to try to drive about 200 cattle on the Trail. He had calculated that there would be demand for beef in Dawson City and hoped to make some money so he could make a trip back to England. He wrote that "Every half hour, one or more packtrains [sic] would go on up the trail. All kinds and varieties of horses, all sorts and conditions of men."[37] Lee described the difficulties of the Trail, and Roger was indeed somewhat shaken by the condition of the trail and the travellers, which he described as

> a string of mud-holes walled with bush, crowded with
> thousands of people all pressing northward in grim silence.
> What with the starvation of their animals, sore backs, stray
> horses, squabbles, bankruptcy, and endless rain, most of the
> pack-trains were just on the verge of collapse. We were near
> the end of our own resources, and had barely funds enough
> to re-provision.[38]

Roger blamed the Canadian government for leaving adventurers to their fate, but the members of his group did not share that view. They later blamed Roger for poor advance information, poor planning, and poor leadership. Roger did admit that "the only thing wrong with the Star Outfit, was my unfortunate leadership; I had splashed too recklessly with the funds"; he was less forthcoming about other issues, however, saying only, "the other fellows confessed the remainder of my sins."[39] While on the trail, Adamson demonstrated a lack of respect for Roger as leader. On 24 May, Roger wrote in his diary, "there was fear of the horses breaking back so I walked 2 miles back & spent the night with fires at a bridge over a creek.... Morning [I] walked back to camp & had a sleep while the outfit loaded. So photograph was taken of me by Adamson." This image was published in August as representative of Roger, "at work."[40] Adamson was not the only participant who would have had trouble showing respect for Roger, for he was not only thought of as a paid employee, he was also from a slightly lower social class. Curtis probably had a low opinion of Roger's leadership skills. The two men also did not get on well personally. Roger wrote about him:

> A. C__ [Arthur Curtis] came of a naval family who
> must have hated horses from time immemorial. Of most
> engaging humour, chivalrous, and unselfish, C__ was
> a born sportsman, an enthusiast at mining, yet seemed
> only at home on the water. Therefore I was apt to be rude
> when our success, our very lives, depended upon learning
> horsemanship and woodcraft. But still he was patient with
> me, his dignity too fine and deep a thing to ruffle easily upon
> the surface, and I never guessed how sore he was at heart.[41]

Adamson, on the other hand, wrote that "Sir Arthur was very sensitive and Pocock's insolence at times made him furious."[42] At the time, Curtis appeared to have much on his mind, and it became apparent later that he had problems he did not share with other members of the group.

Late May brought torrential rain to add to their problems. It was not a happy outfit. On 31 May Roger wrote, "Sacked Bill Bent my cargador for being drunk & useless. He tried to take proceedings for recovery of wages. No magistrate would serve him. 6 pm 10 horses lost by carelessness of Whetham left in charge of herd. 22 horses left for 34 riggings & eight saddles." Seven of these horses were recovered for them on 3 June, which cost $24. On the previous day Roger wrote, "$200 left. Situation desperate." There was a meeting on 3 June to discuss the problems. Duties were changed so that "Hilton becomes Cargador, Sheppard is Horse Wrangler, Curtis and I cooks. Marched with 37 horses, cash $105 left."[43] On 8 June they crossed the Blackwater River and camped by the Mud River, where they were plagued by mud, blackflies, and mosquitoes.

The missing horses, along with Roger's amateur cooking, led to frayed nerves and tempers. It was at Mud River that the conflict between Curtis and Roger came to a head. In his diary Roger described this succinctly:

> June 9 Lay off. 10 horses missing in the dense willow bush. All day cooking, baking & showing the boys how to mend apparejos. Had time for a bath & a smoke in the afternoon. Curtis sulking.
>
> June 10 Up at 3 am work well underweigh [sic]. All hands hunting horses. At about 6 am to 7 am a little after breakfast—Curtis strolled out of camp. Wouldn't have any food.[44]

In his account of the expedition that appeared in a Vancouver newspaper, Roger described that situation in more detail:

> We made our drive of seventeen miles from the Blackwater, forded Mud river, camped, and lost a day over ten strayed horses. For fear of losing a second day I had all hands out early next morning, remaining in camp myself. Being at the time cook and baker, with the mending of apparejas [sic] and other harness to fill any spare moments, I could not well leave camp in any pretext.
>
> Sir Arthur Curtis was still in camp after the rest had left. Indeed I did not expect him to take part in the search because he had always shown a curious ineptitude for brush work,

getting puzzled and lost very easily. Moreover he had never been accustomed to handling horses. Nature intended him for the sea and his tastes led him always afloat, or shooting, or mining in which he was keenly interested. His work, therefore, was not with the horses but in other directions.

This morning, however, after he had arranged his saddle and gear for the day's march, he lit his pipe and walked briskly out of camp before even taking breakfast, evidently intending to join in the horse hunting, as he had remarked earlier that nobody had looked up the valley.[45]

Still later, Roger described events with more emotion:

C__ had been thinking all day, and when he offered to help me wash up after supper, I told him roughly to "go away and rest."

The words cut worse than a whip-lash across his face, words that could never be withdrawn, never forgiven....

Next morning...C__ would not eat in my company, but after breakfast I noticed him preparing his saddle and gear for the day's march. Then he lit his pipe, and as he walked past the fire I begged him to have some breakfast. Without noticing my presence he went on, and passed between two willow bushes out of sight.[46]

Adamson described the friction between Curtis and Roger in several ways, including what transpired in the last two days:

Pocock undertook to get supper that night. Sir Arthur was supposed to help him. Pocock refused all help and told Sir Arthur that he had better take a rest. Sir Arthur went to bed without supper that night in a very gloomy mood. The next morning we had several visitors for breakfast. Pocock seemed in a vicious humor. Sir Arthur, apparently, forgetting his bad humor of the night before. He offered to do some work and Pocock said: "Sir Arthur, go and have a rest: you look very tired: you must be weary." This was not said in the best spirit in the world.

Sir Arthur took umbrage at Pocock's remarks. He told me that the newspaper man would have to apologize or be thrashed. A few minutes afterwards Sir Arthur walked up to Pocock and said: "I'll make you apologize before the whole

party or I'll give you a damned good thrashing." Pocock
never said a word.

Sir Arthur spoke his last words to me. He said: "Old man,
I understand the horses are up the river. I will go and look for
them."

He lighted his pipe. His face was deathly pale. After
walking a distance up the river he disappeared in the dense
underbrush bordering the forest and was never seen again.[47]

All versions agree that that was the last positive sighting of Sir Arthur
Colin Curtis, and the beginning of a mystery.

In both "He Died in the Bush" and *A Frontiersman,* Roger told how
they rounded up the missing horses and then the customary signal of three
revolver shots was fired to recall the group. The rest of the morning was
taken up by breaking camp, and packing, harnessing, loading, and sad-
dling the horses. Only in "He Died in the Bush," though, did Roger add
further explanation, in addition to all this activity, for his lack of concern
when Curtis walked out of camp, "for on previous occasions Sir Arthur
had walked ahead looking for game…." As usual, Roger rode ahead as
scout. He met a lone horseman and enquired whether he had seen Curtis.
He had not, so Roger rode back to place food and a note by the previous
night's campfire. The group camped that night by Bobtail Lake.[48] The
next morning, Roger sent a man back to fire shots down Mud River valley
and listen for a response. Roger also said he sent back the "doctor" with
camping equipment and medical stores.[49] He wrote in his diary:

> June 11 Sent Newbery back to enquire at camps for Curtis,
> & fire alarm shots. 3 pm a passing outfit reported Curtis
> not seen on trail. At 8 Newbery returned[:] no news. I
> started with Swinburne back to Paterson's camp 5 m[iles].
> Slept there. Found two outfits at dawn. Patersons [*sic*] &
> Adamson's brother's outfit.
>
> June 12 Organized search parties & on to Mud River.
> Organized search parties there[.] Sent Swinburne to bring
> down all hands to Mud River except Newbery & Adamson to
> stay on herd.[50]

Later he said he organized the search parties on 11 June.[51] That these dates
do not match might be due to Roger's memory playing tricks, under stress.
It is also uncertain exactly when he wrote the diary entries or whether he
had the diary at hand when he was writing his autobiography. On 14 June

Roger reported "Deluge of rain all day," which would have made tracking very difficult. Colonel Wright, with a Toronto outfit, was passing and his whole group joined the search, but with no success. Finally, Roger accepted Wright's suggestion that he send one of his men for Chilcotin trackers, who were so skilful that the BCPP often employed them to run down fugitives.[52] The trackers found Curtis's trail, which they followed eastward for fifteen miles until it ended at a small river. They were even able to report that Curtis had spent the first night resting against a tree, and that a big grizzly bear had crossed the track, although it apparently had not harmed Curtis.[53] In his diary for 15 June Roger simply reported that the trackers "returned with hopeful report in the evening" and that after the next day's search they returned "hopeless [and] refused further search."[54] Although some of Roger's party lacked experience with wilderness conditions, Roger, and probably Hilton, understood the difficulties of that country. Why did he wait so long before raising an alarm and arranging search parties? Roger said he expected Curtis to catch up, but he also said that Curtis was on foot. We can only assume Roger was so infuriated with Curtis, and so wrapped up in the logistics of the expedition, that he failed in the duty of care owed by a leader to the men under his command.

After these days of fruitless searching, Roger held a conference of the remaining expedition members. This was necessary because they had used most of their food to provision their own and other search parties' efforts. Roger resigned his leadership on 19 June and renounced his share of the expedition's profits.[55] The next day Adamson, Pern, Sheppard, Boddam-Whetham, Swinburne, Jeffcock, Hilton, and Newbery signed a document absolving Roger of any blame: "The expedition to the Klondyke [sic] district led by Roger Pocock having broken up, and the loss and death of Sir Arthur Curtis being the principal cause, we, the members of the said expedition hereby exonerate Roger Pocock from blame, and are of the opinion that in general conduct he has acted honourably throughout."[56] Unfortunately, this declaration was of little value in the court of public opinion. The members of the expedition then split up. While Roger headed for Vancouver, all the others, "though nearly starved to death, reached the Stickeen [sic] in safety, with sixteen horses out of the fifty-one which [they] had bought, and in this fared better than most men on that disastrous trail."[57] That they survived at all was quite a feat for these essentially inexperienced men, but they still suffered criticism:

> At the Lepann [Klappan] river (80 miles from T.C.) were
> two men selling grub. They had originally come out to meet
> the Curtis party (having come up the coast by steamer) but

getting tired of the bad trails were now selling out their flour and bacon at enormous prices to people who came along. Many of the pilgrims had helped to hunt for Sir Arthur Curtis when lost at Mud river [*sic*], at their own expense for several days, and were not very well pleased to find one of the party waiting here to sell flour to them at seventy five cents a lb., and other things in proportion.[58]

While the others continued north, by 25 June Roger was in Quesnel.[59] He then spent several days travelling to Vancouver: "Arr Vancouver wired Lady Curtis offering help. She cabled insisting on full details[.] The reply reduced me to $8. H B Co lent me $30[.]" The cable, dated 3 July, from Lady Curtis to Roger, who was then in Victoria, read, "No necessity come home insist on Knowing [*sic*] worst explain fully by wire cannot bear suspense have you proof death also write."[60] Despite her words, Roger later wrote, "my presence would be needed in England, where I must get probate for C—'s widow"; he also added, "It is still rather a puzzle to me how I got home to England."[61] The inference is that he went immediately to England, whereas according to his Klondike Diary, he actually first made his way across America to his brother:

> Spent 7th July in giving information to H B Co to direct their search for Curtis body. At Vancouver there arrived loan of $100 from Frank, & message to hurry home if I wanted to see Father alive. Paid back $30 to H B Co. & started via Victoria[,] Seattle & Northern Pacific[.] At Fargo, Dakota, I broke down very ill. Went on next day[;] reached Frank July 18 & went smash for a fortnight before I was well enough to travel.

In a letter to Frederick White of the NWMP, Roger addressed his stay in Pennsylvania: "On the way to England I stopped here to see my brother, & am now detained by sickness."[62] This letter was also designed to ensure his pension cheque would reach him, so that, as he wrote, "as soon as I can get the money I shall sail for England." Perhaps he did receive that pension cheque, for he sailed from New York on 30 July, aboard the Cunard SS *Aurania*.

Roger's distress after the loss of Curtis did not prevent his writing "He Died in the Bush" before he left for Philadelphia. It is a clear and lucid account of what he thought happened on the expedition. Obviously he needed to earn money wherever he could, but the article did provoke comment among other expedition members:

You may imagine that after all our disasters none of us feel exactly friendly towards you. All our money gone, and nothing to show for it. We cannot blame you for taking us over the trail, as, after all, hundreds of others in their ignorance did the same. But we can and do blame you for putting forward pretensions to being a "tough frontiers man [*sic*]," and knowing the country etc., and by these pretensions, luring us into joining your party. And we think it was most foolhardy of a man, who knew nothing of horses, and had never packed onein [*sic*] his life, to start a large pack train with green hands. It was courting disaster. And it is only thanks to the energy and perseverance of each individual of the party, that worse hasn't come of it.

I read your account of the sad loss of Curtis, in a Victoria [*sic?*] paper, and I only voicetherest [*sic*] of the party, when I say that it was written in the worst tastepossible [*sic*]. We are all very sore about it. Surely such a serious thing need not have been treated in a flippant, penny-a-liner, style, such as you used. An Ashcroft paper says that you refused to be interviewed by him, and then *sold* your information to a Victoria paper![63]

Sheppard's letter is understandably harsh, but Roger was in fact very knowledgeable about horses. His overconfidence in his own ability in every other aspect of frontier life, though, regularly led him to claim experience of many trades in which he had only dabbled. Throughout his life his overconfidence led him and companions into many scrapes, but this was the only time it resulted, however indirectly, in a man's death.

Meanwhile, acting on legal advice, Lady Curtis sent a cable to Alex McNabb, manager of the Hudson's Bay post at Quesnel, and requested him to hire more Chilcotin trackers to renew the search.[64] These trackers were also unsuccessful, and she was told it would have been impossible for her husband to survive. Lady Curtis then petitioned the Probate, Divorce, and Admiralty Division to have her husband declared dead. Part of the printed account from that undertaking differs somewhat from Roger's version:

On June 4 the expedition left Quesnelle, and four days after encamped on the Mud River. Some horses strayed, and most of the party went out to find them, Sir Arthur being left behind in camp to act as cook. Feeling hurt by some chaffing, in which it was suggested that he had let the Mud

River get into the porridge, Sir Arthur asked for an apology
and not receiving one that satisfied him, he appeared to
brood seriously over what he considered an insult. On June
10, at breakfast at 5 A.M., Sir Arthur received a slight apology
and about 8 P.M. he lit his pipe and left the camp, and had
never been heard of since. The camp was situated 30 miles
from anywhere, Sir Arthur had no food or arms with him,
and it was believed that he had lost his way and perished.
Search parties were sent out, and Indians engaged to track
any possible traces of Sir Arthur, but no vestige of him was
ever discovered. Letters of an affectionate character had
been received by Lady Curtis from Sir Arthur, the last dated
only a few days before his disappearance. Advertisements
had been inserted in various papers to try and discover his
whereabouts, but without any success.

    MR. JUSTICE GORRELL BARNES, on proof of these
facts, held that they were sufficient, and granted leave to
swear Sir Arthur's death on or since June 10, 1898.[65]

As part of this hearing Roger made a sworn statement. There was also an
indication of the state of Curtis's wealth:

    Mr. Justice Barnes asked what Mr. Pocock had sworn to.

> Mr. Barnard said Mr. Pocock stated that he believed Sir
> Arthur Curtis was dead, having regard to the nature of the
> country and the fruitless searches which had been made, and
> he was of [the] opinion that Sir Arthur lost his life by getting
> off the track, and being bewildered.
>
>   Replying to Mr. Justice Barnes, Mr. Barnard said that the
> value of the estate was £1,600.[66]

Lady Curtis had her husband declared dead with what, in Victorian times,
could be considered indecent haste, particularly when one takes into account that she immediately married Robert Maziere Brady (1854–1909).
Some light was thrown on this marital situation by G.W. Cole:

> Colonel Cole says: "I travelled with Sir Arthur and his party
> for four days, being a close companion of his all the time.
> He kept away from the party saying that he had supplied all
> the money and had been treated shamefully in return. The
> day of the night he disappeared, he says, 'I am going to slip

away from the party tonight, and with a good Indian guide, lots of grub and blankets, make for Klondike alone, changing my name when I break away from the party.'" This plan was carried out, says Cole. A man could not be lost in this country where Sir Arthur and his Indian guide started on their lonely tramp. Cole believes the English Baronet is now in Klondike under an assumed name, or reached Atlin, in the early rush, and is wintering there.[67]

Ten years later Cole wrote to one of Vancouver's daily newspapers:

> "I knew," he said, "before they left Vancouver that Curtis would disappear before reaching the Klondike."
>
> "Curtis told me," he went on, "that family complications led him on the Klondike venture. Proof is, that within six months of leaving the party, Lady Curtis applied for an order declaring him dead and shortly afterwards married Col. Robert M. Brady, an Irishman, the real cause of Curtis' disappearance."
>
> Said Cole finally, "Sir Arthur Curtis right now is living the life of a trapper hermit. This should clear Pocock of a 10-year stigma."[68]

Much of this is probably true, apart from the suggestion that Curtis survived and lived as a hermit. Cecil Clark considered this suggestion a ridiculous idea:

> He didn't have the traps, or know how to use them and he would have to sell his furs somewhere on the outside. Besides, he would have to come out for fresh supplies. And in that country every trapper is known—a stranger would be instantly sized up—especially by Indians. To put it simply, where the population is sparse a stranger sticks out like a sore thumb. No, if Curtis lived, someone would have come across him, some trapper or prospector. They may not have known who he was, but they would have talked about him.[69]

As time passed, baseless rumours abounded that Curtis had been seen in Malaya or England, or that some of the First Nations were holding him (either dead or alive) for ransom. The ransom sums mentioned ranged up to $5,000. It was also suggested that skeletons found in British Columbia were his. Even the usually accurate London *Times* announced "SIR ARTHUR CURTIS'S SKELETON FOUND.—A Dalziel telegram from New York, dated yesterday, says:—A telegram from Vancouver, British Columbia, states that the skeleton of Sir Arthur Curtis, of London, has been found in a cave at Klondike, where he perished last winter."[70] We can be quite comfortable in the knowledge that Curtis never reached the Klondike, despite such reports. One Vancouver journalist was more sensible of this than some. After providing an account given by the leader of the party on the Ashcroft Trail, Maurice B. Atkinson, which outlined how difficult the Trail was, the reporter declared: "Nothing has been heard of Sir Arthur Curtis, the Englishman who wandered away and could not be found. They had seen nothing of him for several weeks when Mr. Atkinson left the party and it was generally conceded that the unfortunate baronet had met his death."[71] Other stories about the disappearance of Curtis appeared, mainly in British Columbia newspapers, and then spread around the world to places as distant as Rangoon, Singapore, and Melbourne, as well as various cities in North America and Great Britain. None was particularly friendly to Roger, and some were scathing about the skills of the men in the outfit. A member of another outfit, who did not sign his article, was disparaging:

> They packup [*sic*], and instead of looking for Sir Arthur,
> Pocock left a note, thus: "If you do not turn up by evening
> I shall send out a search party. You will find a lunch in this
> bag. We are going to Nine-mile camp." Of course Sir Arthur
> didn't turn up, and Pocock didn't make any effort to locate
> him until Saturday, then eight or ten Englishmen went racing
> up and down the trail like mad, afraid to go into the bush for
> fear they too would get lost, and it is the greatest wonder in
> the world they are not all lost. Saturday went by, Sir Arthur
> still in the woods. Pocock came to our camp during Saturday
> night and asked if we would assist in the search on Sunday.
> Certainly we would and did, but in vain. Most every party
> coming along the trail joined in the search. Col. Wright has
> put his men on, and sent for Stoney Creek Indians, who
> camped with us a couple of nights ago. They were confident
> they would find him; they had found men for Col. Wright
> before, but he was five days out then, and will surely be dead,
> and if so[,] Pocock is much to blame for leaving him in such
> a wild country, along the Mud river [*sic*], the nature of which
> is swamp, muskeg, black willow, densely thick, then fallen

timber ten or twelve feet high in places, where an immense
fire has gone through many years ago.[72]

Sheppard wrote a strong defence of his fellow expedition members in
response to this attack. Sheppard agreed that, in the main, the story was
correct, but gave this explanation of the initial events:

> June 10, we were leaving the Mud river [sic], but were six
> horses short. We had one or two men out looking for them,
> and they were recalled, as soon as the horses were found,
> by revolver shots—a preconcerted signal. Curtis not being
> a packer, his absence was not noted while packing went on:
> and he knew that we were going because he got his saddle
> ready and his blankets done up.
>
> We started off in due time, and imagined that Curtis was
> either on ahead or behind, but would soon join us. This was
> not an uncommon thing: with 37 horses ready to start, one
> hasn't much time to look to anything else. We went 13 miles
> (not 8, as the Sentinel informer states). When Curtis didn't
> come in that evening, we thought he must have stopped at a
> camp six miles back, where friends of ours were camped.[73]

Many accusations were also directed at Roger. Perhaps he had murdered
Curtis for his money. Was Curtis wearing a money belt? These allegations
were made without Roger's knowledge, for deliberate murder would have
been utterly against his character; nor would money have served to mo-
tivate such an action. He was only interested in having sufficient money
to live simply. A lady who knew him well, when she worked for his sister
Lena, observed that if Roger ever had any more than was necessary for
his immediate needs, he would give it away to the poor and he was generous to a fault.[74] It is also highly unlikely that Curtis would have carried a
large sum of money in a belt. Nevertheless, these accusations attached a
stigma to Roger that endured throughout his life. It was often whispered
behind his back, by those who disapproved of him, that he might be an
un-convicted murderer. Interest in the Curtis mystery continued, particularly in Canada:

> Fundamental rule in this country is; when you are lost in the
> bush ("turned around" is the popular term) stay where you
> are, light a fire (if you can) and wait for the rescuers. If you
> have a gun, fire it occasionally....

We don't know what Curtis took with him; if he carried nothing, he was a goner. For you cannot exist alone in the bush without an axe, matches, bacon, beans, tea and a rifle. These are essentials. In fact the experienced never go alone; they have a partner. So Curtis had everything against him—including the lack of experience which would have made him stay put and wait for rescue.

Cecil Clark also said there were only rare occasions when bodies were found many years later, and that he had such a high opinion of the Chilcotin trackers that he was sure nothing would escape them. Clark speculated: "But why didn't their powers of perception turn up something definite. One of the imponderables. A man, alone, can fall and break a limb, especially trying to walk across a windblown tree bridging some gully, without caulked boots. Then he would crawl under something to shelter from the elements, die of starvation, and thus escape the searcher's notice."[75]

As well, Clark checked out an element of the Curtis story that arose in 1934 when George McKeracher said he was in the Cariboo at the time and remembered a packer employed by Roger's Star outfit. The packer got into trouble with Curtis for ill-treating a horse; he was subsequently fired and swore revenge. According to McKeracher,

> [Curtis carried] about $10,000 in gold in his money belt and after Sir Arthur's disappearance the packer was seen around 150 Mile House with money to burn.
> Later, said McKeracher, he was witness to the holdup [sic] of two men with a sack of gold in a rig. The masked bandit was the half-breed whom McKeracher recognized by his eyes, and who was subsequently caught and jailed.[76]

Clark, an experienced researcher, could find no record of an armed robbery charge at the Clinton, British Columbia, Assizes in that year. Also, $10,000 in gold would have required a very big money belt. Clark interviewed Fred W. Foster, who was born in Clinton in 1876 and had met Roger and his party when they were in Ashcroft. Foster told Clark, "I think that story about the money belt originated with a half-breed named Sage. One of the Pocock party, a very nice fellow called Sheppard, left his money belt behind in a Hat Creek stopping place. Sage found it and went down to Ashcroft and got on a drunk. Sheppard reported the loss to Provincial Constable Joe Bury who rounded up Sage and got back the belt and most of the money."[77] In his diary entry for 19 April, Roger mentioned the theft "by the Hat Creek loafers" of Sheppard's belt containing £200, as well as some rope, blankets, and a revolver, but he did not record recovery of the belt.[78] Money entered into another attack on the Star outfit. "It is also alleged by the miners that Sir Arthur's partners seem now to have plenty of money, although they confessed that at a certain point on the trail they had been 'broke.'"[79] However, Sheppard may have provided an explanation for that money in his letter to Roger: while the money contributed by the participants may have been depleted, the men on the expedition were carrying money of their own and were also able to sell some of the excess gear as they disbanded. Indeed, it was raffling off some of the gear that enabled Roger to pay for his journey home.

Clark acquired some more information from Alex McNabb, the Hudson's Bay manager. He said that an American group, driving horses on the same trail a few days after Curtis disappeared, was camped on almost the same spot near the Mud River. The group heard an unearthly cry from a swamp across the river, which they took to be hostile First Nations, so they broke camp hastily. They told the story when they reached the next settlement, and it got back to McNabb. The cry had come from the direction in which the Chilcotin trackers had followed Curtis, and McNabb thought it could possibly have come from Curtis. There was a strange claim by two men from Montreal that "everyone on the trail states that the Indians know where the body of Sir Arthur Curtis is lying, half covered with mud and leaves, near a mountain stream, but that they want $1,000 before they will locate the remains, and insist upon communicating directly with the friends of the dead man, refusing to 'wawa' with others." There were also doubts raised that the original trackers had actually found Curtis's tracks. Roger received information, via Lockyer of the Hudson's Bay Company in Vancouver, that the tracks were in fact bear tracks, although it strains the imagination to believe that experienced trackers would confuse the tracks of a bear with those of a human. Adamson did not have faith in the trackers, either: "We employed Indians to hunt him and offered a reward. They claimed to have followed him, but I believe never did."[80]

What did happen to Curtis? When Roger was asked in subsequent years, he usually replied with the disclaimer "I have no facts or theories," or something similar.[81] As for Cecil A. Clark, he initially discounted Cole's comments completely; it should be noted, though, that he knew nothing of Lady Curtis's speedy re-marriage until we began corresponding. However, Clark was able to interview some "old-timers" who had firsthand knowledge of events, and after he and I pieced together the circumstantial evidence from England and Canada, we agreed on a probable explanation. Curtis confided in Cole some of his family problems, and told Cole that he intended to seek a new life in Canada. We will never know for certain the story of the triangle formed by Curtis, his wife, Sarah Jessie Curtis, and Brady, but we do know that divorce then was far from easy and carried a considerable stigma, particularly for the wife. Both Curtis and Brady held, or would hold, hereditary titles, and moved in fairly high echelons of society. One can only speculate about what was said in society gossip regarding Lady Curtis, but a revealing indication is evident in a syndicated society column of the time. The Marquise de Fontenoy wrote that "Lady Curtis, of course, will be unable to marry again until she secures positive proof of her husband's death, or else resorts to the extraordinary expedient of obtaining a divorce from him on the ground of desertion."[82] This would be a somewhat peculiar statement to make publicly, so soon after Curtis disappeared, unless the writer had heard some gossip about Lady Curtis. From a distance, the idea of a new life on this frontier of empire in Canada could have appealed to Curtis, particularly given the number of rivers and lakes in that part of the country. If Curtis had decided there was a relationship between his wife and Brady that had become intolerable, he might have considered it gentlemanly to disappear so that he could be declared dead, leaving his wife free to marry Brady without scandal. Curtis would have made such a plan in England before he knew about life in the backwoods of Canada. The terrible difficulties of the trail, added to his personality conflict with Roger, would have built up the stress to an intolerable level.

In addition, if we look again at Roger's description of Curtis's behaviour during the final few days, we have the classic description of a man suffering from clinical depression. This mental illness was not fully understood at the time, and although Norman Pern, a partially qualified medic was in attendance, he would only have been able to deal with physical illness. The Victorians did recognize "melancholia," usually among the upper classes, but someone in Curtis's situation would simply have been told to pull himself together. Sitting silent all day deep in thought, preferring to be alone, and suddenly walking off into the bush as Curtis did, without apparent care for personal safety, are actions that may be expected from a man in the grip of mental illness. This would explain why the trackers apparently found that Curtis had walked fifteen miles without any supplies or provisions: he would not have cared whether he lived or died. The unearthly cry heard by the American group also fits in with the diagnosis of clinical depression. The idea of suicide did appear in newspaper accounts of Curtis's disappearance as early as 27 September 1898, when Ambrose Attwood, whose outfit he claimed had met Roger's along the way, made this claim:

[His] informant was confident from what he had heard in
the camp, that Sir Arthur deliberately took his own life. He
thinks that the nobleman walked into the woods and possibly
threw himself into one of the sluggish dark streams that flow
through the dense forest in that vicinity. It was well known
that Sir Arthur was despondent over the apparent failure
of the expedition, and he was a man who could not stand
bickerings [sic].[83]

Roger wished that the story would fade away and cease to haunt him,
and yet by writing about it himself for *The Province* and *Lloyd's Weekly
Newspaper* in 1898 he helped keep the story alive. By 1936 Roger felt,
somewhat unwisely, that the story and the accusations levelled at him
had been sufficiently forgotten for him to earn some money by telling the
story in a British national Sunday newspaper.[84] This paper had earlier
published "The Lone Wolf Pioneer," Roger's account of his early days
in Canada. After telling his side of things in "A Drama of the Klondike
Trail," he was shocked when the following week brought a response from
James John Martin, who had been Hilton's servant from 1906 until 1910,
when Hilton was an officer in the Middlesex Regiment. Martin claimed
that Hilton had confessed to him one night in 1908 that he had murdered
Curtis:

> On a bad night I lay asleep with Curtis.
>   We had fastened the mules securely and safely stored our
> gold in bags.
>   I woke to find Sir Arthur gone—and the mules and the gold.
>   I went on the track of him alone, and, coming to a tree by a
> stream, miles from the night camp, I found him asleep with the
> mules and the gold.
>   There in that moment I shot him dead and buried him
> against the tree.
>   They will never find him, Martin, but one day I will take
> you there and show you.[85]

The newspaper asked Roger for his view and he very politely discounted
the story. The only faint possibility that Roger could accept was that

> "Doubtless Hilton and his party reached the Stickeen
> River, and found there the stores which I had caused to be
> deposited at a trading post called Telegraph Creek.

"Hilton may have taken to gold-mining, but much more probably to 'packing' (transporting goods by pack animal).

"It is barely possible, but wildly improbable, that he encountered Sir Arthur Curtis there...."[86]

This "confession" could have no basis in fact, as there was no gold and they did not use mules. Martin's story is also impossible for a number of reasons. First, *News of the World* always had the reputation of paying well for any sensational story, and loved reporting on scandals. Second, although the newspaper said Martin was of the highest character, in those years it was usual to have only one or two employers in one's lifetime, since jobs were so hard to find, yet Martin had had quite a number of jobs. Third, and perhaps most important, given the class structure in the Edwardian period, it would have been unheard of for an officer to confide in his servant. However, Martin might have overheard something or read something he was not supposed to and misunderstood. Martin would not have cared to admit this behaviour. Fourth, Martin was probably only ten or eleven years younger than Hilton, which is not a significant age gap, yet Martin said he was quoting Hilton: "you are a much younger man than I am. You have a lot longer to live." While it was true that Martin lived longer, given that Hilton was killed in 1915, this would not have been a factor at the time of the "confession." Indeed Hilton's death meant that there was no way Martin's story could be checked.

It can safely be assumed that the bones of Sir Arthur Curtis will never be found, but perhaps one day someone will find the impressive gold ring Curtis wore on his finger, proudly bearing the Curtis family crest. As for irrepressibly optimistic Roger, despite the disaster that befell his expedition, he later wrote of his Klondike plan, "It still looks nice on paper."[87] In fact, not much more than a month after the expedition was disbanded Roger could write: "You must not think that my expedition has failed. It is reorganized, & I left my boys fully satisfied with the arrangements I was able to make for financing & reprovisioning them. They are going ahead thoroughly competent & well equipped, & are provisioned for sixteen months after reaching Glenora with their horses."[88] The major consequence of this great tragedy was the enduring cloud of suspicion that hung over Roger's head for the remainder of his life. This Roger could not have anticipated.

THE GREAT RIDE
TO MEXICO
and the
WILD BUNCH

ONCE ROGER WAS BACK in his rooms in London, he spent months trying to get over the disappearance of Curtis. Although Roger's general health improved, he could not escape the rumours about Curtis that swirled around him and troubled his mind. Even before he returned to England he complained about "trying in vain to get back to a literary way of thinking."[1] As he tried to find distraction from the world in his writing, he drew on his recent experience in British Columbia as well as more fanciful ideas.[2] The death of his much-loved father may also have provided some impetus.[3] Eventually he decided he must get away to achieve something really remarkable or die in the attempt. His father had also been prone to moving when times were difficult, but Roger added adventure to that idea when he decided to ride a horse from Canada to Mexico. He wanted to attain a place "in the annals of horsemanship," but "It was not to be done for a bet, or for advertisement—I wanted to get back my self-respect."[4]

The idea of making that journey had not been far from his thoughts since 1888, when he had failed so spectacularly after only sixteen miles. Initially he was probably inspired by the exploits of Kit Carson; eleven years later, he still found Carson's ride "from the Mississippi to California, twenty-two hundred miles through wild country among hostile tribes," impressive, but he also specifically mentioned Dmitri Peshkov's ride of "five thousand five hundred miles in one hundred and ninety-three days…."[5]

Roger Pocock leading four horses away from a lodge.
[RCMP Archives, 1779-1]

Roger decided to attempt the Canada-Mexico ride again, because "Neither
of these records could be broken; there is hardly room for such a road distance in the one case [Peshkov] or for such hazard in the other [Carson],
but a third standard might be set, perhaps, of horsemanship and scouting in difficult ground."[6] Spending time on the frontier would also have
appealed to him. The route he chose posed notable hazards, but money
was not one of them. This was one of the few times he did not have to
worry about money, because the editor of *Lloyd's Weekly* was so pleased
with the popularity of Roger's "Into the Great Dominion" series, he was
happy to pay Roger's expenses plus a fee for each article. Roger also felt
he did not have to worry about getting seriously lost, since he could use
the Rocky Mountains as a guide.

Roger began his ride at Fort Macleod on 28 June 1899. Fort Macleod,
which Roger knew well, was a favourite posting for members of the
Mounted Police because the winters were shorter and the weather generally milder than at most other NWMP posts. Although Sam Steele, who
over the years became Roger's friend, had been sent to the Klondike, the
other members of the Steele family were still at Fort Macleod, and Roger
enjoyed visiting them. As always, the Mounted Police treated him with
great warmth and friendship. He rode with several NWMP patrols through

Roger Pocock with the two of the horses he used all the way from
Canada to Mexico. Taken at the end of the ride, probably in Mexico.
[RCMP Archives, 1779–2]

"Blood Indian country and the Mormon settlements" until he reached
the American border.[7] There he parted from these generous friends, who
gave him saddle wallets, silk handkerchiefs, and useful advice on horse
ailments. He felt genuine regret at leaving his beloved Canada: "From the
foot of the hill I looked back, and there against the sky the trooper sat[,]
his horse motionless, while the sun lighted in glory on his harness, and
glowed in the warm colours of his cowboy dress."[8]

Although the American West Roger rode into had been largely tamed
by the late 1890s, it was still, at least in some areas, far from friendly for
the lone traveller. This was particularly true along Roger's route, because
he chose to ride through the desert. Indeed, in his first article for *Lloyd's
Weekly,* Roger made it quite clear to readers that his ride was to be something special: "Nobody had ever ridden the length of the Great American
desert from north to south, from Canada to Mexico. To do that was to
break a record in horsemanship; to fail—there are lots of bones lying about
on that desert." While Roger began the American part of his ride alone,
he soon joined quite a throng of people. Forty miles into Montana he
fell in with a group of cowboys headed for a celebration of American
Independence Day, 4 July, at a Blackfoot camp. Roger, always fascinated

by horses, noted that the horses seemed to be communicating more with each other than did their riders, for "only the most loquacious [man] would interrupt us all with a remark or so to the acre."[9]

Roger's detailed description of the Blackfoot would have captivated readers of *Lloyd's Weekly,* who were hungry for news of a way of life so far removed from their own:

> Far off at the other side of the camp we could hear soft-footed drums measuring a dance, and one other big drum having a good time all to itself. The lone drum lived in the Medicine Lodge, a huge round house of boughs, where young warriors were proved by torture, where prayer was made to the Great Spirit, and the pipe went round among the chiefs and sorcerers. Towards the little drums we rode at a rousing gallop, and drew up beside an enclosure of waggons [sic]. The squaws were doing the Grass Dance, all dressed in bright robes and adorned with little mirrors, dyed grass quills, and beads sewn to the cloth, little feathers, brass cartridge shells, and penny paper fans. They stood in a crescent, shoulder to shoulder, shuffling with bent knees sideways, all to the melancholy rumble of the drums, singing some wild song too old to mean anything at all, but stirring vague emotions until one wanted to cry.[10]

Participants moved on to pony races and, as the sun went down over the Rocky Mountains, dances and fireworks. Roger slept in a hayloft, then in the morning he rode south into sheep country. He possessed the cowboy's distaste for sheep and their herders, for like them he maintained that sheep damaged grazing lands. He did admit, however, that he had been ill-mannered in refusing to speak to the shepherds, when he later learned how many of them had died in sudden autumn snowstorms while they guarded their flocks. When he stopped for the night, wild stallions came close to inspect his own placid horses.

Much of what he wrote for *Lloyd's Weekly* he used again, only slightly altered, in the first volume of his autobiography. Occasionally, however, he thought better of including some comments in his book. For example, although some Americans criticized his autobiography because of the anti-American sentiments he expressed, he did not repeat there some of his stronger comments articulated in *Lloyd's Weekly.* Thus in the book he praised the hospitality he received during a 400-mile ride through Montana, but in *Lloyd's Weekly* he added, rather caustically, that "Once this country was wild, for at this cabin a man burned his wife; at that house three people were killed in a shooting scrap; at yonder grog shop a horse thief was lynched by vigilantes; and often along the road there were abandoned town-sites, little bantling towns which had died in infancy." This colourful description was well suited to the readers of *Lloyd's Weekly*, as was his account of Three Forks, then a virtual ghost town, "placed at the meeting of the Madison, Gunnison [*sic*], and Jefferson rivers.... [Q]uite a large town with shops and churches, hotels and stables enough for two thousand people; but there were three families left, the others driven away, I think, by the mosquitoes." He also described "Western Montana as something akin to a half-boiled ham, promising but not matured. I was glad to press on to the gates of the Yellowstone Park."[11]

Roger was impressed by the scenery in Yellowstone, but not by the tourists who had already started visiting the area in considerable numbers:

> Of course the park swarms with tourists, dragged through the blinding dust in waggonettes. The drivers—locally known as liars—are tame farmers, loaded up to the muzzle with Wild West tales for their "dudes." The dudes believe everything, suffer everything, photograph everything, and pay a great deal more than they expected....
>
> Nobody may use a gun, there are patrols of United States Cavalry to see to it, and the forest swarms with game.

Roger found the dust choking and the mosquitoes and horseflies menacing, but was still able to describe the spectacular scenery of a fifty-mile ride until he reached the Grand Canyon:

> after travelling for a week through wonders and marvels, you come to the Grand Canyon of the Yellowstone, and think you must have gone crazy. A big river comes out of a big lake, and leaps thundering down into a gorge 1,200 feet deep. The sides of this chasm are prickly with towers, spires, and pinnacles; it is all scarlet and salmon, orange and olive, ruby and topaz, snow white, golden brown, colour run mad, Heaven turned loose until even the godless tourist is hushed to reverent awe.[12]

As in this example, Roger had some skill with descriptive writing and could be relied on to paint evocative word pictures for eager readers of *Lloyd's Weekly*.

Roger was fascinated by the geological features, but the bears, protected even then, caused him much distress as they foraged everywhere. One bear raided his camp and left him with only coffee and tobacco. Although Roger did not mention it in his articles in *Lloyd's Weekly,* "The troopers of the 7th Cavalry saved me from subsequent hunger, behaving most brotherly." On the other hand, he complained that their military duties seemed to consist entirely of policing the tourists, whereas, "within fifty miles I came into a community of outlaws who live by robbing trains, banks, coaches, and trading posts, by stealing bunches of cattle, and shooting sheriffs...."[13]

When he reached Jackson Hole, Roger was greeted with suspicion by men who may have been involved in lawlessness. Roger wrote of Jackson Hole:

> ...I had seen no woman, [it] is an outlaw stronghold, not a fortified place or anything sensational, but a district frequented in part by professional hunters, and in part by men who rob railway trains, coaches, banks, who hide fugitives, conceal stolen cattle, who live by robbery under arms. Of these robbers I managed to identify four, but may not betray them because I was their guest; they were very nice men, too.[14]

Yet later, when he was a guest of outlaws at Robbers' Roost, he was happy to name them and use some of them and their adventures in his fiction. Also, in spite of saying they were "very nice men," Roger gave the impression that he was rather wary of them, including Butch Cassidy.[15]

Roger's trail then took him eastwards to the upper pastures of the snowy Gros Ventre Mountains and down into the valley of the Green River, where he was able to camp at Dog Ranch and listen to the tales told by visiting hunters. The July weather was dreadful and it was a relief for him to sit in front of a blazing log fire until everyone was called on to help with the supply wagons, which had become stuck in the mud. Roger described how a stranger arrived at the door, exhausted and soaking wet. Unusually, he did not seek refreshment—only directions to Jackson Hole. No questions were asked, but "he rode a superb horse without a saddle. We watched him ride down to the river—not sauntering like a town tenderfoot, but riding...a robber flying from justice."[16]

Roger later stopped at the camp of a forest ranger, but there, too, he needed to exercise caution. The ranger had stopped the illegal supply of venison to a lumber camp, and a rumour was circulating that the hungry lumbermen were seeking revenge on the ranger. Roger recognized that whatever the situation, he had to be especially watchful, for he was extraordinary in that he did not carry a gun, claiming that he was a dreadful shot. It is also possible, however, that letting it be known he was an eccentric, unarmed Englishman may have saved him from becoming involved in any local unpleasantness.

From there, his route was mainly across desert, but because he was travelling with saddle and pack horses, he needed to find grass and water every day. Roger joined an itinerant barber who seems to have been a tiresome companion, but Roger recognized that it was generally better not to be alone on many of the trails that he followed. They crossed the track of the Union Pacific Railway by Green River City and forded the Green River with some difficulty. They passed through Red Creek Canyon and arrived at Brown's Hole, Colorado, also known as Brown's Park:

> This district is like Jackson's Hole [*sic*], an outlaw stronghold tenanted in part by respectable, well-to-do robbers. To the westward of it in the canyons of Green River there is a meadow fenced by colossal cliffs, a hiding place for stolen herds of cattle and robbers in retreat. Descending Red Creek Canyon, we must have crossed the dim trail which leads to this mysterious pasturage. The trail enters the mountains from one of the Brown's Park ranches, the owner of which is an expert in staving off awkward inquiries.[17]

Nonetheless, in March 1898, three posses arrived from Colorado, Wyoming, and Utah and rounded up three robbers: Patrick Louis Johnson, Harry Tracy, and David Lant. This was an unusual event, because one of the appeals of the area was its proximity to three state lines, which helped outlaws by ensuring that they could easily move beyond a pursuing posse's jurisdiction.

The outlaws Roger met later, in a more relaxed way, were also at home at Brown's Hole: "There seems to have been an unwritten agreement between the Brown's Hole settlers and the outlaws whereby the former kept their mouths shut about the 'strangers' who circulated among them, while the latter reciprocated by never molesting the local people's livestock or other possessions."[18] Roger's experience confirmed this:

> My partner and I had made camp in the ranche [*sic*] meadows, and at sundown I strolled to the house to buy potatoes. While I was there four cowboys came down out of the hills, and at their appearance my host became flurried

and uneasy, making hasty excuses to get rid of me. Later in the night I heard the strange horsemen clattering up the loose stones of the hillside, bound, no doubt, by the hidden trail to the outlaw camp in the canyons. That was my second meeting with desperadoes in hiding, and I had the additional pleasure in Brown's Park of dining with a notable robber—I may not name him, the guest of a public enemy eats under flag of truce.[19]

After noting the beauties and the difficulties of travelling through Lodore Canyon, Roger and his partner headed in a more easterly direction. Crossing mountains and valleys, Roger recorded that "In one hundred and eighty-three miles we met fifty-four persons, and felt that we were entering a crowded country; when swinging down out of the Roan Mountains[,] we saw the steel rails gleaming in the Grand River settlements, and cantered through the farms to the city of Grand Junction, Colorado."[20] Roger's companion saw that he could pursue his trade again, so he decided to stay in Grand Junction. Roger rested himself and his horses for two days there, and enjoyed some luxuries, such as honey, fruit, and chocolates. Then he climbed out of the Grand River valley into woods, grassy meadows, and running water at a height of 10,000 feet. The sudden end of this comfortable three-day ride left him faced with no alternative but a steep, 4,000-foot descent into the Unaweep Canyon and on to Dolores Canyon, which was even more difficult to escape. After three days in suffocating heat on the canyon floor, he saw "cattle tracks up the edge of a knife-like ridge, the way swinging across to some projecting ledge which hung in space, then back again, and up to something worse."[21] The "something worse" he later described as his "worst climb":

[The climb was] made in twelve hours, with three horses up a 3,600 foot cliff where a trail would have been a convenience. The pack and spare horses pulled hard at times because, although ambitious animals, they would have preferred some other way to heaven. That is why the lead rope got under the saddle-horse's tail, which made him buck on a ledge overhanging blue space where there really was no room. A little later the led horses pulled my saddle horse over the edge of a crag. I got off at the top, and the horse lit on his belly across a jutting rock about twelve feet down. He thought he was done for until I persuaded him with the lead rope to scramble up again. Near the summit the oak and juniper bushes forced me to dismount, leading the horses one at a time under or round stiff overhanging branches on most unpleasant ground. They showed off a little because they wished to impress me, but I found out afterwards that horses or even cattle, held at the foot of that cliff until they are hungry, will climb to the top for grass. The place is known as The Gateway and leads up out of the Cañon Dolores in Colorado to the Mesa la Sal in Utah.[22]

For the readers of his autobiography, Roger rather smugly wrote that when he reached the first ranch at Mesa la Sal he was met with a query: "How had I come? Asked the cowboys. 'Followed your tracks,' said I; 'where you drove cattle any fool could ride.' 'We didn't,' said the cowboys; 'we headed cattle into the bottom at sundown. They worked their way up hunting grass, and we found them on the rim rocks in the morning.'"[23]

After seventeen miles of rather easier travel, he reached the first ranch on the La Sal mesa in Utah. The following day he encountered a large herd of sheep with a solitary shepherd. Roger rode hard that day until he met some cowboys so he could warn them about the sheep. He identified so closely with the cowboys that he felt no qualms that the shepherd and his flock would be run off the land, and possibly even butchered. "If you ever hear of thousands of sheep butchered at night by masked riders or driven headlong over a precipice," wrote Roger, "that only means the saving of the stock range. The sheep owner has the lawyers at his back, even if he destroy the whole industry of a country and replace a score of hardworking cowboys with one half-witted herder. I side with the masked riders because human rights are stronger than the law."[24]

Navigation was now easier because he could follow the trail of the young mail riders, "who in these parts ride to outlying settlements 50 or 100 miles across the Desert."[25] Somewhat naïvely, however, when he arrived at Monticello, Utah, he asked for a guide to take him to Robbers' Roost. The Mormon bishop made it known that Roger was a desperado seeking refuge at the Roost, which meant he could find no help—or even anyone prepared to supply him with food. Roger did not explain how he nonetheless found that outlaw stronghold, but find it he did.[26] In his article he gave very clear directions and, most surprisingly, in his autobiography he repeated those directions nearly word for word:

The headquarters of the bandits may be easily located on a map. See where the Green and Grand Rivers meet to form the Colorado. Just below that the west bank of the Colorado

is a precipice called the Orange cliffs. To the north is the San
Rafael canyon, to the south the Dirty Devil canyon, torrents
of rushing mud lost in profound gorges. The tract of land on
top of the Orange cliffs[,] entirely surrounded by canyons,
can only be reached by one of two difficult trails. Here stands
a log house, the Robbers' Roost, with its corrals and spring of
water, with pasturage for horses to ride, cattle to eat and for
sale: the cliffs are a fence, the whole district a secure retreat
from justice.[27]

The mainly working-class readership of *Lloyd's Weekly* would not have
been in a position to travel to America and follow the directions. By the
time *Following the Frontier* was published in America, Roger knew that
fewer outlaws were active in the area and probably felt it had no attraction for a casual tourist. Many years later it was described as "a fortressed
triangle of deep canyons, rivers and mesas and perfectly suited the needs
of the outlaws."[28] The casual tourist at the beginning of the twentieth
century might not have been interested, but in the years since, a great
many tourists and historians of the West have been beguiled by Robbers'
Roost, as well as Hole-in-the-Wall and Brown's Park, the three major way
stations on the Outlaw Trail.

Roger did his share to nurture interest in the Outlaw Trail by collecting stories. He said he had to exercise extreme tact, though, when he
interviewed those he knew to be robbers. He even felt it was necessary to
get the honest men out into the desert where "things were said in a low
undertone, for they spoke at the risk of their property—at the risk of their
lives."[29] He was certainly not a man one would generally praise for his dip-
lomatic skills, yet his credibility was bolstered by the fact that he was alone,
unarmed, and presented no obvious threat to any of them. We can also be
fairly certain that both Roger and his actions, including the warning about
the sheep, were known to the people he met. He had repeatedly shown
that he was strongly in favour of the cattlemen and quite prepared to turn
a blind eye to their unlawful behaviour. That he was extremely sociable
and always keen for a yarn, as well as a skilled and knowledgeable horseman, would also have stood him in good stead with the robbers. Possibly
the men he interviewed were quite intrigued to learn that the stories they
told Roger would be printed in a newspaper in faraway London. Such
notoriety might have appealed to them, as long as it was not too close to
home. If they embellished their stories for his benefit, no one in London
would be in a position to correct them:

Frankly I asked them for information about the robbers, with
equal candour they gave me most valuable help, or, if the
scent got too warm, they lied. That made the inquiry difficult,
but suppressing all facts told in confidence, all names of
informants—some of whom placed their very lives in my
hands—and all details useful to the law, I can still give verified
evidence throwing light on the whole system of outlawry as
it was up to January 1900. If I leave out the best parts of the
story it is because men's lives are at hazard.[30]

The problem with most of what we read about these men is that accounts
were passed by word of mouth or written down from stories told years
later by old-timers. Consequently there are conflicting stories. Further,
the outlaws did not want the whole truth to be known, wished to keep
one step ahead of the law, and used aliases they changed regularly. Roger's
account has the advantage that he wrote it down at the time and he was an
independent observer. He wrote an honest account of what he saw and
what he was told, however much "embroidery" may have been added
by those he interviewed. He also felt he had special credentials for this
investigation:

No man dared to help me, nor dare I hazard men's lives by
telling how I got the facts which are now for the first time
published. These may be dreams of a tenderfoot, but I
have been fourteen years on the frontier, working in thirty
trades, and know the west from Behring [*sic*] Sea to Mexico.
Working and living among desperadoes, I have in the past
been once nearly marooned on a desert island, once nearly
lynched as a spy, once nearly shot in a gun-fight. I ought to
know outlaws by this time.[31]

Roger had earlier read in a New York newspaper an imaginative account
of "the stronghold as a fortified cave, equipped with machine guns,
guarded by sentries, only approached by one trail, and that death for in-
truders. This vision is furnished with a grand piano, electric lights, and
telephones."[32] He, on the other hand, described what he actually found
as nothing more than common ranches where the residents enjoyed less
comfort than in most homes in the general area. On the basis of his travels he maintained "There are 400 professional thieves in the west living
by robbery under arms and hunting in regular packs under discipline.
Their strongholds are in Jackson's Hole [*sic*] and the Hole-in-the-Wall,

Wyoming; Brown's Park in Utah; near Wilcox, Arizona; on the Texas-Mexico border, and in the Indian territory. All work in connection with the central stronghold, the famous Robbers' Roost in Utah."[33] Roger wrote that at Robbers' Roost, "The garrison generally numbers about 10 out of the 34 members of the gang."[34] Certainly in August 1897, about two years before Roger arrived, "The character of the Wild Bunch underwent swift metamorphosis. Although they attracted a host of idolaters, emulators, and assorted hangers-on, at no time did the reconstituted Wild Bunch ever number more than a dozen men, all of whom were hand-picked by Cassidy and Logan and trained for the roles they were to play."[35] Roger did not use the now famous name Wild Bunch, but Pearl Baker provides one explanation of how the name was created:

> they raised such hell when they came to town to celebrate
> in Baggs [Wyoming], Vernal [Utah] or other frontier towns.
> Saloon keepers called them 'that wild bunch from Brown's
> Park' and let them shoot up the place as much as they pleased,
> well knowing that they would come back and pay for all
> damage.... Butch had planned to call the gang he was going to
> organize the *Train Robbers Syndicate,* but history has sort of
> bypassed that title for the more descriptive "Wild Bunch."[36]

As with so much else about the outlaws of the West, there is some dispute about just who led the group. Roger described Butch Cassidy as "second in command," at least at Robbers' Roost, while a later writer declared that "Although Butch Cassidy is given the credit for leadership of the Wild Bunch, old-timers maintain that Lay was actually the brains of the group, and Butch followed his lead."[37] Several others describe Cassidy as the one who formed and led the Wild Bunch, and no less an expert than William A. Pinkerton, the detective, claimed at the time that "The Train Robber's Syndicate is composed of outlaws and thieves headed by George LeRoy Parker, alias Butch Cassidy...."[38] Horan's opinion was that "The Wild Bunch riders frequently changed in personality and numbers, but the hard core usually included Butch Cassidy, the gang's leader; Elza [*sic*] Lay, Harvey and Lonny Logan, Tom O'Day, Harry Longabaugh, the Sundance Kid; Ben Kilpatrick, the Tall Texan; and Will Carver."[39] Another perspective is offered by Matt Warner (born Willard Erastus Christianson, aka the Mormon Kid), who, when he needed money in 1896 to "buy justice" as he put it, sent word to Cassidy. His faith was rewarded when Cassidy, with the help of Elzy Lay and Bob Meeks, robbed a bank in Montpelier, Idaho, to raise the money to pay lawyers and to support Warner's family while he was in jail.[40] A very different view is that "Whether either of the two [Butch Cassidy and the Sundance Kid] ever occupied a position of real leadership in the gang remains doubtful. The murderous Kid Curry (Harvey Logan) probably exercised more authority."[41]

Roger named several of those resident at Robbers' Roost when he visited. "Captain McCarty, described as general manager of the Robbers' Roost is…a cowboy, horse-breaker, and expert roper, inclined to 'play tough,' and has one murder to account for, that of an Indian."[42] If Roger used the proper name here, Tom McCarty (c.1855–c.1900) was not telling Roger the whole truth. McCarty had taken part in the Delta Bank Robbery in 1893, with his brother Billy and nephew Fred. Some onlookers said that Fred killed the bank clerk, but others claimed it was Tom. Both Billy and Fred were gunned down as they tried to escape, so Tom was the only one to get away: "The Delta robbery finished the McCartys, with the killing of two of them and the outlawing of Tom. Never again did he ride with the Wild Bunch; in fact, there is no reason to believe he ever saw Butch Cassidy or Elzy Lay again."[43] Other writers have supplied diverse descriptions of Tom McCarty's later life, but Roger seems to have been somewhat impressed by him, for he turns up, slightly changed, as McCalmont in Roger's novel, *Curly: A Tale of the Arizona Desert*. It could be that McCalmont is a blend of McCarty and Butch Cassidy, since most popular chronicles celebrating Cassidy claimed that he was affable rather than violent and may not even have personally committed any murders. Indeed Baker wrote that "practically every killing laid at the door of the Wild Bunch was committed by Harvey Logan."[44]

Roger, who seems to have got on quite well with the outlaws, later reported with some interest that the outlaws planted "little bunches of ponies here and there in pasture. When they happened to be in a hurry they would travel from pasture to pasture, and at each of these take a fresh mount. Six hundred miles in six days was not unusual they told me, and, from what the sheriffs said who tried to catch them, I think that the robbers spoke in moderation. They were much the most truthful men I have met on the stock range."[45] The system had been inspired by the pony express, but with notable improvements:

> With the daring Castle Gate robbery [21 April 1897] Cassidy
> perfected the technique developed by Tom McCarty in
> relaying horses along a planned escape route. Several weeks
> before a robbery Cassidy would gather, train, and harden
> the horses to be used in the getaway. Blooded animals were
> selected, grain-fed, and exercised rigorously. For the robbery

sure-footed horses capable of fantastic speed over short distances up to fifteen miles were chosen. When the first relay was reached the saddles were switched to deep-chested, long-legged thoroughbreds able to maintain a man-killing pace, hour after hour. The unsaddled initial horses were driven ahead, able to keep up once relieved of their load. If necessary, a second, and even a third, relay of horses with stamina were stationed along the route. Fine horses were Cassidy's trademark; no impromptu posse could keep pace past the first relay.[46]

Roger also described how they used newspapers to communicate.[47] In *Curly* he used what he had learned about a heliograph signalling system employed to contact the lookout that was constantly posted at any stronghold, and he also addressed the methods that ensured that no posse caught outlaws on the run. For example, the ashes of a campfire were buried and the tracks smoothed, leaving only one set of tracks. A rough note was left by the campsite to the effect of "Dere Bill, I'm gawn with the buckboard for grub. Back this even,'—B. Brown."[48] This was designed to make any posse believe that some simple cowboys had been there, rather than escaping outlaws.

Roger liked to tell a particular Butch Cassidy story, which also gave him the opportunity to express his admiration for the gang's horsemanship:

> Tracing their more recent movements I found that they usually travel each with six or seven shod ponies for saddle pack and remounts: hence the amazing speed of their movements. For instance, at 6 P.M. on July 12th, 1899, Butch Cassidy and Johnson, from Robbers' Roost by way of Dandy Crossing, rode into Bluff, Utah. They had some trouble in getting hay for their fourteen ponies, so it was eight o'clock before they supped on bread and milk at the stopping place. Later in the evening they offered to sell or trade horses with the Mormon townsfolk, but those would not accept their bills of sale as being of doubtful title. In the morning they rode away. Some days later, a party of detectives arrived in the town, spent a week making inquiries, and finally departed with only one horse apiece *on the wrong trail.*[49]

If Roger meant "Johnson" to be taken literally, this was probably Patrick Louis Johnson, an itinerant farmhand and one of the lesser members of the gang, "a fool as well as a coward" according to Burroughs, who also wrote, "If Cassidy, Harry Longabaugh [Sundance Kid], [Matt] Warner, and their ilk were the aristocrats of banditry, such men as [John aka "Judge"] Bennett and [Patrick Louis] Johnson could be said to be its panderers and two-bit bums."[50] Pinkerton detective Charles Siringo who, like those he chased, frequently travelled under an alias, believed he was following Butch Cassidy and Elzy Lay, but he identified thirteen as the number of horses.[51] Although it is generally accepted Cassidy planned the Wilcox, Wyoming, train robbery of 2 June 1899, no one seems to have been certain whether Butch Cassidy was directly involved in the robbery itself. This story, however, makes it appear that Cassidy was not there. Roger also reported the initial hunt for the robbers in lively detail and that "the robbers got away with the treasure chest—some 16,000£."[52]

Thanks to the Wilcox robbery, Roger did not meet some of the major members of the Wild Bunch. They had spread out and were in hiding. So, for example, Cassidy and Lay (under the aliases Jim Lowe and William McGinnis) were believed to be working on a ranch in Alma, New Mexico. As a testament to the horsemanship that played such an important role in their success as outlaws, they travelled "so far and so fast they discouraged any possible pursuit and made it easier to pass some of the hot money [from Wilcox].... The date of their arrival [in Alma] was almost an alibi."[53] The others on the run then included the Sundance Kid, Ben Kilpatrick (The Tall Texan), and Bill Carver. Harvey Logan had killed Sheriff Joe Hazen and was definitely lying low, as was George "Flat Nose" Currie, who was in fact not far away, hiding in a cave in Rattlesnake Canyon. Thus, some of the men that Roger met at Robbers' Roost could probably have been listed among the "idolaters, emulators, and assorted hangers-on," but one or two were rather important and even surprising to find mentioned. One of those was David Lant, whom Roger described as one of the original McCarty gang.[54] Lant had been captured on 4 March 1898 and was involved in several jail breaks before he seemed to disappear in July. One story was that he "joined the army in 1898, served in the Philippines, was promoted for bravery in action, returned to Utah, and left the Outlaw Trail."[55] Another account had it that Lant was living, under the alias Dave Stillwell, in the Vernal, Utah, area.[56] Some of the other names Roger mentioned were clearly minor members, or gave him false names and are not recorded in any major book about the Robbers' Roost gang. These included "Messrs. Mickleson and Cofod [who] are Danes, sheep herders and Mormons...[and] John Wesley Allen, Methodist...."[57] Roger rather strangely referred to the religious backgrounds of the outlaws he met, possibly to emphasize that these men were not entirely bad.

Although Butch Cassidy came from a Mormon family, Roger noted him as Roman Catholic.[58]

Train robberies, and particularly the Wilcox train robbery, received significant attention at the time, but Roger thought they were relatively uncommon. "Several trains are robbed every year, now and then a coach or a bank, or specie in transit on the road. Yet those are special occasions, whereas the stealing of cattle is a recognised routine which pays much better. The methods of the robbers in collecting their neighbours' stock for shipment and sale, are rather rapid than careful."[59] He then told two rustling stories that exemplified his point. Roger clearly enjoyed the company of the robbers, and reflected a view that still has some currency:

> The robbers are popular heroes, and not the least alarm
> is excited in the Mormon towns of Bluff, Montecello [sic],
> and Moab by visits of neighbours from the Robbers' Roost.
> These frequent visitors always pay their way, behave 'like
> gentlemen,' and treat the women respectfully. They never kill
> men except in extremity, they never rob the poor, they dare
> not foul their own nest by making themselves unpopular....
>
> It is at Moab that the outlaws buy their supplies, loading
> an occasional pack-train to provision their stronghold on the
> cliffs. The Moabites seem to be a queer tribe, some of them
> probably retired or semi-retired robbers....
>
> In the whole desert region I met only one man who openly
> expressed his abhorrence and contempt for outlaws. One day
> a cowboy called at his camp, and said from the saddle, "Shut
> your mouth about us, or clear out of this country."
>
> He cleared out.[60]

The names of people and places Roger reported to his *Lloyd's Weekly* readers would have meant nothing to them, but the story of an Englishman actually meeting with outlaws in the Wild West would have intrigued them. So Roger was generous with colourful detail as he rode southwards on the Outlaw Trail to the Red Lake trading post. The Trail crossed a reservation where Navajos lived who were annoyed with the outlaws, who had stolen 600 cattle from them. That meant rustlers had to take extreme care along the Trail. Roger found a use for this story in *Curly:* "Yes, we stole six hundred head of cattle from the Navajos, and you should just have seen the eager way they put out after us. They was plenty enthoosiastic, and they came mighty near collecting our wigs."[61]

Roger's inquisitive nature brought him many good stories, but it also nearly led him into serious trouble. For example, he heard of a Mr. Preston who traded out of Willow Springs, Arizona. Preston had reported a man to the law and collected the reward. That man was soon captured and hanged, and as a result Preston was forced to go into hiding. Despite his frequently expressed fondness for robbers, Roger wrote that "when I knew that he still dared to live alone on the Painted Desert distant but four days' march from the great stronghold, I felt that it would be an honour to meet with him."[62] The opportunity arose when Roger was crossing the desert and came across a cowboy camp near a little water. As they all sat chatting around the campfire, a man came into the camp. One of the cowboys whispered to Roger that this was Preston. Eager to interview him, Roger walked up to him:

> "Mr. Preston, I think?"
> "Yes."
> "The gentleman who got that robber?"
> Thinking, no doubt, that I came from the Robbers' Roost to kill him, the trader let out a rough growl, his hand went to his hip, and in another instant I should have been shot. The boys jumped straight at him, held him back, and explained. Then I ate my words. Bad manners in a drawing-room are detestable enough, but a breach of etiquette among the free men of the Desert is a thing beyond excuse.[63]

Roger addressed the matter again, saying that "Nearly every outlaw is a retired cowboy: and the relations between the robbers and the cowpunchers are based on exact rules of etiquette. The cowboy is an armed retainer who is paid to work and to fight for his employer; but he will always warn an outlaw against the police, and it is considered bad manners at a cow camp to ask any questions of a guest."[64] It was probably only the others explaining that Roger was an eccentric Englishman, who was sometimes too curious for his own good, that saved him.

Prospectors and townsfolk at Bluff, Utah, warned Roger against going ahead, without a guide, into country where water was very scarce, so Roger took on a Navajo named Manito. Manito spoke only Spanish and Roger virtually nothing but English, so communication was limited. Manito brought his own horse, which was little more than a skeleton. His job was to find water, grass, and fuel, for which he was paid six shillings a day and all his food. Roger dealt with the cooking, packing, and driving. As

Roger told it, Manito killed off rattlesnakes where they camped, stole any of Roger's goods he fancied, and one night "made me a dry camp within a hundred yards of running water."[65] Manito took great pleasure in telling the Navajo they met about his new servant who did all the work and paid him, as well. One warrior, who spoke some English, asked Roger where he came from. When Roger replied England, the Navajo asked, "Is that a fort?"[66] Roger recorded Manito's shortcomings, but he also described the subjugation of the Navajo with sympathy for their plight, and he went to some effort to mention the remnants of earlier peoples in the region and stress how advanced their cultures were.[67] Roger did not report how and where he parted company with Manito, but before very long he was alone again: "The sun blistered my hands, my mouth was sticky and uncomfortable, the glare made my eyes sore, and furnace blasts of wind lifted the sand in my face. Then the tracks played out and I was lost."[68] Things looked bad until his weary pack horse, Burley, tired of a shortage of grass, set off at speed in a south-south-westerly direction, followed by Roger on Chub, his saddle horse. Roger soon realized that Burley's natural instinct led them from the sand, up bare rock, to a range of Lombardy poplars that indicated the Mormon oasis of Tuba, Arizona.

Roger admired the "stubborn courage" of these Mormons and their willingness to tithe, but he was somewhat disparaging about some of their beliefs and practices:

> I have seen their stores, their ditches for irrigation, their mills, their dairies, all co-operative; a people abstemious, with clean homes, and many signs of living religion which restrains from sin. Without being in the least self-righteous about it, they pay tithes of all they possess.
>
> Now I belong to a Church which would consider such a demand nothing less than extortion. We reserve our smallest silver for the offertory, our warmest advice for the poor, and temper our piety with enlightened avariciousness as an example to all Jews, Turks, Infidels, and Heretics. We are, therefore, in a position to throw stones at these horrid Mormons, who believe in bigamy as a means of grace.
>
> From a secular point of view, I think that the Mormon prospers at the price of his liberty. The Church co-operative store, underselling the little tradesmen, kills out all private enterprise. The Bishop, pious rather than literate, is a deadly enemy for the man who dares to think. There is plenty of physical vigour, dancing, love-making, laughter; but books,

magazines, and newspapers, I seldom managed to find in a Mormon home, and the people were in a state of mental death. It was a relief to find a Gentile village, drunken, profligate, wildly licentious, but alive, full of brave little business ventures, prosperous, growing, where men could think, debate, and fight with hope in their eyes.[69]

From Tuba, Roger headed into the deadly heat of the Painted Desert. There, he met an old prospector who had gone mad with the heat, swearing that voices of the dead were leading him to a cave of gold. Indeed, it was easy in that shimmering heat haze to see things that were not there. Roger was rather proud of the geological knowledge that preserved him from such a fate:

Sometimes a big, bright diamond has been seen on the face of a cliff. I saw one myself the other day, a star of vivid white light far up on the Yaco of a mountain: and perhaps might have started a tragedy of my own, but that I saw some flakes of mica on the trail. A slab of mica shining in the sun has bewitched the prospector, who fancies that precious stones are found ready cut in the rocks, but a real diamond is like a bit of gum Arabic, which he would pass disdainfully by.[70]

A fifty-mile trail out of the heat led up to a large, cool pine forest, but there was still no water, only rabid skunks to be strictly avoided. In fact, one night in the Coconino Forest he awoke to find one of the skunks "trying to reach that eager nose which has so often led me into trouble. I shooed him away, and threw rocks, so that, maybe, he also was alarmed."[71] Eventually, Roger was able to find somewhere safe to leave his horses in the shadow of the San Francisco Peaks, which have the highest altitude in Coconino, for a week's well-earned rest. Roger decided to visit the Grand Canyon by joining the tourists, "queer people in linen dusters, spectacles, and kodaks, ever so pleased with themselves. I felt as if I had come out of the Valley of the Shadow of Death into a pantomime."[72] When the coach arrived at the hotel after a seventy-mile journey, his red-blooded heterosexuality was stirred by what, today, would be considered a discovery hardly worth mentioning: "I was lashed to frenzied excitement by a discovery made the moment I entered the bar-room. On pegs hung three pairs of green-duck bloomers and three pair blue, on hire at a shilling a time for the solace of ladies riding down into the canyon."[73] Roger was interested to find that 400 members of what he called the "Female Christian Endeavourers" had been there trying to hire the bloomers. Roger's fantasies were much simpler than those of the twenty-first-century male.

Roger was skilfully able to describe some of the extraordinary scenery of the Grand Canyon to *Lloyd's Weekly* readers, and put it in a perspective familiar to them:

> I sat on the rim rock at dawn, staring down into space, into thin, blue mist which had no bottom, as though the floor of the world had dropped out. Only when the rose flush caught the further wall could I see dim shapes of mountains far beneath. That Northern wall was twelve miles away, as far as the Hampstead Heath from the Crystal Palace, and in the depths between all London might be lost.
>
> Those mounds down in the mist were mountains bigger than the Grampians. I had travelled of late through many gigantic canyons, but they were only like the little cracks in the bottom of this most awful hollow. I was sitting in a pine forest like those of Norway, but the depths down there were in the climate of Central Africa.
>
> After breakfast we rode down by a trail blasted in the face of the cliffs, which cost two thousand pounds, and is so steep that, rather than haul up water from the river, the hotel sends waggons [*sic*] forty miles to the nearest springs. It was like riding down the outside of St. Paul's cathedral from cross to pavement, multiplied by fifteen.[74]

Roger described more of the landscape, then felt that he had to substantiate his description: "Though I have wallowed in frantic description, please do not think that I am getting up on my hind-legs and pawing at the moon. It is all true."[75]

After the splendour of the Grand Canyon, it was back to the desert for Roger. He had deliberately chosen to ride desert routes to prove that he could succeed in something spectacular, and the next desert, the Gila, was the hottest of all. The heat and solitude certainly played on him:

> [I] had an impression of riding through time, through ages, a wild jumble of shuffled centuries. This Desert is the scrap-heap of world making, the dust-bin of History, full of sweepings thrown from the mills of God. The cowboys are cavaliers left over from Cromwell's wars, the Navajos are spare barbarians from ancient Asia, the tourists are

shopworn goods from the twentieth century, the outlaws, soiled knights from King Arthur's chivalry. So far my mind had tenure of what I saw, a basis for some sort of reasoning. The Yellowstone Park was a discarded garden from the New Jerusalem, the rock monuments in the Navajo Desert a sketchy design for some thirtieth century metropolis, the Grand Canyon an experimental cataclysm from the second Day of the creation. Even so far my brain could accept the facts reverentially, with little prayers for help to understand. But when at last I fought through the red-hot valley of central Arizona, reason revolted in open mutiny. This place was a mistake, a fragment from some other planet, thrown on the wrong scrap-heap.[76]

To his *Lloyd's Weekly* readers he confessed that "Words cannot tell how lonely, how terrifying in its silence, is this red-hot waste of Arizona.... [E]very plant, every beast, every reptile an armed and deadly enemy. The clouds bring forth dust instead of rain...."[77] These responses to the desert illustrate Roger's increasing sense of mysticism. In later years it emerged more in his fiction, although it was not always popular with his readers.

Eventually, after much solitude and heat, he came to Phoenix, "a town of twelve thousand people, with electric street-cars and electric lights." He found the hustle and bustle quite a culture shock. The saloons were crowded, and residents were talking about a robbery at the Palace Saloon two weeks before Roger arrived, during which two men robbed the gaming tables. The big excitement in the local papers was the story of Pearl Hart. Hart and her partner, "Joe Boot," robbed a stagecoach on 29 May 1899, at Cane Spring in the Dripping Spring Mountains, just south of the Pinal Mountains. The passengers reported a big robber and a little robber. The little one seemed very uneasy and fumbled with the trigger of his revolver. After they were caught, it was discovered that the little one was Pearl Hart, which caused much amazement, for even on the frontier it was highly unusual for a woman to take to such a life. Roger was so impressed with the tale of the small woman who dressed as a man to become a robber that the story went home to his newspaper readers,[78] and was also the basis for the girl who dressed as a boy and became a robber in his novel, *Curly.*

After this interlude of city life, Roger headed out into the desert again. He was unsure of his route until he encountered an old man with long silver hair, who introduced himself as "Texas Bob." Roger had been searching for grass for two days, avoiding a golden ridge that looked like more sand drifts, until Texas Bob pointed out that what he was looking at was, in fact, grass. Texas Bob gave him safe directions to Naco, on the border with Mexico, and also a fragment of charred skull. Texas Bob said it was from an old white man killed by the Apache.[79] Roger kept that piece of skull, on his mantelpiece, as an unusual memento and conversation piece until his death. Most probably his sisters then disposed of it with alacrity. While Roger was passing through southeastern Arizona, he met a famous gunman, John Horton Slaughter (1841–1922), who was said to have killed 27 people in self-defence.[80] At Naco, he described a baseball match in October 1899 against Bisbee, a nearby copper mining town, which appeared to have descended into a cross-border raid: "So I found the border lined on both sides with National troops, and a hundred and fifty cowboys preparing to march on the city of Mexico."[81]

Keeping to his plan to ride the desert, Roger employed a Mexican to guide him across the mountains. As usual, Roger was not a good judge of men. As soon as their canteens of water were empty, the guide abandoned him. Fortunately, Roger had learned some tracking skills from Native American friends and was able to pick up a recent trail, which he followed until he met an American cowboy. After the cowboy had given Roger a drink from his own canteen, Roger inquired if the cowboy had seen his fire the previous night. The cowboy had, and pointed out that the Apache might also have seen it and that they were still collecting scalps from lone riders. For his *Lloyd's Weekly* readers Roger then articulated part of his admiration of cowboys:

> The cowboy is something more than a herder paid with
> dollars to work and to fight for his master. By the gorgeous
> colour of his leather gear, the glitter of his arms, the clatter of
> his spurs, the sun tan of his hide, the gallantry of his bearing,
> the manliness of his life, he is a gentleman, a cavalier, and
> something more. Civilisation is the clear daylight, very good
> and full of hope for mankind, but as the day is bounded by
> the glamour of the morning and the evening, so on these
> boundaries of human life, this frontier of the world, there are
> intenser lights and deeper shadows. The world is still young
> as in forgotten centuries, the man-at-arms has independent
> strength for good and evil, is angel and devil in one body.[82]

When Roger reached the first town within Mexico, he sadly sold and said goodbye to his pack horse, Burley, because he could now rely on stopping at the fortified houses that were usually less than a day's ride apart on his route through Mexico. He did have to acquire a gun, though, for he found that while not wearing a gun had caused him no problem as an eccentric Englishman in America, the lack of a gun was drawing unwanted attention in Mexico. He therefore purchased an elderly Colt:

> Everybody had chaffed me for not carrying a revolver, which
> to my mind is a worse nuisance than the umbrella as worn
> by civilised man, a thing which gets wet and unpleasant
> every time there is rain. I am a rotten bad shot, have always
> got the worst of it in gun-fights, and for my weapon would
> prefer a cold boiled ham. A swipe across the face with a cold
> boiled ham would be most discouraging. Anyway, I carried a
> revolver for moral effect in Mexico.[83]

As he made his way through the state of Chihuahua he was most impressed by the ranch owned by Don Luis Terrazas, which Roger claimed was "bigger than Wales, a pasture laced with a loose skein of mountain ranges. Where I crossed it this ranche [sic] was 200 miles wide. At several round-ups I watched the Mexican cowboys at work in the corralls, and it was more fun than a bull-fight."[84] At the town of Chihuahua he bought a thoroughbred Arab gelding. His judgement was good, and the horse took him superbly down the country. As he rode he found Mexicans did not trust Texans, but there was plenty of hospitality in the little homesteads for an Englishman. Finally, Roger had finished with the desert and ahead stretched miles of maize fields in civilized country, all the way to Mexico City. With civilization came other things, such as influenza, which he contracted at Zacatecas. Thieving was rife, and he became so incensed when forage for his horse was stolen at Silao that he became embroiled in an argument with the hotel manager. As a result, Roger was thrown in jail. Fortunately for him, a number of kindly Americans, including Dr. George Byron Hyde (1863–1939), witnessed his arrest and created a considerable fuss until he was released. The spell in jail had exchanged the influenza for a severe bout of dysentery, which made the remaining miles a nightmare for him, and his arrival in Mexico City was not quite what he had envisioned:

> I had built up a day dream in the desert that, entering the city
> of Mexico, I would ride to the doors of some big hotel, leave
> my horse with the porter, ask the office clerk for his book,
> and register my name from Fort Macleod, Canada. But when
> I came to the reality the hotel man, looking me over, decided

that all his rooms were full, that he could not have his tourists
scared by a travel-worn cowboy, with a probable propensity
for casual shots at the waiters—I went elsewhere.

So that was the end. My ride from Fort Macleod on the
Canadian plains to this city of Mexico measured 3,600 statute
miles. A like distance would be from London to Timbuctoo,
or Damascus, or, perhaps, Chicago. 3,100 miles of the way
was desert, too dry for farming, but with few marches of over
40 miles without water. I rode nearly the whole way on three
good horses, but, including pack animals, used nine, at a cost
of ($213.50) £44, 9s. 7d. The time—from June 28, 1899, to
Jan. 21, 1900, was 200 days at 18 miles a day; but for 147 actual
travelling days the average was 24 miles. The longest day
was only 51 miles. Other travellers have ridden further and
done better, but I have added one more record to the annals
of American horsemanship, hoping that in so doing I might
bring the Desert home to my own people.[85]

Even today, Roger's journey would be a considerable achievement. With
all the backup that could now be provided, there are still very few willing
to attempt to re-enact such a ride in its entirety, particularly since Roger
deliberately routed the major part of his journey through the deserts of
western America. Given the advent of dams and other development, it is
no longer even possible to follow his route. That he succeeded is excellent testament to his horsemanship. Casson cites Jim Dullenty, an avid
writer on the Outlaw Trail, as the source who "confirmed that nobody
had authentically ridden the full length of the Outlaw Trail on horseback
from Mexico to Canada."[86] It is hard to understand how Dullenty could
have ignored Roger's ride, which Roger described in such effective detail. Subsequently there has been a claim that Gustav Hinrich Schoof,
a member of the Legion of Frontiersmen, "duplicated" Roger's feat on
horseback.[87] However, many who have ridden the Outlaw Trail since have
only completed parts of it on horseback or have used motorized vehicles
exclusively.[88] Simon Casson, who rode most of the Trail on horseback,
developed a strong respect for the horsemanship required in the region:

Despite our catalogue of errors as tenderfoot travellers, we
had learned a great deal you could never get out of books.
We had now proved that the Wild Bunch were finely honed
experts at much more than just robbing banks and trains.

Without straddling a horse for weeks on end, experiencing

the conditions at first hand, no-one could truly understand just how hard it was to ride unsupported along some parts of the Outlaw Trail. Butch and his fellow outlaws displayed a remarkable feeling for geography; their ability to remember vast tracts of land in close detail was extraordinary with only rudimentary maps or none at all. They also excelled at horsemanship and horse management of course, and in their ability to cope with adverse terrain, climate and supply situations.[89]

Roger not only achieved success in this terrain in 1899–1900, he took the considerable extra risk of dropping in unannounced on outlaw groups that were, and have remained, notorious. The northern tribes would have presented little risk, but the southern Apache could, and Roger was, to all intents and purposes, unarmed. Roger had to rely on his own skill in the wilds, for if he became lost nobody would come searching for him. Yet his remarkable feat was only recognized on page fourteen of *Lloyd's Weekly*, which is now largely forgotten, because at that time most public interest was focussed on the Anglo-Boer War. Instead of front page head-lines, Roger had only the personal satisfaction of the record he achieved and held for the rest of his life, and a complimentary remark by Buffalo Bill Cody: "His description of the West is true to life, and I know a lot of the men he mentions. As to his ride from Canada to old Mexico I envy him the trip."[90]

This success did something to counter, in Roger's mind, the failure of his Klondike expedition. It may also have influenced later long-distance horse riders, just as Roger had been influenced by Carson, Peshkov, and perhaps Stevens. As well, his experience with range horses on this journey deeply informed his book *Horses*, particularly the chapter "Horsemanship," and influenced his "Equipment of Horsemen" in *The Frontiersman's Pocket-book*. There, he provided sensible advice on clothing based on his experi-ence of the extremes of climate and temperature on this ride. Many years later a Legion of Frontiersman publication published a brief account of Roger's ride to serve as an example of the "qualities required of the origi-nal Frontiersmen."[91] Roger's love of adventure was not quenched by this journey. He was soon seeking adventure on another continent.

WAR;
and the
WANDERER WRITES
POPULAR WESTERN YARNS

AS SOON AS ROGER ARRIVED safely in Mexico City he cabled his sisters to tell them of his success. He received, in return, an urgent message from Lena, asking him to return to London at once. She had risen rapidly in her profession, and under her stage name, Lena Ashwell, was beginning to be counted among the leading actresses of the time.[1] However, she was being tormented by detectives employed by her husband, Arthur Playfair, who was persistently seeking evidence he could use to petition for a divorce. In addition to that impending social scandal, her beloved father, who had been in failing health for several years, had recently died, and she was probably still trying to break free of cocaine, which had been prescribed about 1895 by a physician, with the innocent aim of helping to ensure she would not sneeze during a performance.[2] All this stress was bringing her close to breaking point and she desperately needed her brother's support. As an actress at a time when acting was not very socially respectable, she needed him as her champion and support. So Roger returned to London immediately, and his presence helped to ease the pressure on her. Within ten years their positions would be reversed.

Roger then spent over a year in London using some of the stories he had acquired on his travels as the basis for a number of pieces for weekly magazines. One of his serials, "By My Own Hand," was featured in *Lloyd's Weekly Newspaper,* and a twenty-four-part series entitled "Great Adventurers" was also published.[3] As usual, however, it was not long before he felt it was time to go off in search of adventure. He had read about the Anglo-Boer War in South Africa, but his wanderlust and inquisitive nature made him want to see it for himself. He could not secure a commission from a newspaper, which is not surprising, since they all had their own correspondents, and by this time public interest in the war was waning. Nonetheless, he arrived at Durban in December 1901. Years later, from the perspective of the activities of the Legion of Frontiersmen, he complained that the British tramp steamer on which he travelled to Durban had transported war stores for the Boers:

> The officers, all married men with families whose livelihood depended upon their silence, showed me proof that the vessel was actually loaded to the hatches with war stores for the Boers. At Durban I reported the facts, and was snubbed. The unloading proceeded, even after a case marked "pianoforte" broke in the slings, covering the quay with mauser [sic] ammunition. That was but one of several such cargoes sent by "underground railway" to the fighting Commandos.[4]

While he clearly was distressed by the gun running, the manner in which he exempted the officers from blame coincides with the principles described by his friend C.J. Cutcliffe-Hyne in the Captain Kettle stories.[5]

As Roger wandered around Durban in the December heat, he found that his letters of introduction to newspapers and other publishers brought little response. He elicited more interest from two recruiting sergeants:

> I went up to the sergeants and asked them, "What time does the twelve o'clock train leave?"
> "At noon."
> "Come-'n'-have-a-drink?"
> They responded to the password of the Lost Legion, and we had many drinks.[6]

This was not the first time Roger claimed a special importance for Kipling's "Lost Legion." Indeed, "Pocock's fraternity was composed of 'poor devils, who tried and failed, and tried and failed again,' who, as sailors, troopers, gold-miners, or 'any kind of frontiersmen,' were all 'of one tribe,' sharing the common password 'Come-'n'-have-a-drink.' The Lost Legion's story was their own, they swore by its rough code, and yet could believe in an Empire which stood superior to all."[7] This spirit was evident at Roger's hotel the following morning, when Sergeant-Major Hawk came to visit. It was Sunday, and the other bars were closed, so they had recourse to the hotel bar where a man claiming to be an officer stood. He said that he belonged to one of the bands of irregulars serving in South Africa. He talked expansively about "his corps, Sutler's Scouts, a gang of robbers licensed to plunder the Boers, getting no pay, but allowed three-fourths of all they could steal. Troopers earned a hundred pounds a month, but as the corps had just been cut to pieces, there were vacancies."[8] The plan appealed to Roger's romantic nature. Sergeant-Major Hawk was almost at the end of his service and the idea of making decent money also appealed to him. Roger mentioned that he was ex-NWMP and was immediately recruited. Roger continued his reference to the "Lost Legion":

> The South African War had become an industry, with a fair
> demand for labour, and steady wages. So the Lost Legion,
> gathered in its thousands from the ends of the earth, was
> rather pleased, took kindly to the trade, preferred six months'
> engagements, and only visited the coast for a wash and
> a drink before returning cheerily in some new regiment.
> Compared with sailorising [sic], stock riding or prospecting,
> the job was a well-paid picnic, and if a few of the fellows met
> with accidents, the usual thing on the Frontier, that was a
> providential arrangement.[9]

Roger retained a copy of the enlistment form he signed when he joined the National Scouts: "50% of all the value as assessed by Military Authority of all Stock Transport, Vehicles, and Horses captured by my Corps shall be credited to the accounts of my Corps and half that sum shall be distributed monthly among members of the said Corps as an addition to the daily pay."[10] Nonetheless, Roger earned nothing from his few weeks with the Scouts.[11]

To what extent such groups of irregulars were officially authorized was a matter of dispute then and remains so. While they were effective against roving bands of Boers, voices were raised in England against such units. The Secretary of State for War, (William) St. John Fremantle Brodrick (1856–1942), preferred to disown them, and official records are sketchy. However, on 7 December 1901 the National Scouts were officially formed, relying heavily on Boers who fought for the British: "The fact that a fifth of the fighting Afrikaners at the end of the war fought on the side of the British was a secret that has remained hidden till today."[12] On 31 December 1901, Roger's unit was disbanded, and on 1 January 1902 he and his comrades were sworn in as part of the 4th National Scouts. Roger disapproved of the disbandment of these units of irregular bandits: "Strengthened, disciplined, supported, such robbery as ours could have starved the Boers to subjection, ended the long campaign, stayed the shedding of blood."[13] It did bring him into closer contact with Boers, though. His opinion of them was somewhat patronizing, but also prophetic about their support in time of war:

> Apart from their vague sense of honour, and a dread of harm from overwashing themselves, these Boers were glorious men, innocent and unworldly, never quite grown up, their literature the nice bloody parts of the Old Testament, their pleasures, dancing, hunting, scouting, fighting. I found them gentle, patient, and humane, and their Kaffir servants loved them. As they fought a grand campaign against us, they will rally like brothers to our side in time of danger; for England's only friends are the fighting men who have felt our hearts in war.[14]

The conditions under which this war was fought enabled Roger to make good use of the skills he had learned from Canada's First Nations. For example, his ability to move silently brought his comrades an excellent Christmas dinner:

> It so chanced that Waldron's Scouts, those master-scroungers, were camped at Platrand, South Africa, on Christmas Eve, 1900 [*sic*], and had a sharp eye on the cooking preparations of the irregular cavalry camped near them.
> When darkness came that Christmas Eve, Roger crept like an Indian into the adjacent cavalry camp. How he seized and kidnapped the plumpest sucking-pig in the cook's pen, without making a sound, is one of the great stories of Roger's pre-Legion days, and I have seen the grin split his white head in two at the memory of it.
> On Christmas Day Waldron's Scouts fed royally on roast pig. The crackling was particularly choice, and they offered bits of it to famished cavalrymen from the other camp who came sniffing suspiciously, with glowering faces, among them a Hercules of a trooper with a seaman's roll in his gait, whom his companions called "Klondike."
> "Somebody stole your pig?" said Waldron's Scouts, sympathetically. Butter would not have melted in their

mouths. "Those thieving Kaffirs again, no doubt of it. Try a
bit of our crackling, chaps. Very tasty."

The chaps departed, muttering beneath their breath.
Pocock was very busy helping the cook scrape grease off tin
plates, his head well down.[15]

This was not the end of the story for Roger, because the "Hercules of a
trooper" was Alfred Basil Lubbock, who later marched into the Legion
of Frontiersmen office in London to request an enlistment form. Roger
filled in the details:

> Then came a question which electrified the big man, who
> gave his name as A. Basil Lubbock.
>
> "South African War Service?" mused Pocock. "Platrand?"
> "Yes."
>
> "Ever have a suckling pig?" murmured Pocock.
>
> "Yes! And one of those blankety-blank such and such so-
> and-so's of Waldron's Scouts stole it!" thundered Lebbock
> [sic].
>
> Pocock rose and held out his hand.
>
> "My Christmas dinner!" he smiled. "And now you'll come
> out to dinner with me!"
>
> So two great adventurers met officially for the first time,
> and "Klondike" Lubbock, deepsea [sic] sailor, soldier of
> Empire, joined the Legion of Frontiersmen.[16]

Roger began his service in the National Scouts with a fortnight's rest
in a camp on foul ground, which gave them all dysentery. Roger was sent
to hospital with two friends, both of whom died from what Roger termed
neglect but was listed as enteric fever. He was either fortunate or tough, or
a mixture of both, but he survived and managed to get himself transferred
to a convalescent camp, probably before he was sufficiently fit to travel.
This was a healthier camp, where he indulged in his own favourite cure:
food, fresh air, and exercise. After five weeks he was given leave to join his
unit at Middleburg, but as is often the case with the military, his unit was
not there, so he was re-directed to Pretoria. There he became involved in
the kind of skirmish all too common in that war. Roger and a man known
as Irish, under the command of an officer named Barquely, with fifteen
pro-British Boers and five black Africans, went out on a scouting patrol.
They checked a number of abandoned Boer farms until at one they were
ambushed. The ambushers retreated and, after attending to the wounded,

Roger's patrol prepared to defend the farm against reinforcements they were sure the retreating Boers would summon. That attack never materialized. A yell that the Boer Commando were attacking proved to be a unit of 250 British troops coming to their aid. As Roger recorded, "A few more weeks of the Great Sport ended my term of service, and now the Boers were tired of the game, their leaders were discussing the surrender."[17] Thus his actual military experience was somewhat limited, which hindered him later, when he was forming the Legion of Frontiersmen, but his careful observations of how horses were used informed his writing.[18]

At the age of thirty-six he realized the time had come to take his discharge. His damaged foot and elbow, added to prematurely grey hair and lingering dysentery, caused him to be known to every soldier as "Dad," even at that relatively young age. The missing toes also made it difficult for him to march and affected his balance when he stood. It was time to return to London, he decided, where his many trophies and mementos could stimulate memories and encourage him to write:

> I took off my spurs to hang them on the wall of my den—and the bandolier, for England may need me again, me and my Brothers. There hangs my cowboy harness, saddle, revolver, rifle, bridle, shaps, the Mexican gear, the deerskin coat and sash of the Far North, and on the mantelpiece are medals, with the bit of charred skull which Texas Bob gave me out in the Desert.
>
> It is not easy to leave all that. In the watches of the night one hears again the dip of the paddles, the crash of the surf, the thunder of the horses, the making of Empires. It is better yonder than this mere scratching of pens, where there are guiding lights ahead, the lights of Heaven.[19]

After he reached London, Roger wrote some short articles but concentrated on the first volume of his autobiography, which was published as *A Frontiersman* in July 1903 in London, and as *Following the Frontier* in October 1903 in New York. He had originally wanted to call it *The Trails of the Lost Legion,* which would have been a link to his hero, Rudyard Kipling. Neither publisher would accept this title, but both thought the book would benefit from a preface by a well-known author, such as H.G. Wells or Morley Roberts. Roger thought the very best person to write a preface would be Kipling, since he had been such an inspiration, so Roger wrote to tell Kipling that "It did me a lot of good when you wrote to me five years ago asking who had written about 'Almighty Voice,' a

Cree warrior in the Pall Mall Gazette. It was me." He then asked Kipling to read the proofs of his book and write a preface, saying, "You are the only expert on the whole topic—The Trails of the Lost Legion."[20] No doubt Kipling received many similar requests from minor authors, since his endorsement would be bound to increase sales. Kipling politely declined. Nonetheless, there was a flurry of attention when the two versions were published.

Lloyd's Weekly published a review of the London edition very promptly. Under the subheading "A book to thrill the reader," the reviewer enthusiastically described Roger's account of his adventures and concluded that "Such books as this stir the blood in the veins and make one glad that they have been written."[21] However, in the *Times* on 7 August 1903, a Methuen advertisement carried a brief description of *A Frontiersman:* "As exciting as a novel." That may have been a good way to attract readers, but it may also have provided encouragement for some detractors. One reviewer, in response to other descriptions of the book as a "romance" or a "novel," felt compelled to write that there was a "solid substratum of truth beneath these traveller's tales. Mr. Pocock has carried a camera in his pocket as well as in his head. He can show you the spot where he was led out to die at Gaetwangak, and a dozen snapshots of inaccessible outlaw camps." That reviewer, who described Roger as "half journalist, half cowboy," then lavished praise on the book:

> If anyone wishes to realise the meaning of Imperialism, he cannot do better than read this stirring book. The magnificent work done by the mounted police in Canada is admirably depicted by Mr. Pocock, who shows with vivid word-pictures the difference between the Wild West of the States and the Order of the Dominion. And yet Mr. Pocock does not hate the Yank. To him all white men are white—even the outlaw with his desperate and often bloodthirsty raids.
>
> As to the style, the style is the man, a man who has had a life chockful [*sic*] of incident and excitement, and at the same time has kept his eyes open to the wonder, the beauty, the humour, the tragedy of life. There is not much art in it, except the art of impulse and strong feeling. Another man might have written with more finish, but would any other man have won half so much sympathy?[22]

Despite such praise from someone Roger may have known, when it was reviewed elsewhere as fiction, he could not let that pass. Thus in the "new books and new editions" classified advertising in the *Times* on 28 August 1903, there was an announcement:

THE AUTHENTICITY OF A FRONTIERSMAN:
AN AFFADAVIT

In the matter of an Autobiography entitled "A Frontiersman," written by Roger Pocock, and published by Messrs. Methuen and Co., on the 16th July, 1903.

Whereas certain Journals have reviewed my book entitled "A Frontiersman" as if it were a novel, to the grave detriment of its chances of public favour, I, Roger Pocock, of Adam-street, Adelphi, do solemnly and sincerely declare that my said book is an Autobiography and a literal statement of facts, save that to avoid causing pain or injury, certain names and dates have been suppressed. And I make this solemn declaration conscientiously believing the same to be true, and by virtue of the provisions of the Statutory Declaration Act, 1835.

Declared at 2, Clement's-inn, Strand, in the County of London, this 23rd day of July, 1903.

ROGER POCOCK.
Before me, H.H. SHEARD, A Commissioner for Oaths.

Very conveniently located, immediately below this announcement, was a small advertisement for the book, indicating the price. This affidavit ensured Roger even more press coverage. Interest had faded, however, by 1952, when Roger's sister, Hilda, sent a synopsis of *A Frontiersman* to Col. Louis Scott, Dominion Commandant of the Legion of Frontiersmen, because she was "anxious to have [it] re-published in a cheap edition. This will be possible," she wrote, "if I can get a certain amount of promises of sales. I have one for 100 from the London Headquarters, and am writing to other addresses." The journal published the synopsis, an encouraging note from the editor, and an enthusiastic comment from an unnamed representative of the High Commissioner for Canada. However, there is no indication the book was reprinted then.[23]

The New York edition also attracted some attention. A letter and a review appeared under the leader "Pocock's Prejudices." The letter writer angrily quoted some of Roger's comments on Americans out of context:

Sir: There has been issued in New York this week a book called "Following the Frontier." It is an English book by an Englishman calling himself Roger Pocock, and is published in England under the name "The Frontiersman" [*sic*] but it is filled with such foul abuse of the people of this country that I am amazed that any American firm of publishers could be found to issue it. For its attack upon Americans there has been nothing like it since the days of Basil Hall and Mrs. Trollope and it far excels them in coarseness and deliberate falsehood.

In the language of Mr. Pocock, all Americans are "dirty rags," "thieves," "scoundrels," "murderers," "liars," and the like. Yet I am continually reading in the English press that there has never been any obstacle to the friendship of the United States and Great Britain except the attacks upon the English by the Americans. I have never seen anywhere in any American book or newspaper anything approaching in virulence or mendacity Mr. Pocock's book. If the English like this sort of thing, if they are so jealous of the Americans that they enjoy coarse attacks made upon them, let them have their entertainment; but I cannot understand why such things are spread before the American people.

The reviewer then responded to this letter:

This vigorous bit of writing had the effect of impelling us to take up Mr. Roger Pocock's book…[and] we are impelled to say that its principal faults are precisely those of the letter harshly condemning it, namely, a too strenuous expression of fancies and opinions and an overindulgence quite out of place in a prose narrative of personal experiences, of the figure called hyperbole. It is perfectly true that Mr. Pocock does say some harsh things of the habits, manners, and morals of some citizens of this Republic whom he has met in a life of adventure, but we must also admit that Mr. Pocock says some very harsh things of his own country and its institutions…. He spares nobody. His book is violent from beginning to end. It has the effect of seeming to have been written in a fever heat of passion….

It is an example of the impressionistic kind of writing about out-of-door life which has come into vogue since some eminent men, of whom Rudyard Kipling is not the least, though not now the most conspicuous in the public gaze, have uttered many words about the glory of Nature as she is before Civilization sullies her. It is all violent, as we have said, and the impressions of men and events it records are not to be taken for a moment as the observations of a mature, judicial mind, and will not be so taken. Why any patriotic American should protest against this author's expressions of opinion about Americans we cannot understand.

Of course, we have not seen the English edition of the book, and it is possible that the American publishers may have suppressed some passages that our correspondent has read, and that may more nearly justify his ill-feeling for the author. But, even in that case, it would not be worth while to take Pocock seriously enough to condemn his book on patriotic grounds.

Yet there is a certain sort of merit in Mr. Pocock's book, quite enough to justify its republication here and to secure for it some vogue. It has some really splendid bits of description. Its frankness and audacity lend an appreciable charm to many of its passages. It is not a work of genius, to be sure, and only genius could sustain its high-strung key from first to last. One closes it doubting the author's sincerity. But no human being could expect the world actually to believe all the cruel things Roger Pocock says of himself, of his aims, his accomplishments, and his performances.[24]

This was a somewhat critical review, very different in tone from the one in *Black & White,* but Roger would have been content to be granted so many column inches in such an important newspaper, and particularly pleased to be compared to Kipling. Even today we can appreciate that although Roger could be a good descriptive writer, he was often unable to present events in which he had been involved in a detached manner. His self-deprecation, and some of his attacks on groups of people in general, and Americans in particular, could also be irritating.

About this time Roger also completed *Curly: A Tale of the Arizona Desert. Curly* was an immediate success and was reprinted several times over the next twenty-six years. Other than the cliché of a girl passing herself off as a young man, it had an authenticity that was lacking in many of the other "western" yarns of the time. Roger could project that authenticity because he was writing of places and people he had visited very recently. *Curly* was perhaps even somewhat ahead of its time, since it resembles the popular westerns of the inter-war years and Hollywood stories. It was also a story that appealed to all ages, but most particularly to boys. Among the enthusiasts was Louis, Earl Mountbatten of Burma, who wrote, "I liked his books very much, particularly 'Curly.'"[25] The succinct quotations used to promote *Curly* in an advertisement in another of Roger's books capture some of its appeal: "*Daily Telegraph.*—'The book bristles with adventure.' *Birmingham Post.*—'A wonderful stirring story.' *Spectator.*—'It is full of life and action, without a halt in the interest from the beginning to the end, and thoroughly wholesome–an eminently readable volume.' *Daily Mirror.*—'A real good tale, thrilling from the first page to the last.'"[26] In *Curly* Roger's personal experience, particularly his ride from Fort Macleod to Mexico City, was a great asset that helped him to set a high standard he found he could not meet in later books. It was unfortunate for Roger's later search for success as a writer that he generally had to base his fiction on the places and events that he had either seen himself or heard about from men who had been involved. As his experience of adventure became a more distant memory, and as reading tastes changed, his fiction suffered in both content and sales.

However, in *Curly* Roger's prose was particularly good, and the illustrations by Stanley L. Wood were exemplary. In the Boston first edition there are ten illustrations from Wood's drawings. They are atmospheric and hew to Roger's description of events, clothing, and places. They may even have been drawn under Roger's direction, since the two men were friends, and Roger himself had some drawing skill. Wood told of their meeting to discuss the illustrations:

> [Roger declared:] "You think you know a cowboy! Why, you'll go and get things all wrong!"
>
> He crossed to a piece of furniture like a wooden hotel, drew out various drawers, and slung an armful of envelopes as big as paving slabs on the table and at me....
>
> "Stop!" I cried. But he hardly noticed me, and went on dealing out photographs and newspaper cuttings all over the table....
>
> Then he sighed, and gazing dreamily at the ceiling remarked: "Don't you think for a moment you know what a cowboy is like unless you possess plenty of documentary evidence to go on...."[27]

Sadly, most of the other editions contain only Wood's frontispiece, though in the 1931 edition that frontispiece is in colour, while in other editions it is black and white.

Wood's drawings, along with Roger's words, have contributed to continuing interest in the Wild Bunch and Robbers' Roost. Roger's clear description of the area and the men who lived there, although possibly slightly romanticized, is one of the best of those written at that time. We can be grateful for Roger's accurate and evocative descriptions, including that of the route to the stronghold at Robbers' Roost:

> Then away to the left I saw a big corral, with a dust of horses inside, and men sitting round on the top rail, maybe a dozen of them. Beyond it lay a streak of open water, and right in front loomed a house, set in the standing woods, where one could hadly [sic] see a hunded [sic] paces. It was a ranche [sic] house of the usual breed, log-built, low-pitched, banked up around with earth as high as the loopholes, and at each end against the gable stood a dry stone chimney. Two or three men stood in the doorway smoking, and but for the fact that they packed their guns when at home, they looked like the usual cowboys.[28]

Roger also had first-hand knowledge of ranches in the West owned by British nobility, who had been caught up in "the cattle gold rush."[29] He set part of this tale on a ranch owned by an Irish lord. The central characters were also based on people he met. Thus McCalmont is close to the folk-hero status often attributed to Butch Cassidy. Roger's characterization of McCalmont probably also owes something to his meeting with Tom McCarty. Another character from Roger's past, Mutiny, whom he met in the NWMP, is also a character in *Curly*. That McCalmont's daughter, Curly, posed as a boy until she was around twenty may appear to be a cliché or an improbable subterfuge, but some of Shakespeare's plays, as well as the story of Pearl Hart, may have provided inspiration. Both Roger and his sister, Lena Ashwell, were admirers of Shakespeare, who often used this device within his plays.

In *Curly*, written only a few years after he met the various outlaws, Roger reflected the history of the American West and the mythic quality of those outlaws. He achieves this through Curly's comments to the young hero:

"Father says that the worst crimes is cowardice, meanness and cheating. The next worse things is banks, railroad companies, lawyers....

"Father says that robbery is a sign that the law is rotten, and a proof that the Government's too pore [*sic*] and weak to cast a proper shadow. He allows we're a curse to the country, and it serves the people right....

"Do you know what made us bad? All of our tribe was cowboys and stockmen once; not saints, but trying to act honest, and only stealing cows quite moderate.... Then rich men came stealing our water-holes, fencing in our grass, driving our cattle away."[30]

Several years earlier Roger had attacked mining capitalists in his writing. In *Curly* it was the turn of the big ranchers.

The success Roger achieved with *Curly* could not keep him home. While he used the image of "hanging up his spurs" to end *A Frontiersman,* he made it clear he had not developed an immunity to the yearning for adventure. So he did not spend very much time in London before his wanderlust returned. He became determined to visit Greenland, which was virtually closed to visitors by the Danish government. Roger persuaded his friend Lord Mountmorres, who was also a journalist, to write to the Foreign Office on his behalf. The response was prompt, though not overly encouraging:

> In reply to your letter of 14th instant enquiring as to the possibility of obtaining a recommendation to the Danish Government for Mr. Roger Pocock, who is desirous of joining a Danish Expedition to Greenland, I am directed by the Marquess of Lansdowne to inform you that His Lordship would be willing to furnish that gentleman with a letter of introduction to His Majesty's Minister at Copenhagen, but that he is unable to give him any further assistance.[31]

Despite this lack of support, Roger was able to engineer a passage to Greenland in the barque *Thorvaldsen,* which sailed from Elsinore (Helsingør) on 17 May 1904. This journey enabled Roger to provide copy on yet another place that was almost unknown to magazine readers. Perhaps partly inspired by his time among the First Nations in British Columbia, he strongly supported Danish efforts to protect the Inuit of Greenland "from disease, from alcohol, and from interference with the hunting on which they depend for existence." He found the coastline gloriously beautiful and was able to visit Jakobshavn, "a metropolis of nine white people and four hundred natives," and several other places, including "Tassiusak, the most northerly house on earth."[32] The trip also provided him with an idea for a business venture. He was so enthusiastic about "a dish called mattâk (the skin of the white whale), a hard fat with a delicious nutty flavour, which would be highly esteemed by epicures in Europe," that he brought three tins back to England.[33] He sent one of these tins to Queen Alexandra in the hope that, as a Dane, she might like to support trade with the Royal Greenland Trade Company (Kongelige Grønlandske Handelskompagni), which had had a monopoly on trade with Greenland since 1774. Sir Dighton Macnaghten Probyn (1833–1924), privy councillor and keeper of the privy purse, replied that this put Queen Alexandra in a difficult position; nonetheless, he sent Roger "a Queen's shilling, a trophy which, with my war medals has outlasted serious famines."[34] No one, however, wanted to put any capital into Roger's venture, so nothing came of this business opportunity. Some years later, though, one writer thought Roger's trip had lasting value: "His sketches, maps, and drawings of the coast of that country are the best existing, and are valued possessions of the Danish Government."[35]

Another source of money did turn up, though. Roger received an important assignment from the weekly *Illustrated Mail* to visit Russia early in December 1904 and report on the troubles in that country and the effect of the Russo-Japanese War. Roger had steadily improved his camera skills and was able to bring back photographs of quality and interest, together with stories of the lives of ordinary Russian citizens. That assignment was also part of what triggered one of Roger's major tasks in the second half of his life, founding the Legion of Frontiersmen. The *Illustrated Mail* trumpeted his appointment:

> What is the true state of affairs in Russia? Will there be a revolution? Those are the questions everybody is asking. With a view to learn what the people of the great Russian Empire think of the disastrous war, the "Illustrated Mail" sent Mr. Roger Pocock to Russia, and his observations, gathered on the spot, will be read with especial interest.
>
> The choice of Mr. Pocock for such a task was particularly appropriate. He is admitted to be one of the finest descriptive writers of the day. Not only is he a capable writer, but a great traveller, who has seen and depicted life in all parts of the world.[36]

Roger generated a careful and thoughtful description of the country and its people that stood in contrast to the few public signs of awareness of the war:

> In the sublime cathedral of St. Isaac I saw the peasant women buying farthing candles to light up the picture of some popular saint, while they prayed for their sons on the battlefield. When the offertory procession came round I saw poor men put a three-farthing piece in the plate of the Red Cross Society; more than they could spare, for they took out a halfpenny in change. Prayers, candles, offerings—the rich and the poor are standing side by side in the churches and making their honest supplications at every shrine in the streets—Russia with one voice is praying for help in this her time of trouble.
>
> Although patriotic, the poor did not understand the purpose of the war.
>
> "Why should we fight?" say the peasants, "for lands which are useless to us—lands which we cannot farm because they are crowded already?" "If we take this country from the Japanese, it will do no good to the Emperor. The Englishmen will grab the whole of the plunder, and the peasant will get nothing."…
>
> If the merchants of Russia were Russians, the people at large would have rejoiced in the spread of their trade into China. But the merchants of the Empire come from three tribes who are hated by every true Muscovite, because they are not of the Orthodox Church or of Russian blood or speech. The traders are mostly Jews, Germans, and Poles, and if all of them were massacred to-morrow there would be national rejoicings.

Roger then told of the sacrifices the peasants made:

> The Reservists, torn from the land and leaving their families to semi-starvation, disguise their joy and gladness with rioting, mutiny, and wholesale desertion. So the raw troops are herded by regulars to the seat of war, treated more or less as convicts on the way to punishment, displaying some symptoms of heroism, but more of martyrdom. And the Grand Ducal party, seated in perfect safety at St. Petersburg,

is making patriotic sacrifices of all available troops, for their own honour and glory but not for the public good.

Roger predicted a grim outcome to the internal conflicts that characterized the peasants' relationship with the country's leaders:

> in the spring there is likely to be an unusually bad famine in the midst of a disastrous war. The nation will lay the blame upon the statesmen who have so badly advised the Emperor as to bring about all this trouble. There is likely to be a general rising of the peasants to rescue a beloved Sovereign from his evil counsellors and in such a revolt it is not likely that the Grand Dukes will escape with their lives; indeed, the dull mutterings of present discontent sound very like those of the French peasantry on the eve of a revolution which swept away King, Government, and nobility alike in general chaos.[37]

Roger was very perceptive, for on 22 January 1905 the revolution broke out in St. Petersburg. In his other articles on Russia, Roger described Father Ivan of Cronstadt and belief in his cures, the religious and social customs of Russian peasants, and the behaviour of Tolstoy and Gorky.[38] Each of his articles was well illustrated with photographs.

As well as gathering information for these articles, in St. Petersburg Roger indulged in another bout of amateur espionage:

> I put up at the one hotel frequented by my countrymen, and here, at one of the tables in the vestibule, made friends with a British subject, an engineer. He told me that he was engaged in construction work at a new and very secret naval base near Libau.... Convinced as I was that the Russian Fleet was perfectly harmless, built only for residence in harbours, I still felt that our Admiralty would be none the worse for a little information on current topics. I asked the engineer for a plan of the naval base.[39]

In addition to a desire to help the Admiralty, some of his usual inquisitiveness and desire for story ideas may have come into the equation. The engineer pointed out that they were probably being watched. Roger was well aware of this for, in his article on peasants, he referred to the fact that police spies were constantly watching the population. His solution was to send the waiter for paper and pencils, and under the pretext of a game of noughts and crosses he elicited details of the base. Later, in his bedroom, Roger stuffed the paper into the space in his right boot where his toes should have been. Without thinking, he followed the custom that evening of putting his boots outside his room to be cleaned. Fortunately the paper was still there when he suddenly remembered and brought his boots in at 3:00 A.M.

Realizing that he was in danger if his amateur spying came to the notice of the authorities, Roger left Russia on the next available ship. He then had to find a way to get the plans to the Admiralty:

> Back in London I met Jack Brotherton, who was private
> secretary to Admiral Jackie Fisher. I told him to place the
> plan of Libau where it would do the most good, and a
> week later I got a most wonderful letter. It seems that the
> War Office had a plan of Libau, and was making fun of the
> Admiralty because they hadn't got one. So the letter was
> from Admiral Prince Louis of Battenberg, Director of Naval
> Intelligence, just busting with gratitude and demanding more
> information. Well, I sent him the photographs I had taken of
> a flotilla of little two-by-four submarines, a battleship having
> a re-fit, the forts at Cronstadt being faced with armour plate,
> and a brace of destroyers protected from heavy lee by tugs on
> either bow.[40]

It appears that Prince Louis asked, in his second reply, if Roger could be of any more help. He had no more photographs, but he suggested that Prince Louis should take some admirals to the Natural History Museum and see the "invisible duck" at the Museum. This enabled Roger cheekily to claim the credit for introducing the British Navy to the art of naval camouflage.[41] The enthusiastic response from Prince Louis also encouraged Roger to proceed with his idea for an organization. Roger had been thinking for years about Kipling's "Lost Legion." The most succinct account of these original ideas appears in the article he wrote in 1941 for the Canadian Division of the Legion:

> I was but one out of thousands of British subjects scattered
> to the remotest corners of the earth and quickly informed of
> any menace to our peace. I had been properly introduced,
> but somebody might send important information to the
> Government without being introduced. The Government
> would say: "Who the Hell is Jones?" and the letter would

go to the waste-paper department. But suppose there was a Society or Association which could write to the Government and say: "This is our Mr. Jones. He's all right." The officials could always accept information which was known to be reliable. We must have an Association.[42]

Through his travels and discussions with men in other countries of Europe, and those who had travelled widely, Roger became convinced that there would be war with Germany within ten years. He decided to take action, so on Boxing Day, 1904, his letter to the editor appeared in a major national paper under the heading, "The legion that never was 'listed":

> Permit me in your columns to suggest the formation of an organisation of frontiersmen resident in the Kingdom. An applicant for membership would offer evidence that he has done real frontier work in such employments as the following: explorer, scout, hunter or trapper, prospector, or alluvial miner, cowboy or stock rider, cargador, or trader among savages, pearler, sealer, whaler, seaman or sea apprentice, trooper in Irregular Cavalry or Mounted Police, or War Correspondent. All members must be prepared to subscribe. The organisation might begin as a dining club with the hope of getting a club house when funds permit. Its objects would be good fellowship, mutual help, and possibly service to the State in time of war. I should be glad of letters from qualified men, with a view to a general meeting, which would appoint a committee. It is time that the Legion was 'listed.[43]

At the time, Roger was a good four years ahead of the formation of any formal, dedicated, and official military intelligence service, but he intended to put into action his version of the ideas that had been thought about by many other men. He admitted in 1907 that "The idea had been ripening since 1897 that a society for holding Frontiersmen together would be useful to the country in time of war."[44] To implement his great idea he had "twenty three pounds in the bank, twelve hundred invested, and some small earnings...."[45] He would spend all of this during the first year of his personal crusade.

THE LISTING
of the
LEGION

FOR SUNDAY, 1 JANUARY 1905, Roger wrote in his diary: "Began year working hard on League of Frontiersmen. Hilton & Fyfe consulting in my den." This entry reflects his focus, as well as his first choice of name for his organization. Even though "league" was soon replaced by "legion," the term *league* has been mistakenly used in books and articles more than once since. That entry also provides the names of the first three members of the Legion. According to Roger's list, he, of course, was number one. Herbert Philip Hilton, his companion on the Ashcroft Trail, was number two, and "Fyfe" was number three.[1] Whereas Hilton's name appears a number of times in Roger's diaries for this period, Fyfe is only mentioned there twice. Roger's many friendships with newspaper men suggest that Fyfe could possibly have been Henry Hamilton Fyfe (1869–1951), then editor of the *Daily Mirror*. Certainly a number of other newspapermen became members, including Thomas Catling of *Lloyd's Weekly*, for whom Roger wrote many articles. Perhaps Fyfe's name does not appear later because he was caught up in Roger's enthusiasm in the heady early days of the Legion but then backed away from the idea. Number four on Roger's list, Fred Bowers, shows up in Roger's diary on 10 January 1905—"Bowers joined & spent night here"—but he is not on the 1906 and 1907 printed membership lists. These names in Roger's diary give the impression that only a handful of men were consulting in Roger's "den," which became the Legion office. It is just as well there were only a handful, since it was a fifteen-foot square room on the top floor of 6, Adam Street, Adelphi, London.

Percy Burton was number five on Roger's list, formerly in the Imperial Yeomanry, and number six was Sir William Charles Eldon Serjeant (1857–1930), whose name first appeared in Roger's diary on 13 January 1905: "Col Serjeant asked." Serjeant, a barrister who had commanded a battalion in South Africa, was a hunting, shooting, and fishing gentleman in the Victorian mould who did not really approve of Roger and considered him to be in a lower social class. This class consciousness was one of the many problems that beset Roger in the formative years of his Legion. Nonetheless, Serjeant, who was involved in reform plans for the Army, was a keen supporter of the ideals of the Legion and was appointed "General Adviser to the Council." Still, Roger seldom mentioned Serjeant in his diary until problems arose in 1908 and 1909. In addition to these men, Roger's list of the first twenty-five members of the Legion contains five men Roger described as war correspondents—Frederick Arthur Mackenzie (1869–1931), Edmund Candler (1874–1926), Walter Kirton, Frederick Ferdinand Moore (b.1877), and Howell Arthur Gwynne (1865–1950)—as well as novelists Edgar Wallace (1875–1932), C.J. Cutcliffe-Hyne, and Morley Roberts. Also on that list were Harry de Windt (1856–1933), who was well known at the time as a traveller and writer, and Owen Vaughan (born Robert Scourfield Mills, 1863–1919), a writer and fervent Welsh nationalist. Two other men on the list became very important in the early Legion: number eight, Sir Henry Seton-Karr, and number fourteen, the Earl of Lonsdale.

To augment these numbers Roger worked hard to publicize the Legion, but achieved only limited success initially. He became frustrated when he attracted members who soon lost interest when they found that the Legion had big ideas but little direction and no major figure at its head. Consequently, Roger spent much time pursuing Seton-Karr, despite the fact that he broke some of the appointments Roger made with him. Seton-Karr was keen on hunting and fishing and had written a book, *The Call to Arms.* Like Serjeant, he caused Roger considerable anguish within a few years. From what he read in *The Call to Arms,* Roger may have felt that Seton-Karr was a kindred spirit, but again he did not take into account the class barrier. Roger would have been in full agreement with some of the ideas Seton-Karr expressed; for example, Seton-Karr was strongly pro-Canadian and had concerns about the United States of America. This parallel is reflected in an imaginary conversation Seton-Karr wrote for a chapter entitled "War Talk," which could well be based on real conversations he had had. The conversation of Jeremy Jones, a politician, John Brown, an Imperial Yeoman who had lost an arm in South Africa, and Sam West, a Canadian officer and sometime trooper who was lame due to a bullet wound in the shin: these support Roger's ideas about the close links between Canada and Britain. The character of Sam West provides these thoughts:

> When we saw the old country was in a bit of a tight place, and that a Canadian contingent had been offered and accepted, that was good enough for me. I'd been Christmassing [*sic*] with my wife's people down Winnipeg way when I first heard of it, and came straight back to the ranche [*sic*], after fixing things with the wife (she took it fairly well, mind you), and was on board ship with the rest of the boys in a fortnight.[2]

Later in the chapter West articulates this sentiment:

> I'm Canadian born and bred, but come of the old stock, as you know; and right glad was I to fight for the old country when she wanted me.... It was a fair fight between Dutch and English, and we're on the side of the English every time, and don't you forget it. Why is that, d'you say? Well, I'll tell you. Blood is thicker than water to begin with, and I'd always fight in a good cause for my own people and the land they came from.... The poet Kipling puts it in a nutshell:
>> Now this is the Faith that the White men hold
>> When they build them [*sic*] homes afar;
>> Freedom for ourselves and Freedom for our sons
>> And, failing Freedom, War.[3]

In his pursuit of other important members, Roger had more success outside London, particularly in northeast England, where he gained a firm supporter in the Hon. Geoffrey Parsons after they met on 3 February 1905 in Newcastle. That same day Roger met Horace Shafto Orde, who became a great friend, as well as Edward Hamilton Currey, a naval officer whose naval-themed books were first published between 1909 and 1917. However, in March 1905 Roger secured his biggest prize, Lord Lonsdale. Lonsdale was so valuable because he was both highly respected, at least in the sporting world, and a highly visible public figure:

> In the days before...the whole network of instantaneous communications which is available today, there were few national figures outside the Royal Family....and the only glamour in the lives of workaday people was provided by

stage beauties, the stars of music hall, and to a lesser extent the sporting figures of the day, such as leading jockeys and boxing champions. There were no film stars, no jazz bands, no international playboys and playgirls variously to entertain, divert, shock or scandalize the public....

Hugh [i.e., Lonsdale] had in his nature all the elements of a great showman. It did not require a vacuum for his talents to flourish, but because the vacuum was there his image was thrown into even higher relief. And the public lavished on him all the affection which they are capable of bestowing on their heroes. In their eyes there was no one quite like the Yellow Earl.[4]

In his diary for 11 March 1905, Roger proudly wrote: "Went to Oakham weekend at Lord Lonsdale's who is Chairman of Legion." It may have helped Roger's cause that Lonsdale was enthusiastic about uniformed organizations:

Hugh was never happier than when he was playing at soldiers. Brass bands, waving flags and colourful uniforms could bring tears to his eyes. No Yeomanry Regiment had a more splendid annual camp than the Cumberland and Westmorland Yeomanry whilst he commanded them. If his approach to the whole business was rather amateur, his men loved him all the more for it.

Moreover, "He was an inveterate joiner of Clubs.... When other men were content to go on the waiting list to join the fashionable clubs, Hugh was really only interested in clubs which invited him to join as President." Although Roger wrote in his diary on 12 March 1905 that he "got wet seeing Oakham," he also recorded that visit as a "Happy time." This is somewhat surprising, perhaps, because "Altogether[,] staying at Lowther was an experience from which some guests did not recover very readily. It was very much a matter, for most of the guests, of staying *at* Lowther rather than *with* Hugh and Grace Lonsdale—and staying at Lowther meant the strictest observance of all the unwritten rules." One of those rules was that "Virtually nobody who came to stay would dream of arriving without a personal servant."[5] Even with the difference in class and the lack of a "personal servant," however, Roger seems to have managed to fit in. Perhaps his ready fund of tales of Western life made him interesting company. He certainly received another invitation in May.

The public support and financial aid Lord Lonsdale provided to the infant Legion was a great help, but generally support came less from the rich and famous than from visitors from the frontiers of Empire who stopped off in London, the Empire's hub, for a brief visit. These men would join the Legion there, and then leave to spread the word around the Empire. Thus there are records of early Legion units not only in Canada, Australia, South Africa, and New Zealand, but in the Malay States, Falkland Islands, South Sea Islands, and Argentina as well. These men could and did offer enthusiasm, but other than paying their small annual subscription, they could supply little money to run the Legion. Thanks to those financial limitations, everything had to be administered from Roger's rooms at 6, Adam Street. He told the story of those early days to the inaugural meeting of Suffolk Command:

> "About three years ago," said Mr. Pocock, "a very small
> crowd of us met in a bedroom over the Strand. We were all
> very hard up; one man always slept on the hearthrug, because
> it was warmer than the Thames Embankment. (Laughter.)
> We were not influential, not powerful, nor wise, nor good,
> nor anything meritorious, but we began to think about this
> business, and on some days I used to notice that one could
> tell which men were the soldiers—they would be on the bed;
> and the cow boys [*sic*] would invariably squat on the floor,
> and, if there was a sailor man present, ten to one he would
> perch on the table. (Laughter.) He [*sic*] noticed, too, how
> carefully a match was husbanded for lighting a pipe—how the
> striker held his hands round it, how it was passed from hand
> to hand, and finally put out with great care, by men who had
> been accustomed to scarcity of matches in wild countries,
> and had known the danger of throwing a lighted match into
> dry grass. Later on, the meetings were held in more splendid
> rooms; great lords and gentlemen, very illustrious persons,
> joined with us; and from that little nucleus grew the Council
> in London."[6]

Since these early members in London could not have a campfire under the open sky around which to tell their yarns and tall tales, the fire burning in the grate had to suffice.

Having Lonsdale in the Legion helped substantially, and Roger's friends and fellow Frontiersmen, writing in newspapers and magazines, ensured steady publicity.[7] He still needed other powerful supporters, however, and his Legion still needed a leader. Roger was not a natural leader, but had he been, even as an ex-corporal of Irregular Scouts, and with a sister who was a prominent actress, he was not of suitable military or social standing. To help remedy this, he developed one very valuable connection—Prince Louis of Battenberg:

> In the winter of 1904–5, Captain Roger Pocock, the principal organizer of the Legion of Frontiersmen, forwarded to Prince Louis some secret information with regard to Russia. This led to his taking an interest in the Legion of Frontiersmen, and joining the Council of the Movement....
> At the time that Prince Louis took notice of the Legion and became a member of its Council, the body was not recognized by the Admiralty or War Office, and it was typical of his practical imagination to see how useful they were going to be in the near future, and to give them encouragement.[8]

So Prince Louis of Battenberg was supportive, but as a serving naval officer he could give little active help. That meant still more work for Roger, and the pressure often told on him. His diary includes a number of revealing comments: "I was feeling very ill," on one day and on another, "Relapse. Rush of work all day[;] evening tried to get drunk & couldn't."[9]

Another complication was the inaugural dinner he was organizing for Monday, 10 April 1905. He had to deal with many problems connected with the dinner, but he noted in his diary on 27 March the fundamental one: "Lonsdale tried to postpone dinner, but I held him to it." Even on 10 April he faced troubles: "All the Generals backed out of dinner. Replaced them from the Reserve list, & then made them come. Saw Lonsdale in the afternoon." Nonetheless, he was able to end that entry in his diary with the satisfied note: "Lord Lonsdale's dinner, inauguration of the Legion." Roger prepared an eighteen-page document for circulation at the dinner. By listing Lonsdale as the "Founder" of the Legion on that document, Roger paid the sort of compliment that would have met with Lonsdale's approval. The document also lists all the generals, admirals, and senior officers who supported the Legion and were due to attend the dinner. Although not all of them actually attended, Roger was satisfied. However, attendance at the dinner and support for the idea of the Legion did not indicate how active that support would be. It may have been helpful having Sir John French and Frederick Rimington on the list, but there are doubts about the value of their actual support. As well, Sir Frederick Maurice and Sir Percy Scott appear as members of the General Council in the Legion's literature over a number of years, although neither of them would have been happy with Roger in their social circle nor he with them around his campfires. As for the press, Roger wrote exultantly that "The whole of the London daily papers except one, are directly represented on Committee, and behind that are Sir Alfred Harmsworth, C. Arthur Pearson, Esq, and Baron de Reuter, the three men who own and run English journalism."[10] Thomas Henry Marlowe (1868–1935), editor of the *Daily Mail*, one of Harmsworth's papers, was associated with the Legion for thirty years, and C.B. Fry, one of England's best-known sportsmen, was listed as a member of the General Council.

Accounts of the inaugural dinner appeared in London newspapers, but one in Cumbria gave the clearest account of the events of the evening:

> Letters approving the project were received from General Sir Redvers Buller, General French, General Rimington, General Pole-Carew, Lord Methuen, Lord Tweedmouth, and Admiral Kennedy. A resolution, proposed by Sir. F. Maurice and seconded by Lord Brudenell-Bruce, was carried, pledging the meeting to assist in the organisation of those "self-reliant, adventurous, and expert frontiersmen of the British Empire willing to be enrolled for sport in preparation for war." On the motion of Sir Reginald Hart, V.C., seconded by General Sir E. Hutton, the meeting resolved itself into a committee, with the Earl of Lonsdale as chairman. On the motion of Sir Alfred [*sic*] Hime, late Premier of Natal, seconded by Colonel Serjeant, the president was empowered to nominate a general committee for the purpose of organising the legion. Among those who spoke in support of the proposal were Sir H. Seton-Karr, M.P., and Sir Gilbert Parker, M.P. The general opinion was that in many parts of the empire are men whose experience and training fit them to be of service in war, and that they may be enrolled and used in moments of national danger. The representative character of the gathering may be accepted as an augury of success.[11]

The *Daily Telegraph* also reported on the inaugural dinner, and listed many of the notable men at the dinner:

> Among those present were Lord Chesham, Lord C. Brudenell-Bruce, the Right Hon. Sir Albert Hime, Sir Percy Girouard, Sir Gilbert Parker, M.P., Commander Hamilton

Currey, Lieut.-General Sir Reginald Hart, V.C., Major-
General Sir E. Hutton, Major-General Sir F. Maurice,
Colonel Eldon Sergeant [*sic*], Colonel Weston Jarvis, Mr. C.J.
Cutcliffe Hyne, Mr. G.L. Jessop, Sir H. Seton-Karr, M.P.,
Mr. H. Lowther, Captain Vaughan, Mr. C.E. Stevens, and Mr.
Roger Pocock....

Roger came last on the list and no mention was made in the report that the
Legion was his idea. The reader would have received the impression that
the whole project had been instigated by Lord Lonsdale, who "explained
that they hoped to sweep into their net every sort of wild individual who
loved enterprise. There must be no kind of militarism in their ranks; the
men they wanted could be led anywhere, but driven nowhere; they were
the men who hunted and fought, the men who had done real frontier
work."[12]

As a result of that gathering, Roger was sidelined as the organizer and
the man who would do the hard work. He was not to be in any position
of real influence on the committees set up to control the Legion that he
had first envisaged and then brought into being, for he was of the wrong
social class. Still, at the end of that week, Roger wrote Frederick White,
Comptroller of the Royal North West Mounted Police, that "the time
[had] come now to explain the matter of the Legion of Frontiersmen in
the hope of winning [his] interest." He told White of the inaugural dinner
the previous Monday and of the "fiery enthusiasm of the 30 men present as
representatives of the frontier trades...." He was also happy to cite some
particular gains he had made:

> On the military side I have had the private help of the War
> Office, Generals Roberts, Buller, French, Hart, Hutton,
> Maurice, Methuen, Rimington, Pole-Carew; two officers of
> the Intelligence Department, War Office, are on Committee,
> and for some time I have been in contact with the Intelligence
> Department of the Admiralty. The Colonial Minister sent me
> a friendly message; I am in personal touch with the Foreign
> Office set, which is the core of Society.

As to the details of his plan, he enclosed a draft that represented the views
of all those involved and explained his own position:

> You will observe that the Legion is defined as enrolled
> for sport, prepared for war, but the sports are a direct

preparation for war, and the competitions in those sports will discover which are the best teams in the British Empire of guides, scouts, fighters, (raiders) and pioneers. When the Government or any Colony of the Empire has need of the Legion, these champion teams get the first call for war. The whole Legion must be civilian, self-supporting, and self-reliant, and it certainly cannot come under military authority.

You will understand how deeply and how strongly I have been influenced by two short years of service in the Mounted Police, when I confess that the whole project of the Legion is a device for catching and holding in the service of the Empire, ex-policemen of all the Police outfits like myself. We are all intolerant of British tactics of surrender, and strategy of flight, as we saw them when we fought in South Africa. If we fight again for the Empire, we must have our own organisation, our own methods, not those of any civilized army.[13]

In this letter Roger raised several issues that were guaranteed to cause problems. For example, his qualification that the Frontiersmen not submit to military authority made the group a challenge for any government, which cannot have a self-governing collection of amateurs charging around in time of conflict. Clearly Roger's heart was still with the Mounted Police, but his statement about "British tactics" was guaranteed to worry any high official. Nonetheless, Frederick White replied courteously that "In theory the idea is admirable from an Imperial point of view, but in practice I am afraid you would meet with almost insurmountable difficulties—particularly during an extended period of peace."[14] White also said he would be pleased to meet Roger if he came, as he suggested he might, to Canada.

The enthusiasm of the guests at the inaugural dinner (although certainly aided by good food and wine) calmed Roger for a few days; however, the pressure of publicizing and recruiting took its toll on his health, so he sought his usual cure of a short sea voyage. On 20 April he sailed on the SS *Toward* for Glasgow via Plymouth and Waterford, Ireland. On 26 April he took the train from Glasgow to Euston, and the next day he reported in his diary: "arr Euston 7 am feeling well again." Because Legion uniform had been selected—either a slouch hat or a Stetson, a shirt of either navy or khaki as suitable to the climate, a belt, breeches, and boots—on 1 May he wrote he was "getting Legion Kit" and the next day "Photo in legion [*sic*] dress by Bassano."[15] He used this as his publicity photograph and it has often been reproduced over the years. That weekend the new uniform played a role when he was again a guest of Lord Lonsdale. He arrived early enough on Saturday, 6 May, to be invited to take breakfast with Lady Lonsdale. That Sunday he attended Church Parade at a camp of the Imperial Yeomanry and dined at the officers' mess. On Monday he was pleased to report he "rode in the Legion dress as Lord Lonsdale's orderly—mistaken by Yeomanry for Major Burnham. dropped [sic] S[outh] A[frica] medal & offered prize, gave guinea to finder."[16] The size of the reward shows that he was probably allowing for the wealthy company he was keeping.

Possibly the influence of Lord Lonsdale was taking effect, because on 12 May 1905 Roger was able to report in his diary: "Got Salvage Corps, City Police, & Commission Chief of Jahore." He was Lonsdale's guest again that weekend. He rode with Lady Lonsdale on Saturday, 13 May, and was delighted to dine with the Duke of Lancaster's Own Imperial Yeomanry that weekend. On Monday he wrote: "Rode with Lonsdales, lunch, went out in motor car to see trial of [Lonsdale's] race horses. dined mess, Lancasters present[.] splendid day. left midnight."[17] Roger, the ex-policeman and ex-corporal, was being treated as an officer at last, and he found the experience to his liking. In his diary, on 16 May, he recorded optimistically: "[The interest of the] NWMP captured & [that of] Prince Louis of Battenberg, also county constabulary." Lord Lonsdale retained his interest in the Legion and Roger saw him regularly on Legion business. One of the other early members, Biscoe, claimed that he had secured Army officer Garnet Joseph Wolseley, first Viscount Wolseley (1833–1913), although Roger seems to have been doubtful: "Biscoe at lunch meeting alleged to have secured Wolseley." Within a week his suspicion of the man proved correct when "Biscoe wired demanding money. Wired discharging him from the Legion Staff."[18]

Even with his success as a recruiter, money was an immediate problem. Roger was not a good financial manager, and when a cheque was dishonoured on 23 June he had to wire Lord Lonsdale at Ascot for assistance. In addition, Roger's foot was still causing occasional problems with heavy bleeding, and he was finding that voluntary organizations without recourse to military discipline could have major personality conflicts. Thus many of the men he had enrolled in London thought that they were better equipped to be in a position of leadership than Roger, for he was more at ease with the rougher frontier types who looked in at the office on their way through London. Lonsdale was also beginning to find Roger exasperating and was steadily cooling to the idea of the Legion. That Roger constantly wrote to him and sent him wires might have played a role. Roger also wrote to Lord Esher asking for his help, and was nothing if not persistent. For example, in his diary on 14 July 1905, he noted that he spent "all day at [House of] Lords...trying to raise a crowd of bigwigs to force Lonsdale into committee meeting. Wrote warning Lonsdale that I was going to hold meeting anyway at Savoy next Friday. Wrote to Esher asking help." The next day Roger noted that "Lonsdale wrote consenting to my time & place of meeting." He called on Lord Esher on 19 July, and his pressure on Lonsdale succeeded, for according to Roger's diary, on 21 July there were "Councils & meetings all day long 9.30 A.M. to 7 P.M." As well, Lonsdale chaired a major meeting the following Friday, in the White Room at the Savoy: "Constituted General & Executive Committee, & appointed officers. Lord Freddy gave a dinner to executive.... After Executive dinner Kernick was nominated secretary of the Legion."[19] The following day Roger sailed for Newcastle where there was a strong Northern Command of forty-five members under Orde, which Roger officially inaugurated.

On 3 August Roger reported in his diary that he had "closed L[ondo]n Command for the season [&] read to them the story of Canada to Mexico ride." He complained in his diary the next day that he was "Completely worn out, head gone silly." It appears that the pressure had brought on a migraine, which lasted for several days until he travelled to Shrewsbury on 9 August, where he hired a horse. He began a leisurely journey by horse, train, and foot through Wales and across southern England, recording the mileage, scenery, and people he met, just as he had done on his rides in North America, until he arrived in London on 14 September. While he was enjoying the curative effects of travel, he was still receiving and writing letters. Thus on 1 September he recorded in his diary that he had received "Letters to say the King has asked for particulars about the Legion." However, as he travelled between London and the country he suddenly became very ill. His sister, Hilda, diagnosed his symptoms as erysipelas and as a senior nurse, she was able to advise him what to do.[20] All his sisters also told him that he should get a flat, rather than try to live and work at Adam Street, and in October he took their advice.

Despite the turmoil of ill health and a move, he was still delighted to attend dinners given to the officers of the Legion by its wealthy supporters. For example, "Sir H. Seton-Karr gave dinner at Gaiety to Legion officers, decided [to] approach War Office." Later Roger recorded that "Seton-Karr sent completed War Office petition to Lonsdale for signature."[21] In his diary Roger continued to record notable supporters recruited to the cause, including Sir Edward Ward, Sir Neville Lyttelton, and Lady de la Warr.[22] Roger managed to meet (Henry) Spenser Wilkinson (1853–1937), journalist, military historian, and spokesman for volunteer forces, on the third try, on 22 December 1905, but reported no success. In fact, in spite of all these eminent supporters, the Legion was bleeding money so severely that on 21 December Roger noted in his diary: "Legion balance on hand £0.0.0. Banker refuses further overdrafts." On 27 December he wrote, "Messages from Lady De La Warr that Lyttleton says 'Don't worry. I'll look after y[ou]r Frontiersmen.'" The next day Roger noted, "Lady Barrington began to help the Legion."[23] None of this influence really helped, however. Thus Roger's final diary entry for 1905, on 29 December, was "£123 left of my capital[;] took over payment of staff & office."

Money was not Roger's only problem. Conservative Members of Parliament had been well represented in the Legion hierarchy, so when the Liberals were elected in January 1906, Roger found that he had to start again with a new administration that was less inclined to see the value of the Legion. Lawyers consulted by the Legion's General Council advised that it would be unwise to proceed too far without official recognition from the War Office. So, "In December 1905, the Secretary forwarded to the War Office a statement showing the aim and objects of the Legion with a request for the 'tacit approval of the Crown and Imperial Military Authorities.'"[24] A deputation from the Legion was ordered to appear before the Army Council, where they were asked some searching questions, particularly by Sir Neville Lyttleton. Members of the Army Council may have been taken aback by Roger's reply to Lyttleton's query:

> Sir Neville Lyttelton, Chief of the General Staff, asked what
> we proposed to do in the event of war with Germany. As
> the only man present who knew, I was afraid to suggest the
> slightest interference with the Army. It would be less offensive
> if I mentioned one of our maritime projects, so the answer
> was: "Blow up the Kiel Canal, Sir."[25]

On 15 February 1906, Haldane (1856–1928), Secretary of State for War, replied to the Legion's request for approval. In that letter, Haldane's office informed the Legion:

> The Secretary of State for War desires me to inform you that
> he is in sympathy with the aims and objects of the above
> Legion and the formation of an organisation on the lines
> suggested appears to him to be free of difficulty.
>   Mr. Haldane also requests me to state that he thinks the
> Legion well advised as regards its principles of organisation,
> set forth in paragraph 4 of the private and confidential
> circular which you have submitted, providing that "the

Association shall be self governing and self-supporting,
in time of peace." He therefore, recognises the Legion as
a purely private organisation, in no way connected with
any department of State, but one which, should a suitable
occasion arise[,] he might be able to utilise.[26]

For very many years the War Office deeply regretted that letter, since it had not been worded as carefully as it should have been, particularly in its use of the word *recognise*.

Both Roger and the Legion were delighted to claim that the Legion was "officially recognised on 15 February 1906."[27] That led the War Office to deny "recognition" regularly, and often plaintively, and to insist that the phrase "take cognisance of the Legion" should always be used in any correspondence and never "recognise," although the difference in meaning is slight to the average reader of English.[28] This issue also arose as newspapers regularly printed news of the Legion, such as, "We are informed by the secretary of the Legion of Frontiersmen that the formation of the corps, which is to be a civilian, self-governing, and self-supporting force, has been officially approved by the Secretary of State for War, and that 6,000 men with colonial, frontier, and sea experience, have applied for enrolment."[29] In light of the War Office's regular denials of "recognition," it is surprising that as important and trusted a newspaper as the *Times* was not requested to publish a correction. Despite the disputes over the correct word, the letter was just what Roger needed, and he recruited with even greater effort. The letter also meant that instead of having to finance everything either from his own money or that of his wealthy backers, he felt able to request subscriptions.

The letter from the War Office also meant that the Legion could play a role in the arguments that were raging in official circles regarding the best way to reform the Army. Lord Roberts and others were firmly advocating conscription, but the path taken was a volunteer army and the formation of a Territorial Army of part-time reservists. "Such ad hoc units were hardly what Lord Roberts and his cohorts at the National Service League had in mind.... However, these new circumstances did create an opportunity for advocates of quasi-militaristic training for young people—among them Rudyard's friend Robert Baden-Powell...."[30] Roger was a supporter of the Territorial Army. He always wrote that any man eligible to do so should join the Territorials; otherwise, whatever his age and however distant the frontier where he laboured, he could be of service to his country in some way. Roger shared with Baden-Powell and Rudyard Kipling this belief that every man should play a role in the Empire:

Over the next couple of years [i.e., after May 1906] Baden-
Powell developed his ideas, mixing his own army scouting
experience with fashionable interest (which Rudyard
had helped create) in such subjects as the outdoor lore of
American Indians and the lives of frontiersmen.... Into this
cultural hotchpotch Baden-Powell also drew the popular
sense of a need for alertness in the face of the danger of
German invasion. (1906 saw the publication of the best-
selling book, *The Invasion of 1910,* by William Le Queux, a
journalist on Northcliffe's *Daily Mail.*)[31]

Indeed, there was always a linkage between the Legion and the Boy Scout
movement, but it was far more tenuous than either group would originally have liked. How much discussion occurred between Roger and
Baden-Powell has not been ascertained, nor is there any mention of Baden-
Powell in any of Roger's surviving diaries. However, James "Jungle Jim"
Biddulph-Pinchard, a Frontiersman who died in the 1980s, clearly remembered Baden-Powell saying, as an old man, that he had discussed the Boy
Scouts and the Legion of Frontiersmen with Roger. Biddulph-Pinchard's
father had also been a Frontiersman, and many early Boy Scout leaders
were Frontiersmen.[32]

In addition to the similarity of ideas, there are other links between
the Legion and the Boy Scouts. For example, Roger's sister Hilda had
been Nursing Superintendent at a Stationary Hospital at Mafeking. Sam
Steele, Roger's friend, had worked with Baden-Powell in the South African
Constabulary: "He [Baden-Powell] and Steele worked together on plans
to convert the S.A.C. from a military to a police and peace-keeping organization. Steele set out to train the officers and recruits along the lines
of the N.W.M.P."[33] This, of course, was also very much along the lines
that Roger was thinking for his Legion. Back in England, Steele worked
under Baden-Powell again in the Army, and for 24 February 1907, Roger
recorded "Supper 6.30 *Sam Steele*" in his diary. While there were probably no formal meetings between Roger and Baden-Powell, the many similarities in their organizations show a meeting of minds. There were also
probably other links through mutual acquaintances, such as those Roger
selected for positions of authority within the Legion. As well, one of the
Legion camps Roger attended in early September 1908 appears to have
been a joint gathering with the Boy Scouts. He thoroughly enjoyed himself
around the evening campfire, telling the Scouts stories of his adventures.
One of Baden-Powell's biographers was convinced of the influence of the
Legion on his subject:

the Legion undoubtedly made a considerable impact upon
Baden-Powell. The emphasis which he would soon place
upon "frontiersmen" as role models and heroes to the boys is
plainly due to the Legion. "Besides war scouts, there are also
peace scouts," he would write on the first page of *Scouting
for Boys* directed exclusively at boys rather than their
Scoutmasters. "These are the frontiersmen…the 'trappers'
of North America, hunters of Central Africa…the bushmen
and drovers of Australia, the Constabulary of North-West
Canada and of South Africa…." He might have been listing
the former avocations of typical members of the Legion of
Frontiersmen. When Baden-Powell launched the Boy Scouts,
many members of the Legion became Scoutmasters and
named their troops "Legion of Frontiers' Boy Scouts." Roger
Pocock would be a contributor to the very first edition of the
Boy Scouts' newspaper *The Scout,* in which Baden-Powell's
boys were described as "The Legion of Boy Scouts." The
fact that this name was ever seriously considered is another
indication of the extent to which Baden-Powell had been
influenced by Roger's creation. Nevertheless this was never
acknowledged; and the only direct reference to the Legion in
Scouting for Boys would be a recommendation to boys to read
The Frontiersmen's Pocket Book, first published by Roger in
1906 [*sic*].[34]

This is an example of how it was Roger's fate, throughout his life, seldom to be credited for his ideas and plans. There was also the link with
Rudyard Kipling. Although Kipling was a friend of Baden-Powell and
"both inspired and assisted" in the establishment of the Boy Scouts,[35]
Kipling would not have been keen on Roger's Legion, for his own efforts
were channelled to the National Service League, for "One issue Rudyard
never tired of harping on about was national service."[36] Kipling was, however, the spirit behind both the Scouts and the Legion.

Even with this respectable lineage, in order to recruit for the Legion
effectively, Roger still needed some form of rank or title other than just
"Secretary and Founder." He justifiably thought that society would not
approve of a man who had never held the King's Commission giving himself military rank, so he suggested that he be called Commissioner, feeling
that nobody would associate this with military rank. It was, in fact, a rank
used in his beloved NWMP in Canada, and the equivalent of Colonel.
Although some may have noticed this, nobody seems to have objected

Bivouac, Legion of Frontiersmen.
[Author, scan from the digital photographic archives of the
Legion of Frontiersmen (CMO) of a "Philco" postcard.]

publicly when he was described as "Founder and Commissioner" in a 1907 pamphlet. This addressed Roger's concern, but the concern of the gentlemen who governed the Legion that their Founder and main public figure was neither an officer, nor a gentleman, nor a war hero was eased towards the end of 1906 when Lt. Col. Daniel Patrick Driscoll (1862–1934) came into the Legion. Following a failed business venture, Driscoll arrived in London penniless, armed only with a letter of introduction to Roger. For once, Roger judged character correctly and gave Driscoll a paid job in the Legion. By the time of the first annual general meeting of the Legion on 24 June 1907, Driscoll had become London Commandant, and he eventually became Chief of Staff. He was by far the finest leader the Legion had in its first century. Driscoll worked constantly for the Legion and was often at Roger's side at recruiting meetings.

Throughout 1907, Roger's diary records his presence throughout the British Isles, attending inaugural meetings and also—his greatest delight— taking part in Legion summer camps where he could note, "Merry time in camp. Signalling drill"; "walked miles to a pub and got a skinful of whiskey"; "Worked all day, got eggs & mushrooms for camp"; "sing song 11 men in camp evening."[37] The only real problem early that year was the London Commandant, Manoel Herrera de Hora, who "assaulted Willard, who reported at club." That led to a "Meeting with SK [Seton-Karr] re[.] de Hora. Called meeting. SK suggests de Horas resignation"; "Executive meeting re[.] de Hora"; "de Hora trial expelled"; and "officers broke up de Hora's mutiny."[38] The pressure of all the work, travel, and meetings did take its toll on Roger later that year, but even on holiday he could not forget the Legion: "Health broken down with Brain fag. Went to the Grays at Bradford for holiday. Yorkshire Command was out on manoeuvres."[39]

While Roger was travelling throughout Britain to promote the Legion, Lena Ashwell, his formidable sister, was using her contacts within London theatre society to drum up support for the Legion. In both 1906 and 1907 she organized entertainments in London. For example, at a Garden Fête in support of the Legion at the Royal Botanic Gardens, Regent's Park, on 10 July 1906, Albert Chevalier and Lena Ashwell were among those who performed, but "The chief contribution by the legion itself was a performance called 'The Bivouac,' by the London command of the legion, under the direction of Commandant de Hora; this showed the arrival of a party of scouts at a camping ground, supper, songs, and slumber, and then the alarm and 'saddle and off.'"[40] January 1907 provided another demonstration:

> [The Legion] gave an assault-at-arms at Manchester.... The
> Lord Mayor attended in state to receive Lord Lonsdale, who
> presided over the proceedings. An interesting feature of the
> programme were two despatch rides—one from Newcastle-
> on-Tyne and the other from Portsmouth.... The assault-
> at-arms, which was witnessed by a large number of people,
> included sword, bayonet, foil, and singlestick combats, tugs
> of war, boxing contests, and exhibitions illustrative of camp
> and frontier life. It was announced that the Legion numbers
> 2,000 men in England and 800 in South Africa.[41]

Another entertainment, on Empire Day, 24 May 1907, was particularly spectacular, with an audience of 2,000 people and the band of the Coldstream Guards: "Fifty of the leading swordsmen in England, under the direction of the greatest of English swordsmen, Captain Alfred Hutton, gave a display of 'Combat in all Ages.' Two of our London Command men, Captain Graham Hope, R.A., and Mr. R.A. Smith, fought in suits of plate armour, weighing over 70 lbs."[42] Lena persuaded the well-known actor Norman McKinnel to direct a benefit for the Legion. Another public figure was also involved:

> Mr. C.J. Cutcliffe Hyne, the author and traveller, last night
> inaugurated a Bradford command of the recently formed
> Legion of Frontiersmen.... [He believed the] legion
> would form an admirable auxiliary to the existing forces by

providing scouts, pioneers, and other material which would
not be subjected to ordinary military discipline. Commands
had been formed in London, York, Newcastle, Manchester,
Cambridge, Plymouth, and other places. The King had
expressed his approval of the idea, and they were going to
make it a great success.[43]

Roger was thus successful in securing support from many people, but
government officials were never sure how to treat the Legion, with its mixture of eccentrics and men of power and influence in the highest circles.
Another issue was weaponry. It is interesting that the early Legion members seemed to be able to get away with the wearing of arms in public.
Photographs of Roger at the time usually show him armed, despite his
having asserted in *A Frontiersman* that he never liked carrying a gun, even
on his long rides through Canada and the United States. Later, Roger
agreed that they were contravening

> the Law as to Armed Assembly, for when three of us met
> bearing sidearms we were liable to a term of imprisonment.
> Moreover such is the Law that it was legal to carry ball
> ammunition, but illegal to carry blank cartridges. So
> Counsel's Opinion advised us to play at being rifle clubs....
> If we were good and played at rifle clubs, the whole of our
> propaganda to get men would be at advertisement rates in the
> newspapers, costing millions of pounds; whereas if we were
> bad and broke the Law we should have the free use of the
> news columns. And here we were outwitted, for the police
> had orders to leave us alone, because—Counsel's Opinion
> again—it is the unsocial motive which constitutes an offence,
> whereas our conduct was above reproach and our intention
> loyal.[44]

Nonetheless, during this period the War Office was not solely concerned
about the matter of "recognising" the Legion. It also had some concerns
about carrying arms:

> May, 1906. Enquiry as to whether the Legion could wear
> uniform, carry arms, and drill.
>   Reply that the wearing of uniform would not be illegal,
> but that drilling and carrying arms are a matter for the Home
> Office.

It was subsequently pointed out by Treasury Solicitor that it is illegal to raise an armed force without due authority from the Crown.

April, 1907. Request for authority to purchase ammunition at service rates.

Refused on grounds that the Legion is not affiliated to the National Rifle Association, and is recognised as a private organisation only.[45]

Despite the trouble over recognition and arms in this period, in Roger's diary, crowded with meetings and travel, on 24 June 1907 he simply recorded "Annual General Meeting. Dinner. Smoker." However, a newspaper account of that meeting, under the section head "Naval and Military Intelligence," made a point of naming some of the notable people involved and carrying an account of Lord Onslow's praise of the Legion's potential value in time of war:

> He could not help thinking that the idea, which he believed originated with Mr. Pocock, of forming a great Imperial force wholly separate from the Regular forces of the country, who would desire to act as the Legion wished to act, as guides, pioneers, and general helpers of the Regular forces, was of the greatest value, not only to Great Britain, but to the whole of the Empire, over which he hoped the movement would spread.[46]

So this first annual general meeting ended on an optimistic note, and Lord Lonsdale was re-elected president of the Legion. However, after Roger's three successful years of building the Legion and recruiting members, his critics became more active in 1908.

GERMAN SPIES
and
TROUBLES

BY FEBRUARY 1908 THE DISCORD over Roger's leadership became
very apparent in his diary. For 7 February he recorded, "S-K [Seton-Karr]
very brusque. Wanted my resignation. Wanted me to give the Council
a free hand, & to trust to its honour. Told me a retired major had been
found to take my place." Later Roger attributed this situation to German
spies,[1] but Seton-Karr was probably largely responsible for the decision
to replace Roger as head of the Legion. So despite several days of con-
sultations with others, on 10 February Roger noted that he "Drafted &
sent my letter of resignation & began to clear office for my successor. Got
wind that he was a distinguished ex administrator." Then on 13 February
it was clear that his critics had succeeded in relieving him of many of his
Legion responsibilities: "Ex[ecutive] Council. My resignation accepted.
Am appointed same rank & pay for promotion work. Met Major Forbes
the new Chief Ex[ecutive] officer." The appointment of Major Patrick
William Forbes is somewhat surprising, for although Roger called him the
"conqueror of Rhodesia," Forbes had taken the blame—or was simply the
scapegoat—for the Shangani Patrol affair in Rhodesia.[2] Although Roger
kept the title Commissioner, he was to concentrate entirely on promotional
duties and Driscoll was to continue as London Commandant.

Roger accepted his new position meekly and made friends with his new
superior, but he also found an escape from the pressures of the Legion
at the Imperial School of Colonial Instruction, an institution established

by Evelyn ffrench and Cecil Morgan at Shepperton. Morgan and ffrench built a log cabin on the school grounds, which they turned into a club they called El Desperado. There Roger, and his friends and acquaintances who had spent time in the Canadian and American West, could dream again that they were back in the wilderness and tell yarns around a camp-fire in the evenings. Often Roger would also sleep there in an imitation of frontier life.[3] About this time they also staged a demonstration of the pack-saddle and pack-boat, which Morgan invented, and in April, H.W. Koekkoek published a series of sketches of the pack-boat in the *Illustrated London News*.[4] Later that year Roger mentioned providing information for another Legion-related article: "photos for Sketch article on Scout Signs. Sam White, Mordaunt, Piggott, Burry, Tobrett & Daily Mail cooking demonstration, baking, roasting in earth, & clay cooking without dishes" (12 September); "Sketch article appeared on scout signs" (23 September).[5] Roger, Morgan, and ffrench were also interested in trying their hands at the new moving pictures. In his diary for 24 July 1908, Roger noted, "We did the Texas Elopement show for the Biograph. Hot day & great fun." They may have had fun, but they also had problems using the Thames as a stand-in for a Texas river:

> The Heroine had to embark over and over again because
> of things which happened on the Wild Texas River, such
> as a flotilla of swans or a wherry full of girls.... Afterwards,
> when we saw our picture presented at the Palace Theatre[,]
> even we could not tell what it was all about, or why the little
> people on horseback were bobbing up and down in the far
> distances of the Boundless Plains, while the pretty Jersey
> cows grazed undisturbed in the foreground.[6]

Roger needed these distractions, for the adverse press publicity he received made members of the Governing Council again feel that Roger had outlived his usefulness to the Legion. He never had universal approval for his position in the Legion he had worked so hard to bring into being, and stories in the *Daily Mail* and the *Times* late in 1908 regarding the disappearance of Sir Arthur Curtis did not help. Roger noted in his diary that the "Mail & Times brought up story of a new search for Sir Arthur Curtis. Express tried to interview me & published extract from A Frontiersman. Mail sent a man to my camp. All the papers worried me." A month later he wrote: "Rumours of Curtis alive in Ashcroft Dist. Curtis case up again in press. Interviews in plenty. Libel in Daily News. I referred to Langton."[7] Also, according to Roger, a colonel within the supporters of the Legion, whom he did not name, told King Edward that Roger was a notorious murderer who would have been hanged had the body been found. Fortunately, "Lord Lonsdale instructed a woman, and when the subject came up again at a dinner she said, 'Don't you think, Your Majesty, that a man must have a beastly mind to spread such slanders when anybody is trying to render a public service.' The King thought for a while. 'Perhaps so,' he said, and the matter was dropped."[8] Roger was quite impressed when he learned that he had been discussed in such company, but the cloud remained permanently over him. Thus, whereas in 1917 his sister Lena was appointed an Officer of the new Order of the British Empire (OBE) for her Concert Parties for the troops in the First World War, Roger never received any official recognition or honour for all his service to the British Empire. Roger's service through the Legion should certainly have qualified him, but the constant rumours of his alleged part in the disappearance of Sir Arthur Curtis, and the fact that the War Office, in particular, held a permanently low opinion of the Legion, would have countered any suggestion of an award for Roger had anyone suggested it.

As if the bad publicity about Curtis were not enough, in February 1909 Roger made such a silly and very public mistake that only his closest friends could disagree that it was time for him to leave the Legion. A new, fairly small circulation magazine, *The Modern Man: A Weekly Journal of Masculine Interests,* launched a scathing attack on the Legion under the heading, "The Legion of Humbugs": "From time to time Londoners and inhabitants of other parts of the country are startled by the apparition in their midst of weird horsemen, whose attire suggests that they are the advance guard of a Wild and Woolly West circus show." The writer called Legion members "preposterous humbugs" and "patent frauds" who wore "grotesque garb which no real frontiersman ever wore..." The author of the piece then made the following dismissive suggestion:

> If the Legion of Frontiersmen want to soldier as civilians, let them join the Territorial Army and be merged in the crowd.
> But with their ridiculous costumes, their fondness for posturing in public processions, their theatrical amblings about the countryside, they simply make fools of themselves, and are recognised at their true worth as pinchbeck warriors.[9]

A month later the editor of *Modern Man* published Roger's reply, prefaced by the statement that "His name must be familiar to every reader, for, whether the Legion is or is not what Mr. Gray-Reid asserts it is, there can be no doubt that, but for Mr. Pocock's initiative and powers of organisation, it would never have had an existence at all."[10] Roger defended the uniform in detail and addressed the question:

> What in thunder are we doing here?
> Earning our living.
> Each week members come home on business or pleasure, reporting to our Home Commands.
> Each week members sail from England who will bring news to our Commands overseas.
> So we manage to keep touch between say, the White Horse, Newchang, and Blantyre Commands; Leeds has news of outlying men in Thibet; and the man just in from Banksland meets the chap from Tierra del Fuego at a Legion meeting in Glasgow.

Unfortunately, Roger preceded his calm and reasoned account of the objects of the Legion and the background of its members with a foolish challenge:

> We cannot pretend to meet in verbal debate so alert and witty a writer, and it would be beneath his dignity as a gentleman to challenge us merely to a duel of words.
> We ask him rather in what exercise of manly skill he prefers to make good his personal challenge.
> In all courtesy, and under the rules of his own special variety of pugilism, wrestling, or of any other lawful combat, we would like to make him known to a member of the Legion of his own size, weight, and degrees of training.
> In all details we will conform so far as we can to his wishes.[11]

Making such a challenge, without first seeking the advice of wiser men, or even considering what response it would bring, has to be considered an act of monumental stupidity. Of course the author of the original attack delightedly took up the challenge and turned it back on Roger. He wrote that he was thirty-seven, bald, with false teeth, and a liver complaint:

> All I know about Mr. Roger Pocock is that he has written some admirable books; of his physical qualifications I know nothing.

He has challenged me to combat, and I am ready to take him on. I do not want to fight any other member of the Legion. He is its representative, and he shall be my adversary. Unless his challenge was made in mere bravado, he must meet me.

Gray-Reid chose swords as his weapon, Belgium as the place, since duelling was still legal there, and the editor of *Modern Man* as his second.[12] For some weeks this story made front-page copy for *Modern Man* and very bad publicity for the Legion. Roger and the Legion wisely kept publicly silent, although at the next meeting of the Executive Council Roger was taken to task in the strongest possible terms. A month later the Legion did make a public statement:

Mr. Roger Pocock made this challenge on his own authority, without any official sanction, and the Legion of Frontiersmen is not responsible for his action, neither should it suffer for his ill-considered impetuousness.

He had no authority for challenging you, and the ridicule which he has called down on himself must be borne by him alone. The challenge was not made by the Legion, and it is unfair that we should suffer for Mr. Roger Pocock's errors of judgement.[13]

The editor of *Modern Man* then moved on to attack Baden-Powell and the Boy Scout movement. The only positive point that can be made is that both the Boy Scouts and the Legion are still active, while *Modern Man* is long forgotten. However, in the months after the challenge, much of the energy of the Governing Council was directed at removing Roger from the Legion.

There were some writing distractions for Roger during this troubled time. His book *The Dragon-slayer* was re-issued as *Sword and Dragon* (1909) and he was also working on a "scientific romance," *The Chariot of the Sun*.[14] It is almost unreadable now, but it does have interesting but inaccurate predictions about war in the air. Years later, Roger was quite proud that he "had long foreseen" war in the air.[15] We might wonder whether he had read *The War in the Air* (1908) by H.G. Wells before he wrote this book.[16] Roger's tale is set much further in the future, however, in 1980, the year of the "World-Storm," with the narrator's prologue dated 31 December 2000. In his narrative Roger introduces airplanes with "gauze" propellers and monorail trains that leave London at 9 A.M. and arrive in

Cornwall by noon. By 1980 London's population has increased to 10 million, all slums have been replaced with decent housing, and democracy and equality have expanded so that "a carpenter can chat with a Colonel." Thanks to treachery, Russians invade Britain with their allies, the Germans and the French. This war is fought by airplanes in fleets, like naval ships in the air. However, Britain and Queen Margaret are saved by John Brand III with his "etheric ships" and some Yukon frontiersmen. Queen Margaret then sends her viceroys out to secure world peace.

Roger was also in the early stages of thinking out *Jesse of Cariboo*, which he began writing in October 1909. Most of his publishing efforts in this period, though, were directed at a book that became a best seller, *The Frontiersman's Pocket-book*. Sales were ensured because it was treated as the Legion training manual, so every member would have wished to own a copy. As well, it was required reading for Scoutmasters, and Baden-Powell recommended that boys read the book.[17] Roger, as compiler and editor, persuaded forty-six Legion members and twenty-two non-members, some of them quite famous, to contribute articles on their particular interests. Even with this success in rounding up contributors, as early as April 1909 Roger was soliciting comments that could be incorporated into a second edition.[18] This was his final major contribution to the Legion before he left it. There can be no doubt that he gathered together some of the best experts of the time and produced a startlingly practical book for its intended purpose. To make this very point, a declaration was added to the second impression:

> This is a volume of instructions given with clear brevity by
> experts and distinguished authorities, on every phase of
> wilderness life, and travel by land and water in all climates.
> Apart from the individual training which produces a
> Frontiersman and instructions for making all appliances
> needed by travellers, there are chapters on Scouting,
> Shooting, Signalling, and other military subjects, the conduct
> of irregular campaigns, the art of administration in savage
> countries. The book is, in fact, a brief summary of the art of
> pioneering and empire-building. It contains a Dictionary
> of Medical and Surgical Treatment in camp, without drugs
> or instruments. Prepared for the use of the Legion of
> Frontiersmen, this volume will be of great value to Explorers,
> Travellers, Soldiers, Campers, and Yachtsmen.[19]

The preface, probably written by Roger, was more direct: "For a man on the frontier in time of need, the conditions are: That he is broke, and beyond reach of shops, while he wants water, food, guidance, fire, shelter, clothing, and equipment."[20] This book was designed to provide help on all those counts. "Simple medical and surgical treatment when no doctor can be obtained" is particularly fascinating. The book also shows something of the ideas of Roger and his friends in the Edwardian era. While to our eyes it may be little more than a curiosity, at the time it was considered a very useful book.

The names of quite a few of the contributors appear in Roger's diary for 1908, as well as such statements as "Legion Book accepted by John Murray" (29 July); "Legion Book proofs all day" (14 September); and "Lord Muskerry & FC Selous have promised articles in Book. Setting illustrations into text" (16 October). Hamilton Matthew Tilson FitzMaurice-Deane-Morgan, 4th Baron Muskerry (1854-1929), yachtsman and Irish Representative Peer, and Frederick Courteney Selous (1851-1917), hunter and explorer, did indeed contribute ("The Empire on the Sea" and "Game Preservation" respectively), as did Roger's personal friend and fellow Legion member, Cutcliffe-Hyne (who provided several brief pieces in the "Appliances" section and one on reindeer). Other Legion members who contributed are now little known, but a number remain familiar. Erskine Childers (1870-1922), who contributed "Boat Sailing," was a member of the Governing Council, although for many years after his execution in Ireland the Legion tried to distance itself from him.[21] Ewart Grogan (1874-1967), then famous primarily for his journey on foot from the Cape to Cairo, contributed an intelligent article on "Heat: Dress, Equipment, and Management."[22] Roger persuaded Sam Steele to contribute "Conduct of Irregular Horse." Among the non-members who contributed was Sir Frederick John Dealtry Lugard (1852-1945), then governor of Hong Kong, who wrote on "Administration." Henry Hutchinson Montgomery (1847-1932), Secretary of the Society for the Propagation of the Gospel and father of Bernard Law Montgomery, the Field-Marshal, wrote a stirring introduction to the "Morale" section:

If you die, no matter. There is a Watcher above, pen in hand.
When the call of the Empire sounds, you will know your
duty. Wounded enemies and prisoners will learn what British
chivalry is; women and children of the foe will come over to
you for protection even while you fight: and when peace is
restored again the enemies of yesterday will enrol themselves
under you.[23]

John Walter Edward Douglas-Scott, second Baron Montagu of Beaulieu (1866–1929), wrote "The Value of Motor Boats in a Naval War," while Selwyn Francis Edge (1868–1940), automobile entrepreneur and race car driver, wrote "Motor Cars and Modern Warfare." Two women also contributed to the book: Elizabeth Robins (1862–1952) wrote "Women on the Frontier: Dress, Equipment, and Management," while Roger's sister Hilda contributed her nursing expertise to the medical section. Some other articles varied from the intriguing to the gruesome, such as some of the medical treatments to be used on the frontier "when no doctor can be obtained." A substantial portion of the text is credited to specific people, even if that person wrote only a few sentences with a narrow focus, and a few small portions are credited to "the editor," including, appropriately, part of the entry on "frost bite." However, it is highly likely that Roger wrote the text that is not specifically attributed. He was probably not able to lay claim to all the text he wrote because that would have offended the Legion officials, since it was supposed to be an authorized Legion book. He mentioned in his diaries seeking his share of the proceeds of its sales, which supports the significance of his contribution.

In addition to the immediate success of *The Frontiersman's Pocketbook,* things looked brighter in May when the Military Correspondent of the *Times* wrote on "The Territorial Force," and suggested "a subsidy of £1,000 a year might enable the executive council to make the Legion a success."[24] In response, Roger's sister Lena wrote on behalf of "this splendid corps":

> They belong to the class which made the Empire, and are
> trying to organize for its defence. They have never asked
> for help, but they are much too poor to meet the cost of
> increasing their numbers, and their funds—never more
> than £700 a year—are now at an end. Unless they can get
> support the office which raised the Legion must be closed.
> Surely there are sufficient people who have the heart and
> imagination to save this valuable force from being lost to the
> nation. Could a patriotic fund be opened to save the Legion
> of Frontiersmen and make it a success? If so, I shall be very
> glad to subscribe £50 to the fund. Should a public *matinee* be
> of use, I shall be only too glad to organize one.[25]

On 12 May 1909 Roger noted in his diary: "Organizing Patriotic Fund." One repercussion followed almost instantly:

We have learnt with surprise that the following appeal has been somewhat widely circulated:—

PRIVATE AND URGENT.
May 12, 1909

A Patriotic Fund is to be opened under the auspices of *The Times* to finance the Legion of Frontiersmen. Support is being organized on a large scale, but in the meantime the interest must be sustained. Mr. Roger Pocock appeals to his personal friends, and asks everybody who cares for the welfare of the legion [*sic*] to get sums of money from a shilling upwards, with letters, in support, addressed to the Legion Fund, care of Miss Lena Ashwell, Kingsway Theatre, London, W.C.

The statement that a Patriotic Fund is to be opened under the auspices of *The Times* to finance the Legion of Frontiersmen is entirely unfounded; and Mr. Pocock has expressed to us his sincere regret for circulating it. All that *The Times* has done has been to print Miss Lena Ashwell's appeal, which, it will be seen, Sir Henry Seton-Karr supports.[26]

Beneath this statement was Seton-Karr's letter expressing gratitude for Lena's support and reiterating how the Legion had "made remarkable progress on very slender resources." He went on to argue for the Legion's importance and the need for stable funding for the next three years. As a postscript he mentioned that he had "received a promise of £50 for three years towards the £1000 per annum required from a well-known and phil- anthropic peer, whose name I am not yet at liberty to mention."[27]

Despite this proposed support, the Executive Council wanted to see Roger removed from the Legion. Roger's 1909 diary provides a vivid pic- ture. Rival faction within the Legion jostled for power and key members resigned.[28] As matters deteriorated, Roger escaped briefly to join Orde's camp at Warkworth on 29 May, but as soon as he returned to London on 1 June events began swirling around him again. On 2 June, he wrote "Gen Hildyard declined command of Legion. Lena told me to wait till after Ex[ecutive] meeting. Issued Ex[ecutive] Notice 'to receive important letter from Sec for War.'"[29] And then suddenly events seemed to be taking a turn for the better, and on 11 June Roger noted "11 am Esher's secretary told me call 3[.] Forbes disclosed rumour. 3pm. Esher said that subject to abolition of Council & Appointment of his nominee as Commandant Gen[eral] he would grant £500 a yr for 1 yr trial. I to have £300 a yr. Wired Forbes. Wrote SK demanding dissolution of Council." However, Roger was not to be satisfied. On Saturday he "Wrote to various of the Council, tamed Driscoll completely. 5.50 [train] to Cookham to find Col Ricardo, Esher's nominee. All my wolves are smiling now because I gave them the Council to eat instead of me—bless 'em. Called on Col Ricardo at Cookham[;] first impression bad appointment" (12 June). He spent an hour on Sunday morning placing his "Legion scheme" before Ricardo, who told him that he would consider the proposition. However, Roger noted various other meetings in his diary, including on 15 and 16 June, when he simply wrote "alarums & excursions" and "ditto."

So Roger found himself in an unequal power struggle with Seton-Karr, but he did find time to dine a couple of times and to visit the theatre with a Miss Crawshay.[30] She must have been unusually independent for the time as she appears to have owned a motor car, but he never again mentioned her in his diary. In addition to this presumably pleasant time with her, Roger relieved the pressure of Legion events on 17 July by taking a tent and camping out in Wembley Park, where a number of his friends came to visit him. One of those pressures was money, since the Legion had been paying him, but he reported in his diary: "12th last payment of salary."[31] At the end of that month, Roger wrote that "Esher appointed Currey in Charge of L[egion of] F[rontiersmen] & handed over £500 a yr" (28 July). As Hamilton Currey was no more than a retired naval Commander who became a popular author, this appointment looks as if Esher was willing to take the first safe pair of hands he could find within the Legion.

An interesting question is why Esher agreed to lend a hand and find a use for the Legion. The explanation may be that Legion members had been at the enthusiastic heart of the German spy mania that gripped Britain, and had been vigorously forwarding details on "German spies" to any government department that would accept them. The roots of this activity may be traced to Erskine Childers, an early Governing Council member and author of *The Riddle of the Sands: A Record of Secret Service Recently Achieved* (1903). His book was very effective because "The story seemed as if it ought to be true; and for this reason it caused a sensation when it came out.... It inaugurated a new and even more sensational fiction about German intentions which was developed in many later works, especially in Le Queux's notorious *Invasion of 1910...*."[32] Many of the public figures who were loudest in their complaints about Germany, such as William Le Queux and R.D. Blumenfeld (1864–1948), editor of the *Daily Express*, were also keen members of the Legion. Le Queux's books were all bestsellers:

As he travelled around Europe, dropping names as he went, hinting at confidential missions on which he was engaged, striking up acquaintances in the underworld of part-time agents, Le Queux gradually built up a reputation "to his obvious delight" as a "man of mystery." He persuaded Gustav Steinhauer, the German spymaster, that he "had more than a nodding acquaintance with most of the spies of Europe." But his most important conquest was Lieutenant-Colonel James Edmonds, who became responsible for counter-intelligence and "secret service" at the War Office in 1907.[33]

Le Queux's *The Invasion of 1910* was treated by fellow Frontiersmen as foreshadowing the future, for they were convinced that England had hundreds of German spies among the working population. Le Queux claimed to be the first person to warn Great Britain that the Kaiser was plotting a war:

> I discovered, as far back as 1905, a great network of German espionage spread over the United Kingdom.[34]

Roger was one of the most fervent believers in the German threat: "Along our coasts an astonishing number of respectable 'Swiss' residents had houses overlooking the sea, possibly with apartments to let. In one such house the billiard-room had skylight blinds, opened or closed by working a lever beside the fireplace. From the lighted room one could thus flash signals in the Morse code to a submarine in the offing."[35] War Office records list many "intelligence reports" sent in by the Legion, usually over Roger's signature. We may accept that some of these had value, but the Frontiersmen were among the foremost scaremongers at a time when many newspapers and magazines were warning of the German menace. Blumenfeld, for example, was convinced of the existence of German spies:

> The Germans are "mapping out" East Anglia for future reference. I learned to-night that several mysterious strangers—one of whom I have met near my own place in north-west Essex—have been bicycling and driving and photographing all over the county, particularly along the coast, making sketches and taking notes. Looks like a staff ride. The War Office has been told about these activities. Every time a report is made the spying ceases mysteriously,

and then a week or two later it begins again. There is little doubt that the German Army is well represented in East Anglia; but every time I call attention to their spy system I am assailed by the Radicals and called a mischief-maker.[36]

A week later Blumenfeld and Roger met, and most probably discussed this.[37] As a sample of his fascination with spies, Roger made a number of notes about them in the front cover of his 1909 diary: "4 m[iles] inland from Stranraer or Port Patrick Private firm have meadows—This is a blind German expert Depot. 2 Zeppelin ships—being tested in suitable places. hilly.... For 3 yrs a wooden air ship has been building & testing, at Friern Barnet, of London, German. Opp[osite] an Institute called the Freehold." He was not entirely taken up with spies, however, for on the endpapers in his 1908 diary he wrote information on when to contact various periodicals with articles, and on a page meant for addresses he wrote such useful frontier tips as "Kit Carson sat back to fire, to keep eyes in focus. Acacia tree has suckers always reaching to fresh water within 15 ft. Whereas the bed of a creek may be salt."

While Roger could also focus on other matters, he was—very much in the spirit of the times—certain that waiters were involved in spying: "When our Legionaries dined at a restaurant they would often pretend to talk military secrets, just for the fun of collecting a perfect buzz of attendants. Members who spoke German with the proper rasp would order a waiter-spy to name his reporting station, and with a click of the heels the German would respond. It was always a town on the coast."[38] There were typical elements within these accounts:

> The one feature common to all invasion stories was the ubiquitous activity of spies and saboteurs. Resident aliens, usually masquerading as waiters or barbers, would pave the way for an invading force by supplying vital intelligence. Nor was this theme confined to the lucubrations of febrile journalists in penny novels and the half-penny press, but appeared in articles in ostensibly serious journals of opinion.[39]

Baden-Powell was also easily deceived by some of the "intelligence" that could be purchased from a "spy bureau" in Brussels,[40] but it was evidence from Edmonds, some originating from Le Queux, that convinced Haldane, and the Committee of Imperial Defence (CID) on which Esher served, that the time had come to set up a secret service bureau.

The sub-committee of the CID was satisfied that "an extensive system of German espionage exists in this country, and that we have no organisation for keeping in touch with that espionage and for accurately determining its extent or objectives."[41] The opinions that may have led the CID to look towards the Legion for intelligence work were strengthened because "The desire of His Majesty's government to disassociate itself from the opprobrium of spying was reinforced by the wish for a mechanism that prevented unscrupulous information-peddlers from thinking that they were on to a good thing by being directly in touch with government."[42] So the Legion could offer a system of information gathering controlled by the officers and gentlemen of the Legion Council, and no Army officer would have to sully himself with any distasteful spying activities, as long as a way could be found to dispose of the troublesome Roger or find him a job where his blunders would not be so public. It was also necessary to be sure that the information would, in fact, be directed via the gentlemen of the Legion Council, so that the sillier stories Roger thought valid could be filtered out. What was not considered, however, was the personal support that Roger believed he enjoyed from the rank and file "range" men on the frontiers:

> Daily for four and a half years I had letters or visitors to
> keep me in contact with frontier affairs: with the pearlers of
> Thursday Island, the trappers of Lake [sic] St. Anne, the
> ranchers in Patagonia, sea captains at Rangoon, gold miners
> in Chihuahua, or some last remotest prospector in the Vale of
> the Kamschatka, or behind the Karakorum.[43]

Roger considered himself one of these "range" men, who were "trained through initiative for field intelligence," rather than one of the ex-soldiers "trained through discipline for fighting."[44]

At a meeting held on Saturday, 28 August, which was recorded as the "First Annual General Meeting of 1909," both Roger and Hamilton Currey were voted out. The powerful London Command, which would have included among its members most of the Legion officers with influence in the British corridors of power, had already caused problems for Roger. London was the centre of the British Empire, so events affecting London Command always held pride of place in the Legion magazine, and London considered itself the senior Command. Consequently, although Roger had to be invited to meetings of the Legion Governing Council, London Command would probably no longer have considered it necessary to involve their independent-minded founder in every one of their meetings. In his notes he identified one of those meetings he might have preferred not to attend: "Notes of the London Command Bear baiting when I was the bear: London Command to represent the other Commands by proxy."[45] In his diary for 28 August Roger wrote as follows:

> Ann[ual] Gen[eral] Meeting 3 pm Currey & Committee outvoted 250 men against, those in support silent. Currey, Orde, WE Smith & I left meeting & went to Scarboro for northern meeting. Orde very ill in train. left [sic] him at York. Arr Scarboro camp 10 pm. informal [sic] meeting in tent.
>
> Scott's wire arr[ived] reporting London Council with Col. Walker sec. Hilda had taken possession of office & wired.

On Monday, 30 August, Roger returned to London to find that Hilda, one of his redoubtable sisters, and a Miss Brewer had removed all records from the Legion office, probably illegally. After discussions with a number of Legion members, Lena lent Roger money so he could travel to Scotland to talk to Esher, a meeting he later he described in more detail: "Lord Esher was at breakfast while I reported, standing, very tired, cold, and hungry, not at my best. Once he interrupted, shouting to his son in the next room: 'Come here and listen. It's the Middle Ages.'"[46] Esher told Roger to return home and do nothing until he contacted him again. While Roger waited for word from Esher, he spoke to more people, attended more meetings, and described more betrayals, which led him to seek some relief by going sailing after Esher's orders arrived on 20 September. This meant there were several quiet days in his diary.

Roger's diary may have been relatively empty, but the Legion Council members seem to have been adamant that they wanted Roger to be excluded from any power within the Legion and Serjeant to replace him as overall Commandant. Roger began plans for legal action against Serjeant, although the cost of civil action would have been well beyond his means. Finally, the "Second Annual General Meeting of 1909" was held on 15 October according to Roger's diary, but the Minutes of the meeting show it was held on the evening of 16 October. Roger said that as a result of this meeting he was finally expelled from the Legion, but the Minutes do not confirm that. What they do show is that Roger was not elected to either the General Council or the Executive Council, which left him with no official position within the Legion. He became just an ordinary Frontiersman. It seems that he could not accept this demotion and equated it with expulsion, which it was not. The impression given by the Minutes is that the vast majority of those present were on the side of the chairman, Sir William

Serjeant, and opposed to Roger. In Serjeant's address to the meeting he played down Roger's importance to the formation of the Legion, and re-ferred to the "so-called annual general meeting, held here on August 28 last." Serjeant continued:

> certain events which led up to that meeting, which, in addition to the incidents which occurred at the meeting, it will be necessary for me to deal with to-night. The time has come when it is absolutely necessary to proclaim the truth. It is not my intention to pain anyone, whether he be absent or present, but we have to disclose a sore on our body in order that we may treat it. Hitherto it has been kept more or less a secret and under cover, and we have not been able to get at it. But we are now about to effect a cure, and we intend to treat it accordingly. Some years ago, when this organisation developed into the Legion of Frontiersmen, I believe Mr. Pocock, though he possessed no monopoly of the idea, was the first to discuss it in the Press, and I was one of his first correspondents. I saw a great future before a movement of this sort, and invited him to come to my chambers in the Temple, to exchange ideas. We discussed it at length, and at last it took definite shape and form. Commander Hamilton Curry [*sic*], R.N., managed to interest his old friend and chief, Lord Lonsdale—a fine sportsman, as you all know—in the movement. Lord Lonsdale very generously found the preliminary funds to support the project, and we owe a great deal to Commander Hamilton Curry [*sic*] for securing that support. But his Lordship did more than this. Having secured a list of names of very distinguished men interested in works of this sort—patriots to the backbone—Lord Lonsdale invited those noblemen and gentlemen to his house in town at an inaugural dinner, and thus the Legion was started.
>
> Mr. Roger Pocock, the founder of the Legion, had practically a free hand from its commencement, and he had the loyal support of everyone connected with it.

After thus downplaying Roger's input, Serjeant also attacked Roger's need to draw remuneration from the Legion to cover the costs of his time and his travel recruiting for the Legion:

I do not believe there is a single man on the Council of the
Legion who desires to get any credit or any remuneration, or
any advantage out of the Legion, beyond the satisfaction of
knowing and feeling that he is assisting men like ourselves to
perform their duty to their King and country in emergency,
and Mr. Pocock had the advantage of the assistance of these
disinterested noblemen and gentlemen, who supported
him to the very best of their ability by their intelligence and
experience, and with their financial resources, from the very
start.[47]

Serjeant and many others within the Legion of his social class were men
of independent means, and Serjeant was not prepared to take into consideration Roger's limited means or how much he had spent from his own
funds. Serjeant then quoted from a "surprising" letter he had received
from Roger on 24 June. Roger wrote that there had been a decline in financial support that he blamed on the activities of the Council, and that "At
the beginning of this year we had to surrender our salaries—(laughter)—
and the staff has been working without salaries or other tangible means
of support."[48]

It became even more obvious that Serjeant, not Roger, had the support
of the meeting when Serjeant prompted the group: "The question has
been put by Mr. Pocock in a private letter to his friends: 'Are you to be
ruled by Serjeant or by Pocock?' (Cries of 'Serjeant.')." Further questions
were raised regarding finances:

Sergeant-Major Fenwick: Are we to have a balance-sheet
so that we may know, sir, what is to become of the 15s.
subscriptions we paid in?

The Chairman: You must be aware that prior to this
crisis something was evidently wrong with the management.
The financial arrangements were such as not to conduce to
the complete understanding we should like and which we
intend to promote in future. One of the first duties of the new
Executive Council, when formed, will be to inquire into the
financial arrangements of the Legion and to give everyone
satisfaction as far as possible.[49]

Roger's concern that Frontiersmen around the world were being disen-
franchised would have been answered, he suggested, by a motion proposed by Alfred Bottomley: "That in all important affairs of the Legion

a postal vote of all members of the Legion should be taken." Roger told the gathering that if such a motion were passed, it would help the Legion become "an authorised force." Nonetheless, those present considered that it would take far too long to receive a reply from Frontiersmen in far-flung countries, so a watered-down amendment was passed that did nothing to address Roger's concerns: "That a postal vote of members in the United Kingdom may be taken on all important subjects in such a way as the Executive may direct."[50] Roger's later account is contradicted by the Minutes. Roger claimed, "I submitted a motion prepared by Alfred Bottomley, who had lately been killed on duty. Jeers at my 'dead friend' from the Chairman were followed by my formal expulsion from the Service...."[51] There is no reference in the Minutes to any offensive comments about Bottomley by Serjeant, who in fact said that "He [Bottomley] was a most promising officer, and his loss we all very much deplore."[52] Nor is there any mention of expulsion. In fact Lord Mountmorres said, "To-day we have finished, I hope, the whole confusion the Legion has been in during the last two years. (Cheers). Let us bury the axe."[53]

Roger could not bring himself to write the details in his diary, which had previously been full of notes, meetings, and names of supporters and opponents. All he wrote for that day was: "2nd General Meeting 5 pm. Lt. Fortune of Dublin arr[ived] 8 am break-fast." However, several months later, when a Legion member commiserated with him, Roger described his feelings positively:

> Please set aside any illusion that I have personal interests, or personal quarrels. By leaving the Legion I return from destitution to prosperity as a novelist. I fought for a principle, a policy...honest government—and was expelled.
>   Even if I could accept the acquaintance of the men who expelled me I could not compromise with dishonesty, or tolerate a tenderfoot administration.
>   Convalescent from six months of illness I am now free.[54]

On 16 October Roger wrote plainly in his diary: "Went to live at Westgate with Ethel." His departure from the Legion he had formed was so traumatic that he could no longer face his London friends and needed to escape to Kent to live with his sister. He made no more entries in his diary until more than a month later, on 22 November: "Peggy coming. Couldn't wear boot to meet her, she called in doctor, & wound breaking out." His next note read: "to Town to see about wound" (25 November). Through all this the family had heard nothing from Esher, until he visited Roger on 6 December, "in response to a stinging letter from Daisy & offered to make peace between Serjeant & me. Daisy declining, he said he'd 'see about it.'" The next day Roger noted in his diary that "Scott found out that Esher had subsidized the enemy—£300. He called at the office & verified the fact."[55] There was no going back.

It was not just the Legion that presented problems. Roger's frost-damaged foot was again causing trouble, so on 8 December he underwent a ninety-minute operation under chloroform to remove decayed bone in his foot. The operation was carried out by Donald Armour, a Harley Street surgeon. Presumably the influence of Roger's new brother-in-law gave him an introduction to one of the best specialists available.[56] After the surgery on his foot it became apparent that Roger still had many friends. He was able to write the names of fourteen visitors who called the day following surgery, including Ada Wright, Lady Barrington, Hugh Pollard, and several Frontiersmen.[57] He decided to draw a line under the painful events of recent months and start afresh, so above 16 December 1909 he wrote "resumed diary," although he actually made no further notes in 1909.

Roger found it hard to believe that the Legion he had formed could exist without him, and thus took a long time to compose a farewell letter to the Legion. He was approached in July 1910 about a reconciliation, but pride made him insist on a full apology. There was no way that this would be forthcoming, particularly since the Legion was thriving under the natural leadership of Driscoll and without Roger's meddling. Roger nonetheless did meet a number of Legion members socially, particularly since many were fellow members of the Savage Club, where he occasionally spent time. In his diary he reported meeting Driscoll, but more often he met Evelyn ffrench, Fife Scott, Lord Mountmorres, and H.S. Orde. His friendship with Ada Wright seems to have blossomed, and he noted their appointments for tea, supper, and dinner.[58] Yet again, there is the impression that the relationship was not allowed to proceed, because her family would have disapproved of Roger's colourful past, particularly the stigma of the disappearance of Sir Arthur Curtis.

Roger began his diary for 1910 at 36 Grosvenor Street, London, which was Lena's home with her new husband. "Henry [Simson] is pulling me through after operation on my foot," wrote Roger. "Wound healing rapidly. Able to use crutches & go down to meals. Working at the Jesse stories & a farewell letter to the Legion."[59] This new book was published in Britain as *Jesse of Cariboo*, but it gained greater sales and success in North America under the title *A Man in the Open*, and was even made into a silent film.[60] Hughes Massie, Roger's agent, thought it also had more potential: "My dramatic manager thinks well of the chances of 'THE [*sic*] MAN IN THE

The cover of *A Man in the Open*, Roger's most successful book.
[Courtesy of the University of Alberta Libraries.]

OPEN.' Will you drop in by arrangement some day after January 1st, when my dramatic office formally opens and meet her?"[61] In this book Roger returned to his strengths by writing a western-style adventure set mainly in North America. Some of the characters are from Roger's experiences in Canada, but the passing of the years had taken away the sharpness of the characterization, so that unlike his *Curly,* which is a rattling good adventure, this book was an average Edwardian western adventure/romance sunk into fantasy. In his diaries Roger mentioned working on *Jesse* a number of times, whereas he mentioned the American edition primarily to report on money he received.[62] Roger saved one review of *Jesse* used in a John Murray catalogue:

A famous yarn, and the young man who cannot thoroughly
enjoy it should consult his doctor—or the nearest Sandow
exercise specialist—for there must be something wrong with
him; he must be ailing badly. Women, too, will like the book,
especially young women, lovers of hockey, girl guides, and
all the wholesome outdoor family of both sexes.... This
book will just delight scouts and scoutmasters. It is a real live
Western romance, yet as realistic and modern in tone and
fibre as tomorrow's newspaper.[63]

One reason for the success of the American edition is that the publisher
made significant efforts to promote it. As evidence of the many review
copies distributed, Bobbs-Merrill printed a broadsheet with the names
of fifty-seven newspapers and brief extracts from each of the reviews. One
of these reviewers declared of the work, it "stands apart in contemporary
fiction. It carries strength and conviction" (*Bookseller Newsdealer and
Stationer*). Another thought it "An extraordinary story, autobiographical
in form. There is a curious fascination about the author's semi-staccato
style, and the tale he tells is wild and full of primitive passion" (*Detroit
Free Press*). His central character was praised in the *Richmond Palladium*:
"Here is an interesting story of a flesh and blood man—not a clothes-prop
or a prig or a chump or a cad or one of the fifty-seven other varieties of
masculine incunabula—but a man as he should be in the sight of God."
And the reviewer for the *Standard Union* found the book "Original, novel,
filled with bristling incident possible only to the wilds, yet sanguine, and
convincing in its wealth of local color and character, the plain detail of
everyday life and description of locality, it is at once a sensation and a
relief, so absorbing are its adventures and so capable its incidents and
portraiture."[64] Perhaps Roger was even more pleased by a letter he received from a reader:

> I wish to express my heartiest appreciation of your fresh,
> virile, interesting, original book, "The [*sic*] Man in the
> Open." It has given me a very pleasant week, as I only have
> a chance to read piece-meal after working hours, and I
> therefore have to take a "good thing" slow to fully enjoy it.
> I started out not to like your book, for as a rule I donot
> [*sic*] care for this rugged type of story, related in the first
> person, for I usual [*sic*] read more scholarly constructed
> works, but the theme and style both caught me in a grip that
> did not relax until I had turned the last page.[65]

These reviews mention what is in the book, but perhaps another reason for the success of the American edition is what is absent. Roger's manuscript may have been submitted independently to the British and American publishers. They certainly edited it differently. The biggest difference is that the American edition removed most of Roger's writing on fairies. Roger was deeply depressed by the events of his departure from the Legion. He was also always influenced by others, and perhaps in this case by one of his heroes, Rudyard Kipling. Had Roger been reading Kipling's *Puck of Pook's Hill* (1906) and decided, in his rather depressed state, to use a rather darker form of fairy? Whatever the source, Roger's fairy references did not sit well with the American editor.[66]

Writing did not take up all his time, for that year Roger also found time to travel. He believed so strongly in the recuperative effects of travel that he decided to go by sea to the Mediterranean. His voyage began on 24 March 1910, but some very wet weather, and then a sheared shaft and the loss of a propeller in a gale on 13 April, turned the trip into more of an adventure than a rest, even by his standards. In his diary he reported on what he saw and painted, but he also mentioned difficulties with his foot.[67] He travelled northward by train, stopping quite a number of places, then made a rough crossing of the Channel and "borrowed money from a frontiersman [*sic*] got to Grosvenor St" on 24 April. By 26 April he was at his sister Ethel's cottage at Westgate, Kent, where he lived as much of an outdoor life as possible by taking up residence in "the Peter Pan house a studio at back of garden."[68] He did not write in his diary again until 7 July when he noted that "Henry [Simson] called up. Job offered me at £3 a week running a caravan lecture tour for a womens [*sic*] health society."

Among the probable appeals of this job for him was that it was a horse-drawn caravan and he would be outdoors so much. His job for the Women's Imperial Health Association was to travel across the south of England from Buckinghamshire to Somerset. Some members of the Association's committee may have doubted that he was the correct person to run the caravan, as he noted "Hell cat on the committee very spiteful."[69] Nonetheless, he became part of the staff on 25 July and on 30 July "Went to Bath, arr[ived] 1 pm got a carpenter & studied alterations of van." Roger also went into some detail in his diary over the next few days on fitting out the caravan. This, the "first caravan of the association," was to be inaugurated on 20 August by Lena Ashwell, who would break "a phial of pure water against the side. The caravan [would] proceed on its pilgrimage at once, the first lecture being given at Maidenhead on Wednesday next." On that Wednesday Roger noted, "Maidenhead lecture[.] Mayor presided. Miss Gill & Dr. Leslie. Henry & Ethel came."[70] The admiring newspaper article made a point of mentioning the condition and purpose of the caravan:

> [It will be] adequately equipped and manned, from which lectures and demonstrations on all health subjects, and particularly those relating to children, will be delivered by competent speakers. The lectures will be free and open to all, and there will be no collections.
>
> Local enthusiasm will be aroused by advance agents that all may have the chance of attending. Technical language will be tabooed, and the lectures will be made comprehensible and palatable by a series of biograph pictures and views.[71]

In his diary Roger recorded some of the places he and his assistant camped until the last lecture on 30 November, as well as comments on his own health and the replacement of his damaged false teeth.[72] Those few months of touring with the caravan provided a reliable income, but otherwise he was constantly dependent on loans from Henry Simson until royalties from his books arrived at irregular intervals.[73]

After these months with a regular income, at the beginning of 1911 Roger decided to move back to "my old chambers at 15 G[rea]t Ormond St to live there again just as in when I began to prosper."[74] To help ensure he prospered again, he wrote in a diary the names of the editors for various publishers and what sorts of stories several journals wanted.[75] Not all his writing efforts achieved publication, however. For example, earlier he had begun working on another fantasy novel, "The Serene Spirit," which came to nothing, and his publisher, John Murray, rejected an idea for a book called "Building Forces."[76] He even made an attempt at "writing music hall sketch stockade theme" but noted "Daisy to criticise my first music hall sketches" and "Beryl & Billy criticised sketches & took me to Empire Music Hall."[77]

All this criticism and comment seems to have been effective, for within a few days he began a new novel, a format with which he was more familiar. Roger even worked with familiar material. He first noted in his diary that he was writing another Blackguard novel on 2 April 1911. Roger this time used not only his own experience but many elements of the story and characters from his earlier work, *The Blackguard* (1897), as the foundation of the new work published as *The Splendid Blackguard* and *The Cheerful Blackguard*.[78] The same Blackguard is the central character, but this time he is half Irish and thus named José de la Mancha y O'Brien. He again shared Roger's birth date and regimental number. The NWMP were also a very important element in these two novels. Flora MacDonald Steele was delighted that "The whole yarn deals with the Force and some of the Originals are very slightly disguised, which all makes palatable reading. One chuckles as one skims the vigorous lines. And there is poetry and beauty in it, too."[79] In addition to the Blackguard, some other characters return, such as Violet Burrows and her uncle, but their backstories and roles in the Blackguard's life are different. The names of some characters also differ slightly: for example, Violet's uncle is called Loco Burrows (more formally known as Eliphalet P. Burrows), and not Lunatic Burrows; and the Englishman interested in the mine is Augustus Rams, rather than Charlie Ramsay. *Splendid* and *Cheerful* differ significantly from *The Blackguard* because Roger made more extensive use of his knowledge of First Nations life, and because of the central role of the character Rain.

Rain, a Blackfoot, is the most intriguing First Nations character to appear in Roger's books. In addition to playing a central role in *Splendid* and *Cheerful,* she appears in his last published novel, the very strange and justly forgotten *The Wolf Trail.* He describes her with uncharacteristic intensity and passion: "In Rain, the glamour of God's wilderness had taken human form as a Red Indian girl with youth's delicious gravity of bearing, the childlike purity of the untainted Savage, hale strength, athletic grace and eyes derisive."[80] He also described her dressed as a warrior, which was "beautiful to illustrate youth, lithe, wholesome strength and grace, the clear-cut loveliness of a face coloured like glowing bronze, the fearless gallantry of bearing, the spiritual purity and power."[81] Here we have the "noble savage," but, unusually for the time, Rain was a feisty girl with the hero under her command and tuition, and mostly in awe of her. Young First Nations girls were freer in their ways and attitudes than were European girls, who were bound by the rules of European society. To the young, and often frustrated, Roger, this type of girl had come as a breath of fresh air. His story was unusual in presenting a First Nations heroine in that way, so unlike "Pocahontas [who] saved John Smith's life, and was rewarded with a kind of marriage, a trope, which, repeated in dozens of adventure stories, cast the 'savage' in the submissive feminine posture, and signalled the recognition of white superiority."[82] Indeed, the majority of the era's adventure stories put women, if they appeared at all, in the role of passive supporter:

> The adventure story takes up as a recurring motif the heroine
> who before she comes to learn true devotion prays every

night that she may turn into a boy; patriarchy robs a woman of her self. As imaged by her father and brothers[,] the good woman grows in time into a defender of the faith and a keeper of the hero's conscience, a girl loyal to the core, one more "little mother" of England. She is sexless, and has earned that highest of male accolades, the reputation of a "good sport."[83]

Rain was far from submissive, and the author's assertion—"Passion I had for many, devotion I had towards all things beautiful, but Love for only one woman, and her I might not marry"—indicates where Roger's heart lay.[84]

A CAPTAIN
AT LAST

AS USUAL, THE WRITING LIFE was not enough to sustain Roger. In the spring of 1911 he contacted major newspapers and a railway seeking, unsuccessfully, sponsorship for another Canadian trip. He even "applied to Canada Govt for trip as correspondent" and "met John Murray re Canadian trip."[1] It could well be that English newspaper editors had decided that Roger was yesterday's man. He was now in his middle forties and no longer the young adventurer. The days when Roger's articles regularly appeared in a variety of periodicals had faded. It is also significant that immigration to western Canada had increased dramatically, so Canada was no longer the wild, untamed country of Roger's youth. Readers would have been far more interested in tales from comparatively exotic and distant lands. Publication of his magazine and newspaper articles seems to have ceased, perhaps because he was concentrating on writing books. Roger's two major public mistakes—his recent departure from the Legion of Frontiersmen, and the lingering scandal of the loss of Sir Arthur Curtis in 1898—could also have made editors hesitant to use his work. The men on the Governing Council of the Legion of Frontiersmen were not at the absolute centre of power, but they walked the corridors of power and exerted considerable influence through their social position and friends. If any conscious decisions were made to discontinue using

Roger's journalistic writing, they would not have been made formally. Conversations or gossip about Roger over drinks in clubs and among friends within the newspaper publishing world could have been sufficient to persuade editors that it was no longer expedient to feature his work. He had his small circle of loyal friends, such as H.S. Orde, Hugh Pollard, and particularly Harry Fife Scott, but Roger had succeeded in irritating too many powerful acquaintances. Perhaps his early efforts to encourage interest in his writing by hinting at a mysterious past had backfired on him? It may have led the men of influence he had worked so hard to attract to the Legion to wonder whether there was something even more unsavoury in Roger's past.

Of course the greatest mystery in his past was not hidden at all. What happened to Sir Arthur Curtis? The subject even cropped up when he was on his way to Westgate by train for Easter: "Miss Curtis (silence) sat opposite me in train. She knew me by photos. I wondered who she was but she didn't speak." A little later Roger reported that he "Met Miss Curtis," but he did not record the result of the meeting, nor what relation Miss Curtis may have been to Sir Arthur.[2] The summer of 1911 was one of the hottest of the new century, so he spent as much time as possible in camp at Harwich with his friend Orde. On the occasions when he visited London, he found it unbearably hot. The heat also had an adverse effect on attendance in London theatres, making finances difficult for Lena. Fortunately for Lena and Roger, she now had a wealthy husband. In June, Roger met many old friends and colleagues from the Mounted Police who were in England for the coronation of King George V. He specifically mentioned "Commissioner Perry, Insp[ector] Wroughton, Sergeant Alexander of Fort Macleod, & Insp[ector] Doppas, who used to be in charge of Banff in 1897."[3] In March 1912 his thoughts again turned to Canada, when he "met Bellamy, D'Oyley [sic] Carte's manager who was in Riel Rebellion."[4]

Roger was still convinced that war with Germany was not far off, so he enlisted in the National Reserve on 9 March 1912. He was delighted to be in a disciplined, military organization again, and very proud to be "appointed Colour Bearer to Battalion," then "promoted to Colour Sergeant N.R." in spite of his damaged foot.[5] However, Roger spent most of 1912 in a quiet social life, visiting theatres and friends, and receiving regular visits from Ada Wright. A few times the names of other unmarried ladies appear in his diaries as guests or companions at the theatre, but none as regularly as Ada Wright. He also endeavoured to supplement his income by letting out a room at his chambers at 15 Great Ormond Street for a while to a friend, referred to only as "Hope," who often had difficulty paying his rent. Roger made frequent reference to this in his diary until, at last, he noted Hope still owed £14.4.0 but was leaving "to learn vetting & far-riery in Canada next spring."[6] Roger never indicated whether the "Hope" who was leaving was Linton Hope or Graham Hope, both of whom were acquaintances. Neither of these men was young, but it seems unlikely to have been Linton Hope, the yacht designer (1864–1920).

Most Frontiersmen sought new adventure, whatever their age.

In this spirit, Roger was always proud of the number of trades in which he claimed experience. During the summer, Roger spent as much time as possible camping. Often, he would make new friends who would show him something interesting:

> During holiday "Putty" the Painter, Petty Officer of the Blenheim took me all over the ship & a repair ship, & I saw much of the machinery at work.
> I made friends also with the Dhosie (tailor) & the Corporal's Mess of the Royal Fusiliers; spent one day in their camp.[7]

Royalties were coming in from his books, and though they were enough to make him feel prosperous, they seldom completely covered his debts to his brother-in-law. So apart from a few ideas he abandoned, following advice from friends, he "Began the Book of Adventurers for Cassells." However, "Walter Smith of Cassells rejected, Annals of Great Adventure on seeing 5 chapters. Supposed the book to be to order wrote to agent."[8] It was published in 1913 as *Captains of Adventure.* However, because most of the chapters were virtually identical to the articles in his "Great Adventurers" series for *Lloyd's Weekly News,* which had such massive readership in Britain and among British citizens around the Empire, it was an exclusively American publication. Roger was also having some dif-ficulties with Gilmer, his agent. After his October letter to Gilmer, Roger "Borrowed £10 from Henry [Simson] to pay Gilmers [*sic*] typing bill & told him I cut the agency connection." Several weeks later he had made his "final decision: Massie my agent."[9]

After a year with no major travel, Roger was restless. On 1 January 1913 he borrowed £20 from Henry Simson to fulfil his ambition to visit Norway, although it was not the best time of year for such a trip. He bought a round trip ticket to Trondheim and joined the SS *Zero* on 4 January.[10] After ex-periencing mostly rain and strong winds, he returned home 16 January with an idea to make some money. He thought fish skins, obtainable at very little cost in Norway, could be tanned to use for shoe uppers. This was an idea he toyed with again after the First World War, but as with the mattâk from Greenland, at no time could he raise much interest.[11] Roger's diary does not convey enthusiasm, but he did write in praise of Norway. He described the rugged scenery and approved of it:

> All that is very restful when one's soul has been getting rumpled with too much civilization & fuss.
>
> But the best part of the tonic is to meet Norwegian people, to know for once that everybody in sight is honest....
>
> We are indeed descended from this people.... They taught us their seamanship.... They gave us our sense of justice, fair dealing & clean sport....

He then expressed respect for Roald Amundsen's trip to the South Pole, and went on to articulate misgivings that Denmark, Sweden, and Norway were exposed to the "grabbing Power" of Russia, Germany, and Britain. His solution was for the three Scandinavian countries "to forget their little differences, & form a Joint Committee of Defence with their three Kings for alternate presidents."[12]

Not surprisingly, this trip just whetted Roger's appetite for travel. Or, as Roger put it: "The civilized life is good enough until the Spring Fret sets the blood racing in one's arteries, and the town becomes wholly unbearable because the Sea and the Wilderness are calling."[13] In print Roger said Morley Roberts introduced him to Randle Cecil in April, while in his diary he said he "Met a cub of the Cecil family with Pollard, & asked him to come to the Western states. Asked Fox to get him Morning Post commission."[14] Randle Cecil thought he would like to be a journalist, perhaps inspired by his grandfather's youthful career. The meeting went well, and Cecil's father decided that Roger was the right person to toughen the young man up: "I think you will find some difficulty keeping Randle up to the work and I hope you will be severe. If he gets left on a Railway Station I shall not blame you. At the same time you will find him a pleasant travelling companion.... He is a *spoilt* boy."[15] Cecil's father probably commissioned Roger to escort young Cecil to Canada and show him the country, travelling mainly on horseback. Roger later wrote that he designed a geological journey largely for his own benefit and challenged young Cecil to raise his share of the funds, "sharing expenses," without any reference to the Cecil family's wishes.[16] Roger was probably using "literary license," though, for an entry on the January 1914 cash page of Roger's diary says "Deposit with Henry [Simson] £50," with the superscript addition of "Cecil," which suggests that Roger made a profit from the £200 supplied by Randle Cecil's father and that Roger was less than accurate when he claimed that expenses were shared. Roger held the purse strings over a theoretically comfortable £200. He soon decided that Cecil did not have the makings of a journalist, was concerned that Cecil was constantly seasick on the sea voyage, and had grave doubts over his fitness for living rough, but concluded Cecil was charm itself. The letter from Cecil's father had relieved Roger of any blame for most things that could befall the young man, but Roger still had to be very careful not to be too severe or, worse, carelessly land himself with another Sir Arthur Curtis scandal.

Roger and Cecil appear to have looked in on the Steele family in Winnipeg[17] as they travelled by rail to Calgary, where they bought horses and began their journey through the Rockies. In his book *Horses,* Roger wrote that he had "ridden from Regina in Saskatchewan to Red Bluff in California," but this is almost certainly an exaggeration.[18] His account of the expedition in *Chorus to Adventurers* is more detailed and likely more accurate. Roger spent some time persuading Cecil to ride like a stockman instead of an Englishman. Deciding to travel by horseback was usual for Roger; however, for the first time in his travels in Canada, he sought no publicity. His departure from the Legion, which he defined as expulsion, was sufficiently recent to cause him pain and embarrassment.

> All the way across Canada, I had been furtive, avoiding journalists, writing illegibly in hotel registers, sneaking through the many places where Commands of the Legion might tender a public reception. I heard that the Ste[.] Anne and Edmonton Commands tried to intercept me at Calgary; but since my expulsion from the Corps, meetings of that kind would have been distasteful, with too much heartache in them. How could I face the trappers of Lac Ste[.] Anne, who had been brothers to me. Everywhere I had met Legionaries, and still older comrades of the Royal Canadian Mounted Police [*sic*]; but the Commands were to be dreaded, and it was an immense relief to escape out of Vancouver without having been caught, to get back to the horses in pasture, and to cross the boundary into the United States, where I was only a novelist.[19]

He did not manage to escape all publicity, however. A Calgary newspaper described Roger's response to the changes there since he last visited in 1897, and the pair's literary and travel plans for the journey: "Their route was mapped out for them by officials of the Canadian Pacific department of natural resources."[20] Clearly, while the men with power at Legion head-quarters in London had lost faith in Roger's ability, the Legion members in Canada had not. These men still respected him as the founder of the Legion of which they were so proud.

Roger was neither the first nor last to return to an area after many years only to find that it had changed beyond all recognition:

> I had known this very region of East Oregon as a land
> of perilous adventure, of gorgeous romance, with all the
> glamour of the frontier, where men wore steel and leather
> with unconscious grace, delighting in furious riding and
> brilliant marksmanship. The real range men spoke little,
> but in liquid English, were gentle in their manner, with
> something of high courtesy, headlong in generosity, terrific in
> wrath, almost superhuman in endurance, chivalrous towards
> women, loved by children, in everything an aristocracy, with
> the natural habit of cavaliers in any land or age. All men were
> lawless then, but none were mean.[21]

He retained his romantic view of the past but was unable to show Cecil the wide frontier lands he had so loved. The changes also meant that he could not collect any adventurous tales that might persuade editors to publish his stories once more. Indeed, things had changed so much that "among the young gallants of the farms, dressed up as cowboys, playing circus tricks, and trying to be 'tough,' one smelt vulgarity, such stuff as films are made of. Even the few real stockmen were dressed for show, and not for handling stock."[22] Though the journey gave him no new stories, he enjoyed the long ride from Calgary, Alberta, to Red Bluff, California, largely at someone else's expense. During this journey Roger also indulged in geology, another of his passions, by studying the Rocky Mountains. Much as he would have wished, though, this never resulted in a book. From the grandeur of the mountains Roger returned to London, to find that his charwoman had pawned his clothes, household linen, and bedding. Fortunately for Roger, given his usual penurious state, most of his possessions were restored to him with the aid of the police.

Roger spent time and effort in the early part of 1914 on an idea that did not involve travel. He tried to become involved in the growing motion picture industry, and he even wrote to Rudyard Kipling, asking if he would consider writing scripts and offering to show the great man how it was done. Kipling briefly and politely declined the offer.[23] Despite this show of confidence, Roger's ideas achieved little success, so in July he went to camp near the village of West Mersea in Essex. He was taken out dredging oysters on 8 July, and three days later noted in his diary, "News of a yacht off to Norway[:] wrote offering services," but he did not record a response to his offer. He was able to return to sea, though, in the crew of a trawler out of Brightlingsea, Essex, for the last two weeks of July: "Mr. Stoker took me out trawling" and "we sailed to Osea island." For several subsequent days he was also on water: "midnight. sailed trawling with Stoker"; "into Brightlingsea to sell fish noon"; and "Into Brightlingsea to sell fish." Up to 31 July he was still "trawling."[24] On 28 July Stoker complained that the day-time light on the North Bench Head buoy was out, for the first time in twenty years. The light had been extinguished in anticipation of the coming conflict.

> The hour was high noon, of Wednesday the 28th of July, 1914. Faint airs played lightly over the glittering sea, an airplane soared above in the high azure, and far away inland the sunlight caught the flank of a small airship. Easing the sheet before a flaw of wind, we ran on silent into Brightlingsea. We drew in to the quay, landed our baskets of fish, and carried them through quiet streets to the fishmonger's shop as usual, then did a bit of shopping, put out to sea again, and shot the trawl.
> Mr. George Stoker was Owner-skipper, I was Mate, and a small boy was crew, in a little beam-trawler. Once in each watch we hauled, getting a ton of weed, small crabs and a few fish, and daily took our catch into Brightlingsea. Work must go on as usual everywhere, and I for one felt miserly in the spending of those last brief days of peace.[25]

Inevitably, Roger's pleasure in being at sea was interrupted by events. His response to those events was practical: "The European crisis acute," and "Decided to go to town ready for military service. Had a right brew of punch with Knight after a merry singsong with the three pretty secretaries."[26] His eye for a pretty girl had not left him, even on the brink of war. On 3 August 1914, all the sailors who were naval reservists left by bus and Roger took a train to London. The next day he tried, without success, to find his National Reserve Officer Commanding (O.C.), Capt. B. Granville Baker, but by 5 August he was hard at work addressing envelopes in the Orderly Room of the Paddington Battalion in Harrow Road. The banks had been closed, but re-opened on 7 August, which enabled him to cash his Mounted Police pension cheque for some much needed money. London was in a fervour: "Grey's speech in Commons. Waited at Greenroom Club (Savage closed) & walked with [Walter] Kirton to Central News where we got synopsis. French exodus. Strand full of starving American millionaires. Mobilisation of army."[27] While Roger frantically tried to join the Army, even though he was forty-nine, he was still doing what he could as a volunteer clerk. His experience was not unusual. Leo Amery reported his visit to Birmingham on Saturday, 8 August, where he was shocked by the inefficiency of recruiting.

> I thought I would try and see what was doing at the
> recruiting office. I eventually tracked this down in a narrow
> side-street blocked from end to end by a crowd of thousands
> of men standing patiently in pouring rain while waiting to
> be admitted, one at a time, into a poky little house, on the
> second floor of which a sadly bewildered recruiting officer
> was dealing with the problem on approved red tape lines. In
> other words each would-be recruit had to have a cold bath
> in the only bathroom before being examined by the only
> doctor, and then taken laboriously through pages of print on
> the official attestation form by the only recruiting sergeant.
> To add to the crisis there were only about a dozen attestation
> forms left![28]

This sort of thing was repeated in many towns and cities around the country, but few had the advantage of someone like Leo Amery to cut through the red tape. Unlike Roger, Amery was in the fortunate position of being able to take immediate action and commandeer the Town Hall: "We went round to an office which someone had opened for National Reservists, i.e. for ex-reservists who had registered their names as willing to re-enlist in an emergency. We found a couple of hundred of these crowding round, and soon collected a score of old sergeants with recruiting experience, telling them to be at the Town Hall early on Monday."[29]

After declaring on 24 August that "The whole week [was] spent trying for a job in the army," on 2 September Roger travelled to Grimsby to try and enlist in the Navy. He did not succeed, but the very next day Granville Baker was given a position as interpreter and so left the office in Roger's charge. Finally, on 19 October, his persistence was rewarded to some extent when he managed to enlist in the County of London (Royal Irish) Defence Corps, where he was made orderly room clerk, as a corporal, and set about organizing the office. On 21 October he "shaved off [his] beard." On 2 November he met an old friend, Captain (later Major) Marquis Ivrea.[30] Ivrea offered him a position as quartermaster-sergeant in the Warwickshire Royal Horse Artillery (Territorial) at Leamington, where Ivrea was forming the second line Battery. All Roger needed to do was persuade his O.C. to grant him a transfer, which took a few days of pressure. Roger was able to spend the weekend before Christmas with the Ivreas at the country house of one of the other officers, Lt. Croxall. It was not socially acceptable for Roger, an N C O, to attend a country house weekend at an officer's house in uniform, so he had to send to London for his civilian clothes. After a very pleasant visit he returned to duty and the correct social position for his military rank.

Roger had a period of Christmas leave, beginning 8 January 1915, but his O.C. sent him to visit General Palmer at Cheltenham, who approved him for a commission, and he was "In London Gazette as Lieut from 3d [February]."[31] He was fortunate to have Henry Simson to fall back on for money, however, for he reported that his new officer's kit cost £53.[32] Much of his time as a British officer was spent riding, although he took little pleasure in the British saddle—apparently needing quantities of violinist's rosin to stay in the saddle. In addition to manoeuvres and training the men who were to go to France, he was required to ride to hounds with the North Warwickshire hunt. The gun drill he had learned aboard his father's ship, T.S. *Wellesley*, seems to have stood him in good stead. At times he would take a draft of trained men to Southampton. The unit was ordered to Diss, in Norfolk, where they arrived in April. Croxall had become a captain, and he and Lt. Dixon were posted to France, so Roger became acting adjutant, and then received orders to take the advance party and assume temporary command. He had already begun to acquire a reputation as "Ali Baba" for his ability to acquire what was needed for his men by any means available. Major Duncan was first to use the name, which immediately stuck, particularly as Roger liked the idea and kept telling people about it. His experience as an irregular scout in the Anglo-Boer War, and sometimes living off the land, gave him the necessary cunning. His Anglo-Boer War methods even seem to have been adopted by the unit: "My looting system is adopted officially with Cecil as OC loot."[33] His record identifies him thus:

[A] capable and good Officer.

He is popular with N.C.O.'s and Men and never tired of trying to improve their circumstances.

In like manner he has displayed great ingenuity in improving the surroundings and standings of his Stables and general comfort of his Horses about which he is somewhat of an authority.[34]

One example is how quickly he set about improving the hutting for the men. Roger went to visit a camp of the Leicesters, probably trying to acquire equipment. On his return the same day, he found that the camp had received an unannounced visit from Col. Candless, "a cracked Division Staff officer," as he confided in his diary, who "pretended the guns were unguarded. He found Sergt. Maj. Weir on sentry & sent me a note. I posted an armed guard."[35] Evidently, the senior officers were concerned that there might be a German invasion. When Major Ivrea heard that Roger was to write his second volume of autobiography, he wrote to Roger to remind him of that month when Roger was in command:

> I hope you won't forget to describe the "Commune" that
> I found on my arrival at Diss....nor how you invited the
> Battery to high tea, for which I had ultimately twenty-four
> hours' notice to pay out of my own pocket....nor how you
> gave a man 'fined 10s.' for being asleep on sentry-go in
> wartime—and the General's fury thereat.[36]

In fact, Roger's diary shows that the matter was not as serious as that. Gunner Kelly was sentenced to five days and fined ten shillings for striking Bombardier House on 3 April, "the fine being afterward disallowed."[37] It appears that Roger had some sympathy for Kelly's action. Later, Roger was always highly complimentary about Ivrea, but he did not always feel that way. While Ivrea was on sick leave, Roger complained that "This week was filled with insane letters from Major Ivrea which had to be dealt with by a Board of officers."[38]

Following orders that the unit was now the second-line and not the third-line Battery, Roger was detailed by Major Ivrea to return to Leamington and there set up and command a new third-line Battery. It might be cruel to think that a time-honoured way had been found to remove an over-enthusiastic officer by promoting him elsewhere, but Roger wryly wrote that he "had won a Captaincy in just five and a half months.... Provided that I stuck faithfully to Home Service, at the same rate of promotion another six months would find me a Field Marshal, whereas a fellow who wasted his time at the Front would be lucky if he earned one chevron as Acting Bombardier."[39] Roger applied for his own choice of men to form the core of his unit. Although there is a note in his War Office file that "He has also the gift of being able to estimate character in men and thereby attract to his Battery some of the best and most experienced men as N.C.O.'s that there are in the School,"[40] we again have evidence that he trusted too easily. He requested two of his old Legion of Frontiersmen friends, who were probably also fellow Savages: Bernard Hamilton as an officer and Edward Else as Battery quartermaster sergeant to recruit partly from contacts in London. These men had not been accepted by Driscoll for the 25th Battalion Royal Fusiliers (Frontiersmen), and it was soon evident that Driscoll was the better judge of character. Edward Else had come to the attention of the War Office in 1909 when Roger, on behalf of the Legion, sent information on gunrunning in Colombia and on the North West Frontier, and also suggested that a Scotland Yard Inspector was leaking important official information.[41] Unfortunately, both Hamilton and Else had problems with excessive drinking. Roger also brought Corporal Clarke with him from Diss and made Clarke a sergeant, and eventually his sergeant-major, in spite of the fact that in Diss he had reduced Clarke from sergeant to corporal for drunkenness.

Roger's temporary captaincy was gazetted from 1 May 1915. He was still troubled by Major Ivrea, who sent him recruits of dubious quality. Roger was prepared to resist, though, and recorded that he "sent back Major Ivrea's tourist party of invalids & imbeciles numbering 6 rejected by my Doctor."[42] Despite all this activity, Roger was able to take a weekend leave to visit Major-General Sir Sam Steele, who was commanding the 2nd Canadian Division at Shorncliffe. Roger stayed at the Metropole Hotel, Folkestone, as Sam Steele's guest on 12 June. He took the opportunity to ask Steele for a good man as subaltern. Steele gave him Hal Jarvis, "a bushman from North Ontario, standing about six foot six, strong as an ox, with brains and manners besides, and a sense of humour."[43] According to Roger, Jarvis shared his attitude towards the unofficial acquisition of anything likely to be of use to the unit, and so the two men got on famously. Roger did make a tentative inquiry whether there might be a place for himself in the Canadian Army, serving under Steele, but received a polite "Letter from Steele to say no vacancies in Canadian army."[44] Roger did take one man from the Canadian Army, though, when he found that Randle Cecil was serving as a private in a Canadian Highland battalion in France, and arranged Cecil's transfer and commission into his own unit.

Training for the unit was so strenuous that Roger collapsed on 6 and 7 September, and was granted a week's leave by the physician. He went to the Savage Club, but his sleep was interrupted: "Many refreshments. Went to bed very sleepy. 11.20 awakened by the Zep raid all around. View from window at Club was superb." Early the next morning he went to see the bombed ruins on the corner of Theobalds Road and Red Lion Street and met R.A. Smith, one of the original members of the Legion, who had also witnessed the raid: "Penny Bank smashed...saw Wood St. on fire."[45]

On 13 September Roger "came back to duty[,] despite MO's extension of leave," and found he was to appear before General Sir J. Perrott, Inspector of Royal Horse Artillery (R.H.A.) and Royal Field Artillery (R.F.A.) at Leamington, mainly about the matter of the pony he had commandeered on 31 July. Even though the pony was too unwell to be used for military duties, the matter generated some correspondence and discussion.

> Here is another case which has been badly handled. If all
> these allegations are true I think Capt Pocock should have
> been dealt with in a proper military way. There seems very
> little more than hearsay to go on, and all I know of the case is
> that I have heard Captain Pocock badly spoken of. I should
> like to transfer him to T[erritorial] F[orce] Reserve, but it
> may be difficult to defend this action if he appeals.[46]

Roger took the opportunity to seek Perrott's advice about Lt. Hamilton, who was "on a drunk." It must have been a common problem, for Roger not only punished Hamilton, he "put…all pubs & the Club out of bounds. Destroyed all liquor at HQ."[47] It seems that problems with drink were rife within the Home Service in the First World War, although this is a subject infrequently discussed by military historians. Roger was still finding it difficult to cope, so the Medical Officer put him on medical leave again on 15 September and sent him to a Medical Board at Northampton, which gave him a month's sick leave on 22 September, according to his diary. There he also noted on 22 October that "sick leave expired," but the next day he went to visit Sam Steele at Folkestone, with permission.[48] There he was shown around Shorncliffe by Steele and by his aide-de-camp. The day after his fiftieth birthday, in London, the "Medical Board at Caxton Hall sent me to duty." The next day he found there were serious problems over the unit accounts: "Else drinking & hysterical when the accountant & S.M. Cotton arr[ived] 6 pm spent evening till midnight on the claim against me of £28. Else useless. Applied for Wadham of 2d Battery to examine acc[oun]ts." Then Roger "Made the Medi[ical] Officer put Else off duty, but to stay in Leamington. Put Cecil in charge of enquiry with Bomb[adier] Taylor to help. Wired…for Lt Wadham of 2d Battery because 2 Lt Hunter is coming in a month."[49] Once again, Roger's faulty judgement of character had landed him with problems, for only he could be blamed for taking on and trusting Edward Else. On 25 November Roger had to call in a Chartered Accountant, and the next day he learned that his "deficit" was £31. Yet again Roger had to send a message to his brother-in-law for money to help him out of a very difficult situation.[50] As the officer commanding the Battery, Roger would have been personally responsible for any financial discrepancy in the Battery accounts.

In January 1916 matters were improving. The problem accounts were settled and refunds from the Pay Office enabled Roger to pay his brother-in-law. Plans were in hand to transfer Else away, but Roger "Reduced Else to Sergeant for incompetence. Sent cheque for £13 towards Else's Brewery Bill. The Sergeants mess exonerates Else of this charge." The next day a new bill of Else's arrived for £29.5.4, and Else complained to the commandant, Major Duncan, who confirmed Roger's action in reducing him.[51] All was not well, though, for Roger admitted that he made mistakes and his officers, particularly Lt. Brokenshaw, were upset by some of his ways. Roger even "Resolved to apply for release from Army."[52] Slowly and steadily, though, despite bouts of influenza and measles, his men and officers were drafted, with the fit ones going to active duty. In April he learned that "My command, the 3/1 Warwick RHA ceases to exist from this date."[53] Finally, in May, Roger got the opportunity he had always wanted—to take a draft to France, if only to Le Havre. He took forty men to Southampton and, as the senior officer present, was made O.C. Troops on the SS *African Prince,* with 470 men and 250 horses. He claimed that he had to create a fuss to have companion ladders to the hatches installed before he would embark, but he did not mention that in his diary. He was given "All sorts of confidential orders," which he claimed were mainly to do with the sanitary arrangements at sea. He was up all night and the next morning clearing the draft, completing the business by noon. Soon after he landed in France, though, he was struck down by a fever, which he thought was heat stroke. This put him into the officers' hospital for a few days and caused his sisters to be concerned when they received a telegram reporting he was "slightly wounded." He also was "More or less lame from a bruise [sustained] on [the] outward passage."[54]

After he returned to England, Roger learned on 30 May that his unit was being moved to Bulford, on Salisbury Plain, but that did not get in the way of his social life. Ada Wright no longer appeared in his diaries, but he still had an eye for the ladies. He met a Miss Mayne at the YMCA and seems to have enjoyed her company: "Miss Mayne & another YMCA waitress to lunch at the Mess. Miss Mayne & I walked to Stonehenge. Tea at YMCA."[55] Back in London on leave, "Blumenfeld Ed[itor] of the Express told me at 7 pm of the Jutland Naval Engagement." The next week he noted, "Kitchener reported drowned. Profound gloom in town." By now Roger's duties were much reduced, since the Batteries were being merged into one school and had only limited vacancies for officers. He therefore spent more time in London, recording such activities as "Shopping. The Kitchener Memorial Service going on at St[.] Pauls. Lunch [at] Club. Shopping afternoon. Dined with Ethel in Oxford St. because Princess Victoria dining with Daisy. Play. D'Israeli."[56] He then learned his services would no longer be required. He was rather sarcastic about the Army's failure to use his skills with horses; it is more probable, however, that his tendency to break down under pressure made them realize that at his age he was not fit for the task.[57] Col. Yorke took him to Salisbury, where there were initial discussions about Roger's involvement in a Labour Battalion in France, but this did not come to fruition. He lost his captaincy and reverted to unpaid lieutenant on the Reserve List.[58] A follow-up report requested by the War Office made this statement:

> His knowledge of accounts and mathematics generally is undoubtedly his weakest point.
> On account of age and certain physical deffects [*sic*] he is not fitted for service in the field, but as a Battery Commander at home I have found him eminently satisfactory.[59]

This was probably a sensible conclusion by the Army, and it also gave Roger the chance to finish his much admired and consulted book, *Horses*. Nonetheless, he wrote to the War Office to request another posting: "I have the honour to submit, and beg you to forward, this application for employment in any organising capacity. At the age of 50 I am rated unfit for active service, but might be useful with horses, shipping, or in anti-aircraft organisation."[60]

Roger's request brought no immediate response, but he received some pleasure in completing his book *Horses,* of which he claimed, "It became the text-book used by Battery Commanders at the Front."[61] Roger also described *Horses* as his "first work of scientific research."[62] Shortly after it was published he tried to use the book for his own benefit, to "show that I can be of service as an Instructor & adviser in Horsemastership. I seek employment with the Expeditionary Force."[63] Roger recorded very little about the writing process for this book in his diaries, but perhaps his desire to keep track of military activities took precedence.[64] One testament to its quality may be that he, or far more likely the publisher, was able to persuade J. Cossar Ewart to write the preface and to advise him on the text. Ewart, from the perspective of wartime, wrote the following:

> The chapters on the History of the horse and on horsemanship are highly suggestive and interesting, but at the

Roger Pocock with no beard, *c.*1916.
[Author; copy of original photograph in the Dudley Archive kindly
supplied to the author by the late Capt. Charles Dudley.]

moment those on the Pleasure Horse and the Soldier Horse
claim and deserve most attention.... If the suggestions made
by a horsemaster who knows more about Range than Indoor
or Pleasure horses—suggestions as to the breeding, rearing,
and management of military horses—are duly considered[,]
we may have an ample supply of suitable horses for our next
war.[65]

There is no doubt that Roger loved horses, and that his scholarship on
the subject was as good as, if not better than, that on his other favourite
topic, geology. He shows his usual irritating jocularity and even, at times,

dry wit throughout what was meant to be a textbook, but it is nonetheless entertaining and thought-provoking. Three examples demonstrate his attitude.

> The material used in making a horse consists of grass and water. We cannot make one because we are too ignorant.
>
> [Faults and remedies in horses:] Propping. This is balking at a gallop and taking a series of springs in that position, each with a rigid crash on all four legs. The rider has a tendency to continue his journey alone. Propping is much favoured by range horses.
>
> Moreover, the animal has "instincts" which impel "it" to beget a foal or a litter of puppies. Humans, with the same instincts are impelled to beget a bumptious young bacteriologist, or a pair of curates.[66]

Roger was also somewhat inclined to anthropomorphize the horse, and even to suggest immortality: "Are all the Hosts of Heaven infantry?"[67] The influence of First Nations peoples on his life, particularly the Blackfoot, led him to suggest that conversations between man and horse occurred via thought transference. This reflected his increasing research into psychic matters, which significantly affected his writing and the book's saleability. He went into some detail regarding how different countries with their different grasses would, in his opinion, produce different sizes and colours of horses, and went on to give examples. He continued to preach vociferously against the English saddle and riding method; he thought the weight of that saddle was carried on too small an area and that the way of riding allowed too little for the horse's intelligence. From the perspective of a frontiersman, he even provided a list for the contents of saddle wallets:

> For the general purposes of travel I carry in the wallets a tin of gall cure, a medicine case containing chlorodyne, and tablets of quinine, carbolic acid, cascara, a salicylate and permanganate of potash, with a lancet, forceps, surgical needles and silk, and a dressing; a mosquito salve such as oil of pennyroyal, and some netting; a toothbrush in a case, soap in a tobacco pouch, and a towel; toilet paper; a little sealed bottle of matches for emergencies; an emergency ration such as cake chocolate; luncheon; something to read; notebook and pencil.[68]

After *Horses* was accepted for publication, he started work on another book, a novel, but it was never published.[69]

On 7 August 1916 he was delighted to receive a telegram from Number 8 Artillery School, ordering him to report for duty with the 13th Labour Battalion, Berkshire Regiment, at Freshwater, Isle of Wight. He left London the next morning and found the camp. When he reported, the surprised brigadier told him the telegram was incorrect, for he was at the 12th Labour Battalion, and the 13th Battalion was stationed at Purbrook, near Portsmouth. Following six changes of car, train, and steamer he arrived at the fort and found the adjutant, Captain Lee. The next day Roger was in for another surprise when he met Colonel Searle. It is fortunate that Searle, as with many other senior officers, never saw Roger's description of him:

> Col. Searle turned out to be tall, handsome, distinguished,
> stupid, senile, a bore, & a tedious exponent of etiquette,
> futile as an organizer, unable to trust anybody to carry on,
> constantly interrupting, interfering with, and delaying work,
> so that every job had to be done several times over. My
> Co[mpany] Sergt. Major Williams hopelessly incompetent,
> but it was a fortnight before I got Foster in his place.

Roger made further comments ten days later: "During this period the Colonel wasted the whole morning time of Co[mpan]y officers & sergt. major standing around. The rest of the day being a muddle of impossible orders piled one on top of another. Colonel peevish, everybody else hysterical, no real purpose."[70] Many of the men were unfit for active service, and in some cases seem to have been unfit for any sort of military service. Alcohol was still causing problems, and its abuse presented Roger with some odd tasks: "Sat on Court of Enquiry with Capt. Cookson & 2d Lt. Abraham on Pte. Wornald of A Co. who cut his throat while enjoying D.T."[71] Roger's duties were reduced, the "Med Board reported me fit for Horse work," and then on 19 September the Battalion left for France, leaving Roger and another officer with the remnants.[72] Roger was sent first to Colonel Lord John Cecil in charge of Portsmouth Defences, "who had no use for me," and then to Major Beasley of the Defence Corps at Fareham, "who didn't want me." The remaining men were posted, so Roger returned to London to try to gain another posting. He had a number of interviews without success, and in his last diary entry for November he wrote that it had been "Two months since 13 Batt[alion] left & still no job."[73]

After a few rather typical Army non-jobs, he served as Quartermaster at Fort Nelson, near Portsmouth, until February, when he was ordered to hand over his stores and go to Rowbarton, near Taunton in Somerset, where he was to join the 1st Hampshire Infantry Works Company. The practice of having Works Companies attached to regiments was in the process of being changed and the Labour Corps was being formed in its stead. Roger noted, "I'm to go to a Labour Battalion" and then reported to the O.C. Captain Palmer.[74] He took over the quartermaster duties aided by a "sick Q.M.S." who soon broke down. A new sergeant-major arrived, but his health immediately failed. They were sent 2nd Lt. Morris, but Captain Palmer also broke down. The depot sent a replacement who arrived completely drunk. The new man was ordered away and, perhaps in desperation, Roger was given the command on 2 March 1917.[75] He immediately set to organizing things and appointing his own senior NCOs. On 5 March they entrained for Folkestone, where Roger was able to call on Sam Steele the next morning. After a rough crossing later that day, they rested at Boulogne and entrained again. They arrived at Hazebrouck, Flanders, at 9 A.M. on 7 March, in bitter cold with snow, to find that there was no food, no fuel, and no blankets. He could do nothing but settle the men as best he could in barns. The next morning they found two men had died. Roger sent out his officers with instructions to stop and loot every vehicle that passed, and to tell the driver to report the robbery at once. He found a telephone and made the wires hum with his comments to Headquarters, knowing that a temporary captain might get away with actions that a regular officer could not. In this way he made a big start on building a reputation as a rebel in Flanders, to add to that of an eccentric robber that he had acquired in England. He "demanded & obtained med[ical] inspection. 32 to Hospital." The next day his Company was moved to a disused prisoner-of-war camp near Poperinghe, where the prisoners had been evacuated due to its proximity to the front lines. Roger's Company found it reasonably safe as the shells seemed to fly right over them. He reported that there were "only 17 to Hospital today & 4 more during evening. Influenza virulent but no more spotted fever. Quarantine enjoined."[76] The camp may have been considered too dangerous for prisoners, but members of Roger's Company were quite content, as it was far better equipped with hot baths and stoves than most other camps. Only one dangerous incident was recorded: "7 am. Anti aircraft firing at a German plane fragment of shell fell at QM store doorway & a bullet through No. 10 hut roof. heavy [sic] firing culminating towards evening in prolonged & tremendous bombardment."[77]

Very little has been written about the Labour Battalions and Companies, in contrast to full accounts of all the fighting units. Yet there was a desperate need for men for every kind of unskilled work on railways, roads, handling ammunition, and digging trenches and graves. The tasks were unpleasant, dangerous, and often very close to the front line. The men in the Labour Battalions had been wounded and were unfit for active service, had some physical disability, or were volunteers beyond the age of combat service. Some of the men proved to be either medically unfit or mentally unsuitable for such duties, but others approached their duties calmly. Roger actually boasted of his men and their pride in their unit:

> Our work was unloading trains, building light railways, or mending roads which shells had made untidy; and steadily our invalids gained in strength from outdoor living, good food, and moderate labour.... [U]nder gusts of shell-fire... our men would walk to the nearest cover, smoke cigarettes, and watch the shelling with interest while they rested. The spell improved their work; but of much greater value was their interest in the drum-fire, in the movements of troops, in the aerial dog-fights overhead, in the burning of kite balloons and parachute descents, but most especially in the processions of German prisoners, to whom they would give the whole of their cigarettes.[78]

Brigadier Alfred Mack (1898–1990), later a commandant of the Canadian Division of the Legion of Frontiersmen, served on the Ypres Salient at this time and clearly recalled the notoriety achieved by Roger, "the rebellious Labour Company Commander," although he never met him. Mack also wrote that "Men of the Labour Units in that area were accepted by the men of the line of [*sic*] comrades on equal footing, and respected as such. They were exposed to just as much shelling havoc as the rest, and 'carried on.'"[79]

Roger wrote down some maxims for war service, which he kept in his scrapbooks: "The man who nails pictures in his hut will be transferred elsewhere. If one unit plants a garden, another will reap the fruit. Buy a new tunic and you will get shoved in the Reserve. If you want to get to the Front, pretend that you don't."[80] All these were inspired by what happened to him during his military service, and the first two occurred at the disused prisoner-of-war camp. On 3 April, staff officers came to take over his splendid camp. He protested vigorously, even travelling to Division Headquarters at Reninghelst to protest, but without success. His official "orders arr[ived] 11 am to move at 10am. I got a lift & inspected new camp…called Kenova camp. All rats. Marched the men over very cold evening."[81] Kenova, about a mile from Headquarters, was completely infested with rats, so it took some time, and a number of ratting parties, to get their numbers down. Roger was delighted to learn on 9 April that his captaincy had been restored "from Date of taking command," and on 20 April the unit was officially re-named "as 178 Labour Co[mpan]y."[82] When an advance party of the 23 West Surrey Labour Company arrived to share the camp on 10 April, Roger's Company moved out of their huts into tents, which were less warm in a cold spring but also less troubled by rats. He found that he had racing trainer Joe Kelly in his ranks and made him staff sergeant in charge of transport. Soon the Company's horses were the envy of all other units. Campbell, Roger's sergeant-major, was puzzled that he had been given the position, since he had been only a navvy all his life, but he was the strongest and fiercest man in the unit and also had leadership abilities, so he was the best man for the job. One escapade during this period nearly resulted in Roger being shot as a spy: "Walk with Morris. Arrested for German spies by Col Hales, 8 Glosters. Marched under guard to Brigade HQ on Windmill hill. dined [sic] with HQ mess. Handed over to a Pm 19 Div. who took us in car to West Outre & obtained our release from Div HQ. back to camp 11.15."[83]

On 4 May the Company was told it was to move three days later. Suddenly the weather became very hot, so they turned in their winter clothes and Roger gave orders for all ranks to bathe in a nearby stream, the Grootebeck, which, within a few days, brought him an official complaint from a senior officer, General Legge. The men were working day and night shifts at Ellarsyde railway yards, but he obtained authority for a day of rest on Sunday, 6 May. That day a British plane made a forced landing in a nearby meadow, so they entertained the plane's observer to lunch. In the afternoon Roger met General Legge who, together with the pilot, accepted an invitation to tea.[84] Orders to move arrived at 4:30 P.M. on 14 May, so Roger made the arrangements and cancelled the working parties in order to obey orders, but this did not stop Major Whiddiquake and Captain Gall from making an official protest at the withdrawal of the working parties. Everyone stood ready to move the next morning until further orders arrived at 1 P.M. stating that everything was cancelled, so the working parties went out again. Even in Flanders the problem of drunkenness had not completely disappeared, as Sgt. Hurst disgraced himself on 20 May. Two days later Hurst tried to forestall matters by applying for reduction to corporal. Roger granted that request, but also made Hurst "swear off all drinks 3 months."[85]

On 1 June Roger "Saw a balloon (Brit) in flames. We expected the Big Push." On 6 June he recorded this note:

> No. 3 Platoon, [Lt] Lavender, special duty shelled unit at
> Kemmel. 4 men wounded. Parties walked 6 m[iles] back
> arr[ived] up to 3 am. 3.10 *Big Push* at Wycherta Ridge. Hill
> 60 blown up.
> Guns roll in earthquake.[86]

Five specialist tunnelling companies had been mining the area for some time, and nineteen mines, involving approximately 600 tons of explosive, were detonated simultaneously. The sound of the combined mines was heard in London, but Roger described the feeling: "There came earthquake so that I could scarcely keep my foothold."[87] By 8 June he was able to note:

> News of general advance & all well.
> Tremendous artillery fighting but much further away.
> Balloons forward some miles.
> Cancelled rest party to send 300 men in two shifts up to
> Kemmel extension. Morning & evening shifts out about 14 to
> 16 hours.
> Medical rerating ordered.

For the following day he made this observation:

> Newspapers in, describing capture of the German Messines
> salient.
> Sgt Cook on leave. Sgt Lewis back.
> Capt. Pullen took me to Messines ridge[,] saw craters
> 80 ft. deep, tanks passing the ruins of Ypres, Messiol &
> Wycherta & Hill 60 near horizon. My working party of 165
> grading close up to skyline. Picked up relics[,] saw burial
> parties at work & guns taking position. Anti aircraft guns
> firing close by, & big shells streaming overhead.[88]

On the following day he was detailed to escort Col. Davenport and Major Wallace to the battlefield where they had a picnic. Roger wrote, "never saw I such a quaint event as the Staff picnic next day on the Château grounds ten yards from Suicide Corner, with myself employed as a Guide to officers visiting the craters, and looking down over the head of Hill Sixty to the shattered wreck of Ypres."[89] On 12 June orders arrived, so the next day they moved to a new camp in the old British reserve trenches one mile in front of Kemmel, where they dug in deeper. He noted that the "average day's work 16 1/2 hours[,] no rest from shelling," which was a long day for men who were officially unfit for active service.[90] He kept the men digging in even deeper, but it was there Roger claimed the first of the many premonitions that were to change his outlook on life. On 16 June a shell hit the ammunition dump where his men were working. Three men were killed, three wounded, and three shell-shocked. He applied for authority to move his camp, as he believed its location was too dangerous. A telegram arrived the next day with the new location, but he had no map to work out the coordinates, so he took it on himself to move the Company to a "good camp with dugouts for all behind Kemmel Hill." The next day he received a visit from his group commander who was "furious & threatening.... Expected to be relieved of Command even cashiered for disobedience of orders." Roger stuck to his opinion and insisted that the commander visit the vacated camp to see for himself how dangerous it was, suggesting that he would make his own report to higher authority to the effect that the men had been placed in unacceptable danger. Although Roger received another black mark on his record for exercising the sort of initiative that was not allowed in the army, on 22 June many vehicles arrived to move the men to a much better camp, "out of Kemmel Hill to a field n[ea]r Brandhoek."[91] Roger was granted leave the next day and went to Boulogne to visit his sister Lena, who was there with her highly successful Concert Parties for the troops. His leave did not begin well, for he "missed leave train at 2 pm caught freight train arr[ived] Boulogne 10.30 pm. A porter tried to lure me into a doubtful house. Got clear. Slept at a small pension."[92]

After Roger returned to his camp on 30 June, he noted that the German kite balloons were in full view and directing shell fire. He ordered the sergeant-major to pitch the tents at random, rather than in the neat and orderly lines required by the Army, and to camouflage them with branches. On 2 July, two other companies moved in to share their camp and Roger made the grave mistake of protesting to Headquarters that the new residents had pitched their tents in a neat and orderly manner, which would draw the attention of the German spotters in the kite balloons. He was ordered to align the tents neatly. He noted, "Group Commander unbearable," and the next day "aligned tents."[93] He did, however, get away with leaving the guy ropes slack, which meant that the loose canvas acted as defence against shrapnel. Shortly thereafter, "Group Commander Cordeaux confessed orders to examine into my fitness to command. 1 hour's torture."[94]

His independent ways, which generally followed the ideals of the Legion of Frontiersmen, might have been acceptable in a senior officer such as Lt. Col. Driscoll, and in the less structured campaign of East Africa with the 25th Battalion Royal Fusiliers (Frontiersmen), but it was not tolerable within the ordered discipline of the Western Front. Roger even received a reprimand for the incorrect colour of his shirts. Had he been younger, fitter, and able to go with Driscoll, his conduct would not have stood out. Roger had been desperately keen to see active service, but his age and hard life helped the horrors of the war to have an effect. Lt. Col. Edward Kyme Cordeaux (1866–1946) disliked and disapproved of Roger's unconventional ways, but eventually Cordeaux "owned up to no Confidential Report against me. He has lied." Nonetheless, the next day the "Group Commander insulted me. Resigned my command."[95] His official letter of resignation is somewhat poignant.

> I have the honour to report that the duties of my post are beyond my strength, compelling me to resign the command of my unit.
> Respectfully submitted herewith is my record of service. The founding of the Legion of Frontiersmen gave me a training in organization and in Intelligence Work. My Work "Horses" published this year by John Murray, which I seek leave to submit, may show that I can be of service as as [sic] an Instructor & adviser in Horsemastership. I seek employment with the Expeditionary Force.[96]

However, Lt. Col. Cordeaux insisted on having the final word of vengeance, so his letter recommending that Roger be permitted to resign his command concluded, "I consider that Captain Pocock is lacking in the initiative and energy requisite for the command of a Labour Unit."[97]

All this time Roger's men were working valiantly under heavy enemy fire and some heavy rain, which caused flooding in the camp. Roger wrote letters and made contact with a number of senior officers as he inquired about other vacancies, including as "director remounts." Roger was deeply upset about the bombing of hospitals, either deliberately or accidentally. In a big bombing raid on 17 August, one of his men was killed and three wounded from a working detachment at Remy Hospital.[98] Throughout, Roger noted the number of men ill, wounded, or killed, but there were still little stories to amuse him. For example, King George V was to visit the area on 6 July, and a "Very Secret" dispatch arrived to tell him of the visit and the correct protocol. Roger had a platoon working nearby and informed the officer, swearing him to secrecy. Meanwhile Sergeant-Major Campbell was waiting to tell Roger all about the visit, about which the men had heard everything from the Belgians. The Germans also knew, for they launched a bombardment. Roger was also amused that when they found a spring of good clear water, permission had to be sought to drink it. The result was a thick file of correspondence and, by the time the request came for a sample for testing, the spring had dried up, so Roger sent the contents of a soda water bottle that had been allowed to go flat. The Army has always been frustrating for those who have no time for unnecessary red tape.

On 19 August Roger had business at Vlamertinghe Yard, because he thought the Yardmaster had been treating the men of his Company badly. He had another premonition while saying his goodbyes to the Yardmaster:

> "This ground's bad. Get out!" The Yardmaster turned back,
> and a few yards brought him to cover. I ran for all I was
> worth, waving my cane to a lorry, which slowed down. As I
> climbed to the seat a shell burst precisely where I had been
> standing when the warning reached me. It killed two and
> wounded two of my men, as I learned afterwards....[99]

While it does not show up in his diary, Roger later wrote he was badly shaken, and the premonitions that he had been having made him decide he should return to the fold of orthodox religion.[100] The day after this incident Lt. Col. Cordeaux achieved what he had been working for, and Roger noted that he was "Invalided as too old & infirm for General Service to Proceed to Eng[land] & report in writing to War Office."[101] At a General Parade he said goodbye to his men and they said goodbye to him, with sadness. Not all the senior officers were pleased to see him go, and next morning Col. Gordon provided him with his official car so he could catch the train to Boulogne.

Roger reached London on 22 August to find that the theatres and entertainments of London were still very busy. He threw himself into a social round of meeting old friends and seeing shows. On the first evening he went to see the spectacularly successful musical *Chu Chin Chow,* which had opened on 31 August 1916. In his diary he also listed a great many others he saw. The effect of all the months under bombardment, though, meant that he found it impossible to sleep indoors on the first night, so he sat on the windowsill. One of his social engagements was visiting his old friend Hugh Pollard on 26 August. Pollard was working in Military

Intelligence and he arranged a job for Roger in that department, beginning on 1 September, although Roger only noted this event six days later:

> I went to work for Military Intelligence 7B & worked hard with great success until Dawson applied for me to W.O.
> Capt. Edge also applied for me to be messing officer at RFC camps.[102]

According to his diary, Roger "left Military Intelligence Dept" on 1 December. Perhaps his writing was too journalistic and over the top for the propaganda department, and this persuaded the War Office against changing the initial temporary three-month appointment to a permanent one. Roger seemed to think so when he wrote, "My masterpieces were put into a special drawer, to be disinfected, and never one saw daylight."[103] In any event, it did not interfere much with his social life.

Another old friend and Legion member, Selwyn Francis Edge, arranged a further transfer for him, this time to the Royal Flying Corps (RFC), where his peculiar skills and abilities were much appreciated, particularly by its more adventurous and free-thinking young officers. He went "to join RFC" on 13 December and spent the remainder of the war there, reverting to his old rank of lieutenant, having yet again lost his temporary captaincy. He served as a "penguin," that is, a ground officer. Life became joyous again for him, especially when another old friend, Guy Ashby, applied for him to be transferred to his unit at Chattis Hill, near Stockbridge. On 1st April 1918, the same date that the Royal Flying Corps became the Royal Air Force, he was delighted to have his temporary captaincy restored for the remainder of the War. Here Roger was in his element: "Only in the Air Force, or on the frontiers, where everything was new, one could take thought and action in perfect freedom, with the result that all one's work proved useful. The whole atmosphere was buoyant with youthful health and vibrant energy."[104] He never forgot the experience, and for the rest of his life was fond of preaching to the young that flying and the flying services were the future. He made many new friends, including Norman Macmillan. The escapades of the young pilots delighted Roger with his sense of adventure and lack of respect for those senior and staff officers whom he thought had failed to earn respect. Roger enjoyed living under canvas at Chattis Hill, although Macmillan considered the facilities too basic in comparison with other training aerodromes. Roger had time to recover from his ordeal at the Front and enjoy the history and geology of the area while thinking about his magnum opus, "The Great Design," which was going to be, in his opinion, his most important work of non-fiction. When the church bells rang out across the Wiltshire Downs in November 1918 to herald the end of that terrible war, he could turn his mind back to what had happened to the world many thousands of years ago and his own particular theories. Despite his age and frequent clashes with Army bureaucracy and military discipline, Roger's patriotism and thirst for adventure sustained him through numerous assignments and unit transfers. Once more he had the satisfaction of campaigning in defence of his country.

"THE GREAT DESIGN"
and the
WORLD FLIGHT
EXPEDITION

ROGER RETURNED TO CIVILIAN LIFE after he was discharged from the Army with the rank of lieutenant. Although his captaincy had been temporary, and only for part of his war service, he used the title for the rest of his life. He had been wounded earlier by some of the pointed asides, and even open comments, made about him by early Legion members who had held the King's commission and came from a higher social class; he wished, therefore, to retain the rank as a quiet reminder to those who may have looked down on an ex-irregular corporal. As a captain he should, at least in theory, be considered an officer and a gentleman, rather than an adventurer with ideas above his station in life.

Not long after his discharge he went to sea, this time to the deep-sea fisheries, the herring-drifters, and the trawlers, and to painting pictures of fish and painting fish on glass vessels:

> In June, 1919, I was sent to the Crystal Palace to get my
> release from the Army, and wandered about that wonderful
> place, which has exits leading in many directions. Which way
> should I go? In the whole world of adventure, where could I
> learn most?

The Sea was calling me, ready to greet a son with the lash of her winds, the sting of her salt spray.

Here was a province in the world of adventure, where men very deeply tanned, wore rough blue guernseys and thigh boots, and the best of them had earrings to improve their sight. Not that one should ever judge a nut by its shell, for a very good nutshell may have a bad nut inside, or even be quite empty. But in the Deep Sea Fisheries an empty or a rotten man wouldn't last.[1]

Other than his war service, the main feature of Roger's life between 1914 and 1924 was the lure of the sea. A natural sailor, who was at home in almost any weather, a life on board ship with simple, hard-working fishermen may have given him respite from mental demons caused by the Curtis affair, his departure from the Legion, and the horrors of the First World War. In the fading days of peace before war was declared, he had passed many enjoyable hours working on George Stoker's little beam-trawler.[2] These would have been happy memories to take with him into the conflict. So it is perhaps understandable that after his discharge his thoughts turned again to life at sea: "In the next year or two I was to be a guest in many different ships, learning the ways of the herring drifters, the trawlers of the shoals, the line-fishers of the deeps, in motor, sail, and steam."[3] Although he worked his passages, he considered himself a guest, and by behaving appropriately he won the trust of the sailors:

Among themselves all men are free and equal, but towards strangers they form a shy, sensitive and most exclusive aristocracy, quite civil, icily reserved. How, then, had I managed to get inside the tribal brotherhood? Of course I never ventured to sea without a big bag of sugar cakes and plenty of cigarettes to pay my footing, but that would not account for the barest toleration, whereas I was admitted to the closest friendship. Puzzled at this, I asked the deckies in one ship why they were so kind. I found out that I was all right, because I was a broken-down swell. I had not been mistaken for a gent.[4]

However, in addition to his ability to get along with all types of people and his ability to persuade people to talk and to be a good listener himself, his calmness in the roughest conditions impressed the sailors. As an example he recalled a trip on a Scottish herring-drifter:

The weather happened to be coarse that evening, and
the ship lively, so after supper I smoked my pipe amid
the warm smells of the engine-room, much to the general
disappointment. Still, they would show me, and this was first
of four vessels out of all the fleet which ventured to shoot the
nets. They had to haul in a hurry and run for shelter behind
Shetland; but still these Scots had one more test for the
foreigner. It was a short cut behind an islet, tide-race between
fanged reefs in a full gale, a crazy thing to adventure. I loved
them for that because it brought back the thrill of good old
memories, for I had shot big rapids in canoes. I had only
to stand in the wheel-house and keep my mouth shut, but
afterwards the deckies called me by my Christian name.[5]

The seamen told him many a fascinating tale, but although he tried to offer
stories of the fisheries to the newspapers, they were not interested:

I hoped to make expenses as a journalist, but never found
a journal which took the slightest interest in the Deep Sea
Fisheries. How strange is the public taste which is ravenous
for stories about cowboys, now extinct, and cowgirls who
never existed, but ignores altogether this picturesque life,
with all its heroism, its glamour and its agony. I have been a
cowboy, and know the North American stock-range, from
the Saskatchewan River to Zacatecas in Mexico, its extremist
[sic] limits; but never did I find one story to compare with
that of an aged Grimsby Skipper.[6]

He could only save the stories and record them in his autobiography.
Readers wanted escapism after the horrors of the war, and although they
might have considered more of his escapist "Wild West" yarns and adventure stories, he had exhausted the fund of tales he had acquired as a
younger man, and he did not have the ability to write fiction from imagination or from research. He did manage, though, to recast some of his
heroes of adventure for boys.[7]

Roger had been working on a book, even though he spent so much
time at sea. Probably fitfully, he had been writing the least successful
of his novels, *The Wolf Trail*, which was eventually accepted and published. Perhaps fortunately for his reputation, it was not a success and
few copies survive. Nonetheless, Roger was, as always, quite generous in
presenting copies of his book. He was sufficiently proud of *Wolf Trail*

to present an inscribed copy of the London edition to a noted explorer: "To Vilhjalmur Stefansson from Roger Pocock. In memory of a happy meeting & a generous action. June 4th 1923." He also presented a copy to the son and grandson of early supporters of the Legion: "To Charles Palmer [from] Roger Pocock."[8] Perhaps unwisely, instead of writing the adventure story Roger's readers expected from him, he provided a not very well written allegory, and returned to his beloved Rain, the Blackfoot girl who first appeared in *The Splendid Blackguard* and *The Cheerful Blackguard.* Roger wrote that as early as 1913, when he and Randle Cecil were riding through the mountains in British Columbia, he had begun to think about this book: "The next march brought us by a switchback trail to the summit of Wells Pass, in an amphitheatre of peaks and glaciers of such surpassing grandeur that I chose it for the scene of my next novel, 'The Wolf Trail.'"[9] In addition, he used quite a number of other places he had come to know in his travels. As usual, Roger based some of the events in the book loosely on his personal experience and stories he had been told.

The scenery may have had grandeur, but in this weird and disjointed story the hero has a dream life as a First Nations young man, in which his astral projection becomes Storm, whose female companion is Rain. The horrors Roger had experienced in the war and his return to Christianity had an effect on his writing. So, for example, Storm takes on other forms, including a centurion at the crucifixion of Jesus and an Icelandic chief. Even fairies make an appearance in the narrative. In a confused way, the story suggests a kind of reincarnation until the second-stage soul is ready to pass into heaven or hell. Towards the end of the book Storm is crucified by an evil white hunter, and Rain dies with him. They are saved from pain by No-man (also known as Hiram J. Kant), an American hunter who at an earlier stage in the story tried to rape Rain, but she plunged a knife into him and prevented him from ever thinking of rape again when "she dragged the wounded man abreast of the hearth-fire, rolled him face downwards, his loins across the belt of red-hot coals, and stood holding him there with her foot, until the awful vengeance was accomplished."[10] Storm and Rain convert No-man to Christianity and he becomes their friend. After No-man is shot by the evil hunter, he, Storm, and Rain find themselves on the wolf trail, the First Nations' view of the way to heaven. There they are greeted by angels.

Roger wrote the mystical sections at the end in 1919, when he was on holiday at Birchington, Kent, with family, where he said, "The life we lived was that prescribed to students of the Unseen."[11] His family's immersion in spiritualism was related to the post-war revival of interest in the idea that the human spirit existed after death and that it was possible for the dead to communicate with the living. Roger described his own wartime experience with some of the elements of spiritualism. After the war, as he was writing *The Wolf Trail,* he said the whole sequence came to him in a vision as he looked out his window towards the sea:

> Through this, flickering through it like double-filming in cinema work, appeared another landscape—wilderness, a dark inland sea, stupendous alps, and in the foreground the characters and action of the story. The two landscapes, normal and abnormal, flickered in by turns, neither completely seen at any given moment. I could leave my writing for a meal or a rest, and come back to it without losing the vision, which belonged to full normal waking consciousness. It was not vision of substantial fact, but what is known technically as an astral reflection, a dramatic presentation in which I could see what was done, hear what was said.[12]

When the vision left him, he suddenly found himself unable to write any more and even unable to speak. On the second day, when he was somewhat recovered, he telephoned the doctor, who suggested another sea trip, where Roger was always content. In light of his claim that he was unable to sleep in an enclosed room for some time after his return from war, Roger was probably suffering from a form of shell shock. He had, however, made a study of many kinds of mysticism and telepathy, and during the war he claimed significant premonitions, and that his "thought-concentration in the form of prayer" had protected his men.[13] He even claimed for himself some of the mystical skills of the First Nations people, probably aided by his studies and his time spent with them:

> On the Great Plains of North America, while in perfect health, I have caught the strong scent of cattle at five miles, the perfume of fresh running water—smell of a wet knife—at half a mile, and seen the bending of grass from a waggon [*sic*] wheel after six weeks. Still I can time myself in sleep to wake at a given hour, and know where North is, except on the Underground Railway.[14]

In the aftermath of the war, many others shared his mystical interests, but for Roger, writing of *The Wolf Trail* may have acted as a catharsis.

Roger Pocock, Spitsbergen, Wood Bay, N. Shore, Porphyrite exposure.
[SPRI 1520.]

However, the book also expressed considerable violence and sexual passions, mainly suppressed. In the social climate of the early 1920s when it was published, it must have caused some surprise among its limited readership, unless they read the acknowledgment that hinted at the nature of this book.[15]

Following a number of voyages on the herring-drifters, trawlers, and line-fishers that sailed out of ports on the east coast of England and Scotland, Roger was pleased to be able to take part in the 1921 Oxford University Expedition to Spitsbergen. Roger is listed among the eighteen men named as members of the expedition, with the description "(Cook; Artist)."[16] Roger claimed he was also responsible for refitting the *Terningen,* which had been chartered for the journey.[17] Some years ago, not one of the few surviving members of the expedition and their families remembered Roger by name, but a few had a vague recollection there was

a cook.[18] The leader of the expedition was the Rev. Francis Charles Robert Jourdain (1865–1940). Roger, however, held that his expedition experience gave him the right to make suggestions to the young men, which rather exceeded a cook's mandate. So at Tromsø, as he listened to stories about the perils of Arctic travel, and watched the members of the expedition arrive, "looking ostentatiously British, eager and inexperienced," he came to this conclusion:

> Considering the high attainments of these men in Science, it would be rather a pity if they all got drowned; so the cook suggested that there should be an Adjutant in support of the Reverend Doctor Jourdain, Oo-ologist Commanding. This being agreed to, the cook proposed that the Adjutant should be Mr. Julian Huxley, and he was duly appointed.

Considering a lifetime of howling error in the selection of
men, I am rather proud of having been wise for once.[19]

Huxley described responsibilities differently. He said that with some pestering from colleagues and help from Jourdain and Alec Carr-Saunders, he
"decided to organize an all-round scientific expedition to the Arctic...."
While the original impetus was to study birds and collect their eggs, there
were also botanists, geologists, a glaciologist, and zoologists on the expedition. Huxley was quite pleased with both the immediate and long-term
results.[20]

Before the expedition left Tromsø to head north, Derek Henry Strutt,
just back from spending two years in Spitsbergen, met Roger:

> I remember him [Roger] as a rather corpulent middle-aged
> man, with grey hair and pince-nez, and a kindly expression—
> but that's about all which does stay in my memory.
>
> We went for a walk together to the outskirts of the town
> and sat down on a hillside, covered with small larch or
> spruce bushes, overlooking the fjord, and I bombarded him
> with questions principally regarding the latest plays, actors
> and actresses, books and authors, which might have made
> a success during my absence from the world, and I have no
> doubt he answered me satisfactorily and was probably highly
> amused at my naivete.

After they parted Strutt learned Roger's name from other members of the
Oxford expedition:

> The episode then practically passed out of my memory,
> and was only revived a long time afterwards when I saw the
> name over a long critique...and connected it with my chance
> acquaintance in Tromsoe, at the same time kicking myself
> metaphorically, thinking of my artless questions put to one of
> the leading minds of his day....[21]

During the expedition, in Roger's spare time, or as he put it, "Apart from
the daily detail of overhauling stores, cooking and baking, landscape painting, photography and journalism, boat work and an occasional run ashore,
I had certain private worries in geology."[22] He needed to pursue his study
of geology so he could prepare for what he thought was going to be his
most important written work. Roger studied fossils, as well as changes in

sea level and climate over the centuries. He spent much of the summer of 1922 in the Shetland Islands, studying changes in sea level. He was convinced that these changes were mainly due to movements of the Earth's axis, but there were flaws in his theories, partly because, as he openly admitted, "I am so hopelessly bad at arithmetic."[23] This study continued to absorb a substantial share of his energy for the rest of his life.

The book he wanted to write as a result of this study would explain his theories of the movement of the axis of the earth over many thousands of years. The only lasting evidence of his time in Spitsbergen, however, are paintings he made as artist of the expedition.[24] Nonetheless, in the years immediately following his return from Spitsbergen, he produced a manuscript he titled "The Great Design," setting out his theories. He approached it as a disciple of William Thomson, Baron Kelvin of Largs (1824–1907), the distinguished mathematician and physicist, some of whose theories were superseded even during his lifetime. Roger was unable to find a publisher and, in spite of his attempt to ensure the manuscript would be preserved after his death, all attempts to discover it have failed.[25] It probably has been destroyed, but Roger did give some hint of his reasoning in his autobiography. He thought Spitsbergen's barren landscape gave him much evidence. For example, he saw two plants, club moss and mare's tail, which he said should only be found in the equatorial belt. Other plants and fossils also made him believe that Spitsbergen had once enjoyed a much warmer climate.

> Has then Spitsbergen travelled out of the equatorial tropic
> into this high Arctic? Rather I think we read…a shift of
> the Earth's axis, amounting to nearly ninety degrees of arc.
> This place was on the Equator, which is now near the North
> Pole, because the Earth is spinning on a different axis. There
> is my little unofficial worry, which makes the current and
> fashionable Geology seem like a pack of nonsense. Perhaps
> I had better leave that subject, with the threat of a third
> autobiography—if I have time.[26]

Unfortunately, he did not have either the time or a willing publisher.

Unable to find a publisher when he had completed "The Great Design," Roger tried hard to find a respected person to sponsor it. Roger claimed that the Arctic explorer Augustine Courtauld showed some interest in his theories and tried to help him. After he had done some re-writing, and possibly at Courtauld's suggestion, Roger wrote to Frank Debenham (1883–1965) at the Scott Polar Research Institute in

Cambridge. Fortunately, Debenham was a kindly man, as well as a distinguished scholar. He was not one to snub or ignore what astronomer Patrick Moore charmingly refers to as "independent thinkers." Moore has investigated a number of scientific and astronomic "independent thinkers," some of whose ideas ran on lines similar to those expressed by Roger.[27] Roger entered into a correspondence with Debenham, which went on from 1932 until 1938. It is from this correspondence that we are able to learn a little more about Roger's idiosyncratic ideas. In his first letter, Roger outlined these thoughts:

> In half a century of travel and research, I have observed certain
> movements of the Earth's axis, from about B.C.200,000 down
> to about A.D.1500. So far as I know, Lord Kelvin was the only
> observer to note the changes of sea-level resulting from the
> presence of ice-caps, and that at a time when their volume
> was less accurately measured than it is to-day. Changes in
> sea-level have an important bearing upon the general theme,
> which seems to be new to Science. It may be defined as a re-
> statement of History in terms of climatic change.
>   In the course of the last two years I have almost completed
> the re-writing of the book, and in another month will have
> a synopsis ready, a very brief statement of the theory. This
> synopsis I am most anxious to submit to a Geographer, and
> I should be very grateful if you would consent to examine a
> rough chart of the axial vibration during the latter half of the
> Quartenary [sic] Ice Ages.[28]

Any scientist would be wary of claims for revolutionary explanations of world history, but Debenham agreed to look at the synopsis. Roger was most grateful for this agreement.

> Courtauld submitted for me to The Times a bare bones
> synopsis, which is too brief to be intelligible, was rejected,
> and is now with the Morning Post. At the Savile Club
> meeting he suggested my theme for a debate, which for me
> would be a great adventure.
>   Your consent to read a synopsis of "The Great Design"
> gave me renewed hope. I send one rather longer and more
> intelligible than that which went to The Times....
>   "The Great Design," despite my utmost endeavours, has
> never had even a reading, but if the synopsis now submitted

wins ever so modified approval, I can try my luck with the Cambridge University Press, and with my publishers in the United States.[29]

Debenham was good enough to read the synopsis and replied with the greatest of courtesy, while pointing out the more obvious flaws in Roger's theories:

I have read through your resume of your book, and am now going to give you a completely frank criticism of it.

I must begin by saying that it is most entertaining, and I enjoyed reading it from that point of view, but I must also add that from any other point of view I consider your thesis not proven.

The trouble seems to me that you have jumped the arguments too much and make statements without leading up to them by proof. Thus in your first chapter you say: "In former times the gyroscopic fly-wheel which we call the ocean had to spin a little northwards of the true equator, etc." How do you know that, and why wasn't the whole of the northern hemisphere drowned at the same time? In fact, I am afraid those horrible scientists will receive your book with a shower of questions as to proof, mathematical analysis, etc, [sic] etc. We're an odd lot, we scientists, but we cannot help asking for figures or equations to support such statements as that the Polar flood was 652 ft. Again, I simply cannot follow your methods of triangulation to find the position of the North Pole. It is delightful reading, that chapter, especially the wanderings of the lobster, the tapir and the hippo, and I almost feel it is worth-while printing for that reason, but it's rather too like "Alice in Wonderland" to really persuade the scientists. By the time we get to Chapter Seven I must confess to feeling somewhat dizzy, for [w]ithout following your argument at all, I find all sorts of explanations as to the history of civilization coming pat in terms of the movement of the North Pole.

As I said before, delightful reading, but I choke somewhat from swallowing it all, partly from amusement, and partly from meeting statements for which there is no tangible proof, such as my scientific soul requires.

To sum up, I am afraid I must confess to doubting the of [sic] your discoveries more on the score of what is omitted than what is stated. I imagine too that publishers [*sic*] readers would enjoy reading your script as I did, but would not be convinced that it would be a saleable book.

I hope this isn't damping to you. I don't think it will be since you are a philosopher, but you must remember also that I have no claim to be a scientist in the strict sense of the word, and it would be better to try someone else as well, preferably one who enjoys your style less, and therefore will give plainer criticism.[30]

As we do not have the manuscript that Roger spent so much of his time over so many years of his later life writing, Debenham's kindly letter is of some help in showing what was in Roger's mind. He was naturally a little downcast when he replied:

A straight, frank, unbiased criticism is the best thing that can possibly happen to an author, curative of swelled head, a tonic to make one fit, a light in the dark to guide one through bad ground.

So I don't want to talk back, but only to express my grateful thanks.[31]

Four years passed and it looks very much as if advancing age had affected Roger's memory, because he wrote again with a fairly concise statement of his case. It looks as if he had forgotten the earlier correspondence and wrote, effectively, a similar letter to a number of distinguished scientists. It is fortunate that he did so, for it gives us a fuller insight into his theories:

The study of the Quartenary [*sic*] Ice Ages seems to come under the general heading of Polar Research.

The astronomical explanations have not appealed to me, because Alaska was never glaciated, and because there is no shred of evidence that an ice-cap in Eur-Asia was contemporary with one in America.

During fifty years of travel and research, I studied raised beaches, ice movements, tilting of continents, migrations of plants, animals and men. These data led me to the conclusion that, about B.C.200,000 the Earth was struck by a meteor or a planet, which set the axis reeling. At about B.C.90,000 the North Pole, moving at one mile in six years, was describing circles which had then reached a diameter of 60° of arc, having a period of about 50,000 years. At B.C.10,390 the movement was arrested and the Pole lurched on an easterly curve, slowing down reaching present position at about A.D.1400.

The Hoerdiger [sic] Institute of Vienna has observed the impact of a planet about B.C.200,000, and the arrest of the polar movement at about the same period as my own estimate.

This theory of Polar Displacement gives the first explanation of the Great Desert Belt now extending from the Atlantic coast of the Sahara to the Gobi. It explains the migration of the tapir between Malaya and Brazil. It serves as a key to unlock many difficulties in geo-physics, archaeology and history. It involves a new conception of human life in terms of climatic change.

There is no longer any hope of getting my book produced as a commercial venture. Let me quote H.H. Howland, late Editor of the Century Magazine: "I have read the manuscript and am tremendously impressed. It is a brilliant piece of writing. One doesn't often see the like these days. On second thought I believe I'll substitute: one *never* sees the like &c. The learning seems to me profound, and the research monumental. I didn't understand it all but that's my misfortune and not your fault. I didn't give a damn however, for the joy of reading such beautiful English carried me gaily along."

On an income of thirty shillings a week, I cannot print the book. The one remaining hope is to win the countenance or support of some learned Society or University, or persuading some journal to print the ten thousand word synopsis. I am attempting to advertise it with a lecture, for which I enclose an invitation without expecting you to visit London for such a trivial occasion.

And yet it may interest you to consider Polar Research as the key which unlocks great mysteries, the clue to the whole story of mankind in terms of Climatic Change. In that case I beg you to read the synopsis, and, if it please you, to have the main book considered with a view to effective support.[32]

Debenham replied to say that he could not attend the lecture because he was going to Australia. He also briefly pointed out what he considered a major flaw in the argument: "My great trouble with your thesis is that geo-dynamics would not permit large meteorites to disturb the earth's axis to such a degree without much more vital effects upon the earths [*sic*] surface. In other words, the splitting of the earth. But that can only be an opinion and I hope you can convince others of your theory."[33] Roger replied that he was not a man to accept defeat and answered Debenham's criticism:

> Before leaving England you wrote that your objection to my theory of Polar displacement was that a direct blow would split the Earth.
>
> The Hoerbiger Institute says that the blow was not direct, but that a small planet, caught by the attraction of the Earth, collided with a grazing or glancing blow, & was shattered.
>
> Professor Roxby of Liverpool accepted my theory & promised to read my manuscript book The Great Design. After eight months I am trying to recover [it], & have also sent for the American copy.
>
> Mr. Edward Lynam, OC Maps at the British Museum[,] told a friend that he was profoundly impressed by the synopsis. He is sending it to you in the hope that you will introduce the book to the Cambridge University Press.
>
> Nobody could regret more than I do that I am a nuisance, but a fellow who accepts defeat is not much good.[34]

The idea that the earth was disturbed at some time in the past by a meteor or planet, or even a comet, was not a new one. It had been put forward by William Whiston, a contemporary of Sir Isaac Newton, at the beginning of the eighteenth century. Whiston's date was either 28 November 2349 B.C. or 2 December 2926 B.C. (He was not sure which.) This interference caused the biblical Flood. His date was considerably different from Roger's 200,000 B.C. Roger cited the Hoerbiger Institute as support for his theory of planetary deflection, but one of the liabilities of Hans Hörbiger's theory was that it was later taken up enthusiastically for a time by the Nazis in Germany. Part of Hörbiger's World Ice Doctrine (Welteislehre or WEL) was that the moon is ice-coated and is spiralling down towards the earth. There have been at least six previous moons, all of which have approached close to the earth, causing major upheavals. Roger adapted Hörbiger's idea of a glancing blow by the last ice-moon to affect Earth. Roger's problem was that he was writing at a time when British publishers had little interest in his type of "independent thinker," particularly when they knew Roger as a writer of old-fashioned western tales. Had he lived twenty or thirty years later and submitted "The Great Design," it is quite possible that it may have been published and achieved some success, as did George Adamski, Erich von Daniken, and Immanuel Velikovsky with their books. As it was, "The Great Design," despite all the years of hard work and thought that Roger invested in the manuscript, was destined to fade into oblivion along with a multitude of other unpublished books written at the wrong time.

Certainly, Roger never gave up. Only three weeks before his death in 1941 he wrote to Flora Steele:

> And now I am busy, with no hopes whatever, on my
> pet hobby, tracking the North Pole through his furtive
> wanderings in the Ice Ages. It is hopeless because I have
> never found a responsible scientist who would even read a
> synopsis. The only other man who tried to follow this trail
> was Lord Kelvin.[35]

He complained, quite incorrectly and forgetfully, that he had never found a responsible scientist who would read a synopsis. He died without seeing his theory brought to the wide audience he considered that it deserved. He would never surrender what he thought was right, but "The Great Design" must go down as another of the failures, albeit a less public one, that he suffered with fortitude throughout his life.

Roger was interested in exploring the earth and its history, but he also became convinced of the importance of flight rather early in its development. Probably the first time he had published this view was in 1907:

> From the moment that the aeroplane becomes a practical
> fact, our men [Frontiersmen], accustomed by seamanship,
> horsemanship, and cycling to a perfect poise and balance of
> the body, will be the most adaptable of men in learning the
> new method of transport. Indeed, we may look forward to
> the aerial age as a golden age of seamanship, for men will be
> tested as to their manhood as they never were in the conquest
> of the sea. We would like to be pioneers in evolving a cavalry
> of the air.[36]

In the 1930s he would encourage young men to consider their own future in flight. In the 1920s, thanks to some friends and his eagerness for adventure, he had the opportunity to participate in an attempt to fly around the world.

Immediately after the First World War, and into the 1920s, there was intense international public interest in long-distance flight. The great prize was to be the first to achieve a flight around the world. Whereas the Americans poured government money into their attempt and eventual success, Britain left all such attempts to amateurs. The great British amateur succeeding (or often failing) in the face of supreme odds has long been part of the national character. The original British plan for a flight around the world entailed using two brothers, Sir Ross and Sir Keith Smith, as pilots. They had been knighted for being the first to fly from Britain to Australia, but tragedy struck when Ross Smith was killed at Brooklands Aerodrome as he was testing a plane in advance of the planned flight. Rather than allow another country to be the first to achieve the flight, the *Daily News* and its air correspondent, Major Wilfred Theodore Blake, decided to encourage a British attempt during 1922 with another pilot. Blake chanced to meet Norman Macmillan, who had a reputation as a brilliant pilot:

> As we strolled down St. James's Street to Rumpelmeyer's for tea, he [Blake] told me he was trying to form an expedition to fly round the world so that Britain should still be first to do it. He had been promised some of the money he needed, and asked me if I would join him to pilot the expedition.... We met several times to discuss the equipment required for the flight....[37]

Blake still needed a third man, because the *Daily News* could not cover the whole cost of the attempt. If the third man were an aerial cameraman, much of the cost of the flight could be recouped by showing motion pictures made during the flight. That third man was Lt. Col. L.E. Broome:

> Broome, although an excellent amateur photographer, was not a professional cameraman; nor did he know anything of value about aeroplanes and aviation; from my point of view as pilot his main claim to participate in the flight lay in his knowledge of the route between Japan and Canada. Between these two countries lie the desolate and frequently fog-bound Kurile and Aleutian Islands, a chain of volcanic rocks separating the Behring [*sic*] Sea from the Pacific Ocean. It was useful to have a member of the crew who knew the local conditions.[38]

The first plane, a D.H. 9 bomber, was purchased cheaply as war surplus and converted for their needs. It was to take them to Calcutta. From Calcutta they would fly a Fairey float seaplane that would be shipped there by sea.[39]

Roger learned about this flight when Macmillan, together with Major Payn, their old Officer Commanding at Chattis Hill, took him out to tea to talk about old times, "while a jazz band played filth," as Roger wrote, with the standard older man's intolerance of younger men's music. They invited him to watch the take-off the following Wednesday, Empire Day, 24 May 1922. Roger spent an evening with Macmillan and, with difficulty for him, kept his misgivings about the North Pacific section of the flight to himself. He felt it best to encourage Macmillan and leave the problems of crossing that perilous area in the hands of Broome, the "expert." Roger admitted, though, "I was jealous."[40] With his lifelong hunger for adventure it would be safe to assume that he would have desperately liked to have taken Broome's place. Roger would have felt that his own knowledge of the route between Japan and Canada was at least equal to Broome's, as was his ability with a camera. Roger's anxiety was increased when the very overloaded plane struggled to take off from Croydon:

> In addition to the three standard petrol tanks there were
> two extra wing tanks carrying another fourteen gallons of
> fuel, an oversize oil tank, spare wheel, kit of tools, ourselves
> (Broome weighed about as much as Blake and I together), a
> cinematograph outfit that weighed over 100 pounds, spare
> films, and our own personal kit—a change of underclothing, a
> suit of pyjamas, toothbrush and shaving gear.[41]

The story of the flight veered between farce and near tragedy. News of it filtered through to Roger. Broome had to be replaced by a lighter man, as the load became impossible, even for a pilot with Macmillan's skill. Probably for financial reasons, a top aerial cameraman was chosen rather than an expert on the North Pacific, and "Finally, it was decided that Broome should go to Japan to organise the route from Tokio [*sic*] to Vancouver, while Geoffrey H. Malins, a professional cameraman and film director, took his place in the aeroplane at Rome."[42] Macmillan and Malins (1886–1940) became friends, but the relationship with Blake became steadily cooler. Macmillan blamed Blake for many of the mishaps, possibly with some justification. The final collapse of the attempt came when the Fairey III.C float-plane, which had taken off from Calcutta, was forced down by equipment failure on a lonely island called Lukhidia Char.[43] They managed to persuade some local people to send a telegram to Blake, who had remained in Calcutta with an inflamed appendix. The telegram advised: "ENGINE FAILURE. ALL O.K. NOW, PETROL SHORT OWING TO HEAVY ADVERSE WIND. ADVISE CHITTAGONG TO KEEP LOOK OUT FOR US FROM HIGH TIDE, TUESDAY AND OBTAIN PETROL. ADVISE ALL CONCERNED. LIVING ON MILK SUPPLIED BY NATIVES IN EXCHANGE FOR CIGARS. CHEERIO. MAC AND MALINS."[44] Macmillan did manage to take off again, but the engine soon failed completely. He was forced to land in the sea and the plane overturned in a storm, so for three days Macmillan and Malins clung to the upturned floats of the plane. Eventually a launch, *Dorothea,* found them, but the two men were furious that Blake had made no mention of their engine failure in his telegram to Chittagong. He had only advised that the two men were on their way and would need fuel. Macmillan felt that Blake's carelessness had nearly cost them their lives: "But there was no chance of continuing the flight, even had we been fit. We had lost almost everything we possessed; the cinematograph camera and its films, our maps, even my passport, were at the bottom of the Bay of Bengal."[45] Relationships between the flyers and the leader, Blake, had totally broken down so the attempt was over. Nonetheless, Blake lavished the highest praise on Macmillan's ability as both pilot and mechanic.[46]

On 21 August, the *Daily News* headline was "CAPT. MACMILLAN MISSING," but on 28 August the story of the sufferings of Macmillan and Malins in the Bay of Bengal, written by Macmillan (although Blake was the paper's official correspondent), took five front page columns with a banner headline: "WONDERFUL STORY OF WORLD FLIGHT WRECK," with two more columns inside the paper.[47] On 21 September the back page of the *Daily News* showed a photograph of Macmillan and Malins in hospital. On 27 September, Blake was back in England. Macmillan and Malins arrived in England on 14 October. The next day "Cordial greetings passed between the three airmen," according to the *Daily News,* in what sounded like an arranged reunion rather than a spontaneous meeting between friends. Nonetheless, Blake was optimistic about another attempt:

> They [Macmillan and Malins] were perfectly cheerful and
> quite willing to try again if we could raise the money for a
> further attempt.
>   We arranged to travel home as soon as possible in order
> to put the film of the flight on the market, hoping that the

profits would be sufficiently large for another expedition to be equipped....

It is no good regretting that the flight did not prove successful, for no one can say what element of luck may be against him; and I think that our disasters may fairly be attributed to sheer bad luck rather than to any fault in the organisation of the flight.... It was a wonderful experience which has brought with it knowledge which will be of use to us should we be enabled to start again; and as none of us are deterred by the hardships we endured, we all hope that we may be able to have a second attempt in order that a British machine with a British crew may be the first to get round the world.[48]

Malins said, "it was only the excellent help of the Royal Air Force and the wonderful piloting of Captain Macmillan throughout the flight that made it possible for us to reach the distance we did."[49]

When Macmillan and Malins had recovered from their ordeal, they went to visit Roger. They had spent much of their time in hospital devising plans for a second attempt, and it would definitely be made without Major Blake. Roger was probably one of the most widely-travelled men Macmillan knew, and one of the few with experience in the North Pacific. After their recent experience, they would have felt confident that they could reach Japan, but they needed Roger's advice for the path of the flight from Japan to Canada. Also, Roger had so many friends and contacts across Canada that he could help with that crossing and advise on the right places to land in Greenland and Iceland, since he was highly knowledgeable about climatic conditions and other problems.

Macmillan and Malins were taken aback by Roger's reaction. He seemed to shed years, and instead of being a man fast approaching sixty, he became young and enthusiastic again, brimming with ideas. He "begged to be taken into partnership.... [T]he first flight round the world ought to be a British venture, for the glory of our Country and the benefit of our aircraft industry."[50] All they had wanted was his advice, but they agreed to appoint Roger geographer for the new expedition. With this official position in mind, Roger at once started drawing up plans and presenting them to Macmillan and Malins. In his enthusiasm, Roger forgot that Britain was weary and subdued after the war and that the Victorian spirit of adventure and empire building was long past. Unfortunately, as with the Klondike expedition, Roger's plans looked good on paper, but the practicalities left a lot to be desired.

Roger agreed with Macmillan and Malins that they should be able to reach Japan without refuelling problems, but after that, he predicted, supplies would be short:

> [there would be only] a few tins of petrol, good enough for motor-boats in the fur trade, but not fit for use by a seaplane. In Yetorup, the first island beyond Japan, there was an area of perpetual fog, and fog would be general through the stormy Kurils, where the harbours are old craters, too deep for anchorage, uninhabited, sketchily surveyed. Kamchatka, under Bolshevist rule, had gone decidedly pink, with the Volunteer Fleet in refuge, short of stores, likely to loot a sea-plane. In the Commander Islands conditions were not reported. The fog-bound Aleutians being actively volcanic, the two sets of charts were opposed on quite important points, and for twenty-two hundred miles there were no known supplies, the nearest petrol being at Unalashka. Along the Alaskan coast there were supplies, but there might be a little trouble with local hurricanes from the Alps of St. Elias, and drift-ice in some harbours.[51]

Roger's answer to the problem was a seaborne expedition to prepare the way for the seaplane by selecting harbours at intervals of approximately 400 miles where they would lay down stores, arrange maps, and gather local knowledge to help the flyers. It soon became clear, though, that Macmillan and Malins made a grave mistake by handing the organization of the seaborne expedition to Roger.

To advance his cause, Roger went back to the Legion, which fourteen years earlier had made his position within the organization untenable.[52] This was a rather odd decision in some ways, but he needed the backing of an organization, and Legion members were highly patriotic. The new president of the Legion was the greatly respected Major-General Edward Douglas Loch, 2nd Baron Loch (1873–1942). Roger and Loch developed quite a rapport. Since Driscoll had immigrated to East Africa in 1919, where he was trying to make a living growing coffee, the Legion had been commanded by a rather ineffective and elderly retired colonel, H.T. Tamplin. To find crew for a ship, Roger suggested they advertise for adventurers who would pay to take part in the expedition. He would ensure potential adventurers knew of the dangers and that there would be only a very slight chance of turning a profit from trading along the route. However, Roger also told the volunteers that they would be taking a specialist with them, "Captain Francis, who came specially from Canada to join us and take charge of this side of the expedition," although only Roger seemed to know anything about this speciality.[53]

Frank Cecil Ransley, one of the crew members, wrote an account of how he came to volunteer. Ransley successfully flew Bristol Fighters during the war, and was awarded a Distinguished Flying Cross in 1918. As with many others searching for an occupation after the war, he went into farming and found life in the open air soothed the nervousness brought on by the war. He was working in Lincolnshire with another ex-pilot, G. Herbert "Bill" Heaton, on Heaton's brother's farm. The year 1922 had been meagre financially, so when Ransley and Heaton read an advertisement for adventurers in the *Daily Mail* they were susceptible. On 26 February 1923 an advertisement also appeared in the *Times:* "ADVENTURERS WANTED for Exciting Sea Expedition; small CAPITAL essential.—Legion, 6, Adamstreet, Adelphi, London." According to Roger, these advertisements were placed by Malins, who "enrolled thirty-eight men, ex-officers with war training from the Navy, Army, Air Force and Merchant Service, subscribing their capital to the funds and serving without pay."[54] Ransley and Heaton decided that "This looked better than hoeing turnips and we both had some of our gratuity left. We took the first train to London and the next morning called in at Adam Street."[55] Roger interviewed them and told them they would be expected to contribute between £200 and £500 each. He said the ship had not yet been purchased, but it was expected to be ready to sail by June 1923. To conform with Board of Trade regulations, the crew would be signed on at one shilling a month. Neither Ransley nor Heaton could afford more than £100, and this was accepted, although they were told that the small contribution meant that they would be given the rather undesirable jobs of coal trimmer and stoker. They returned to Lincolnshire to await the summons to join the ship.

In the early 1920s there were far fewer men with either the money or the inclination to take part in exotic adventures than when Roger had advertised for his Klondike expedition in January 1898; consequently, Roger could not find the forty men he had originally sought, and he had to accept sums smaller than the £200 to £500 he had requested. Thus Ransley wrote that when he and Heaton joined the ship they "learned that the volunteer crew's aggregate contribution amounted to £6,000 and that as several firms were donating supplies we should be able to complete our mission without having to raise more money."[56] Firms may have been willing to donate supplies, but sponsorship would also be needed. Newspapers, however, were unwilling to support an expedition so soon after a splendid story of a great British failure, particularly when it had the same unsuccessful aircrew, Macmillan and Malins. Newsreel photography was still in its infancy, so Malins' skill with a camera did not hold much financial promise, and although the British government could be relied on to make fine comments of support, which it did, there was no chance it would provide financial backing. Of course, if the expedition proved a success, there would be many organizations that would want a share of the credit; all Roger could find, though, were promises of sponsorship once the expedition had proved itself.

Raising money was made yet more difficult because Roger could not turn to his usual financial backer, his brother-in-law, for Henry Simson was then paying for Lena's efforts to turn the dilapidated Bijou Theatre into the Century Theatre. Although Roger, Malins, and Macmillan could not find financial sponsorship, a number of companies were prepared to donate their products, perhaps in the hope that if these samples were traded around the world a demand for them might be created. Photographs in the Heaton Album show crates of Crosbie's jams, pickles, and marmalade being loaded, and they were never short of Player's cigarettes. Roger was always moving around the ship handing them out. Pains Fireworks also donated around £100 worth of their product, which was quite a large quantity then. They also had a rather strange item, "The Shackleton Folding Boat," which received much publicity in England and when they arrived in America, although Ransley had no recollection of ever seeing it.

Despite a shortage of money, Roger pursued the most important acquisition, a ship. He took this as his personal duty and travelled as far as Rotterdam and Antwerp without success. On a frustrating trip to Hull, he saw an advertisement that caused him to take the first available train to Birkenhead, where "lay *Vanduara*, a very dream of loveliness, a schooner-rigged steam yacht, named in honour of a famous racing clipper, and built in 1886 for the Coats people, master spinners of thread, who were very rich, and reputed to have spent three hundred thousand pounds upon this little wonder." Roger was so caught up in his plan he was ready to risk everything. The *Vanduara* was for sale at £1,500, so Roger used his own funds of £630 as a deposit and had the ship surveyed. In light of what he learned elsewhere, it seems surprising that Roger could say that "She came out 100 A1 for hull and engines, but needed a new foremast...."[57] It is not clear in one article based on an interview with Roger whether the reporter was imaginative or whether Roger let slip some idea of how much the re-fit of the ship had cost, but there it is stated that the ship "was purchased for £10,000 and insured for that sum—this amount having been raised by subscription in five and a half months."[58] Not very many months later, just after the ship was seized in California, one newspaper

SY *Frontiersman*, the Expedition Ship for the MacMillan
and Malins round the world flight organization.
[Courtesy of the Bruce Peel Special Collections Library, University of Alberta.]

said that "the Frontiersman was purchased, equipped, and despatched at a cost of just over £12,000."[59] If this was the case, the expedition sailed with a large millstone of debt attached to it. It appears that Roger spent money without first checking with Macmillan and Malins, probably using the good name of the Legion to obtain credit.

Roger was probably the only one who believed the *Vanduara* was suitable for their purpose. During the war she had served in the Liverpool Pilot Service, and her engines were close to being worn out. Roger dismissed this problem, saying that they would be sailing the ship for much of the way, since coal would be difficult to acquire. That they had been unable to attract volunteers with the skills necessary to use the sails, and that the sails were far too small to sail the ship across an ocean, did not affect his thinking. Ransley wrote that the crew members "were a motley lot with only about four who had seen service at sea[,] and it was only thanks to them that we managed to get as far as we did."[60] Roger also totally discounted the fact that the ship was only single-skinned, and thus not suitable for use in icy waters. Perhaps Roger was swayed by the fine quality mahogany fittings in the cabins. Roger had plenty of sailing experience, and he should certainly have been able to see the problems; however, not for the first time, his heart ruled his head. For their part, the volunteers were not happy with the ship when they saw it in London. Ransley, in particular, was worried:

The hired crew who brought the boat from Liverpool to
London considered we were foolhardy to venture to sea in
the yacht. They said that under another name she had sunk
in the Mersey and had been salvaged. The engines were
the same as those she had before she sank. The hired crew
forecast trouble with these triple expansion engines and how
right they were as we found to our cost.[61]

One of the volunteers, Guy Eardley-Wilmot (1893–1966), accompanied the
hired crew on its voyage from Liverpool to London. The son of Admiral
Sir Sidney Eardley-Wilmot, he had considerable sea-going and sailing experience. He had been commissioned in the Royal Navy, but his tendency
to damage any small vessel with which he was entrusted caused him to
leave the Navy and transfer to the Army, where he distinguished himself.
He was a popular and big man, known to all as "Tiny." He seldom had
much money, but his many friends clubbed together and bought him one
share in each of forty companies which gave shareholders a lunch at their
annual general meetings. That way he would be certain of at least forty
good meals every year, no matter how short of money he might be.[62]

Roger's plan was to take a crew of forty and leave a man in charge
of each of the "dumps of stores—these dumps being indicated by pre-
arranged camouflaged landmarks only visible from the air, in order to
prevent them being discovered and looted by the natives." These dumps
were to be left "Along the Alaskan coast to Juneau, the Alsatian Islands,
Kamschatka, the Kuriles, the Liu Ku Islands...."[63] Macmillan and Malins
would begin their flight in February 1924, the plane and ship would ren-
dezvous in Japan, then the ship would follow the plane to Canada, picking
up the men left with the stores as they went, and then sail back to Britain.
The *Vanduara,* re-named the SY *Frontiersman,* "was some 90 feet in
length and somewhat narrow in width. We were sceptical as to how 40
crew could be accommodated in such a small craft."[64]

To publicize the expedition, Roger endeavoured to persuade various
newspapers to cover the preparations. So, for example, the dramatic leader
in *World's Pictorial News* was "Rear-Admiral as Odd-Job Man," a reference
to Eardley-Wilmot, who was, in fact, son of a rear-admiral. This may have
been a little embroidery by Roger to gain extra publicity. Another newspaper ran an item on the expedition's launching of balloons over London:

> Six large balloons are to be sent up today over London for
> the purpose of obtaining special atmospheric data for the
> flight round the world by Capt. Macmillan and Capt. Malins.

The promoters wish whoever secures any of the balloons
to send them back to headquarters, 6, Adam-street, Adelphi,
W.C.[65]

What "special atmospheric data" an expedition would seek to collect to lay dumps across the North Pacific, and that would be available from balloons above London, is a mystery.

Roger said in later years that he was pleased with the members of the crew. He had originally signed Commander Andrew Downes, R.N., as the skipper, but for reasons never made clear Downes was unable to obtain a Board of Trade Master's ticket and became boatswain. Lt. Commander Robin Spalding was taken on as skipper, although the honest members of the crew found him too weak. We do not know whose imagination supplied the description of the previous careers of the crew, but the *Times* recorded that "Among the crew are seven ex-officers of the Air Force, including two flight commanders. A geologist, pyrotechnic expert, photographer, wireless experts, two surgeons, and an eye specialist are also of the ship's company." The *Times* also supplied an account of the main objects of the expedition, as well as how it was to be financed:

The flight and sea expedition are being financed from
public sources. Many prominent trading firms are assisting
by making large gifts of stores and foodstuffs. The crew are
prepared to do trade at ports of call on behalf of any British
firm which cares to accept the offer. Samples of goods will be
carried on board, and a small commission fee will be charged
on all orders received. This money will be devoted to the
expenses of the expedition.

At a luncheon on board the yacht yesterday, LORD
LOCH, who presided, proposed the toast of "The Craft."
COMMANDER SPALDING, on behalf of the crew, responded
to the toast. CAPTAIN MALINS, in responding to the toast of
"The World Flight," said that when Captain Macmillan and
he came down in the Bay of Bengal last year they made a vow
that if they were picked up and got safely back to England,
they would work day and night to organize another attempt
to get round the world, and thus finish the job upon which
they had started.[66]

When Ransley was in his mid-eighties, he was sceptical about Roger's claim that the volunteers were all officers and gentlemen. His opinion was

"Tiny" and Heaton.
[Courtesy of the Bruce Peel Special Collections Library, University of Alberta.]

that the criminal classes were rather well represented. He thought there were also a number of homosexuals who wished to escape from Britain at a time when homosexual activity was illegal. When he gave talks about the expedition, he said that his experiences on the voyage gave him an interest in the criminal classes and led him to join the British prison service on his return.

The ship was opened to the public at St. Katherine's Dock, London, on 16 June. The charge for admission was to help fund the flight. Macmillan and Malins had been working frantically to gain support for the flight, while Roger was working for the seaborne expedition: it seems there may have been competing interests. Photographs taken of the event show that considerable numbers of the public took the opportunity to look around the ship. Lord Loch was in attendance, along with Sir Sefton Brancker.

Silver the cinematographer.

[Courtesy of the Bruce Peel Special Collections Library, University of Alberta.]

Brancker proffered the British government's "moral support" but nothing more tangible.[67] Also at the ship that day was Dr. Fred Thompson. Before the war Thompson and Roger together had attempted to become involved in the motion picture industry. This time Thompson's task was to go to California and create publicity before the ship arrived. In one of the promotional photographs taken in June, Roger was surrounded by a number of unnamed men in Legion uniform. Eardley-Wilmot wrote a curt caption in his album: "Capt. Pocock & his gang." The ship's cook, Mellon, appeared in photographs in the *Daily Mirror* doing balancing tricks with a life preserver and juggling.[68] In conversation Ransley confirmed that Mellon was a comedian and joker. The supposed ship's mascot, a dog named Pog, whose "father was in five naval engagements," was also featured in the *Daily Mirror*, but Ransley said that no dog went with them.[69]

Capt. Malins—The Crowd.

[Courtesy of the Bruce Peel Special Collections Library, University of Alberta.]

The problem was to find men with the correct skills, most particularly engineers. It appears that Roger was getting desperate: it turns out that Pearce, the second engineer, was given the job because he was a skilled motorcycle mechanic. Roger could not find a chief engineer because men declined the position once they saw the worn-out machinery they were expected to use to sail the ship across the Atlantic. So the ship left London without a chief engineer, but it took one on at Gravesend. Paulton came on board wearing a smart bowler hat. He removed it, went below to look at the engines, immediately came back up, and put his bowler on again. The skipper had had the foresight to order the ship to cast off, so Paulton shrugged his shoulders, removed his bowler, and went back down to the engine room.[70] The reluctant chief engineer was soon proved right because the engines failed completely off Dover, and in the hands of a crew greatly lacking in the necessary experience, the ship nearly crashed into Dover pier. Ransley recalled the harbour master jumping up and down at the end of his pier in fury at the crew's incompetence. It was difficult to dissuade Paulton from putting on his bowler and leaving, but fortunately he was persuaded to stay. The ship was in Dover a fortnight for repairs, although Roger only admitted that "some small indisposition of the engines detained us for a few days at Dover...."[71] Some of the crew started to cause problems, and their uniform made them unmistakeable, for it was "very distinctive and it was not long before our worried leader was the recipient of a string of complaints of bad behaviour in the town by the wilder members of the crew. It was with a heartfelt sigh of relief that the skipper was able to ring down for 'Slow Ahead.'"[72] Fortunately, the weather in the Bay of Biscay was kind to them, and they were able to reach Madeira within eight days. There they coaled ship and the crew took rides on the bullock sledges. One member of the crew caused Roger more problems when he decided to go ashore in the heat wearing nothing but his Aertex® undershorts. It was, he said, what the natives wore. As the weave of this garment left nothing to the imagination, he was arrested within five minutes and Roger was forced to bail him out.[73]

From Madeira they had fourteen days of fairly uneventful sailing to St. Lucia in the West Indies. Ransley noted that the flying fish that landed on the deck of the ship during that part of the voyage "were next encountered on the breakfast table as a welcome substitute for bully beef."[74] It had been strictly agreed with Macmillan and Malins that Roger's task was solely that of geographer, and he was to spend his time in the chartroom drawing up charts and maps for the pilots to take on the flight. On no account was he to involve himself in the running of the ship. Of course this soon slipped his mind, and he was all round the ship, wishing to take part in scrubbing decks and polishing. He would have liked to participate in the heavy work, such as stoking, but his age and infirmity prevented that. Spalding proved to be far too weak for his position as captain, but Wells, the first officer, although a small man, was an excellent officer and always prominent and wise in the constant committee meetings that had to be held over every problem. Apart from the rougher elements in the crew, there were some who were totally unsuitable. For example, Ransley remembered one man clearly, Rumball, who was constantly seasick even in the calmest weather. He kept a pocket full of biscuits, which he munched to try to help his sickness.

They anchored at St. Lucia, off what was then the tiny and unspoiled town of Castries. The crew thought the island was close to paradise. The governor of St. Lucia, Col. Houston, invited Roger to bring half a dozen of the crew to dinner at the Residence. Roger had to pick them with great care. Ransley was one of the men he chose.

> The Residence stood on a hill overlooking the shore where the ship was moored. After dinner we took our cigars to a balcony where a short time later we were treated to a fine display of fireworks and were surprised the Governor should so honour us. A few minutes later a panting messenger from the ship arrived. He whispered in Captain Pocock's ear. We learned that B. [Bagshaw] had been imbibing too freely and to amuse the natives had let off the £100 worth of fireworks which Messrs. Paine [*sic*] had so kindly donated to us. When we left the island next morning the natives were in tears. They had so enjoyed having us and the fireworks. B. was also in tears as he went ashore en route for England. We never saw him again.[75]

They then set sail for the Panama Canal, where they had a long wait because there was no cash to pay the Canal fees. Eventually a cheque was accepted, but Ransley was convinced that it bounced. Ransley had been promoted to quartermaster or steersman, and so was able to enjoy the journey through the Canal. They headed for Acapulco. The heat in the tropics proved almost overpowering, particularly for the stokers and coal trimmers. The crew found a use at last for the too-small sails and rigged up a sail bath, attached to the mast. Photographs show the crew greatly enjoyed this, until after a few days someone cut the ropes and they all crashed to the deck. The many gallons of sea water in the sail went straight down into the engine room and doused the fires. The ship wallowed for several hours until steam could be raised again.

There was no coal at Acapulco, so they headed for Manzanillo where coal was available. The sample they tried was acceptable, but to pay for this fuel it was necessary to open the cash box, which contained £350 for emergency use. Early on the morning of 10 August, Ransley wrote, Roger assembled the whole of the ship's company on deck:

> Captain Pocock addressed us. He was in a state of agitation.
> "We have a thief on board. All our reserve cash has gone. Will the thief come forward and save the expedition from disaster?" he said.
> There was no reply from the crew so another cheque was tendered for the coal which was rumoured would "bounce."[76]

In later conversation Ransley expanded on this confrontation. He said that there was complete silence for a while until Roger slowly turned and walked away. There were tears in his eyes and he suddenly looked old. He had taken a gamble that had gone wrong. He had again been found to be a poor judge of men. There was little pity for him in the crew. The honest men were angry with him for his lack of judgement and leadership, and the dishonest were not concerned since they had nearly reached America. Roger went to see the British consul for help, but he was away: "Mr. Aguirre, United States Consul, as an act of private courtesy backed our bill, which I endorsed, so that it became my personal obligation. Afterwards it was paid."[77] This sounds as if his long-suffering brother-in-law, Henry Simson, may have helped him out again. It turned out they were tricked, though, because while the coal sample was acceptable, very little of what they received would burn. Ransley had a clear memory of events and wrote an excellent description:

> Out in the open sea the engines began to make queer "rackety" noises and we were reduced to a speed of about a knot an hour. Examination of the coal revealed a large percentage of sand.
>
> The bosses were long in conference. Charts were studied and distances measured. Captain Pocock announced that we were going to bring up the "gift" axes from the hold and would wallow along to an island called Cerros or Cedros where we should be able to chop down trees for fuel. When we came, after many days, in sight of our "Treasure" Island[,] binoculars were raised and quickly lowered. The island was bare of trees!
>
> The bosses were long in conference again. This time the crew were called in. We were told to keep calm as a Mr. Thompson had been sent to Los Angeles ahead of the yacht for the purpose of getting contributions from the public and the film world.[78]

The crew were told Americans were noted for their generosity, so Thompson had probably already raised a substantial amount. They cabled Thompson to charter a tug to bring them in, but he replied that he had not raised enough money for that. They wired to London for help, but no doubt Macmillan and Malins had discovered how much debt Roger had already run up, so they only sent encouragement to stand firm. All hands were set to the back-breaking task of sifting out by hand what good coal

Mr Wooden's Party, Beverly Hills, Los Angeles.
[Courtesy of the Bruce Peel Special Collections Library, University of Alberta.]

they could find. They were even considering burning the lovely mahogany fittings of the ship, but just managed to reach San Pedro, the port for Los Angeles, with the last of the coal. Ransley wrote that "our spirits rose. We hoped and believed our troubles were over. Little did we know this was only the beginning."[79]

Thompson might not have been able to raise much money, but he had publicized the expedition far and wide. Unfortunately, he had elaborated too much and had persuaded the Americans that crew members were all from British nobility, the sons of dukes and earls. His idea had been to obtain invitations for them to functions and meetings with important people who would then donate generously. They were towed into the dock of the new and exclusive California Yacht Club. The SY *Frontiersman* took up all the moorings, which other yacht owners were happy to allow for a few days, but soon began to resent. The first priority was to arrange for an overhaul of the engines, although they had no money to meet the bill. This lack of money did not inhibit their social life, either. They were taken to visit the ranch belonging to Mr. Wooden in Beverly Hills. There they were able to admire Wooden's magnificent thoroughbred horses. Some of the men also admired Wooden's even more attractive daughters. They also visited the Thomas H. Ince Motion Picture Studios and the oil wells at Signal Hill, "where we saw 'gushers' spouting oil hundreds of feet into the air. A shocking waste I thought, but petrol was then about 7 cents a gallon close to the oil fields."[80] They were also entertained to dinner by

Dr. Thompson, Claire Windsor and others.
[Courtesy of the Bruce Peel Special Collections Library, University of Alberta.]

the Adventurers Club of Los Angeles on 29 August, and each man was presented with a certificate of honorary membership. Gin was mentioned on the menu as an excellent accompaniment to the local orange juice, but "As prohibition laws allowed no alcohol, the guests were informed that this omission could be rectified if they cared to look under the table cloth, where ample stocks were available."[81] The lavish menu granted Roger a new rank with its declaration that the dinner was "in honor of Commander Roger Pocock and the personnel of the British Steam Yacht 'Frontiersman' who are surveying the course for the World Flight by Captain G.H. Malins and Captain Norman Macmillan of the Royal British Air Force." The dinner was held at the Ince Studios where they were treated to the spectacular flooding of a ship's engine room while a film, *Anna Christie,* was being shot. Ransley wrote that "Elaborate speeches were made by some of our hosts describing us as 'scions of nobility' from England who from patriotic motives had participated in this great adventure etc., etc."[82] Some of the notable Californians present also wrote flowery greetings on the backs of the menus.

Of course, the expedition had to return the compliment, and so the most important members of the Adventurers Club, local dignitaries, and film stars were invited to lunch on 31 August. Although Roger had been desperately trying to raise money locally and wiring requests to England without success, somehow they managed to put together a selection of cold meats and some fruit salad. Only picked members of the crew attended because conditions were very cramped. After the lunch photographs were taken of the ship's officers with some of the guests on deck. Ransley was not at the lunch but saw the guests: "Some of the guests were of course film people[,] one of whom was the 'Star' Pauline Fredericks who had several photographs of herself taken standing on the poop deck draped in a Union Jack which did not entirely hide her charms."[83] Eardley-Wilmot's Album has photographs of the ship's officers with "Miss Claire Windsor." In spite of the fact that he was old enough to be her father, Roger showed he was still prey to female charms by the way he looked at the young lady while the photograph was being taken. For Ransley, though, the high point of the visits was one to Clover Field, "a huge flying ground where most of the aeroplanes were privately owned. We were given flights in the air. I teamed up with Bill Fry[,] an ex-American war pilot[,] who allowed me to take over the controls for a brief period. I found I had not lost my expertise."[84] They also visited Goldwyn Film Studios and met Douglas Fairbanks and Mary Pickford.

All the visiting and publicity brought in few donations, and the ship's popularity soon began to wane. The Yacht Club members wanted their moorings back, so the *Frontiersman* had to anchor offshore, which meant that some of the men were more or less confined to the ship. Abundant rumours that they were not all officers and gentlemen were confirmed by the activities of some of the wilder crew members. Roger had begun to include Eardley-Wilmot in conferences with Downes, Spalding, and Wells. In hindsight it might have paid to have been open with some of the men, such as Eardley-Wilmot, much earlier in the voyage. One glimmer of hope came to Roger when into the bay sailed a yacht owned by American millionaire William B. Leeds, Jr. Eardley-Wilmot had crewed for Leeds in the past and would do so again. Leeds, Eardley-Wilmot, and Roger were seen several times walking along in earnest conversation. Roger wanted Leeds to finance the ship as far as Canada, where Roger was convinced he could raise support from Canadian friends and acquaintances. Leeds was a businessman and probably could not see any merit in offering money, particularly since America was about to begin its own attempt at an around the world flight. All Roger's pleading brought no support, especially after disaster struck the expedition in a major way. Ransley gave his eyewitness account of events:

> One evening during a game [of bridge] in the Chart Room
> we noticed three small steam cutters making for the ship
> at speed. On arrival they informed us they were Revenue,
> Prohibition and Police Officers and produced a warrant

to search the ship. In London several barrels of rum were
donated to the expedition and were of course sealed by the
Customs. America in 1923 was prohibitionist. The officers
accused us of rum running which we indignantly denied.
They said they had evidence. All the "speakeasies" in the
district[,] they said, had rum in their cellars and it must
have come from us. A Revenue Officer tapped a barrel and
pronounced it held water. All the other barrels held plain
water. Some members of the crew must have pocketed a good
sum for their stolen rum. The ship was arrested and put in
charge of a bailiff called Bill who nailed a writ to the mast.[85]

Eardley-Wilmot took a photograph of Bill Finn, who stood by the mast
with the writ nailed to it. A Los Angeles newspaper immediately featured
the raid on the yacht as front page news.

One of the raids was conducted by L.J. Tyson, harbor
prohibition officer, and Earl Beach, deputy collector of
customs, who reported that they discovered sixty-five gallons
of first-rate Scotch whisky aboard, and promptly attached the
liquor and the boat.
      At the same time Dep. U.S. Marshal Finn served notice on
the commander, Capt. Spalding, that the yacht was attached
in behalf of the Los Angeles Shipbuilding and Dry Dock
Company, for a claim of $250 asserted to be due for labor,
material and equipment.[86]

There is some discrepancy in reports on whether the casks contained
rum or whisky. Roger claimed it was rum, but Ransley, who witnessed
the raids, was quite clear in his book and in conversation that the casks
contained nothing but water and the contents had been sold by some of
the criminal elements of the crew. If the ship had casks of both rum and
whisky, then they were in trouble with American law for both what they
had (whisky) and for what they did not have (rum). Roger immediately
wired to London for help, but thanks to Reuters, newspaper reporters
reached Malins first. His reaction was astonishment followed by indigna-
tion. Malins claimed

that the quantity of whisky named, roughly speaking,
corresponded to that with which the Frontiersman was
supplied when she left England and was intended to comply

with the Board of Trade regulations for her lengthy voyage, and particularly to provide the small quantities necessary at each supply dump.[87]

Macmillan and Malins changed their hard line and told Roger to hang on and they would file a statement in the Federal Court in California that all outstanding debts would be paid by 10 October.

As to the Legion of Frontiersmen, its leaders quickly denied that the expedition had anything to do with the Legion, pointing out that the expedition had only rented an office at their headquarters. The Legion even refused to forward any further mail for the crew that arrived at 6 Adam Street. Despite numerous explicit connections between the Legion and the expedition in newspapers before and during the expedition, as well as the name of the ship itself (SY *Frontiersman*), afterwards no member of the Legion was prepared to admit to any link with the expedition. This was made rather difficult, however, since every crew member had been expected to become a member of the Legion and wear the uniform. The Legion had covered itself to a certain extent by making the expedition rent a room at its headquarters at 6 Adam Street. The mitigating effect of this was rather limited, however, because a goodly number of Legion members in uniform were in publicity photographs taken before the ship sailed.[88]

Although Roger never admitted in public that any members of his crew were at fault, he must have tried to work out which of them was dishonest. He also placed considerable blame on the Americans, even accusing them of proceeding "to wreck our living quarters, stamping upon such trifles as gold watches, trampling dress-suits into a mixture of oil and coal dust. Nearly all our private property was destroyed…"; crew members such as Ransley, however, made no complaint.[89] In conversation, Ransley maintained that suspicion centred on Pitchforth as the leader of the dishonest crew members. He never seemed to be short of money and in every port was seen with a different lady, who was well made-up and apparently expensive to treat. He also said that Pitchforth could have gained access to the cash box. Some of the crew, however, were quite content the expedition had failed. They had travelled as far as they wished and had no desire to be marooned on some lonely island in the cold North Pacific. Besides, at least a few had achieved a tidy profit on their original investment by rifling the cash box and selling rum illegally. Roger obtained a job as a film extra for a few days thanks to a director, Harold Shaw, whom he had met in London. He donated the $75 he was paid to help buy provisions for the crew, but some were suspicious and thought his absence meant that he had deserted them. Days became weeks and still no help came from London, so even Roger realized that there was no hope of the expedition continuing. Fortunately, the climate was excellent and the manager of the Los Angeles labour exchange was a Scot who found jobs for all the crew members who wanted employment. Eventually, many made their way back to England by working their passage, although in December 1923 Eardley-Wilmot and Heaton maintained that only four of the crew had managed to get home.[90] In spite of the fact that newspapers, encouraged by Eardley-Wilmot, were painting word pictures of the adventurers starving on a California beach, it is probable that many were in no hurry to return to England.

Eardley-Wilmot and Heaton, though, were furious about the way they had been treated, and livid with Roger in particular. Roger had told the crew that they were all equal members, but he did not treat them as such and did not tell them that they were setting off saddled with debt and reliant totally on his optimism that he could solve all their problems on the journey. This foolhardiness later led some crew members to accuse him of cheating, and Eardley-Wilmot bore his bitterness and grudge against Roger to the end of his life. Ransley, however, put the affair down to experience and enjoyed telling the story over and over again. Roger later claimed, with characteristic optimism, that "it was felt that I had played the game, and in the years which followed I had abundant proof of friendship from almost everybody. They would not have me maligned by mere outsiders."[91] Despite Roger's claim, shortly after Eardley-Wilmot and Heaton returned to England, they arranged an interview with the Legion of Frontiersmen and Commandant Col. Tamplin, who managed to persuade them that the fault was entirely Roger's:

> A number of the crew of S.Y. *Frontiersman* called yesterday, all gentlemen, asking what *we* were going to do. They denounced Pocock in unmeasured terms and said he is now a fugitive from the fury of the crew somewhere in Los Angeles. The gentlemen who came here were very indignant and hotly resented that they should be the victims of Pocock's *fraud* and deceit. They described Pocock's grandiloquent orations at the several Dinners of Welcome, of a public character, at which they were entertained in which he appears to have posed as the Representative of the Legion of Frontiersmen!
>
> I must say they were speedily convinced of the real position and we parted on excellent terms.[92]

Tamplin seems conveniently to have forgotten the enthusiasm with which the Legion fully backed the expedition before it left London. The Executive Council had passed a resolution of good wishes to the expedition, which was included in a letter the Council sent to Roger. That letter concluded with the statement that the Legion "will be ever ready to aid here in England as may be required, to the utmost of our ability."[93]

A strongly critical piece in *John Bull*, perhaps encouraged by Eardley-Wilmot, said the Legion, and particularly Lord Loch, had at least a moral obligation to rescue the men, since the Legion's name had been so closely associated with the voyage. Perhaps in response to an earlier piece, Tamplin wrote to *John Bull* "to say that the World's Flight was a completely independent and separate undertaking, in no way initiated, conducted, or financed by the Legion." The writer at *John Bull* followed up angrily:

> How then does he account for the World's Flight appeals
> for money issued from the Frontiersmen's office, describing
> Lord Loch as President, and bearing the symbol and motto
> of the Frontiersmen, "God Guard Thee"?
>   In what capacity did Lord Loch, described as President
> of the World's Flight, see the World's Flight ship off? Did
> the men who sailed know that his benison was a mere pious,
> disinterested and irresponsible gesture? Did they know that
> the ship was loaded to the water-line with debt?[94]

In November Eardley-Wilmot also wrote twice to Brancker at the Air Ministry, but received little comfort from the conciliatory reply.

> He [Lord Loch] will be writing to you, so please hold your
> hand regarding publicity until you have talked matters over.
> In any case, I doubt if paper agitation is going to do anybody
> any good.
>   Naturally, the Air Ministry moral support of the Legion of
> Frontiersmen World Flight has been withdrawn.[95]

Two days later Brancker responded to another letter from Eardley-Wilmot.

> I quite see your point, & I have done so all along. I hope
> perhaps that your meeting with Lord Loch and Macmillan
> may bring forward a suggestion as to what we could do to

restore our loss of prestige involved by this unfortunate incident. Anyway, you can be quite clear that the Air Ministry is not going to support any further funds being collected by the existing organization.[96]

For the rest of his life, Eardley-Wilmot wished to have his version of the adventure told, but said that he "crossed swords with his [Roger's] sister Miss Lena Ashwell," who always flew to Roger's defence; Eardley-Wilmot claimed, "I tried most unsuccessfully to write an account of it for various magazines but I found it quite impossible to dodge the laws of libel!!"[97] By the time Roger slipped quietly back into Britain, though, the furore had died down.

For SY *Frontiersman,* the end was not graceful. To pay the debts they had run up in California, the ship was auctioned there in what Roger thought might have been a rigged auction.[98] He reported that he read a few months later in a California newspaper that the ship had been bought by bootleggers who used her to run liquor from the West Indies. Following a storm off California, and then a fight among the crew, the ship was scuttled. So it was an ignominious end for the ship that Roger had on first sight called "a very dream of loveliness." As for flights around the world, thanks in large part to Roger, the flight Macmillan and Malins wanted to make never left the ground. Another unsuccessful British attempt was made in 1924 under the auspices of the *Times,* with Squadron Leader A. Stuart C. MacLaren as organizer and navigator. The Americans, with government and military support, achieved the first flight around the world on 28 September 1924.

HOLLYWOOD
and a
WORLD TOUR:
END *of the*
"SPLENDID ADVENTURE"

IT IS A TESTAMENT TO Roger's gift for friendship that he did not lose
all his friends after the debacle of the voyage of the SY *Frontiersman,* but
he did need to earn some money rather than rely on friends. He thought
California was a land of real estate developers full of "get rich quick" ideas,
and life was based on credit and the purchase of things by instalments.
This approach was contrary to his Victorian upbringing, but these elements were brought together in one of his first jobs in California, which
was to draw up designs for an English-style village, which prospective
purchasers were told would be built on desert scrubland. Roger duly put
his artistic talent to work and designed an "English village in the half-
timbered style," manor house and all. His employer told him to "pep it
up a bit," so he added a main street 200 feet wide. Still the developer was
not happy, so Roger added the novel idea of lampposts topped by some
attractive angels dressed in nothing but their wings. He left the design for
these lying about in his rooms, which provided incentive for his landlord
to throw him out.[1]

Roger then recalled that in London he had been stopped in his tracks
by an advertising board outside the Pavilion Cinema, in Piccadilly Circus,
which was showing *A Man in the Open.* He had never been approached
for permission or been paid for this use of his book.

Still, theft as it was, here was a jolly good picture as films go, with the firmament raked for Stars to play in it. So now, having come to Hollywood as author of a Feature, an actual Offering, a world-wide Success, I suffered from the quaint delusion that I could sell the film rights of all my books as being guaranteed worth stealing. But why should these people buy when they could steal? It took me thirty months of heartbreaking disappointments to discover that the thefts are made in Hollywood, and the purchases in New York.[2]

Before he learned that hard lesson, he had a business card printed: "Roger Pocock, 6495 Ivarine Avenue, Hollywood, HE 4604. Consultant in Technical and Art Direction."[3] He listed his books and stories and included brief comments on plots and their suitability for use as movies. People in the film industry were not going to actually pay him for anything he had written previously, so they fobbed him off by telling him that all story purchases were made in New York. What did happen, though, was that his resemblance to the late King Edward VII made casting directors see him as just the man to play "the King, the old Prince, or the College Principal.... I thought myself a monstrous fine actor," wrote Roger. "Perhaps I was, but I was actually engaged as an Economy, because a professional would have cost the Management two hundred dollars a day instead of ten."[4]

Roger claimed that he also went into business with a new-found friend, John P. McCarthy (1884–1962), but this partnership was no great success, or, as Roger put it, they were "generally on the verge of famine."[5] They did, however, generate at least one silent film together, *The Brand of Cowardice,* released in 1925. McCarthy directed and McCarthy and Roger were listed as the writers. Among the actors were the marvellously named Cuyler Supplee and Ligia de Golconda. One reviewer described it as "a better than average western. The story is as conventional as the title is meaningless, but in all other respects—direction, photography, continuity, atmosphere and general presentation—the picture maintains a sufficiently high standard." Referring to the title again, the reviewer added that "every one [*sic*] will wonder where the cowardice comes in, as no one in the picture seems to have the slightest fear of any one [*sic*] else." This reviewer found the story somewhat formulaic, with the U.S. Marshal posing as a bandit and falling for the daughter of the wealthy ranch owner: "A departure is the omission of practically all hand-to-hand battling, but there is plenty of pistol play, hard chases and wild riding in the moonlight included in the action."[6] Perhaps Roger's personal interest in westerns is what enabled him to meet the great star of western films, Tom Mix, for "By 1921, Tom was one of the ten top box office attractions in the country," and he "reached the height of his career with Fox in 1922."[7]

> Tom Mix had known and greatly admired Captain Roger Pocock...during the latter's days in Hollywood in the early 1920's. In His [*sic*] own life-story "The West of Yesterday," published in 1923, Tom Mix begins the Foreword to his book by stating "I find myself in perfect agreement with Roger Pocock" and goes on to quote from Pocock's book "Man in The Open" regarding living close to Nature.[8]

While Roger was still focussed on movies, another opportunity arose. In 1922, before the debacle of the world flight, Roger started work on his first stage play, *The Celluloid Cat*. While he was in Hollywood he heard from his sister Lena that she would be staging it. It tells of the contest between two women, both of whom claim to be the widow of a millionaire.[9] The first two acts are set in northern Canada, borrowing from Roger's experience, while the conclusion takes place in New York City. The only known surviving manuscript is among the Lord Chamberlain's Plays in the British Library. That copy shows Roger wrote the play, and Lena annotated it, but it was originally attributed to Anonymous. It was first performed at various borough halls in the London area in March 1924. After the performance at Longfield Hall, Ealing, a reviewer described it as "a melodrama in the sentimental vein but it is well constructed and contains many sparkling lines. The characterisation with the exception of the padre is convincing and the working out of the story produces many effective situations."[10] Another reviewer said Lena "must be congratulated on getting the atmosphere of the North West across the footlights[,] and also in her selection of the cast."[11] That March, Lena's company performed it at Battersea Town Hall, at Sutton, Surrey, and in her newly acquired Century Theatre in London. In May her company performed it at Brighton and Eastbourne.[12] Its success was enough to kindle Roger's enthusiasm for another career, this time as playwright.

Friends loaned him £100 and he returned quietly to London in the winter of 1925 to find, with some relief, that the World Flight Expedition had been forgotten by the British public. Even a Legion publication could remark calmly on Roger's return:

> just back from Hollywood, the American "movie metropolis" where he has been studying the business for two and a

half years as producer and actor. He has been contributing special articles to the *Daily News,* in the course of which he expresses the opinion that Great Britain is the natural home of the film industry, as being most suited climatically and otherwise for the delicate tones so necessary for first-class photography.[13]

Full of his usual eagerness, he set to work with Lena to adapt Dostoevsky's *Crime and Punishment* for performance at the Century Theatre. This would have been a daunting task, even for an established playwright. When it was first performed on 7 February 1927, a reviewer wondered "why it was ever attempted." After further comment on how the play was "a thin representation of the novel's later passages," the reviewer reverted to the idea that "Dostoevsky did not think in terms of the theatre[,] and the theatre cannot imprison him."[14] Roger and Lena continued to work together to adapt Stevenson's *Dr. Jekyll and Mr. Hyde.* This followed *Crime and Punishment* on to the stage of the Century on 28 March, having already been performed at the Public Hall, Sutton, and at Bath, on 14 March 1927. One reviewer seemed somewhat puzzled by Roger's ideas— "This is Robert Louis Stevenson brought up to date, but not greatly improved by the addition of cinemas and aeroplanes"—while another felt there had been "a fatal attempt to bring Stevenson up to date, and to lighten his tale—which it was above all necessary not to lighten—by the introduction of facetious and irrelevant chatter.... The melodrama, which more dexterous treatment might have concealed, appears in violent contrast with these patches of affected modernism...."[15] Nonetheless, it did have some success and was taken on tour in May by Wilfred Fletcher, an actor who had key roles in both *Dr. Jekyll and Mr. Hyde* and *Crime and Punishment.* The cast included a young Godfrey Kenton, who remembered Roger coming into the Century still full of boyish enthusiasm, although he was more than sixty years old.[16] The play was transferred to the tiny Q Theatre at Kew Bridge in August, but by then *The Stage* found it "weak and unconvincing."[17]

Roger did not abandon books. He successfully edited Lena's *Reflections from Shakespeare: A Series of Lectures,* but publishers rejected his own books. His style had become too old-fashioned and his tendency to include his ideas on mysticism in the plots had a detrimental effect on their saleability. This certainly shows in his manuscript "Search-Lights." Roger prepared this so it could be marketed by Hughes Massie & Co., and prefaced it with eight lines from Derzhavin's "Ode to God," then proceeded with his "treatise on the natural History of the Human Soul."[18]

Chapters have headings such as "Consciousness," "The Concentration of the Ray," "The Tele-Cinema," "Echoes Through Time," "The Light of Philosophy," "The Light of Science," "The Light of Religion," "The Light of Spiritism," "The Light of Telepathy," and "The Search-Light of Oriental Theosophy." While Roger's latest book mentioned on the title page is *Horses*, published in 1917, and the latest publication date of books in the bibliography is 1918, he was probably writing this in the early or mid 1920s. He drew upon his own experience to make his point. In a section titled "Suggestion," he referred to his time as a missionary, when "I discovered in myself a mysterious faculty of the mind which enables an unarmed white man to take command and dominate a tribe of armed savages." In "Consciousness Outside the Body," he described the amputation of his toes in 1885:

> Once I was a Constable in the Royal North West Mounted Police [*sic*], had been disabled during a small campaign, and suffered an operation under chloroform. Either the knife or the drug must have disagreed with me, and driven me out of my body, for I awakened in interstellar Night. I had no body, but was a creature of pure thought, whirled on a[n] orbit in Space. Once in each round of the circle I met my *self*, and had communion with *me* for an instant. The orbit changed its figure to a descending spiral, so that the intervals grew shorter between these meetings of self with self. Still, at each contact, knowledge passed between us. Then grew the meetings in their frequency until, at the end of all time one meeting merged into the next. So we twain became one, and in that instant knew all things of heaven and earth. And all was one—God.
>
> On the journey home, threading a way between the planets, I wondered what manner of world I was coming to. When I arrived, alighted into my body, and awakened I was surprised to find the nice familiar surroundings of this earthly life, glad to meet the surgeon, the orderly, and the man who had put me to sleep, delighted with the bed, the room, the view of some log cabins through the window. Then I forgot all about where I had been.
>
> Three days later the hospital orderly made his affected cough, which I had last heard through fumes of chloriform [*sic*]. At once I remembered the vision, and had a bout of hysterics.[19]

This passage encapsulates how Roger's ability to write what publishers wanted had declined so seriously that by 1928 his income had dropped below £100 a year and his health suffered. Roger may thus have felt the need for travel, his usual restorative, which is how he met Grace F. Wilson, an Englishwoman, and her daughter. The Wilsons had been on a pilgrimage to Albert, France, to visit the grave of a relative.

> We had just sat down to dinner in the Hotel [in Amiens]
> when a very courtly gentleman with King George beard &
> all came to our table & bowed saying "may a very lonely
> Englishman sit at your table." We had very happy &
> interesting conversation & as we were going on to Rouen
> he told us of places not to miss & how best to get to them
> easily....
>
> I had of course no idea who he was until he offered me his
> cigarette case & told me it had been given him by the Pilots
> of the Air Force where he had worked on the ground in the
> War.
>
> Then I saw Roger Pocock, his signature cut in the silver.
>
> Later on in England I saw a review of his book "Chorus to
> Adventurers" reviewed in the Press with his photograph &
> recognised him & that it was the man we had met in Amiens,
> & had so enjoyed.
>
> His manner was so kindly & charming. I wrote to him via
> his publishers and had a picture postcard in reply. I did not
> think he would remember us.[20]

He may have been lonely in Amiens, but he still had a number of friends. Some of these friends used their influence to get him admitted as a Brother at Charterhouse on 7 May 1928.[21] This brought about such a change in fortune and dramatic improvement in his health that in August 1928 he was able to write a bittersweet letter to his brother Frank in America.

> You'll see from the above address that there's a big change
> in my affairs. I was admitted to Charterhouse on May 7th,
> and the release from worry may be the cause, or possibly the
> beer, of a complete restoration to health after a long illness.
> It is seven years now since my modest prosperity came to an
> end. Three plays were produced, and moderately successful,
> but they brought in very little money. Since I earned L100
> with Daisy's "Reflections from Shakespeare" my four later

books have failed to get published. Anyway my total earnings had come below a hundred pounds a year, and an apparently complete breakdown in health forced me to seek for cover.

He went on to tell his brother something of the history of Charterhouse, where there was a family link, because their father had been a day boy at Charterhouse School. Roger then explained what Charterhouse was like at the time of his writing:

[It is] inhabited by sixty old buffers [*sic*] like me, and a staff of forty. The pension and allowances are valued at L250 a year for life, with the perfection of quiet, comfort, cleanliness, and an excellent dinner served at the awkward hour of 2 P.M. in the great hall. Situated at the edge of the City, it is within easy reach of the Club, and all the theatres. Besides, I keep on my fine shack in Daisy's garden, for week-ends, holidays, and the month of July when all the Brethren are turned loose to graze. At the moment too, there came a sudden revival of prosperity, with good earnings, which may continue, on a new Encyclopoedia [*sic*], lots of book reviewing, and a few little odd jobs. Most of my time however is devoted to painting flower pictures, which are all the rage just now, and there is talk of an exhibition so soon as I have a sufficient stock in hand. Also I am painting fishes on glass vessels, which may come into fashion and make money. Anyway the days are full, and there is nothing more to worry about.[22]

Harry Leigh-Pink interviewed Roger at Charterhouse and nicely captured the spirit of the place and its inhabitants: "Half an hour [later] I was sitting with my man [Roger] in a tiny apartment, living-room, bedroom, toilet, kitchen in the time-worn Charterhouse edifice which since 1611 has been a home for male pensioners 'Gentlemen by descent and in poverty, soldiers that have borne arms by sea or land, merchants decayed by piracy and shipwreck or servants in household to the King or Queen's Majesty['].''[23] It was a great relief to Roger to have a regular income and a roof over his head. He had to accept that age and the rigours of the life he had led were taking a toll on him. Fortunately, Lena had a house named Ponders End, at Chieveley, Berkshire, and he had the use of the "shack" there, a summerhouse in the garden, where he could dream that he was still leading his outdoor life.

The contrast in his situation after he entered Charterhouse is apparent in the letter Roger wrote to his brother's daughter, Doris, who had sent him a card and letter. While it has a tone of forced cheerfulness, it also reflects his enhanced security. Roger wrote that Francis had been talking about "coming over these fifty years past, and it's time he began to hurry." Roger also told Doris about family activities in England:

> Of Rosalie, no news is good news.... You may remember
> hearing of three theatrical companies called the Lena Ashwell
> Players. After ten years the venture was just clearing expenses
> when, this time last year the King's illness, the influenza
> epidemic, and bad weather emptied the theatres. Indeed the
> Government warned the public against all entertainments
> where they might catch influenza. So the Players lost $15,000
> in a few weeks, and had to close down.
> Hilda is making a little money as a lecturer on health.
> As for me, I had my pocket picked three months ago, a loss
> of $45, which I could ill afford. But that set me hustling as a
> journalist, and I've got much more than even, with a good
> new connection. The dullest journal in existence sent me
> for review a stack of books on all the Sciences. I made fun
> of all the illustrious authors, and expected nothing less than
> assassination. And yet the misguided Editor has accepted
> all the reviews deriding his dearest friends. There are also
> two big scientific articles more or less accepted by learned
> journals. Of course that sort of stuff is enormous glory, but
> my new connection is with three weekly journals which
> pay well, and are read by the vulgar millions. Besides I have
> three books which are being rejected by the most important
> publishers. Its [sic] not all work. There's lots of fun as well.[24]

Despite this new peace in his life, yet again Roger became involved with the Legion of Frontiersmen. Arthur Burchardt-Ashton, a reluctant Commandant-General of the Legion, had no great leadership qualities, but he was wealthy and able to support the Legion financially. His adjutant, and later "chief of staff," Henry Cecil Edwards-Carter was viewed with suspicion by many of the Frontiersmen who had seen action in the First World War. Edwards-Carter had been "in munitions" in the war, and fighting men tended to think that this meant he had made money comfortably while his compatriots had risked their lives. Edwards-Carter also had a high opinion of his own importance and wore unjustified rank on his Legion uniform. Although some Frontiersmen did support him, and he had a number of friends within the Legion who considered him a loyal and supportive colleague, reaction to Edwards-Carter holding a position of authority brought about a breakaway, which began around July 1927 and was complete by March 1928. This breakaway group was first known as the Independent Overseas Legion of Frontiersmen (sometimes referred to as Independent Overseas Command [I O C]), but the name was changed officially in June 1931 to the Imperial Overseas Legion of Frontiersmen. An extravagantly romanticized suffix—Driscoll's Tigers—was occasionally added to this. Roger originally rejected joining the Legion or any offshoot:

> I am sensible of the good feeling which has prompted you to
> ask me to join the Independent Overseas Command, but I do
> not wish to associate myself closely either with the original
> Legion, which I founded, or any offshoot therefrom, lest one
> or other might think I was taking sides in Legion politics;
> therefore, while I have the warmest sympathy with any and
> every body of men who are banding themselves together for
> the defence of the Empire, you will not misunderstand, I
> hope, my attitude in not identifying myself with any party in
> the Legion.[25]

However, publication of *Chorus to Adventurers* that spring set off a chain of events. Among other things, its success boosted his bank account sufficiently to enable him to pursue the idea of a world recruiting tour for the Legion.[26]

In 1931 *Chorus to Adventurers,* the second volume of Roger's autobiography, was published to generally good reviews. The *Times* referred to his founding of the Legion and the Legion's amateur counter-espionage work:

> as founder of the Legion of Frontiersmen he was closely
> involved in the curious activities of those who investigated
> schemes devised to the detriment of his beloved British
> Empire.... As he hates officers and officials and all who
> represent routine as cordially as he loves the Empire which
> the routine is presumably devised to serve, his tales do not
> lack piquancy; but the mellow that goes to their composition

greatly exceeds the acid. There may have been something of
the mountebank in the legionaries whose "tribal customs"
Captain Pocock delights to recall, but he can afford to
admit certain extravagances in these foster-children of his,
for they went with a death roll in the War of 6,000 "from a
membership computed at 17,000 down to the present time."

The reviewer also expressed his opinion of Roger as an explorer, in contrast with Roger the writer:

> he is, for an adventurer, on a beaten track; and the chapters
> that are peculiarly his own have to do with expeditions to
> the Arctic, the Deep Sea Fisheries, and certain experiences
> of the occult. In all these, he shows himself possessed of
> unusually subtle powers of perception. He sees, and can
> make his readers see, the colour in freshly caught fish, and
> when his eye is caught by the marks in the thin deposit of
> mud left by the flood tide he can interpret what he sees with
> the knowledge of the geologist.[27]

A lengthy review of the book and an interview with Roger were also published in *The British Imperial Frontier Man*. That interview was undertaken mainly by Capt. J.H.W. Porter. Porter, who was blinded in the First
World War, was accompanied by one of the co-founders of the I O C, probably Capt. C.W. Hollis or perhaps Major G.D. Hazzledine.

> He [Roger] was just about getting about again after a bad
> attack of pleurisy. Slightly bent at the shoulder, but a majestic
> specimen of manhood yet, he welcomed the visitors with all
> that old-world courtesy which stamps the British gentleman
> with the hall mark of grace and nobility of character and puts
> the stranger immediately at ease. He arranged our chairs and
> we partook of rich syrupy tea and Gentlemen's Relish, the
> latter being exactly the right thing to lend added piquancy to
> the occasion. In a very few minutes after tea our pipes were
> going. At first there seemed a slight reserve as though two men
> of the world were mentally weighing each other up. An almost
> embarrassing silence ensued for a moment or two and then
> the curtain lifted. Mutual confidence had been established
> and we dived back into the old days of the Legion.[28]

In at least one case, either Porter led Roger to expand on what he had written in the book and name names, or Porter made an error. In *Chorus to Adventurers* Roger told the story of an unnamed man perspiring heavily on a winter day because he was wearing a chain mail vest to protect himself from a man who had pursued him from South America. Porter said that the man with the vest was Basil Lubbock.[29] Porter chose to quote Roger's comments on the inaugural dinner for the Legion in 1905: "He recalled a wonderful dinner party, given in London to members of the Legion by Lord Lonsdale, who brought down from Cumberland his Yeomanry Band and his wonderful silver plate for the occasion. The latter reminded us, he said, of the days when we scratched on our old tin plates."[30] Porter also quoted extensively from the book, including the foreword "in its entirety," before concluding that the book "contains so much splendid matter interesting to all Frontiersmen the world over, that we regret that we have not space to deal more fully with the book, which is well worth the price charged for it...."[31]

Over the years, Roger had had little or no contact with Driscoll, but in *Chorus to Adventurers* Roger praised Driscoll very highly. No doubt Driscoll had found it difficult to forget the events of 1909 and the problems Roger had caused with the *Modern Man* affair, but Roger's praise seems to have persuaded Driscoll to ask Roger to work with him and wear the uniform again. Roger's agreement was trumpeted in the organization's publication:

> One of the first fruits of the efforts of Kaid Belton, our new
> Deputy Commandant-General, is the return of the Founder,
> Commissioner Roger Pocock, coming out of his well-earned
> retirement to do what he can for us, on the direct invitation
> of Colonel Driscoll, our Commandant-General, following
> the securing of his re-enrolment form some months ago by
> Capt. Porter in the course of an interview at Charterhouse.
> There was a goodly gathering of real Frontiersmen at the
> Rendezvous on the 7th August to welcome him back....
>
> Kaid Belton, in the chair, proposing the toast of The
> Founder, said we were gathered not to honour Roger Pocock,
> but to be honoured by his presence among us. There could
> be no vestige of doubt as to which body is the real Legion
> of Frontiersmen.... His coming to the Imperial Overseas
> Legion of Frontiersmen might prove to be the greatest event
> in its history....

Roger responded to the toast and threw his support strongly behind this group: "Amongst other things he knew that the good men who were supporting the Craven Street organisation could not be rightly informed as to the position or there would be only one organisation."[32] Roger threw himself wholeheartedly into the breakaway group and their fight with the original (Craven Street) Legion. At times the fight became rather messy with petitions and counter-petitions to the War Office.[33] Belton's suggestion that Roger in London and Driscoll in Kenya would be working "hand in hand" seems somewhat ambitious, but for Roger it was a great joy to be able to don his beloved Legion uniform again and be invited to their summer camps to tell his stories to a captive audience around the campfire. Following the debacle of the World Flight Expedition, the Legion had been very cautious about potential problems he might cause if he were allowed back within their ranks. After he was accepted into Charterhouse, life had greatly improved for Roger. When he joined the breakaway Legion several years later, he became much busier and even more content.

Once Edwards-Carter's failing health caused him to take a back seat in the original Legion, Driscoll, writing from "Ruiru, Kenya Colony, British East Africa," encouraged Roger to work towards healing the breach in the Legion. One instance of this occurred in 1932. Every year the Frontiersmen paraded on Horseguards Parade in London to be inspected by a senior general. It could be that officials of the original Legion were concerned that Roger and Driscoll, the two "big beasts" from the early days, had now come together in support of the rebels, and that they urgently wished for reconciliation. It could also be that the general had cancelled at the last minute. However it happened, Roger was photographed trying to throw off his years as he inspected the immaculately turned out ranks of Frontiersmen on Horseguards in May 1932. In September of that year Henry Simson died, so Lena needed Roger's help.

By the summer of 1934, Roger was trying to heal the wounds between the official and breakaway Legions in the way he liked best. He set up a camp on a seven-acre site near Dartford, Kent, between early July and early September. All British units were welcomed there and he considered it his duty to re-establish friendships around the campfire. However, he was still yearning to travel, and amalgamation of the Frontiersmen in 1934 led him to put a proposal to the Master of Charterhouse.

His seventieth birthday was fast approaching, and Roger wanted one more adventure on this earth. He wished to travel around the world, visiting all Legion units on the way. He only needed enough money for travel by sea, as each Legion unit would be delighted to offer the Founder hospitality everywhere he stopped. His application to the Council that governed

Charterhouse presented a problem, though, since Council members were not used to requests from pensioners who wanted to travel around the world. Of course, not every Brother was a Roger Pocock. The Master of Charterhouse was in favour of granting Roger leave, so he forwarded various leaflets about the Legion that Roger had loaned him to Dr. Cosmo Lang, Archbishop of Canterbury. Lang was a friend of General Jan Smuts, who had become a member of the Legion. Dr. Lang wrote to Smuts:

> Will you forgive me if I intrude upon your time with a
> request which you may think somewhat trivial? But I am
> obliged to write as Chairman of the Governors of the very old
> Charterhouse Hospital intended for Brothers of the type of
> Thackeray's Colonel Newcome. One of them is a somewhat
> remarkable person called Captain Roger Pocock who claims
> to have been the Founder of the Legion of Frontiersmen,
> and I note that you are described as a member of its Grand
> Council. Captain Pocock has applied to the Governors
> for leave of absence for six months in order to undertake a
> tour of inspection and encouragement etc. of the various
> branches of the Legion of Frontiersmen in the Dominions,
> and he informed the Governors that he had every hope
> that you would undertake to be the head of the branch of
> the Legion in South Africa. It is somewhat unusual for one
> of the Brothers to absent himself for six months and to
> leave his retirement for such an exacting programme as the
> good Captain Pocock contemplates, and I was asked by the
> Governors to approach you very privately and to ask whether
> you regard the Legion of Frontiersmen as a body worthy
> of every encouragement and particularly whether Captain
> Pocock was justified in expressing the hope that you would
> give it your special leadership in South Africa. We are only
> anxious to deal fairly with Captain Pocock and at the same
> time consistently with the Rules of the Charterhouse.[34]

Smuts was fairly cautious in his reply: "I am somewhat puzzled as to what to say. I believe I am an Hon. Vice-President of the Legion of Frontiersmen—a quite reputable body of old veterans of pre-war days scattered over the Empire. It would no doubt be very welcome to Frontiersmen abroad to have a visit from Captain Pocock, and the visit may do good."[35] One reason for his caution was that Smuts was concerned that Roger's age could cause problems, and that Charterhouse had a moral responsibility for his well-being. Lang still was inclined not to refuse Roger's request, so he turned to another governor, Lord Hanworth, for his advice:

> I hesitate to act definitely on Smuts' letter and to say that the old man must not be allowed to go as I know that many of our colleagues, and I think the Master himself, felt that he ought to be allowed to go unless there was any evidence that this Legion of Frontiersmen was not satisfactory.[36]

Lord Hanworth replied positively:

> The letter of General Smuts does not give sufficient reason for refusing the request of the old brother. The majority of the Assembly was in favour of giving him leave....
> The old man's health and a possible breakdown ought not to prevent the visit....
> Hence let him go.[37]

This was enough for Lang to recommend that Roger be given his furlough, although he would not receive his pension while he was away. So Roger had to try to get by on what little money he had saved from his recent writings, particularly *Chorus to Adventurers,* as well as the money donated to the Dominions Tour Fund. Hence on 6 February 1935, seventy members of Clapham and other London squadrons of the Legion gathered at Fusilier House, Balham, to bid Roger farewell and wish him a successful journey.[38] This was probably just one of a number of Legion meetings Roger attended before his departure on 23 May. Although such meetings would have been ostensibly to bid Roger farewell, he would have used them as fund-raising exercises.

His first visit was to Legion units in South Africa, which brought back memories of his brief service in the Anglo-Boer War and elicited praise for his efforts:

> The Founder (and Director of Recruiting) has, by his visit to South Africa, completed the first portion of his unofficial world tour. He has had wonderful receptions everywhere and has made contact at the following places where the Legion is not represented at present:—Capetown, Port Elizabeth, East London, Durban, Pietermaritzburg and Pretoria. In addition he has visited the Units located in and around Johannesburg, which entertained him royally. The Founder has certainly

Roger Pocock wearing the buffalo coat presented
to him by the Canadian Frontiersmen.
[Photo in author's possession.]

stirred things up in South Africa and the formation of
new units is confidently expected in the near future. One
at Capetown is already formed under Col. Devine. The
Executive Council passed a vote of thanks to Capt. Pocock at
its last meeting.[39]

It is interesting that although Council members passed a vote of thanks,
they were still unsure about Roger's reliability and insisted on empha-
sizing that it was an "unofficial" tour. The hierarchy of the Legion in
London may have found him an irritant, but he was greeted as a hero
by units around the world and treated with great respect. While his visit

was unofficial, Roger happily reported that "In the Benoni Squadron I met a fellow from the Ladysmith Garrison, one from the Relief Column, and one young Boer who had been firing on both. Here is our Legion at its very greatest, healing national wounds."[40] Next was Perth, Adelaide, Melbourne, and Sydney, Australia. Australian Frontiersmen were spread far and wide; however, once word spread that their beloved Founder was to visit, many travelled long distances to meet him. He then spent twenty-six days in New Zealand, where he attended the meetings of twenty-three squadrons, a gruelling itinerary for a man in his seventieth year. His great delight was to visit his parents' old home there. In a letter he described the home his brother had left as a very small boy:

> I wonder how much you remember of Motueka? Father's house is known as "The Gables." It is built of 9"X9" squared timber posts morticed [sic] into beams of the same size. The panels are filled in with clay & the whole house sheathed as a frame building. It is the most substantial house in the district.
>
> Mother's little flapper maid servant, now aged 87 was so happy over the meeting that she cried her eyes out.... The people have replaced the worn-out tombstone at Lilian's grave.
>
> The Nelson Motueka district is the richest land in New Zealand, farmed intensively & noted for its tobacco. The schools at Nelson are so good that Service people from India settle there to get their children educated.
>
> New Zealand is by far the finest of the Dominions in the character of the people & the splendour of the scenery. Moreover, as the son of a pioneer settler, I was welcomed as an "old identity." There was a certain amount of fun in being given civil receptions by Lord Mayors, red carpet being laid as if I were the Royal Family, guards of honour and all sorts of fuss.[41]

The New Zealand Frontiersmen also made a great impression on him, particularly the "roughnecks" who reminded him of the men he had encountered in Canada and the American West in his youth: "The Squadrons dearest to me were the roughneck outfits, far away in the Bush, who won't wear uniform, but would come say ninety miles, or in one case 146 miles to attend a meeting. Yet one does not forget the magnificent turn-out of a hundred men and a band in such cities as Wellington, Dunedin, and Auckland."[42]

Roger then went back to Australia to visit the squadrons at Brisbane, Townsville, Cairns, and Thursday Island that he had been unable to include earlier. He moved on to Manila, in the Philippines, and stayed a week at Hong Kong, where the squadron greatly impressed him, although he found it difficult to persuade his aged limbs back on a horse to hold a mounted parade. There Roger also made a radio broadcast. On 17 October he talked of his own experiences and those of his friends and colleagues in the Legion: "Before dinner he spoke for 15 minutes over the radio to Hong Kong and listeners were of [the] opinion that this broadcast was one of the most interesting Hong Kong has had."[43] It is evidence of the strength and popularity of the Legion around the world that he went to see squadrons not only in Shanghai, but also in Japan at Nagasaki, Kobe, Yokohama, and Tokyo. He then sailed on RMS *Empress of Russia* to Vancouver. Roger's welcome everywhere he went in Canada would have been an immense thrill to him, but it also acted as great publicity for the Legion and its work. The punishing itinerary he had already carried out would have been difficult for a younger and fitter man, but the great success of every visit carried Roger through, particularly in Canada, which was one of the strongest Commands of the Legion, and particularly dear to him.

The strength of that Command was due to one man. After the First World War the Legion in Canada had suffered the same shrinkage of members as in other countries due to the loss of so many members in the war and the lessening of interest in paramilitary organizations. Indeed it had limped along until 1929 when it was revived by Lt. Col. Louis Scott (1887–1967). The camp, which played such a beneficial role in the revitalization, came to the Legion through Scott's job as district supervisor in northern Alberta for the Soldier Settlement Board (SSB) and as a result of his foresight. The SSB had awarded an ex-soldier 200 acres on the shore of Hastings Lake, thirty-five miles southeast of Edmonton, where Scott was based. This parcel was heavily wooded and had a number of hills, bogs, and holes. The recipient made some attempt at farming the land but soon declared he wished to quit. When Scott went to look at the land he agreed that it was unsuitable for farming, but realized it would make an excellent training camp for the Legion. He was able to negotiate purchase of the land from the government for a nominal sum, and in return it was named Fort Scott. All Canadian Frontiersmen who could easily travel to the camp spent their spare time building a log cabin for use in summer camps. Large rocks were also collected on the site to build a war memorial for the 9,000 Frontiersmen who gave their lives during the First World War.[44]

As with everywhere else he had visited, Roger was treated with great honour, but Canadians, who considered him one of their own, greeted him with special warmth. Apparently officials at Legion headquarters in London were aware of this, and feared that Roger might acquire so much personal support he could make decisions that would usurp their authority. Hence Commandant C.H. Wybrow wrote to Col. Scott in an attempt to forestall such a thing:

> The Commandant-General wishes it to be known by all
> Officers in your command that this Tour is in no way Official.
> Captain Pocock is undertaking it solely as a private venture,
> (or adventure), and it is to be distinctly understood that,
> while it is hoped that all Frontiersmen throughout the World
> will welcome him in a manner worthy of his age and past
> association with the great body he created, everything he
> might say, both in public and in private conversation, must be
> accepted as an expression of his PRIVATE opinion, and in no
> way Official or binding on the Legion in any way.[45]

It is easy to understand, in light of Roger's former activities in the Legion, that officials in London would be very nervous about what he might either do or promise on its behalf; however, this letter was rather strongly worded, and Canadians would be particularly upset about this sort of diktat coming from England. They had always been of independent spirit and prone to writing letters complaining about the autocratic manner of the London officials.

On Wednesday, 6 November, a large banquet in Roger's honour was held at the Hotel Georgia in Vancouver. He spoke of his first visit to Vancouver, "when it was a burned village in the woods," described the Legion and its role in the First World War, praised the vibrancy of the Legion in New Zealand, and "expressed his delight that Vancouver is reorganising."[46] Roger then travelled to Edmonton, where he celebrated his seventieth birthday. While the weather was cold and snowy when he arrived on 8 November, the welcome was warm, and he was received by a guard of honour and escorted to the hotel:

> Edmonton and the strong North re-claimed one of her
> strong pioneer sons Friday night when Commandant Roger
> Pocock...came home....
>   At the King Edward hotel, Commandant Pocock received
> a score of distinguished men before the party went down to
> the Rose Room for a banquet in his honor.[47]

At that banquet Dr. E.A. Braithwaite told of events in 1885 and said that Roger lost toes that day, but "He still served Canada and the Empire with undiminished loyalty and zeal."[48] The *Edmonton Journal* called Roger "one of the earliest Albertans" and said more than 100 were present at that banquet. In that account of his speech, Roger stressed the important role the Legion played in Canada and in the Empire:

> "Now our force has spread throughout the empire," the commandant told the Edmonton squadron at the dinner. "Before the war we used to be regarded as a sort of comic opera outfit. But during the war 17,500 members of our legion served, and 9,000 fell in action. We stood recognized."
>
> He told of glamorous places taken by Frontiersmen in various parts of the empire, and by their sons.
>
> "You have in this city Major-General Griesbach, the son of the Number One member of the Mounted Police, the force which provides us with much of our tradition. When we went to go behind the scenes of officialdom to get something special in London, we interview the son of a Frontiersman; when we attend ceremonials on the Horse Guards parade, we are reviewed by the son of a Frontiersman...." He told of recognition by the home office of the legion as a defender of civilians and of training for defence against gas attacks.[49]

Saturday had been earmarked for discussions with Louis Scott, but Roger also found time to talk with Assistant Commissioner Henry Montgomery Newson of the Mounted Police. On Sunday, 10 November, Roger attended a service at Holy Trinity Anglican Church in Edmonton, where he read one of the lessons, and then a convoy of seventeen cars took the party to Fort Scott at Hastings Lake, where Roger unveiled the Frontiersmen's War Memorial.[50] Before that ceremony, Roger and the others went into the log cabin so that they could "fortify" themselves against the cold. Perhaps Roger fortified himself too well, since it was said that he slipped on the ice and fell.

After he left Edmonton, Roger carried on across Canada, calling at Camrose, Calgary, Regina, Winnipeg, Sault Ste Marie, Toronto, Kingston, Ottawa, Montreal, and Halifax. At every stop he made a speech. That speech was usually reported in the local newspapers, which helped recruitment for the Legion. In a speech in Toronto he put forward his view that air travel would be the way of the future. He recommended young men seek a career in the Air Force and "Always [to] tackle the most dangerous thing you can find."[51] At Ottawa, the RCMP, which held Roger in high esteem in spite of his brief service, welcomed him. He wrote that in contrast to "all sorts of fuss" in New Zealand and Australia, "Canada took me quite calmly. Still I had a gorgious [sic] time with the Mounted Police, & at Montreal they put me up for a week in the hangman's bedroom."[52] Flora Macdonald Steele reported on his stay in Montreal, where he "was put up at the R.C.M.P. Barracks in this city, thoroughly pleased to be with The Outfit. I know that he was bright and cheery and we were glad to foregather with him."[53]

Roger arrived at Liverpool on 15 December, after what he called "37,000 miles of sheer enjoyment."[54] He was elated by the success of his journey and happily became the guest of honour at a dinner held by the Legion at a prestigious venue, the Duke of York's Headquarters in London.

> After the Loyal Toast had been drunk, the Commandant-
> General, in a few well-chosen words, expressed the pleasure
> it gave him, both personally and on behalf of the Legion,
> to accord the Founder a hearty Welcome Home at the
> conclusion of his World Tour—during which he had visited
> practically every Command or outlying unit of the Legion
> overseas. He felt sure that this Tour had been an unqualified
> success and that its results would be of immense benefit to
> the Corps.[55]

Roger was called on to give a summary of his tour, and when he rose from his seat was accorded an ovation.

In the discussions he had with Mounted Police officials during his stay in Canada, Roger recommended closer cooperation between the Mounted Police and the Legion, and he explained how his well-trained and well-run Legion could be a valuable auxiliary to the Mounted Police. The Frontiersmen in Canada were quite convinced that they owed a great deal to Roger's negotiations, which enabled them to announce with great pride a year later:

> Affiliation. Royal Canadian Mounted Police. The following
> extract from General Order No. 695, Part I, week ending
> 26–9–36, of the Royal Canadian Mounted Police, is
> published for the information of all members:
>   By Authority of the Honourable, the Minister in Control
> of the Force, The Legion of Frontiersmen, is hereby affiliated

with the Royal Canadian Mounted Police, in the same
manner as Units of the Canadian Militia are affiliated with
Regiments of His Majesty's Forces in the United Kingdom.[56]

In this way, after the many problems, failures, and setbacks he had experienced with the organization he had founded, Roger achieved one success
of momentous proportions, and the Mounted Police acquired an auxiliary
force that was well disciplined and under the firm command of a trusted
officer, Louis Scott. Further—a consideration of great importance to any
publicly-funded body—that auxiliary force would come free of charge,
with its own recognizable uniform that was different, but not too dis-
similar, from that of the Mounted Police. Although the Legion officials in
London had distanced themselves from Roger's trip, as soon as they heard
of the affiliation, they published it in every pamphlet and handbook. The
affiliation caused some problems for the British War Office, which had
always tried to keep the troublesome Legion at arm's length. The Legion
had made some suggestions in the early 1930s about ways members could
be used in Britain, but the Legion's desire for independence had always
been a stumbling block.

During his world tour Roger found the solution for his concern that
communication between units and Commands took so long. Roger was
always keen to utilize the latest scientific developments and ever forward-
thinking, so he proposed a chain of radio stations:

> Will members or candidates who have radio plants for
> receiving and transmitting messages be kind enough to apply
> to Corporal Bennett, L.F. at Canadian Headquarters, 201
> Williamson Building, Edmonton, Alberta, who will furnish
> wave lengths and times for Legion messages. We are creating
> a chain of stations girdling the planet, putting an end to the
> isolation of Frontiersmen.[57]

Later, Roger explained why Edmonton was the centre of this effort:

> If Australians excel as horsemen, Canadians are born
> engineers.... It is this Canadian gift for mechanics which
> accounts for the new venture of Corporal Bennett at
> Edmonton, who has established a chain of radio stations
> for receiving and transmitting messages. It extends from
> Prince Edward Island to Vancouver, and will soon girdle the
> Empire.[58]

In addition to encouraging radio use, Roger was keen to see the Legion increase its number of air units, for he thought "the future of the Legion will be in the air-ways; and it will be useful if we can find photographers in our membership for aerial photography in time of war."[59]

Roger knew that he had achieved one of the great successes of his life with his world tour, so he decided it was time to rest on his laurels. In February 1937 Frontiersmen were told that Roger, "now seeks to be relieved of official rank and appointments; but, his interest in the Personnel of the Legion is unabated and he will continue to be a member of the Executive Council, so that his experience and knowledge of Legion affairs will not be lost to the directive body."[60] In 1939 the visit to Canada of King George VI and Queen Elizabeth called the Frontiersmen into action as a back-up to the Mounted Police. After the visit, Scott received a letter of thanks from Brigadier S.T. Wood: "The assistance of The Legion of Frontiersmen was of inestimable value and the highest praise is due its members both for the smartness of their appearance and the efficiency with which they assisted the police."[61] Nonetheless, with the Legion, as with Roger, events never followed a smooth course, so the affiliation between the Legion and the RCMP was terminated in October 1939 because of internal squabbles and divisions.[62] After all his efforts in Canada in 1935, it is safe to assume that Roger was devastated by this turn of events. Yet again something monumental in his life went seriously wrong, and a great achievement turned to failure. While no blame could be attached to Roger, this would not have alleviated the distress he felt. Roger even became involved in the controversy: when Canadian Division asked to publish his photograph in its magazine, Roger happily consented. He then received a severe reprimand from Imperial Headquarters for agreeing to this. Roger admitted that his reply "scorched the paper":

> He thought that the I.H.Q. were invading his personal affairs and he would not tolerate such action. In his opinion, their handling of the affairs of the Canadian Division demonstrated incompetence and irresponsibility. He did not want to start any action that would damage the Frontiersmen Image while the country was at War, but he refused to be associated with it. He resigned from the I.H.Q. Council and The Legion of Frontiersmen.
>
> He was offered Membership in the Canadian Division, which he gladly accepted saying that Canada represented an important part of his life.[63]

Calgary Chapter, Legion of Frontiersmen, Calgary, Alberta, 1935.
Roger Pocock is seated third from the right in the front row.
[Glenbow Archives, PB 335-1]

He retained that membership until his death.

As the world moved towards another war, Roger realized that he had little chance of any active service—he had, after all, been almost too old for the First World War. He could do little more than worry, think, and meditate. He was convinced that another war was inevitable and that, as before, Britain was insufficiently prepared. He hoped that well-trained Legion members would again play a part. In the meantime he was still able to attend Legion engagements. He remained very popular with the ordinary Frontiersmen and was pleased to accept invitations. For example, "Wednesday October 7th saw some 50 members of the Essex Area with Commdt. Pocock, Capt. Erswell and T.A. officers, at Troop H.Q. for the purpose of having a good 'binge' on the occasion of the O.C.'s 'Stag' party. What a night!" It seems that Roger was as fond in his later years of an evening's drinking as he had been in his youth. That article does not say whether Roger attended the wedding on 11 October, which was reported as "a pukka Frontiersman affair," but he gave a lecture to the Troop on the following Tuesday evening about the history of the Legion around the Empire, and he was back at Hornchurch again on 22 October for the "first Annual Dinner and Dance."[64]

Roger was a welcome guest at such events at the many Troops round the London area and was happy to attend if they were not too difficult

A recent Photograph of CAPTAIN ROGER POCOCK
(The famous Cowboy-Novelist)

(Issued by London General Press)

"A recent Photograph of Captain Roger Pocock, (The famous
Cowboy-Novelist)," issued by London General Press, *c.* 1934.

[Scanned from an advertising card in the possession of the author.]

or expensive for him to reach from Charterhouse.[65] Roger was particularly pleased to be invited to any summer camp within easy reach of Charterhouse. On these occasions many photographs were taken of him together with other Frontiersmen who were delighted to be photographed with the Founder. Even the children of Frontiersmen wanted to be photographed with such a well-known adventurer and author, and they wished to be allowed to sit around the campfire to listen to Roger's great fund of stories about his adventures. Actress June Tobin, daughter of Roger's friend Vahd W. Tobin, who was a senior Legion officer, remembered being at such camps and Roger telling stories, some of which may have been a little saucy. She was able to recall just the punch line of one story, where Roger said, in a somewhat Churchillian voice, "and from her enormous bosom, she produced—a sofa!" June Tobin said she puzzled about that story and why the adults found it amusing.[66] Roger's image did not appear only in photographs: the Legion commissioned Gerald C. Hudson to paint an oil portrait to hang in Headquarters. Roger found a way to use it to assist Legion finances:

> My portrait, by Gerald Hudson, at Imperial Headquarters,
> has been reproduced by the three-colour process. Copies
> have been presented to units and unit Commanders, and
> may be had at 2/- post free on application to me at my private
> address: Charterhouse, London, E.C.1. If the names and
> ranks of purchasers are sent with the order, all copies will be
> autographed.[67]

Roger also received the great honour of a competition in his name:

> Wishing to encourage riding and scouting in the name of a
> great rider and scout, my brother, Major Harwood Elmes
> Steele, M.C., conceived the idea of an Empire Cavalry contest
> on Empire Day, 1936, and so he raised the necessary sums of
> money collected from friends and admirers of Roger Pocock,
> who had once been described by Fred Burnham, the famous
> scout, as "one of the greatest adventurers of all time." He
> worked out the details for the competition.... A handsome
> trophy was designed and executed by Mappin's Limited,
> and the Pocock Lone Scout Shield became the centre of an
> interesting competition for horsemastership and scouting.[68]

Two competitions were held before Roger's death:

The Pocock Lone Scout Trophy was first won by the Bihar Light Horse, in 1938, and secondly by the Prince Edward Island Light Horse, 1939, and the shield now reposes with that regiment, until such time as competitors will be able to come forward again and renew their interest in scouting and riding.[69]

A newspaper praised the competition for being "in full consonance with the character of the Legion and the record of its founder," particularly his "solitary ride from Fort Macleod in Alberta to Mexico City." The article continued:

> These corporate and personal records have suggested the conditions of the present competition. Candidates will be required to carry out a 70-mile ride, to be covered within 36 consecutive hours along a prescribed route....
>
> The conditions governing the competition require a fair degree of personal skill and of horsemastership.... It is hoped, therefore, that the competition will prove attractive because it calls both for a spirit of emulation and for a full measure of physical fitness among the competitors.[70]

Roger was aware of his good fortune, so in letters to his brother in America he tried to be cheerful, although age was having an effect on his sisters, as well. In 1936 he wrote in a letter:

> Rosalie is now disabled by failing eyesight, unable to read or sew but still able to do a bit of gardening, and in splendid physical health. Daisy [Lena] I saw last night, there has been in the last few days a return of trouble caused by the old abscess in the stomach. The attacks are getting less frequent and less severe. She is reading proof of her autobiography, which will be out before Christmas. She carries on her higher thought classes, reads the lessons at a church of the Old Catholics, and is deeply in research about the newly discovered cosmic ray.
>
> Hilda was lecturing last night at Liverpool and has engagements all over the Kingdom, partly on health, more generally on Eugenics. She is in perfect health and has immense energy for a very busy life.[71]

Roger shared Lena's interest in mysticism and religion. Lena was also involved in the Oxford Group, and Moral Re-Armament (MRA) erected a monument to her at Westminster Theatre in Palace Street, London.[72] Eugenics is considered deeply offensive now, but between the wars it was a subject of broad interest. In 1935 Hilda was the London Propaganda Secretary for the Eugenics Society and published at least one article in that field.[73] Although Roger always made it clear he was opposed to both communism and fascism, the involvement of his sisters with the Oxford Group and MRA, added to a number of very public denunciations of left-wing activities by prominent Frontiersmen, must have caused some concern in official British circles. As a sort of counterbalance to this, Lena was friendly with both Clement Attlee (1883–1967) and his older brother, the Rev. Bernard Henry Bravery Attlee (1873–1943), who was the vicar of Chieveley where Lena had her country home.

On a more personal note, Roger wrote of his activities and concerns:

> I am in riotous health and fairly busy with the Legion of
> Frontiersmen, having about three engagements a week, on the
> average. Lectures, drills, signalling, air defenses, weddings,
> dances, dinners, church parades. Last Sunday I had a rest,
> after nineteen successive Sundays on duty. But there are
> also operas, cinemas or chess on spare evenings. Reprints
> are forthcoming of some of my old books. Apart from
> conferences and parades there is a deal of correspondence—
> promoting new units, or keeping the children in order; and
> there are several thousand of them.
>
> At a time of great prosperity in Britain and general recovery
> in the Dominions, the condition of the United States makes
> one anxious. Nobody here pretends to understand American
> finance and our ideas are vague as to the internal politics.
>
> World conditions drift toward a clash between
> Communism and Faschism [*sic*], with Democracy trying
> to keep out of the impending war between them. In the
> British Commonwealth the Communists and Fasccists [*sic*]
> are dangerous only in time of distress and unemployment,
> but Democracy is perfectly safe while we are prosperous.
> The next slump will be very perilous, but for the present
> our only political interest is in keeping God's peace among
> the nations. My own work deals only with the safty [*sic*] of
> women and children, in the event of war. And I don't think
> there is anything more to be said.[74]

Roger's writings, as early as the late nineteenth century, made it clear the United States made him anxious. As usual, his vision of the future, from his perspective in 1936, contained a mixture of the well-reasoned and the inaccurate. Despite his concern about the coming of war, he was still able to have fun:

> Since my retirement at the age of 72 from...the Legion I have turned craftsman, & am working very hard on monuments for Charterhouse[:] a martyrs' memorial & half a dozen heraldic bas-reliefs. Its great fun & I'm having the time of my young life at sculpting, gilding, jewel setting, carpentry, inlay work &c.[75]

Unfortunately, all this work was destroyed when Charterhouse was bombed.

As he grew older, Roger became more interested in spiritual matters. His approach certainly had impressed Porter, who wrote: "He did not talk about himself but branched into a speculation upon adventures upon which we may all enter after this life and then he relapsed into thought...." Porter even made a point of quoting from *Chorus to Adventurers:*

> To traverse wild countries, to explore dangerous trades, penetrate past ages, see into the future—these are the things which make my life worth living, and the most joyous of adventures was the long and difficult research which led me into the Wonderland of the Mind. Let me compare it to a gigantic mountain, easier to climb if it were only visible.[76]

It would have been normal for an aging man who had lived such a life of adventure to reflect on his own mortality. Roger certainly studied many alternatives and additions to Christianity, but he always returned to Christianity as his foundation, although the First Nations beliefs he had learned about when he was young always had an influence. For example, he often claimed skills that were admired when demonstrated by First Nations peoples who lived in the wilderness and relied on their ability to survive in a hostile environment. So "we discussed the mind and the senses and he told us how he could smell water at a distance in the desert. We suggested that it might smell like damp moss or a wet linen sheet hanging in the air to dry. 'No,' he said, 'It smells like steel. Dip a knife into water and then smell it.'"[77] Earlier, Roger had claimed that

> At half a mile I have smelt a mountain river—like a wet knife.

Once, at about five miles on a windless day my two horses
snuffed a fresh pool and bolted for it at full gallop despite my
frantic protests at their apparent madness. Considering that
we were lost in sand-rock desert, all three of us owed our lives
to that small distant smell.[78]

Although such skills and ability to work with nature owed much to the
influence of First Nations peoples on his early life, it seems that he began
to take a particular interest in spiritual matters and second sight when he
was recuperating and Beryl Mercer told his fortune on 10 March 1910. Yet
a sampling of the diary notes he made of what she told him seem just as
vague as one would expect:

Work on documents & sums of money remunerative work for
a very fair man.
    Sudden rather unpleasant news of a friend.
    Go across London about a cheque which makes me very
angry.
    *News from a distance someone staying near water makes
me anxious.
    Meeting on money matters & violent quarrel with young
fair man. I like him too.
    Leaving a fair woman behind who is fond of me.
    Dark man at my house a very good friend. *Henry*
    Big split between very fair man & one of my colour.
(Serjeant & Esher?)[79]

Although Roger seemed to be able to put names to some of these vague
descriptions, one might view them as standard fortune-telling generaliza-
tions. Nonetheless, it is probably fair to date Roger's inquiries into the
human mind and soul from this time, and it can be observed that including
such otherworldly ideas in his fiction did not improve its marketability.

With the passing of the years, Roger's rapport with Kipling also
changed. In later years Roger seems to have dropped all mention of
Kipling, his early hero, and there is no evidence Roger wrote to Kipling
again after his attempt to involve Kipling in filmmaking. When they
were both younger, they shared a distrust of America and an imperialist
view of Britain as the head of a powerful empire, with Canada at its side.
However, "after the war in South Africa, and especially after the advent
of a Liberal Government, Kipling's role changed. No longer the apostle
whom everyone wanted to hear, he was consigned to the role of Cassandra,

condemned to utter prophecies that no one would heed."[80] One way in which their views diverged was that Kipling was an ardent supporter of National Service, while Roger believed in voluntary service through the Territorials for younger men and the Legion of Frontiersmen for those unable to join the Territorials. Kipling was also strongly against women's suffrage, whereas Roger, although he did not make any public display, would have been expected to share Lena's support of that movement. Kipling's politics steadily moved to the right, while Roger could be called apolitical. Roger had acquaintances from all sides of the political spectrum and listened to their views, while making up his own mind privately on the best way forward. Both Kipling and Roger, though, believed in the benefits of technology, particularly the great future of aviation and the importance of radio. Kipling's Victorian poetry also had a great effect on Roger, as it did on all like-minded men in the Legion. One of Kipling's poems, "Lost Legion," was often quoted by Legion members. Roger was such a great admirer of Kipling's nineteenth-century poetry he even tried his hand at writing similar poetry. Judging by what does survive, it is no real misfortune that most of it has been lost. The words Roger wrote for the original Legion hymn, "Love under Arms," have survived, however. Some Frontiersmen suggested this be sung during the Legion's centenary celebrations in 2005, but wiser counsel prevailed. Possibly "Love under Arms" was looked on more kindly during the early years of the Legion, but it sounds jingoistic now. The last of the four verses provides a sense of the quality of Roger's verse:

> We would not arm to order,
> We would not serve for gold–
> The Freemen of the Border
> Are neither ruled nor sold,
> But from the farthest ranges
> Last reef, and utmost strand,
> A love that never changes
> Shall guard thee, Motherland!

It is not surprising that this hymn was apparently not used after Roger left the Legion. A copy of the published sheet music was only re-discovered by the author among some of Roger's papers approximately forty years after his death. If there had been a copy in the Legion archives, it would have been destroyed in the bombing of the London headquarters in 1940.

Roger may have been apolitical, but he did have many contacts and friends, and he was keen to know more about the abdication of Edward VIII.

One of the last photographs of Roger Pocock in uniform.
[Legion of Frontiersmen (Countess Mountbatten's Own), LOFI2-RP8)]

Unfortunately, his nephew's account of what Roger said he had been able to discover from various sources only hints at the information: "At the 1936 affair, Roger wrote to the effect he had been in touch with the politicians responsible for the abdication, who stated the Wallis Simpson affair was not the cause—rather that Edward was *unfit to reign.*" Ken Pocock would say no more than that "I have never given out the letter or contents as I thought the matter unkind."[81] The only politician of the time Roger is known to have been in contact with was Clement Attlee, perhaps through Attlee's brother. As to which other politicians Roger might have contacted, it is only possible to speculate.

The dark days for Great Britain in 1940 and 1941 left Roger feeling frustrated that his age prevented him from taking a proper part in the defeat of Hitler, which he was sure would happen but did not live to see. He was too old even to be accepted in the Home Guard, which owed much to the Legion and the many Frontiersmen who were too old for active service but found a way to serve their country through what was originally the Local Defence Volunteers (LDV) and then became the Home Guard. Indeed, it was the vigorous recruitment activities of the Legion that spurred the

British government to form the LDV.[82] Roger was concerned that America was dragging her heels about supporting Britain, so he tried to help in the one way he could, by writing to a newspaper in Washington, D.C. Roger told of the young men gone to war, of the gardens devoted to vegetables instead of flowers, of the young children who had been evacuated from the bombing of the cities to the village:

> So there you have the detail of an English country village with 700 people engaged in a great variety of services to the state. Does it suggest enormous official expenditure? It costs the government nothing. Does it suggest a meddling interference with our rights as citizens? We have not even one policeman. Does it suggest terror, anxiety, scarcity, privation, famine, impending catastrophe? We have not noticed anything of the kind. The old beer cult of John Bull, braggart and aggressive expressing contempt for mere foreigners, has faded out, for really the present day beer is too thin and too expensive to give us inspiration. Its place has been taken by the prayer cult, as a tonic for the nerves and something more.

Roger stressed the virtue of prayer because he and his sisters felt that prayer and meditation were probably all they could usefully offer, since they could not be more physically active. He concluded by saying that "Much as we should appreciate American maritime help for our blockade, convoy work and transport of children, we realize that the republic must be fully armed and of one mind before she meets the armed and united Germans in the field. And while there is such a strain upon production it is especially generous of the government and people to let us have precedence in the supply of armaments."[83]

During 1941 matters grew worse. Charterhouse was bombed. Roger wrote, "My home, the ancient Charterhouse, has been destroyed. My private effects escaped, including the buffalo robe which you gave me, but seven monuments, the whole of my work as a sculptor, shared the fate of the buildings. I have been living in the country, too old, they say, for any public service, although only 75 and in sound health."[84] More important than the loss of some possessions was the loss of the financial security Charterhouse had provided for him. Thus Roger wrote to Colonel Wood in Ottawa about missing forms that he required in order to receive his Mounted Police pension:

The matter has become urgent since the destruction of
the Charterhouse estate from which I drew my income, so
that I have nothing left excepting a billeting allowance from
Government of $5 a month....

   If it were possible at the age of 75 to get employment or if
I could get quick returns for my work as a writer I would not
trouble you. As it is, I beg for the pension forms.[85]

Roger was nearly penniless, and the idyllic summer days spent camping out
in the summerhouse in Lena's garden at Chieveley and at Legion camps
were now a thing of the past. Having to leave his home at Charterhouse
hurt him deeply, and he became weaker. The busy days of the 1930s were
gone, and with no sign of an early end to the war, his life lacked purpose
and he could see no more hope of any adventures or even tasks. He was
evacuated to Weston-Super-Mare, Somerset, where he tried to be positive and cheerful. His final letter to his brother rambled, though, and he
dwelled on memories and recounted a lot of the history of the Pocock
family, together with the history of Chieveley. Roger also told him simply,
and quite bluntly, of Rosalie's death:

   I have to tell you news about Rosalie, last summer she was
   still gardening although her sight was very dim, nearing
   blindness. During the winter her health failed gradually. This
   summer she could go out only in a bath chair when there was
   sunshine. For a month or so there has been great pain, which
   came to an end last week.

      Lena and Hilda conveyed the body to a crematorium in
   North-West London, but the actual funeral was followed [sic]
   by a Memorial Service at Chieveley, and there I suppose there
   will be a tablet to her memory. The church was beautifully
   decorated and the whole village attended, for she was very
   much loved.[86]

Soon after Roger wrote that letter his own end came. November brought
in hard weather that would be treacherous for any old man, particularly
one who, like Roger, was seldom seen without a cigarette. The story of
his end is best and most simply told in a letter Lena wrote:

   For the last few months Roger has been living at Weston-
   Super-Mare. He had been quite ill here and then had been

a short spell in Newbury Hospital. He was very happy in
Weston as there are many airmen as well as old friends of the
Legion, several good cinemas, and many good concerts. He
wrote very happily and was surprisingly well in health as well
as mind.

He lectured on Russia on the Friday—was moved to
nursing home on the Sunday suffering from bronchial
pneumonia. My sister and I were telegraphed for on
Monday night. On Tuesday when we reached the home
he was in great spirits although obviously very ill. Later in
the evening he was still very happy, though 'very tired.' On
Wednesday morning at a quarter to four he sailed away to
the undiscovered country in his sleep. He was cremated at
Bristol cemetery....

There was a splendid tribute in *The Times,* and several
references in other papers.

Roger had a grand life and all the people at Weston loved
him. I can hardly realize that he is "away." We were such great
friends.[87]

Roger Pocock departed this world on his last great adventure on
12 November 1941, three days after his seventy-sixth birthday. A memorial service was held for him at St. Martin-in-the-Fields, London, on 22
November, where "Colonel E.G. Dunn read the Lesson, and an address
was given by Captain R.A. Smith. More than a hundred Frontiersmen
were present."[88] Considering the effects of the war, that was an impressive number.

The tribute in the *Times* was an outline of his life, achievements, and
adventures.[89] It elicited a reader's encomium:

Roger Pocock was so modest that few except his closest
friends could guess that life to him was and had always
been a splendid adventure. There can rarely have been a
man so wholly devoted to every good cause except himself:
or so completely undefeated by sorrow and suffering. It is
impossible to imagine that he ever did a mean thing or had
a mean thought. He was immensely proud of the Legion of
Frontiersmen and of his part in its foundation and direction.
But his pride in it had nothing personal, and was due solely
to his knowledge that the Legion had been of real service

to the country which he loved. He felt more bitterly than anything in his life the fact that age prevented him from taking a more active part in the present war—in fact this may be said to be the only bitterness he ever felt. One could have wished that he could have lived to see the victory which he never doubted would come.[90]

As befits a man of broad influence, obituaries were published in newspapers near and far. The *Weston-Super-Mare Gazette* reported his death on 15 November, with a mention of his "many occupations" and some of his adventures, and a week later provided a brief but complimentary obituary, including the statement that "Capt. Pocock was deservedly popular and well-known on account of his work, writings and lectures."[91] The *Bristol Evening Post* said Roger, the "internationally famous founder of the Legion of Frontiersmen," died "from pneumonia, after a life packed with adventure in all parts of the world." A guard of honour of Frontiersmen was at the cremation, and there were wreaths "from the Legion of Frontiersmen all over the Empire as well as from the masters, staff and brethren of Charterhouse."[92] Some obituaries were published in Canada.[93] There were also accounts of the service held in Holy Trinity Church in Cookham in 1945, to dedicate the family memorial plaque his sister Rosalie had commissioned.[94] However, one of the most splendid summaries of his life was written while he was still alive:

> Roger Pocock, traveller, explorer, prospector, pioneer, author, artist, poet, founder of the Legion of Frontiersmen (and soldier of course, during the war), devoted son of the Empire and brother of his fellow-men and member and communicant of the Church of England, in the very widest sense of the word, has been a splendid missionary. He has taken into many parts of the world the qualities that make for the very best of manhood and nationhood, and nothing that is wrong. He has taken religion, valor, enterprise, ambition, patriotism, love of country and love of home, devotion to duty, unbounded faith, unflagging industry, endurance, fortitude and initiative, and as well, courtesy, good manners, and upright dealing, not bad missionary work. He has been a true servant of the Empire in many ways, spending his life in loving and often unrequited service. His work in founding the Legion of Frontiersmen alone, the wonderful association

of British men who have seen and known the strenuous life of Britain's sons all over the world, will be a lasting memorial whose worth can never be gauged in sufficient terms.[95]

Few men have crammed so much into seventy-six years. He also left several legacies. His long-distance horse ride was still a British record over a century later. More importantly, his beloved Legion of Frontiersmen is still extant, although much reduced in numbers. The vibrancy of this legacy was demonstrated over the weekend of 24–25 April 2005, as members of the Legion of Frontiersmen from around the world gathered in London for centenary celebrations. There may have been no campfires, but in the bar of the Union Jack Club many legion "campfire yarns" were told, and men with greying hair from different countries discovered that they had served on the same station in the same foreign country at the same time, maybe thirty or forty years earlier.

On the Sunday, Frontiersmen from many countries marched together through the City of London to the Guildhall, as in past days, preceded by mounted Frontiersmen on fine horses. Canadian Frontiersmen rode with the British mounted troop. The thoughts of the British public watching the Frontiersmen ride through the streets of the City could have echoed those expressed to Roger in 1897 about the NWMP: "Who are those men who can ride?" At the Guildhall they were inspected by the Legion's Patron, The Countess Mountbatten, continuing the family link to her grandfather, Prince Louis. From cadets hardly into their teens to grizzled veterans in their late seventies, they showed their discipline and ability to "do anything" by parading their Colours and showing parade skills that would have graced any regular military unit.

Throughout the weekend the name of Roger Pocock was seldom far from the lips of those taking part, and his spirit imbued all the proceedings. Roger's life may have been a mixture of failures and successes, but here was one lasting legacy. His idea, his dream, and his plan still proudly continued a century after he formed the Legion, and well over sixty years after his death. One statement frequently rang out from this memorial to Roger, which would have given him great pleasure: "Founder of the Legion of Frontiersmen." He would also have been delighted to see the Legion still thriving, most particularly in Canada, the country where he always felt at home and for whose people he always held such high regard and affection.

Appendix

MONOGRAPHS BY ROGER POCOCK

Roger Pocock was a prolific journalist, and a comprehensive list of his journalism appears in the notes. Books published in the nineteenth century normally appeared under the name H.R. Pocock or H.R.A. Pocock. In the twentieth century, he generally used Roger Pocock.

FICTION

Tales of Western Life. Ottawa: Mitchell, 1888.
Rules of the Game. London: Tower Romance Library, 1895.
Arctic Night. London: Chapman and Hall, 1896.
The Blackguard. London: New Vagabond Library 1896. Revised US ed. *The Cheerful Blackguard*. Indianapolis: Bobbs-Merrill, 1915. Repr. as *The Splendid Blackguard*. London: John Murray, 1915.
The Dragon-slayer. London: Chapman and Hall, 1896. Repr. as *Sword and Dragon*. London: Hodder & Stoughton, 1909.
Curly. London: Gay & Bird, 1904.
Chariot of the Sun. London: Chapman and Hall, 1910.
Jesse of Cariboo. London: John Murray, 1911. Revised US ed. *A Man in the Open*. Indianapolis: Bobbs-Merrill, 1912.
The Wolf Trail. Oxford: Basil Blackwell, 1923.

NON-FICTION

Rottenness: A Study of America and England. London: Neville Beeman, 1896. *Canada's Fighting Forces*. Our Fighting Forces 2. London: Newnes, 1914.
Horses. London: John Murray, 1917.
The Frontiersman's Pocket Book. Ed. Roger Pocock. London: John Murray, 1909.
Ashwell, Lena. *Reflections from Shakespeare*. Ed. Roger Pocock. London: Hutchinson, 1926.

AUTOBIOGRAPHY

Following the Frontier. New York: McClure Phillips, 1903. Revised and expanded UK ed. *A Frontiersman*. London: Methuen, 1903.
Chorus to Adventurers. London: John Lane; The Bodley Head, 1931.

NOTES

INTRODUCTION

1. R. Pocock, *Rules of the Game* (London: Tower Publishing, 1895), 278–79.
2. G.R. Stevens, *A City Goes to War* (Brampton, Ontario: Edmonton Regiment Associates, 1964), 12.
3. Jeffery Williams, *First in the Field, Gault of the Patricias* (London: Leo Cooper, 1995), 64.
4. Tim Jeal, *Baden-Powell* (London: Hutchinson, 1989), 375.

1: PUPPYHOOD

1. Harry Leigh-Pink, "Adventure of the Legion: Basil Lubbock, Cape Horn Sailor," *The Canadian Frontiersman* 34, no. 2 (April–June 1964): 4.
2. For a brief but vivid account of several notable Pococks, see T. Pocock, *Captain Marryat* (London: Chatham Publishing, 2000), 73–74.
3. R. Pocock to C.W.K. Pocock, 1927. The Ashwells were a moneyed family, so that name was continued down the generations, which elicited some useful legacies. Ashwell was also a good name for Roger's sister, Lena, to take when she went on the stage, although the senior branch of the family might not have approved, for the stage was not considered a suitable profession for a well brought up young lady.
4. Charles lost the wager, for there was a stair missing near the summit, and the strength of the wind on the last section frightened the ponies, forcing the two midshipmen to dismount (R. Pocock, *Horses* [London: John Murray, 1917], 60; R. Pocock to C.W.K. Pocock, 1927). Two of his excellent drawings of that ride are in the scrapbook of Commander Charles Ashwell Boteler Pocock (National Maritime Museum, Greenwich, X.1999.040, hereinafter cited as Pocock Scrapbook NMM).
5. R. Pocock to C.W.K. Pocock, 1927. Mount Pocock (53°26'00" N –129°15'00" W) in British Columbia was given that name in the late 1850s by a naval survey team.
6. Some sources, including her own children, gave her birth year as 1839; however, the Stevens family Bible says she was the ninth child of James Agnew Stevens, by his second wife, and was born at Holyhead on 29 December 1830 at 5:30 A.M. (insert in Pocock Scrapbook NMM).
7. Ashwell, *Myself a Player* (London: Michael Joseph, 1936), 15, 18–20.
8. Ashwell, *Myself a Player,* 14; R. Pocock to C.W.K. Pocock, 1927.
9. Francis, who shared the Agnew name with his maternal grandfather, was born in Weybridge, Surrey. When he grew up, he took American citizenship and became a noted electrical inventor and specialist in electric traction, particularly in coal mines and "early electric cars and motor boats" (R. Pocock to C.W.K. Pocock, 1927). Francis was later known as Frank.
10. Pocock to C.W.K. Pocock, 1927. On the birth certificate he is simply Henry Roger, but elsewhere, including the 1881 British census and some title pages, he has three forenames. The name Roger may have come from his godfather, Roger Dutton, who lived at Motueka.
11. Roger was not the only one to be creative with his birthplace. Others have attributed it to places as divergent as New Zealand (*Times* (London) [13 November 1941]: 7, col. E) and Labrador (Agnes C. O'Dea, comp., *Bibliography of Newfoundland,* edited by Anne Alexander, 2 vols. [Toronto: University of Toronto Press, in association with Memorial University of Newfoundland, 1986], 1:277).

12. There is an essay by Maggie B. Gale on Lena, as Lena Ashwell, in the *Oxford Dictionary of National Biography* (Oxford: Oxford University Press, 2004).

13. Ashwell, *Myself a Player*, 13, 16–17.

14. Harry Leigh-Pink, "Christmas with Roger Pocock," *The Canadian Frontiersman* 34, no. 4 (October–December 1964): 6.

15. Ashwell, *Myself a Player*, 21–22.

16. Ashwell, *Myself a Player*, 22.

17. Roger was admitted to Ludlow 28 October 1875 and left at Easter, 1880 (R.S. Burns, Principal, to Geoffrey A. Pocock, Ludlow, Shropshire, 27 November 1978).

18. R. Pocock to C.W.K. Pocock, 1927. As Roger put it many years later: "When my father became depressed about his income as a half-pay captain, we always moved, by way of economy, to another continent. To this, his one dissipation, my mother deferred with patience, and shifted her home by turns to Jersey, Bombay, Southsea, New Zealand, and finally Canada" (R. Pocock, "Lone Wolf Pioneer" [19 May 1935]: 5) In "The Lone Wolf Pioneer," *The News of the World*, 19 May 1935. Roger revised, but also to a great extent repeated, parts of his *A Frontiersman*, which was also published, slightly abbreviated, as *Following the Frontier* (New York: McClure, Phillips, 1903).

19. Ashwell, *Myself a Player*, 21.

20. R. Pocock, "Lone Wolf Pioneer," (19 May 1935), 5. In 1927 Roger gave a slightly more prosaic account of the event: "The ship S.S. Peruvian, lost her propellor [*sic*] in pack ice, and was driven for a week in a big ice-pack, reaching Quebeck [*sic*] under tow after a passage of 26 days on 23rd May 1882" (R. Pocock to C.W.K. Pocock, 1927).

21. Ashwell, *Myself a Player*, 24–25. There is a photograph of the cottage with Hilda, Ethel, Rosalie, and Lena on the veranda (Pocock Scrapbook NMM).

22. R. Pocock, *A Frontiersman* (London: Methuen, 1903), 3.

23. Roger Pocock, diary, 1883. The diary is kept in the collection of the late Capt. Charles E.S. Dudley, hereafter cited as "Dudley Collection."

24. R. Pocock, *A Frontiersman*, 3.

25. Samuel Keefer (1811–90) was a civil engineer. Rosalie married Keefer in 1883. After his death Rosalie moved to England where she settled at Chieveley, Berkshire. Keefer's money seems to have supported Rosalie for the rest of her life.

26. Leigh-Pink, "Christmas with Roger Pocock," 6.

27. R. Pocock, "Lone Wolf Pioneer" (19 May 1935), 5.

28. R. Pocock, "Lone Wolf Pioneer" (19 May 1935), 5; R. Pocock, *A Frontiersman*, 5–10.

29. R. Pocock, *A Frontiersman*, 10.

30. R. Pocock, *A Frontiersman*, 10–11.

31. R. Pocock, *A Frontiersman*, 13.

32. Roger began early to collect bits of printed material in his diaries, made lists of slang, and drew scenes as reminders of events he experienced.

33. R. Pocock, *A Frontiersman*, 17.

34. R. Pocock, *A Frontiersman*, 18.

35. R. Pocock, "Into the Great Dominion: From London to Winnipeg," 14.

36. This first appeared as the privately published *Leaves from the Journal of Our Life in the Highlands, 1848 to 1861* (London: n.d., [1865]). It appeared in many editions and translations in the nineteenth century.

37. R. Pocock, *A Frontiersman*, 21–22; R. Pocock, "Lone Wolf Pioneer" (19 May 1935): 5; Leigh-Pink, "Christmas with Roger Pocock," 6–7.

38. Roger Pocock to Charles Pocock, [Winnipeg], 2 November 1884 (Roger Pocock Private Diary, 1885). He enlisted on 3 November (S.W. Horrall, RCMP Historian, to Geoffrey A. Pocock, Ottawa, 1 November 1979).

39. Leigh-Pink, "Christmas with Roger Pocock," 7. In 1883 the name was simply North-West Mounted Police.

1. R. Pocock, "Lone Wolf Pioneer" (26 May 1935): 5; see also R. Pocock, *A Frontiersman*, 23–24. The official record shows that Roger was "Height, 5 feet 9 inches," "Weight, 140 lbs," and "Muscular development, Good," so he cannot have been quite as half-starved as he liked to suggest. There is also a note on that record, signed by Dr. Augustus Jukes (1821–1905), Chief Surgeon of the N W M P: "Re-examined at Regina Novr 6, 1884 and his acceptance confirmed. This man is sound and able bodied for his years but lacks education" ("Medical Examination" [Library and Archives Canada RG 18 G vol. 3347, file/dossier 1107]).

2. John G. Donkin provides a kit list, as well as enthusiastic comments about the quantity and quality of the kit, in *Trooper and Redskin* (London: Sampson Low, Marston, Searle & Rivington, 1889), 30–31. Roger prepared a booklet of information about the N W M P in which he recorded a list of "Kit prices," with the statement "Repay prices are 10 perc[ent] higher than cost," and a list of rations (Roger Pocock Private Diary, 1885). In addition to diary entries, Roger's Private Diary volumes for 1885 and 1886 hold letters, drawings, clippings, and poems, among other things, since he treated them as scrapbooks. Hereinafter these two volumes, in the Peel Special Collections Library at the University of Alberta, are cited as "Private Diary, 1885" and "Private Diary, 1886."

3. R. Pocock, *A Frontiersman*, 24.

4. Roger Pocock to Sarah Pocock, Regina, 16 December 1884 (Private Diary, 1885). Fairly consistently in his letters, Roger had trouble spelling some words correctly and often used American spellings despite his English education; he was also rather scant or casual with punctuation.

5. Roger Pocock to Charles Pocock, Regina, 20 January 1885 (Private Diary, 1885).

6. Roger Pocock to Charles Pocock, Regina, 20 January 1885. Roger added this note, dated 25 January, in the top margin of the 20 January 1885 letter.

7. Roger Pocock to Sarah Pocock, Regina, 21 February 1885 (Private Diary, 1885).

8. For example, in a letter to his mother he included a page with "a Barrackroom monologue, mild enough to put on paper, from my chum Charlie Sinclair." He then proceeded, with parenthetical interjections, judicious blank spaces, and frequent use of slang, to recount Sinclair's words and actions (Roger Pocock to Sarah Pocock, Regina, 21 February 1885 [Private Diary, 1885]).

9. Roger told Mutiny's story in some detail in his "Lone Wolf Pioneer" (26 May, 5 and 9 June 1935), but did not do so in his autobiography or extant diaries and letters. "Mutiny" shows up in Roger's letter to his mother on 12 July 1885 in a list of nicknames, and Roger mentioned "Mutiny Fleming" in his "What Became of Men I Knew in the Force up to 1897" (Private Diary, 1885). For Roger's primary use of Mutiny's story, see R. Pocock, *Jesse of Cariboo* (London: John Murray, 1911), and R. Pocock, *A Man in the Open* (Indianapolis: Bobbs-Merril, 1912). Roger passed Mutiny's experiences to the hero, Jesse. Mutiny also appears by name, but with a slightly altered character, in Roger's *Curly* (London: Gay & Bird, 1904). Surly McNabb in Roger's Blackguard books is also partly based on Mutiny.

10. R. Pocock, "Lone Wolf Pioneer" (26 May 1935): 5.

11. R. Pocock, *A Frontiersman*, 25.

12. Leigh-Pink, "Christmas with Roger Pocock," 7. See also [R. Pocock], "What Became of Men" (Private Diary, 1885).

13. Private Diary, 1885. Despite that statement, Roger referred to earlier diaries: "13th [October 1886] My Diaries of 1884 & 1883 stolen or lost, offered a reward of $10....I offered $20 on the 16th for return of diaries" (Private Diary, 1886).

14. Roger Pocock to Sarah Pocock, Regina, 21 February 1885 (Private Diary, 1885). In his diary entry Roger called this a gazette, which he named "The Growl" (February 1885 [Private Diary, 1885]).

15. Private Diary, 1885.

16. Roger Pocock to Sarah Pocock, [Prince Albert], 15 September 1885 (Private Diary, 1885).

17. Roger Pocock to Sarah Pocock, Regina, 3 and 21 February 1885 (Private Diary, 1885). The "Egyptian war" was the Gordon Relief Expedition.

18. For an excellent, concise essay on the causes of the 1885 Rebellion and why it was prosecuted as it was, see R.C. Macleod, "Introduction," *Reminiscences of a Bungle by one of the Bunglers* (Edmonton: University of Alberta Press, 1983), xiv–xlii.

19. R. Pocock, "Lone Wolf Pioneer" (26 May 1935): 5 (ellipsis in original). A slightly different and expanded version is in R. Pocock, *A Frontiersman,* 31–33. *Nitchie,* in Canadian usage, can refer to either a First Nations person or a pony, but in this instance the reference is clear, and generally if Roger were referring to a pony he used the term *cayuse* (sometimes spelled *cayeuse*). Despite Mutiny's prediction, Crowfoot did not go into battle in 1885.

20. Donkin, *Trooper and Redskin,* 104–05. Roger mentioned the eclipse in his diary for 17 March, but not in his [Account of Journey to Prince Albert] (Private Diary, 1885).

21. R. Pocock, [Account of Journey to Prince Albert]. A typed copy of most of [Account] is in LAC 1107. The commonly cited number is ninety-three, including Irvine. While here Roger said there were ninety-four, elsewhere he said ninety-six (R. Pocock, *Frontiersman,* 34) and ninety (Roger Pocock report, Regina, 27 October 1886 [LAC 1107]). The number in Irvine's official diary was ninety-three (RCMP Museum, Regina, Irvine fonds 935.31).

22. R. Pocock, [Account of Journey to Prince Albert]. That chief's name is also spelled *Piapot, Payepot,* and *Payipwat,* although Kisikawasan was his birth name.

23. Roger Pocock report, Regina, 27 October 1886 (LAC 1107). S/Sgt E.A. Braithwaite was then a veterinary sergeant.

24. R. Pocock, "Lone Wolf Pioneer" (2 June 1935): 5.

25. Donkin, *Trooper and Redskin,* 45 (parentheses in original).

26. Roger Pocock to Sarah Pocock, Regina, 16 and 25 December 1884, 3 February 1885 (Private Diary, 1885). In that 25 December letter, Roger also mentioned he had a touch of frostbite on his nose and wrist and was well aware of how dangerous frostbite could be.

27. Donkin, *Trooper and Redskin,* 113. Roger seemed to agree with Donkin when he wrote that "A light hard-wood sledge was used for traveling the jumper; but woe to the idiot lazy enough to spend the day in it! One must trot alongside until every finger tingled with warmth before it was safe to rest" (R. Pocock, "'Riders of the Plains,'" 12).

28. "Noted Adventurer, Capt. Pocock Dies," *Edmonton Journal* (14 November 1941): 24, col. 2. This text is also in "Feet Frozen as He Read Greek Book: Former Mounted Policeman Dead in England, is Remembered by M.D.," *Lethbridge Herald* (18 November 1941): 6, col. D.

29. T.M.B., "Sir Arthur Curtis' Bones: They Lie Mouldering in the Trackless Forest: A True Story of the Ashcroft Trail," *The Province* (22 October 1898): 5.

30. R. Pocock, [Account of Journey to Prince Albert]. Later Roger praised the speed of that journey (*Horses,* 204–05). Dr. Hugh N. Bain was Acting Assistant Surgeon in Prince Albert in 1886 (J.P. Turner, *North-West Mounted Police 1873–1893,* 2 vols, [Ottawa: King's Printer, 1950] , 2:319).

31. Roger Pocock to Sarah Pocock, Prince Albert, [undated but before 10 April 1885] (Private Diary, 1885).

32. R . Pocock, *A Frontiersman,* 44.

33. R. Pocock, "Lone Wolf Pioneer" (2 June 1935): 5. For an earlier version of this tale see R. Pocock, *A Frontiersman,* 45. Roger did not mention this incident in his extant diaries and letters for the period.

34. Private Diary, 1885. Elsewhere Roger called it chloroform (R. Pocock, [Account of Journey to Prince Albert]. Roger used Morse code five times in his 1885 Private Diary and twice in his 1886 Private Diary to disguise information he wanted to record but keep private. "Miller" is Dr. Robert Miller.

35. Roger Pocock to Charles Pocock, Prince Albert, 19 May 1886 (Private Diary, 1886). His account of the dream itself is not in the diary.

36. Private Diary, 1885. When Roger wrote "Sessamied" he was referring to the sesamoid. He used Morse code for the word *dream.*

37. Roger Pocock to Charles Pocock, Prince Albert, 1 July 1885 (Private Diary, 1885).

38. R. Pocock, *Arctic Night* (London: Chapman & Hall, 1896), 87–100.

39. George F.G. Stanley, *The Birth of Western Canada: A History of the Riel Rebellions* (Toronto: University of Toronto Press, 1960), 372.

40. Stanley, *The Birth of Western Canada,* 376.

41. Turner, *North-West Mounted Police,* 2:223. Others did not agree with Irvine's opinion. He was forced to resign from the NWMP in March 1886 (Beal and Macleod, *Prairie Fire: The 1885 North-West Rebellion* Edmonton: Hurtig, 1984, 341), despite a testimonial signed by twenty-nine men who had served under him (RCMP Museum, Regina, Irvine fonds 73.39.13 a-e).

42. Roger Pocock to Sarah Pocock, [Prince Albert], 30 August 1886 (underscoring in original; Private Diary, 1886).

43. [Roger Pocock], "A Narrative of Riel's Rebellion: How Canadians Fight for Their Fatherland: *Extracted from the 'York Daily Herald' of Monday, February 22nd, 1886.*" The anonymous clipping is from an unknown newspaper included in Roger's Private Diary, 1885. The introductory paragraph attributes the piece to "a young man in active service in the police of the North-West Territory of Canada. He lost several toes on the march in the frost during the late rebellion."

44. R. Pocock, *A Frontiersman*, 52.

45. Roger Pocock to Sarah Pocock, [Prince Albert], 14 March 1886 (Private Diary, 1886).

46. Roger Pocock to Sarah Pocock, [Prince Albert], 20 July 1886 (Private Diary, 1886). Whether this was the same Ada Wright who appeared in his pocket diaries between 1907 and 1914, when he lived in London, will remain a mystery.

47. Roger Pocock to Sarah Pocock, [Prince Albert], February 1886 (Private Diary, 1886).

48. Roger Pocock to Sarah Pocock, Regina, 7 November 1885 (Private Diary, 1885). Forrest was editor of the *Witness*.

49. Roger Pocock to Sarah Pocock, [Prince Albert], February 1886 (Private Diary, 1886). In his diary he noted for 27 January that he "began walking," and for 2 February that "Walking progresses favorably" (Private Diary, 1886). In March he wrote, "I can walk on a smooth surface freely and without effort. I can wear moccasins [*sic*]. I can traverse two miles or more on foot and not suffer from it" (Roger Pocock to Sarah Pocock, [Prince Albert], 14 March 1886 [Private Diary, 1886]).

50. Roger Pocock to Sarah Pocock, [Prince Albert], 21 February 1886 (underscoring in original; Private Diary, 1886).

51. Roger Pocock to Sarah Pocock, [Prince Albert], 28 February 1886 (Private Diary, 1886).

52. Roger Pocock to Sarah Pocock, [Prince Albert], 12 May 1886 (Private Diary, 1886).

53. Roger Pocock to Sarah Pocock, [Prince Albert], 7 July 1886 (Private Diary, 1886).

54. Roger Pocock to Sarah Pocock, [Prince Albert], 20 July 1886 (Private Diary, 1886).

55. Private Diary, 1886. Roger wrote on the clipping of a reprint of that article: "My first published work, 1885 Roger Pocock."

56. Roger Pocock to Sarah Pocock, Prince Albert, 25 July 1885 (Private Diary, 1886). Roger clearly dated this letter 1885, but it is filed in the 1886 diary.

57. Private Diary, 1886.

58. Roger Pocock to Sarah Pocock, 25 July 1885 (Private Diary, 1886).

59. Roger Pocock to Sarah Pocock, [Prince Albert], June 1886 (Private Diary, 1886).

60. Roger Pocock to Sarah Pocock, [Prince Albert], 20 July 1886 (Private Diary, 1886).

61. Roger Pocock to Sarah Pocock, [Prince Albert], 17 August 1886 (Private Diary, 1886).

62. Private Diary, 1886; see also Roger Pocock to Sarah Pocock, Sugar Bush, [27 August 1886] (Private Diary, 1886). Roger began this letter at Sugar Bush, almost certainly on 27 August, but added to it at least until 31 August. It was not unusual for Roger to write a letter over several days.

63. Roger Pocock to Sarah Pocock, Sugar Bush, [27 August 1886] (Private Diary, 1886).

64. The phrase "paper collar" could perhaps refer to excessively formal demeanour or to personal wealth, or it could be inspired by the American slang expression "paper collar soldier." In slang, one of the definitions for *Johnny* or *Johnnie* is police officer.

65. Roger Pocock to Sarah Pocock, Sugar Bush, [27 August 1886] (Private Diary, 1886).

66. Roger Pocock to Sarah Pocock, Prince Albert, 1 October 1886 (underscoring and parentheses in original; Private Diary, 1886). Harry Keenan is mentioned several times in Roger's diaries for 1885 and 1886. He was still in the Mounted Police in 1897 ([R. Pocock], "What Became of Men" [Private Diary, 1885]).

67. R. Pocock, *A Frontiersman*, 53–54.

68. R. Pocock, "'Riders of the Plains,'" 11, 12.

69. Roger Pocock to Sarah Pocock, [Prince Albert], 6 August 1886 (Private Diary, 1886).

70. Roger Pocock to Sarah Pocock, [Prince Albert], 17 August 1886 (Private Diary, 1886). Roger commented on books and reading in fourteen of his extant letters between 25 December 1884 and 1 October 1886. Homer, Dante, and Sir Walter Scott were among the authors Roger mentioned.

71. Roger Pocock to Sarah Pocock, Prince Albert, 1 October 1886 (Private Diary, 1886).

72. Roger Pocock to Sarah Pocock, Prince Albert, April 1885 (Private Diary, 1885). While this letter was written before the 10 April surgery, Roger also mentioned the possibility of being invalided in letters dated 20 July 1885, 28 June 1886, 30 August 1886, and September 1886 (Private Diary, 1885 and 1886). In a letter to his mother dated 7 November 1885, he did not mention being invalided specifically, but he went into some detail about how he might travel to see family if he left the NWMP and responded to an idea his father had apparently expressed about a potential job (Private Diary, 1885).

73. Roger Pocock to Sarah Pocock, [Prince Albert], 7 July 1886 (Private Diary, 1886).

74. Roger Pocock to Sarah Pocock, [Prince Albert], 6 August 1886 (Private Diary, 1886).

75. R. Pocock, "Lone Wolf Pioneer" (9 June 1935): 5; see also R. Pocock, *A Frontiersman*, 57.

76. Charles Pocock to R.J. Wicksteed, Toronto, 7 October 1886 (LAC 1107). Indeed, Jukes wrote that he had examined Roger on 24 September 1886 and recommended he be sent to Regina "to be invalided" (Dr. Augustus Jukes to William M. Herchmer, Regina, 27 October 1886 [LAC 1107]).

77. Charles Pocock to R.J. Wicksteed, Toronto, 7 October 1886 (LAC 1107). Jukes responded that attributing the opinion that the "wound shall take years to heal" to him was "purely fabulous" (Dr. Augustus Jukes to Lawrence William Herchmer, Regina, 27 October 1886 [LAC 1107]). Jukes also requested that Roger address this claim in a memorandum that Jukes included with his letter: "Dr. Jukes never expressed that opinion sofar [*sic*] as I have any knowledge" (Roger Pocock, Regina, 27 October 1886 [LAC 1107]).

78. Samuel Keefer to Thomas White, Minister of the Interior, Brockville, 12 October 1886 (LAC 1107). Later Keefer wrote to Frederick White (1847–1918), Comptroller of the NWMP (1880–1904), asking what he could do to advance Roger's case with the medical board (Samuel Keefer to Frederick White, Brockville, 17 January 1887 [LAC 1107]).

79. Form no. 54, dated 13 November 1886 (LAC 1107).

80. Form signed by Herchmer, Commissioner, NWMP, and handwritten sworn statement (LAC 1107).

81. LAC 1107. It was indeed for life. When Commissioner Stuart Taylor Wood learned of Roger's death, he wrote that "Captain Pocock was the last remaining pensioner paid from our voted pensions 'on account of the Rebellion of 1885' under Vote 322, Main Estimates, 1941–1942" (S.T. Wood to Secretary, The Treasury Board, Ottawa, 24 November 1941 [LAC 1107]).

82. Roger Pocock to Commissioner, RCMP, Charterhouse, London, 10 November 1931 (strikethrough in original; LAC 1107). The tone of his letter suggests Roger was notified that he was eligible to apply.

83. LAC 1107.

84. Roger Pocock to Sarah Pocock, Prince Albert, 1 October 1886 (underscoring in original; Private Diary 1886). One of these pieces was published anonymously, and the other two under the pseudonym Coyote: [R. Pocock], "A Night-Halt"; Coyote, "A Useless Man"; Coyote, "The Ice Cortege." Roger also used the pseudonym Coyote for another story, "Self-Accused," which he wrote during this period, but was published later. He described this as "My first military story, characters from life, incident ficticious [*sic*]" (Roger Pocock to Sarah Pocock, [Prince Albert], 6 August 1886 [Private Diary, 1886]). Roger mentioned beginning to write "The Ice Cortege" and "A Useless Man" in his diary for 12 April 1886 and told his mother he was "delighted at the appearance of 'Useless Man'" (Roger Pocock to Sarah Pocock, [Prince Albert], 30 August 1886 (Private Diary, 1886). In his diary for 17 August Roger noted "The Week accept [*sic*] Ice Cortége" (Private Diary, 1886). Roger wrote that he "sent an account of a 'Night Halt' in the North West to Chambers [*sic*] Journal because they are courteous enough to return rejected contributions. I took for my scene Eagle Creek & for occasion our own halt there on the trip from P Albert" (Roger Pocock to Sarah Pocock, Battleford, September 1886 [Private Diary, 1886]). Two poems he was working on during this period were also published, one under his initials: R.P., "The Weird of the Great Lake"; R. Pocock, "Lights Out!" In "Weird of the Great Lake," Roger tried to capture the brooding menace of Lake Superior. The six-stanza published version is quite different from the four-stanza handwritten version in his diary (Private Diary, 1886). "Lights Out!" is three stanzas of emotional farewell to the NWMP.

85. Private Diary, 1886 (underscoring and capitalization as in original).

1. R. Pocock, "Left the Mounted Police" (Private Diary, 1886). Roger was clearly embarrassed by his behaviour at Ottawa House, as he used Morse code to write "in the evening had a disgraceful drunk" and "very sick all day."

2. H.R.A. Pocock, *Tales of Western Life, Lake Superior and the Canadian Prairie* (Ottawa: C.W. Mitchell, 1888). Of the fourteen stories and poems in *Tales of Western Life*, seven first appeared in periodicals: "A Night-Halt" in *Chambers's Journal;* "A Useless Man," "The Ice Cortege," and "Lights Out!" in *The Week;* "The Lean Man" in *Toronto World;* "Death of Wakuzza" in *Catholic Weekly Record* (London, Ontario); and "The Laurentides" in *Catholic Weekly Review* (Toronto). Another story, "Buck Stanton," was probably also first published in a periodical, since a printed version is included in his 1886 diary. The focus of this one-page story by "H.R.A. Pocock, Ottawa," is the virtue of avoiding alcohol. While citing Ottawa as his location suggests when the story was published, since he worked in Ottawa for less than a year, there is no indication of the name of the periodical from which the page was torn. The differences in the stories in the two formats—periodical and book—are slight. Two of the poems—"The Laurentides" and "The Legend of Thunder"—were reprinted, credited to *Tales of Western Life,* in William Douw Lighthall, comp. and ed., *Songs of the Great Dominion: Voices from the Forests and Waters, the Settlements and Cities of Canada* (London: Walter Scott, 1889).

3. R. Pocock, *A Frontiersman,* 60.

4. Glenbow Archives M-981, box 1, file 3.

5. Gilbert Parker, "Tales of Western Life," *Victoria Daily Times* 11, no. 322 (21 June 1890): 1, col. F.

6. "The Lean Man" has been reprinted in Dick Harrison, ed., *Best Mounted Police Stories* (Edmonton: the University of Alberta Press, 1978), 94–107. In his introduction to the story, Harrison writes, "The ironic tone of 'The Lean Man' suggests the urbane world adventurer, but the ending reveals a concern for the Indian which was unusual in 1887" (94). Harrison placed Roger squarely in the "British Mountie" tradition (3–4). "The Lean Man" also appears in D. Skene-Melvin, ed., *Crime in a Cold Climate: An Anthology of Classic Canadian Crime* (Toronto: Simon & Pierre, 1994), 126–38. Skene-Melvin's favourable introduction notes that "This story... marks what is probably the earliest appearance of a Mountie in fiction" (127).

7. H.R.A. Pocock, "Lean Man," *Tales of Western Life,* see 51, 56, and 62.

8. H.R.A. Pocock, "Lean Man," 51.

9. H.R.A. Pocock, "A Night Halt," *Tales of Western Life,* 77.

10. H.R.A. Pocock, *Tales of Western Life,* vi.

11. Roger Pocock to Lena Pocock, Ottawa, 20 June 1887 (Dudley Collection).

12. Ashwell, *Myself a Player,* 67.

13. Roger Pocock to Lena Pocock, Brockville, 25 May 1887 (Dudley Collection).

14. In August 1888 Roger described his father as being "on the way with the family to Switzerland" (Roger Pocock to Frederick White, NWMP, Metlacahtla, British Columbia, 15 August 1888 [LAC 1107]).

15. R. Pocock, *A Frontiersman,* 60.

16. R. Pocock, *A Frontiersman,* 60–61.

17. R. Pocock, *Horses,* 80–81.

18. R. Pocock, *A Frontiersman,* 61.

19. With less than his usual optimism, several months later Roger wrote: "I got my right arm smashed up by a broncho [*sic*] in the Southern Interior in May and will probably never be able to do hard work again" (Roger Pocock to Frederick White, Metlacahtla, British Columbia, 15 August 1888 [LAC 1107]).

20. R. Pocock, "War on the Skeena," 464.

21. R. Pocock, "War on the Skeena," 464.

22. R. Pocock, "Lone Wolf Pioneer" (16 June 1935): 5. Roger noted on his "Index to letters & Printed Matter" that on "July 18—Appointed Special Correspondent of Montreal Witness—left that day for Vancouver, Victoria & Port Essington—arrived at Port Essington on 27 July" (Glenbow Archives M-981, box 1, file 3).

23. While Roger called him Gaetwinlthgul Jim or Gitwinthgul Jim, the current accepted form of his name is Kamalmuk or Kitwancool Jim (James A. McDonald and Jennifer Joseph, "Key Events

in the Gitksan Encounter with the Colonial World," in William Beynon, *Potlach at Gitsegukla: William Beynon's 1945 Field Notebooks,* ed. Margaret Anderson and Marjorie Halpin [Vancouver: University of British Columbia Press, 2000], 204).

24. The preliminary trial, with Roycraft and Fitzstubbs as stipendiary magistrates, occurred on 6 August 1888 ([H.R.A. Pocock], "Skeena Murder Trials"; source title and August date written in ink on clipping in Glenbow Archives M-981, box 1, file 3]). While this article is unsigned and is not specifically attributed to the "special correspondent," it is probably by Roger.

25. [H.R.A. Pocock], "Skeena Murder Trials."

26. [H.R.A. Pocock], "Skeena Murder Trials." Roger ended one article about his experience in this part of British Columbia by expressing hope that the advance of settlement had not killed all the "savage gentlefolk who once honoured me with their friendship" (R. Pocock, "White Man's Job"). A story Roger wrote earlier, "Black Box," also highlighted the problem of diseases passed to First Nations through the carelessness of the white settlers. Roger wrote similarly of a "black box" in *A Frontiersman,* 91–92.

27. Roger called him *Nealth* or *Neatsk.* Neetuh was suspected of witchcraft.

28. There are several other versions of this tale in print, in which the number of children, among other details, varies.

29. The current, preferred spelling is *Gitwangak* or *Kitwanga.*

30. R. Pocock, "War on the Skeena," 465. Roger earlier told the story in great detail in his series "Gitwinthgul Jim."

31. The Gitksan uprising was provoked by the killing of Kamalmuk, but also by the death of a local man named Haatq, who had been in prison since 1884 for killing A.C. Youmans. Both were instances of the conflict between British and First Nations approaches to justice. For a lively account of Haatq's case, see C. Clark, *Tales of the British Columbia Provincial Police* (Sidney, B.C.: Heritage House, 1989), 19–27.

32. R. Pocock, "War on the Skeena," 466. Just before he left for Alaska, Roger wrote that he "accepted or rather volunteered for the Mission at Kitwingar [*sic*] in the disturbed district up the Skeena River and must go up the country within a month if possible before the water gets too high for canoes" (Roger Pocock to Frederick White, Metlacahtla, British Columbia, 15 August 1888 [LAC 1170]). Later Roger was less clear about whether he was recruited or had volunteered (R. Pocock, *A Frontiersman,* 67).

33. R. Pocock, *A Frontiersman,* 67.

34. [H.R.A. Pocock], "Metlakahtla's Ruins"; [H.R.A. Pocock], "Canadian Exiles"; [H.R.A. Pocock], "Alaska and Its Riches"; [H.R.A. Pocock], "In Far Northern Seas"; [H.R.A. Pocock], "Lofty Mount St. Elias"; [H.R.A. Pocock], "Behring Sea Fur Seal"; [H.R.A. Pocock], "Left to Their Fate" (all *Witness* clippings in Glenbow Archives M-981, box 1, file 3). Roger also described this travel, with his usual sardonic touch, in *A Frontiersman.* He was most struck by how the glacier had receded since Vancouver had described it, yet he felt that from his position on a steamer, "The scene is one of almost unapproachable splendour, perhaps the grandest in the whole world" (62–72). Roger addressed the Muir glacier again more than a year later in "The Muir Glacier."

35. [H.R.A. Pocock], "In Far Northern Seas" (parentheses in original).

36. R. Pocock, *A Frontiersman,* 73.

37. H.R.A. Pocock to Charles Todd, Metlacahtla, British Columbia, 16 August 1888 (Library and Archives Canada RG 10 vol. 3824, file/dossier 59,708, hereinafter cited as LAC 59,708).

38. R. Pocock, "War on the Skeena," 467.

39. R. Pocock, "White Man's Power," 254. Years later he simply said "the two tribes talked and talked" (R. Pocock, "Lone Wolf Pioneer" [16 June 1935]: 5).

40. Leigh-Pink, "Christmas with Roger Pocock," 7.

41. R. Pocock, "War on the Skeena," 468.

42. Quoted in Forrest E. LaViolette, *The Struggle for Survival: Indian Cultures and the Protestant Ethic in British Columbia* (Toronto: University of Toronto Press, 1978), 64. It is interesting that Roger wrote Fitzstubbs was "the only white man present," given that Roger himself was there. LaViolette identified Roger as a missionary: "Rev. H.K.A. [*sic*] Pocock, of the Church Missionary Society...." Roger had no such illusions. He wrote that he "wore a pea jacket and

deerskin breeches lest the people should mistake the mere *locum tenens* for a regular priest" (R. Pocock, "White Man's Power," 253).

43. R. Pocock, *A Frontiersman*, 94.
44. Cecil A. Clark to Geoffrey A. Pocock, Victoria, British Columbia, 26 December 1979. Roger had only expected to be the missionary until May (Roger Pocock to Frederick White, Metlacahtla, British Columbia, 15 August 1888 [LAC 1170]).
45. *Pacific States Newspaper Directory, 1886–1887* (San Francisco CA: Palmer & Rey, 1886), [157].
46. H.R.A. Pocock, "A Great Archipelago."
47. H.R.A. Pocock, "Tales of the Skeena: The Giatkshians' Early History"; H.R.A. Pocock, "Tales of the Skeena. Major Downie"; H.R.A. Pocock, "Tales of the Skeena: Mr. Hankin's Adventures."
48. H.R.A. Pocock, "The Steamer Beaver"; H.R.A. Pocock, "Historical Notes." His later treatment of the story of the *Beaver* was very similar, if a bit more melodramatic (R. Pocock, *Captains of Adventure* [Indianapolis: Bobbs-Merril, 1913], 302–06).
49. Cecil A. Clark, "Frontiersmen Carry on Tradition of Service," *The Islander: Daily Colonist Magazine* (19 April 1959): 8.
50. [H.R.A. Pocock], "Left to Their Fate."
51. H.R.A. Pocock, "The Coast Indians. Their Government by the White People."
52. H.R.A. Pocock, "The Coast Indians. The Practice of Sorcery Universal." In the conclusion he described the "Indian Office" as "doleful and slumbering."
53. Roger Pocock to Grant Powell, Under Secretary of State, Alert Bay, 28 June 1889 (LAC 59,708).
54. Roger Pocock to Grant Powell, Vancouver, 16 July 1889 (LAC 59,708). Roger was referring to the third and fourth articles in his series: H.R.A. Pocock, "The Coast Indians: Evidences of Cannibalism," and H.R.A. Pocock, "The Coast Indians: A Remedy." This series elicited an editorial. The writer was not inclined to blame either the "Indian Department" or missionaries for the problems Roger described ("The Untutored Indian," *Victoria Daily Times* 11, no. 38 [23 July 1889]: 2, col. A).
55. Editorial, *Ottawa Free Press* (17 July 1889) (clipping in LAC 59,708). Under the clipping is a six-line account of Roger's time in the NWMP and his pension, which ends with the statement that "he is extremely eccentric." It is signed with the initials F.W., perhaps for Frederick White.
56. H.R.A. Pocock, "It's the Same All Over" (clipping in LAC 59,708). Much of the rest of this article also appeared in his "The Coast Indians" articles.
57. Department of Indian Affairs to Hamilton Moffatt, Ottawa, 8 August 1889 (LAC 59,708).
58. Hamilton Moffatt to Superintendent of Indian Affairs, Victoria, 19 August 1889 (underscoring in original; LAC 59,708). Roger wrote again on enforcement of the potlatch law and included a suggestion about how to protect the salmon fishery in H.R.A. Pocock, "The Northern Coast."
59. H.R.A. Pocock, "The Lore of Haida: I—The Raven"; H.R.A. Pocock, "The Lore of Haida: II"; H.R.A. Pocock, "The Lore of Haida: VII"; H.R.A. Pocock, "The Lore of Haida: I—The Vikings of the West"; H.R.A. Pocock, "The Lore of Haida: The Raven's Empire"; and H.R.A. Pocock, "Lore of the Haidahs." The numbering and title form in this series is a little erratic, but a thorough review of the microfilm back file revealed no further instalments, although Roger did write another article about the Haida: H.R.A. Pocock, "Indian Fiction."
60. R. Pocock, "Lone Wolf Pioneer" (23 June 1935): 5. Roger's enthusiasm for the sea and its drama is even more apparent in his earlier account of this adventure (R. Pocock, *A Frontiersman*, 101–19).
61. Roger Pocock to Frederick White, Victoria, British Columbia, 10 December 1889 (LAC 1107).
62. Roger tried to use this story later as a screenplay—*The Salvation Pirate: A Story of the Yokohama Pirates, by One of Them*—while he was in Hollywood, and expanded it into a forty-eight page arrangement of scenes as *The Yokohama Pirates, by One of the Actual Pirates*, dated 20 May 1935 (Glenbow Archives M-981, box 1, files 6–7). There is no sign anything resulted from either effort. He also used it in R. Pocock, *Captains of Adventure*, 154–55.
63. Clark, "Frontiersmen Carry on Tradition of Service," 8.
64. While Roger had first-hand experience of sealing, the inspiration behind Kipling's stories and poems set in the Pribilof Islands was probably Henry Wood Elliott, *The Seal-Islands of Alaska* (Washington, DC: G.P.O., 1881) and "his visits to the Yokohama Club.... Into these northern seas he never penetrated, even if he wrote of them with understanding" (Carrington, *Life of Rudyard Kipling* [New York: Doubleday, 1955], 156).

65. R. Pocock, "Great Adventurers: The Laureate of Empire." Elsewhere Roger wrote that "Mr. Kipling had the *Rhyme of the Three Sealers*, he told me, from Captain Lake in Yokohama. I had it from the mate of one of the three schooners, *The Stella*" (R. Pocock, *Captains of Adventure*, 153–54).

66. Roger Pocock to Frank Pocock, Victoria, 3 May 1890 (Dudley Collection). Roger's description of the British Columbia government as a swindler is related to the granting of railway lands in the Kootenays.

67. Roger Pocock to the editor of *The Miner*, Ashcroft, British Columbia, 26 February 1898 (Glenbow Archives M-254). In February 1898, when Roger returned to British Columbia to begin his Klondike expedition, he tried to settle some debts remaining from 1890. He wrote that letter to the editor and placed an advertisement in *The Miner*, of Nelson, B.C., trying to find a hotel keeper and hardware representative to whom he owed money. He also sent the editor of *The Miner* $100 to be given "to a hospital or other philanthropic service in Kootenay" at the editor's discretion. That money went to Kootenay Lake General Hospital (Glenbow Archives M-254).

68. H.R.A. Pocock, "Warm Springs Camp: The Great Kootenay Silver Region"; R. Pocock, "Into the Great Dominion: The Golden West"; R. Pocock, *A Frontiersman*, 122–23. Seven years after this journey, Roger's "Wealth in the North-West" was published with four photographs he took in the Kootenays during the summer of 1890. He called it British Columbia's Klondike.

69. H.R.A. Pocock, "The Road to Kootenay: How to Reach the Great Silver Mines"; H.R.A. Pocock, "The Road to Kootenay: Our Correspondent Arrives at Nelson City"; H.R.A. Pocock, "Kootenay Projects"; H.R.A. Pocock, "Ruining Quartz Mining"; H.R.A. Pocock, "Warm Springs Camp: The Great Kootenay Silver Region"; [H.R.A. Pocock], "Warm Springs Camp: Our Correspondent in the Kootenay Mines"; H.R.A. Pocock, "Toad Mountain"; H.R.A. Pocock, "Kootenay Mines"; H.R.A. Pocock, "A Mining Camp." "Warm Springs Camp: Our Correspondent" is unsigned, but clearly was written by the same hand as the others: "For three months I have been a student of the Kootenay mines" (H.R.A. Pocock, "A Mining Camp: Our Correspondent"). In this series Roger described the difficulties and pleasures of travel from Victoria to the Kootenays and the mining technology of Dr. Wilbur A. Hendryx in contrast to that of the Ainsworth Syndicate, and named the various geologic "belts" and mining claims.

70. R. Pocock, *A Frontiersman*, 130. Elsewhere Roger made it clear that a "scarehead" is an alarmist or overly dramatic newspaper headline (R. Pocock, *Arctic Night*, 84; R. Pocock, *Rottenness*, 2).

71. R. Pocock, *A Frontiersman*, 133.

72. R. Pocock, *A Frontiersman*, 135.

73. R. Pocock, *A Frontiersman*, 135–36.

74. R. Pocock, *A Frontiersman*, 137, 139.

75. R. Pocock, *A Frontiersman*, 139–40.

76. R. Pocock, *A Frontiersman*, 141.

77. Dudley Collection.

78. Dudley Collection. Roger used the last verse in one of his stories, "Man on the Bridge."

79. Dudley Collection, clipping in scrapbook

80. R. Pocock, "Lone Wolf Pioneer" (23 June 1935): 5; see also R. Pocock, *A Frontiersman*, 142.

81. R. Pocock, *A Frontiersman*, 141.

82. R. Pocock, *A Frontiersman*, 154.

83. R. Pocock, *A Frontiersman*, 150.

84. R. Pocock, *A Frontiersman*, 155.

85. R. Pocock, *The Blackguard*; R. Pocock, *Wolf Trail*; R.S. Pocock, *Wolf Trail*.

86. R. Pocock, *Horses*, 108.

87. R. Pocock, *A Frontiersman*, 158.

88. R. Pocock, *A Frontiersman*, 163.

89. R. Pocock, *A Frontiersman*, 164. According to Cecil A. Clark, "There was a telegram for him from England. Not only a telegram but $500 with it. A book of western stories he had written had turned out a best seller. Could he return and talk over prospects of another book?" (Clark, "Frontiersmen Carry on Tradition of Service," 8).

1. R. Pocock, "'Riders of the Plains,'" 13 (brackets in original). This was probably not the only occasion when an editor could not find Roger.

2. R. Pocock, "Left the Mounted Police" (Private Diary, 1886).

3. Ashwell, *Myself a Player*, 41.

4. Ashwell, *Myself a Player*, 46; see also 41.

5. Roger Pocock, diary, 1891 (Dudley Collection).

6. Roger Pocock, diary, 1892 (Dudley Collection).

7. R. Pocock to C.W.K. Pocock, 1927. It is possible that the incorrect spelling "fassion" could be a typographical error in the typewritten copy supplied to the author by the late C.W.K. Pocock.

8. Roger Pocock diary and fragment (Glenbow Archives M-254). The undated fragment is in Roger's handwriting. The Jubilee was in June 1897, and Roger did not reach Victoria, B.C., after riding the patrol, until 28 September 1897, which suggests October or November for his return to London. During those six days, Roger mentioned several times having to "drug" Ethel. These drugs may have been opiates. The correct spelling of the village is Margaret Riding.

9. Roger Pocock, Klondike Diary (Glenbow Archives M-254).

10. Roger Pocock, diary, February 1894 (Dudley Collection).

11. R. Pocock, *A Frontiersman*, 168.

12. R. Pocock, "Western Ocean Drover," in which his main point was that Britain should not have had to import cattle.

13. Roger Pocock to Charles Pocock, at sea on board SS *Bretwalda*, November 1896 (Glenbow Archives M-254). The letters related to this journey are dated from 3 October to 25 November 1896.

14. Roger Pocock to Charles Pocock, at sea aboard SS *Bretwalda*, 5 October 1896 (Glenbow Archives M-254).

15. Roger Pocock to Charles Pocock, Rutledge, Pennsylvania, 30 October 1896 and 2 November 1896 (Glenbow Archives M-254).

16. Roger Pocock to an unnamed editor, Rutledge, Pennsylvania, no date (Glenbow Archives M-254). While he did not name the editor here, in the next letter in the scrapbook, written on board the *Bretwalda*, 9 November 1896, Roger told his father to "Watch the Daily Graphic for an article I sent on the Election in Philadelphia."

17. Roger Pocock to Charles Pocock, at sea on board SS *Bretwalda*, November 1896 (Glenbow Archives M-254). In his letter dated 9 November, with a last paragraph dated 10 November at 3 P.M., Roger wrote that the ship was due to sail at 5 P.M. that day. Given the lacklustre tone at the beginning of this undated letter—"Nothing happens in this month of Sundays, neither incident nor idea, nor work nor play, but a succession of meals[,] sleeps & talks, the reading of trash & some observation of the weather"—he probably started it well into the voyage. Several short paragraphs at the end are preceded by "Wed 25 November/96. Off Anglesea." Roger made a habit of treating letters to his father as surrogate diaries. Thus he kept adding entries with subsequent dates and also asked his father to keep the letters.

18. Lizzie Robinson to Miss Pocock, North Shields, 15 September 1897 (Glenbow Archives M-254).

19. T. Pocock, *Captain Marryat*, 166.

20. Moyles and Owram, *Imperial Dreams and Colonial Realities*, 39.

21. Roger Pocock to Charles Pocock, 1891 (Dudley Collection).

22. *National Observer* (undated clipping; Glenbow Archives M-254).

23. R. Pocock, *Rules of the Game*, 278.

24. R. Pocock, *Blackguard*, 19–20.

25. Roger Pocock to Charles Pocock, on board SS *Bretwalda*, 12 October 1896 (Glenbow Archives M-254).

26. All review clippings can be found in the Glenbow Archives, M-254.

27. C.J. Cutcliffe-Hyne to Roger Pocock, Oak Vale, Bradford, 21 July 1897 (Glenbow Archives M-254). While Charles John Cutcliffe Wright Hyne (known as C.J. Cutcliffe-Hyne, 1865–1944) was famous as a writer of adventure stories, he was also a notable traveller and writer of historical fiction and boys' books.

28. R. Pocock, *Arctic Night*, 5–6. Colonel Hiram W. Giggleswick also appears in Roger's *Dragonslayer* and "Noble Five." Roger made a sketch of Giggleswick (Glenbow Archives M-254). A character named Jim Ballantyne also appears in Roger's story, "Vigilantes."

29. R. Pocock, *Arctic Night*, 12.

30. R. Pocock, *Arctic Night*, 91.

31. R. Pocock, *Arctic Night*, 91–100; R. Pocock, *Blackguard*, 10. This chapter in *Arctic Night* was published, nearly word-for-word, as R. Pocock, "The Blackguard," in *Chapman's Magazine*. Roger used La Mancha again, though this time he was a less heroic figure: "Blackguard's Judgement" (Glenbow Archives M-981, box 1, file 8). The Blackguard made only a fleeting appearance in another tale by Roger, this one set firmly in 1885: [R. Pocock], "Makings of Manhood." See also Roger's *Cheerful Blackguard* and *Splendid Blackguard*.

32. Clippings in Glenbow Archives M-254.

33. Roger Pocock to Charles Pocock, Edinburgh, 29 September 1896 (Glenbow Archives M-254).

34. [Reviews of fiction], *The Athenæum* no. 3611 (9 January 1897): 46 (Glenbow Archives M-254).

35. M. McD. Bodkin to Roger Pocock, Dublin, 2 January 1897 (Glenbow Archives M-254).

36. M M [identified in Roger's hand as C.W. Mason] to Roger Pocock, no place or date (Glenbow Archives M-254).

37. Roger Pocock, diary, 20 February 1897 (Glenbow Archives M-254).

38. In Roger's "A Cowboy on 'Change,'" a few words are different (for example, a policeman in *All the Year Round* became deputy warder in *Arctic Night*), and a few words have been added to the *Arctic Night* version. In Roger's "Silver Chamber," the British lord's name is Augustus Guineapig, rather than John Guineapig, and Giggleswick does not make an appearance by name, but the central tale of betrayal is the same.

39. "Another tale from this period, "Brimstone Pete," was published without a byline, but evidence in papers in the Dudley Collection, as well as some internal evidence of his developing style, strongly suggests Roger wrote it.

40. R. Pocock, "Noble Five." Noble Five was the name of a mining company in the area. The villainous Noble Five syndicate also appears in Roger's "Freiberg Expert." This time, however, the story takes place in Amber, Idaho, a very thinly disguised stand-in for Wallace, and the metal is tin.

41. "Riders of the Plains," for example, which is largely a memoir and celebration of his experience. Roger's "North-West Mounted Police" is a brief account of the early days of the NWMP and its interaction with the First Nations. Roger also used his own experience in several stories, including one in which La Mancha makes another appearance, "Glory of Arms," which is the tale of a recruit named Bob who met an unattainable young woman, succumbed to "visions of great adventure, even of that awful physical suffering which tears away the veil of sense at the open gates of death," and joined the NWMP in September 1884. Roger's "A Capital Felony," is quite a good NWMP yarn with a twist in the tail, which demonstrates how Roger's writing improved.

42. Clippings in Glenbow Archives M-254.

43. R. Pocock, *Rottenness*, 10.

44. R. Pocock, *Rottenness*, 12.

45. R. Pocock, *Rottenness*, 3, 12.

46. R. Pocock, *Rottenness*, 20.

47. R. Pocock, *Rottenness*, 195.

48. R. Pocock, *Rottenness*, 207. Roger defined a *parasite* as "the human being who eats but does not work, who reaps where he has not sown, who takes rent and revenue from the labour of others, rendering no service in return" (196).

49. R. Pocock, *Rottenness*, 89.

50. Roger Pocock to Charles Pocock, at sea on board SS *Bretwalda*, 21 October 1896 (Glenbow Archives M-254).

51. Roger Pocock to Charles Pocock, Rutledge, Pennsylvania, 2 November 1896 (Glenbow Archives M-254).

52. Frank Pocock to Charles Pocock, Rutledge, Pennsylvania, 13 November 1896 (Glenbow Archives M-254).

53. D. Sladen, *My Long Life* (London: Hutchinson, 1939), 163.

54. G.B. Burgin, *Memoirs of a Clubman* (London: Hutchinson, 1921), 128–29.

55. D. Sladen, *My Long Life*, 163.

56. Burgin, *Memoirs of a Clubman*, 130.

57. R.T. Stearn, "Mysterious Mr. Le Queux: War Novelist, Defence Publicist and Counterspy," *Soldiers of the Queen* (Sept 1992), 24. This is probably the most carefully reasoned account of Le Queux's life, although no one has been entirely able to separate the fact from the fiction.

58. D. Sladen, *My Long Life*, 186.

59. Ashwell, *Myself a Player*, 113.

60. R. Pocock, *Chorus to Adventurers*, 13–14. We can date this journey because Charles Pocock wrote to his sister Ella, on 14 December 1894, that "Roger is at Sebastopol on a cruise" (Pocock Scrapbook NMM).

61. R. Pocock, *Chorus to Adventurers*, 14, 15.

62. Quoted in Jeal, *Baden-Powell*, 151.

63. R. Pocock, *Chorus to Adventurers*, 15.

64. Jeal, *Baden-Powell*, 148.

65. Roger Pocock to Charles Pocock, Old Waverley Temperance Hotel, Edinburgh, 29 September 1896 (Glenbow Archives M-254).

66. Roger Pocock, diary (Glenbow Archives M-254). Rudyard Kipling was then living in Rock House, Maidencombe, near Torquay, on Babbacombe Bay, while his parents were living at Tisbury, Wiltshire (Ricketts, *Rudyard Kipling*, 226).

67. MacDonald, *Language of Empire*, 162–63.

68. R. Pocock, "Laureate of Empire."

69. R. Pocock, "Riders of the Plains," 11.

70. R. Pocock, "Laureate of Empire."

71. Rudyard Kipling, "The Lost Legion," *Collected Verse of Rudyard Kipling* (London: Hodder & Stoughton, 1912), 147.

72. R. Pocock, "Laureate of Empire."

73. R. Pocock, *A Frontiersman*, 165 (italics in original). For a slightly different version of this, see R. Pocock, "Laureate of Empire." The quarrelling was over Kipling's fur seal tales.

74. MacDonald, *Language of Empire*, 164.

75. Stewart, *Sam Steele, Lion of the Frontier* (Regina, Sask.: Centax Books, 1999), 202. For Roger's description of the Stetson, see his *Horses*, 165–66. He also praised it in one of his contributions to the book he compiled and edited, *Frontiersman's Pocket-book*, 156–57. Roger recommended the Stetson as part of frontier clothing to the members of the Legion of Frontiersmen. They wear it today only as part of ceremonial uniform, or in Canada with traditional uniform.

76. See also G.A. Pocock, *One Hundred Years of the Legion of Frontiersmen: Soldiers, Spies and Counter-spies, Sacrifice and Service to the State* (Chichester, U.K.: Phillimore, 2004), 20–21.

77. R. Pocock, *Chorus to Adventurers*, 10–11; see also G.A. Pocock, *For Adventure and for Patriotism*, 20–21. The story of the trap in Roger's letter to his father is a little simpler (Roger Pocock to Charles Pocock, 4 July 1897 [Glenbow Archives M-254]). Roger did not indicate where he was when he wrote this letter, but he was probably in London.

78. Roger Pocock to Charles Pocock, London, 25 June 1897 (Glenbow Archives M-254).

79. Roger Pocock to Charles Pocock, London, [28 June 1897] (Glenbow Archives M-254). Always thinking of future writing projects, Roger ended this letter with "To be continued. Keep this."

80. Roger Pocock to Charles Pocock, London, [28 June 1897] (Glenbow Archives M-254).

81. Roger Pocock to Charles Pocock, London, [28 June 1897] (Glenbow Archives M-254).

82. Robert J. Jones, "Old-Timers' Column," *R.C.M.P. Quarterly* vol. 13, no. 4 (April 1948): 379.

83. R. Pocock, *Chorus to Adventurers*, 11.

84. R. Pocock, *Chorus to Adventurers*, 12.

85. Roger Pocock to Charles Pocock, London, [28 June 1897] (Glenbow Archives M-254).

86. Roger Pocock to Charles Pocock, London, 1 July 1897 (Glenbow Archives M-254). In his diary Roger wrote, "Perry gladly consented to taking me west if I could get a job as special Correspondent [*sic*]"; in a letter to his father he wrote, "Perry gladly consented to take me west…" (Roger Pocock, diary, 22 June 1897 and Roger Pocock to Charles Pocock, London, 25 June 1897 [Glenbow Archives M-254]).

87. Roger Pocock to Charles Pocock, 4 July 1897 (Glenbow Archives M-254). In a diary fragment Roger wrote, "[July] 7 Left England" (Glenbow Archives M-254).

88. Thomas Catling, *My Life's Pilgrimage* (London: John Murray, 1911), 231. Catling described this achievement as "unprecedented in the history of a British newspaper." Because this number represents actual copies circulated, rather more than a million people would have been reading *Lloyd's Weekly*.

89. Macleod, *NWMP and Law Enforcement*, 45–46; see also Turner, *North-West Mounted Police*, 2:280–84.

90. Roger Pocock to Charles Pocock, at sea on board SS *Parisian*, 15 July 1897 (Glenbow Archives M-254).

91. R. Pocock, *A Frontiersman*, 178.

92. Roger Pocock to Charles Pocock (Glenbow Archives M-254). Roger did not indicate a place or date, but context indicates he was in Regina, and he referred to beginning his ride the next day. He left Regina on 30 July 1897. If his health did not force a change after he wrote, then 29 July as a completion date for the letter seems probable.

93. The "letter" (as Roger called his articles) that appeared on 26 December 1897 was titled "The Great Home Festival in Canada," but clearly it was part thirteen of the "Into the Great Dominion" series.

94. Roger Pocock to Charles Pocock, [Regina], [29 July 1897] (Glenbow Archives M-254). The "record of names" is his "What Became of Men I Knew in the Force up to 1897" (Private Diary, 1885).

95. Roger Pocock to Charles Pocock, [Regina], [29 July 1897] (Glenbow Archives M-254).

96. R. Pocock, "Into the Great Dominion: Hitting the Trail."

97. R. Pocock, *A Frontiersman*, 185.

98. MacDonald, *Language of Empire*, 168.

99. R. Pocock, "Into the Great Dominion: Gold Mining."

100. R. Pocock, "Into the Great Dominion: Across the Plains."

101. R. Pocock, "Into the Great Dominion: Life with the Mounted Police."

102. Roger Pocock to Charles Pocock, [Regina], [29 July 1897] (Glenbow Archives M-254).

103. R. Pocock, "Life with the Mounted Police." In contrast to his embellishment, Roger travelled with a "roll of bedding and a small valise" (R. Pocock, "Hitting the Trail").

104. R. Pocock, *A Frontiersman*, 181.

105. R. Pocock, "Life with the Mounted Police."

106. R. Pocock, "Into the Great Dominion: The Cypress Hills."

107. For example, on 30 July, "Led horse started dragging me nearly off waggon [*sic*] Heroux took reins & I recovered, & got grip on led horse. Hand burned with rope, but I stuck"; on 20 August, "[horse] bucked me off"; and on 22 August, "[horse] bucked & went down on its belly, my arms round neck" (Glenbow Archives M-254).

108. R. Pocock, "Into the Great Dominion: Horse Records."

109. R. Pocock, diary (Glenbow Archives M-254).

110. R. Pocock, diary (Glenbow Archives M-254). This probably is a reference to the first three parts of his series "Into the Great Dominion."

111. R. Pocock, "Into the Great Dominion: The Red Indians."

112. R. Pocock, "Into the Great Dominion: The Life of a Cowboy: With the 'Lazy H' Round-up." "Lazy H" was the brand of the Oxley ranch.

113. R. Pocock, "Into the Great Dominion: The Life of a Cowboy."

114. R. Pocock, "The Great Home Festival in Canada."

115. Steele, "Great Adventurer—Roger Pocock," 35. In his diary Roger simply wrote on 25 August at Pincher Creek, "Major Steele in from Macleod…. Had an hour with him," and on 28 August at Fort Macleod, "got to know Major SB Steele" (Glenbow Archives M-254). Later, Roger referred to Steele as "my oldest friend" (R. Pocock, *Chorus to Adventurers*, 146).

116. Charles E.S. Dudley (Harwood Steele's nephew), conversations with Geoffrey A. Pocock. Indeed, the relationship was so close that Harwood Steele inherited many of Roger's papers related to Canada.

117. Roger told the story in "The Outlaw," in his "Great Adventurers" series. It was also published in *Captains of Adventure*, 179–85.

118. R. Pocock, "Into the Great Dominion: In the Rocky Mountains"; R. Pocock, *A Frontiersman*, 202–03.

119. R. Pocock, "Gold Mining." Roger did not mention mining for gold in his diary for this period.

120. R. Pocock, "Gold Mining." Roger went into enthusiastic detail about the techniques and geology of mining.

121. R. Pocock, *A Frontiersman*, 209.

122. R. Pocock, "Golden West."

123. R. Pocock, *A Frontiersman*, 185–86.

5: THE CASE OF THE VANISHING BARONET

1. Herbert Currey (1849–1902) was the son of William Currey and his wife, Frances Mary Pocock, who was the sister of Roger's father, Charles Pocock. Above Roger's first entry in his Klondike Diary, which is dated 5 February 1898, he wrote: "I undertook to lead a 'Klondike' expedition & raised it accordingly. This was to pay me £200 for my services. The money was to pay the £290 furniture debt which was owing to Herbert Currey" (Roger Pocock, Klondike Diary [Glenbow M-254]; hereinafter cited as Klondike Diary).

2. MacDonald, *Sons of the Empire*, 32.

3. R. Pocock, *Chorus to Adventurers*, 3–5.

4. Roger reported on a captain who was "told by his owners to have an accident." He then described a later incident of near scuttling by that captain (R. Pocock, *A Frontiersman*, 169–71) that closely resembles Roger's description of his experience on the SS *Bretwalda* (Roger Pocock to Charles Pocock, at sea aboard SS *Bretwalda*, 5 October 1896 [Glenbow Archives M-254]).

5. R. Pocock, *Chorus to Adventurers*, 5. Cutcliffe-Hyne described working with Wood to develop the image of Kettle: "together we made a hundred sketches, working by trial and error," but "Wood said he must get a living model if he was to stick to that one specification." Wood found him "pulling beer in a pub in North London," yet "Scores of small dapper men, with the requisite torpedo beard, have claimed to be the original of Captain Kettle (Cutcliffe-Hyne, *My Joyful Life*, 273–74). Frank Cecil Ransley, speaking of his experience in 1923, described Roger as "a little man who looked, above the beard like Captain Kettle" ("A £100 Worth of Adventure: Prison Governor's Story: Sailed Seas in Broken Down Yacht," *Bournemouth Daily Echo* [23 April 1942]: 7). Later, Ransley intimated that other members of that expedition commented on the likeness (Frank Cecil Ransley in conversation with Geoffrey A. Pocock).

6. Roger was elected to the Savage Club in 1904 (Alan Wykes, Honorary Secretary, Savage Club, to Geoffrey A. Pocock, London, 19 March 1979).

7. R. Pocock, *Chorus to Adventurers*, 5.

8. Clippings and programs of The Nameless Club (Dudley Collection).

9. R. Pocock, *Chorus to Adventurers*, 97–98.

10. Clippings and programs of The Nameless Club (Dudley Collection).

11. MacDonald, *Language of Empire*, 205.

12. R. Pocock, "Into the Great Dominion: The Canadian Yukon."

13. R. Pocock, "Into the Great Dominion: The Canadian Yukon."

14. Price, *From Euston to Klondike*, 58–59.

15. R. Pocock, *A Frontiersman*, 212.

16. R. Pocock, *A Frontiersman*, 211.

17. R. Pocock, *A Frontiersman*, 211.

18. R. Pocock, *A Frontiersman*, 211.

19. R. Pocock, "Canadian Yukon"; R. Pocock, "Into the Great Dominion: The All-Canadian Routes." In the second article, Roger mentioned another all-Canadian route, the "Edmonton" route, which he said "would be an excellent route for the insane, especially if the Government provided asylums at intervals." In 1898 and 1899 Roger condemned that route again (R. Pocock, "Argonauts of the Klondike"; R. Pocock, "Travel in Klondike"). For an account of a more recent trip along the northern part of Roger's route see Pynn, *The Forgotten Trail*.

20. Garland, *Trail of the Goldseekers: A Record of Travel in Prose and Verse* (New York: Macmillan, 1899), 8. While his partner, Burton Babcock, went all the way, Garland (1860–1940) turned aside at Glenora. Garland also used this experience in his novel, *Long Trail*.

21. Garland, *Trail of the Goldseekers*, 54.

22. R. Pocock, *A Frontiersman*, 212. The sum of £250 was probably equivalent to two years of wages for many working men.

23. Lee, *Klondike Cattle Drive*, 26.

24. Glenbow Archives M-254. In addition to the eleven sections of the Memorandum, which clearly were drawn up by a legal professional, there was a page of four bylaws. The bylaws were signed by Roger and Boddam-Whetham.

25. Klondike Diary.

26. R. Pocock, *A Frontiersman*, 213.

27. R. Pocock, *A Frontiersman*, 211.

28. R. Pocock, *A Frontiersman*, 213; R. Pocock, "Lost Baronet."

29. R. Pocock, *A Frontiersman*, 214.

30. Klondike Diary.

31. "Another Story: The Sir Arthur Curtis Party and the Ashcroft Trail," *The Province* (17 October 1898; clipping, Glenbow Archives M-254). This sum appears to be erroneous, however, because on 15 April, several days before they left Hat Creek, Roger noted $200 for "men feed" and another $200 for "horse feed" (Klondike Diary).

32. 24 March 1898 (Klondike Diary).

33. Klondike Diary.

34. R. Pocock, *A Frontiersman*, 212.

35. Klondike Diary; R. Pocock, *A Frontiersman*, 215; see also R. Pocock, "Lost Baronet." In another account he was more general: "Two or three of the larger parties marched for the Fraser, leaving horses dead at every camp…" (R. Pocock, "He Died in the Bush" [Glenbow Archives M-254]).

36. Klondike Diary.

37. Lee, *Klondike Cattle Drive*, 4.

38. R. Pocock, *A Frontiersman*, 218.

39. R. Pocock, *A Frontiersman*, 218.

40. Klondike Diary; drawing of "Roger Pocock, Journalist, Bohemian and Guide of the Curtis Expedition, at Work on the Trail. From a snapshot taken by Mr. Adamson," *Victoria Daily Colonist* (28 August 1898; clipping, Glenbow Archives M-254). That drawing was also published in T.M.B., "Sir Arthur Curtis' Bones."

41. R. Pocock, *A Frontiersman*, 219–20.

42. T.M.B., "Sir Arthur Curtis' Bones."

43. Klondike Diary.

44. Klondike Diary.

45. R. Pocock, "He Died in the Bush."

46. R. Pocock, *A Frontiersman*, 220–21. Here Roger gave the date Curtis disappeared as 9 June, as he did in "Lost Baronet."

47. T.M.B., "Sir Arthur Curtis' Bones." T.M.B. said the story was "substantiated by Mr. Adamson's carefully kept diary."

48. In both *A Frontiersman* and "He Died in the Bush," Roger said he shortened that day's journey to allow Curtis to catch up. However, in the former he wrote they went ten miles (221), while in the latter he indicated twelve miles. Adamson, who was prone to criticize Roger, did not describe the search in detail because "The rest of the story you know. Pocock has told it and has told it truly" (T.M.B., "Sir Arthur Curtis' Bones"). This was a direct reference to R. Pocock's "He Died in the Bush."

49. R. Pocock, *A Frontiersman*, 221.

50. Klondike Diary.

51. R. Pocock, *A Frontiersman*, 222.

52. Cecil A. Clark to Geoffrey A. Pocock, Victoria, 24 November 1979. In his Klondike Diary for 14 June, Roger wrote there were four Chilcotin trackers; elsewhere he said there were five (R. Pocock, *A Frontiersman*, 223; R. Pocock, "Lost Baronet").

53. R. Pocock, *A Frontiersman*, 223; see also R. Pocock, "He Died in the Bush."

54. Klondike Diary.

55. While Roger was being paid, rather than being a paying member, article eight of the contract states: "All profits arising from the said Expedition shall, after payment of all expenses connected therewith, be equally divided between all the parties hereto" (Glenbow Archives M-254). This seems to include Roger. Hilton, who was receiving expenses as horse-wrangler was, however, explicitly included in the division of profits in article six of the contract.

56. Typed copy, certified as correct by D.P. Driscoll, dated 16 March 1907 (Glenbow Archives M-254).

57. R. Pocock, *A Frontiersman*, 224.

58. Lee, *Klondike Cattle Drive*, 23. Lee attributed this comment to a date between 26 August and 29 August 1898. T.C. would be Telegraph Creek.

59. Adamson's chronology is a little different, and includes a cable. "On July 6th we abandoned the search. Sheppard telegraphed his brother in London to break the news to Lady Curtis. While at Quesnelle he received an answer, asking if all hope had been given up. He replied in the affirmative" (T.M.B., "Sir Arthur Curtis' Bones"). Adamson is next quoted as saying, "The party split up then. Pocock went to Ashcroft.... Sheppard and I proceeded to Glenora." According to Roger's Klondike Diary, he was in Victoria on 6 July and Sheppard and Adamson set off on 25 June.

60. Klondike Diary; Lady Curtis cable (Glenbow Archives M-254). The stress appears to have caused Roger to lose track of the days. Since the reply cable was dated 3 July, he probably arrived in Vancouver a day or two before that. His estimate, therefore, that it was the eighth or ninth day after his initial cable on which he boarded the train to Vancouver in Ashcroft is probably not accurate.

61. R. Pocock, *A Frontiersman*, 224.

62. Roger Pocock to Frederick White, Swarthmore, Pennsylvania, 22 July 1898 (LAC 1107); Klondike Diary; and Roger Pocock to Charles Pocock, Philadelphia, 25 July 1898 (Glenbow Archives M-254).

63. Gerald A. Sheppard to Roger Pocock, Fort Wrangel, Alaska, 28 September 1898 (underscoring in original; Glenbow Archives M-254). This is a typed copy of the letter Roger received. It is corrected and annotated in Roger's hand. No account written by Roger could be found in the *Victoria Daily Colonist* or the *Victoria Daily Times*, so the reference almost certainly is to R. Pocock, "He Died in the Bush," which was published in Vancouver.

64. Cecil A. Clark, "Into the Vast Wilds the Baronet Vanished," *The Islander: Daily Colonist Magazine* (26 March 1961): 9. In another account it was stated that "At the request of Sir Arthur's family, who reside in Hampshire, the provincial police shortly after made diligent search, but they also were unsuccessful at that time" (*Times* (London) [21 September 1908]: 6, col. C). Roger noted in his diary that "Mail & Times brought up story of a new search for Sir Arthur Curtis. Express tried to interview me & published extract from A Frontiersman. Mail sent a man to my camp. All the papers worried me" (Roger Pocock, pocket diary, 21 September 1908; hereafter "Pocket Diary").

65. *Times* (London) (31 January 1899): 15, col. A. In "Lost Baronet Found" (*Daily News*, 24 October 1908), Curtis was said to have "impoverished himself on the Stock Exchange" and to have been "a remarkably bad bushman with no sense of direction whatever" and "a capable man with his hands and excellent shot." Roger's response to the *Daily News* piece was "Rumours of Curtis alive in Ashcroft Dist. Curtis case up again in press. Interviews in plenty. Libel in Daily News. I referred to Langton" (Pocket Diary, 24 October 1908). Roger probably objected to this particular paragraph in the *Daily News*: "Instead of organising any regular search Pocock proceeded on with the party merely leaving a note which said 'If you do not turn up by the evening I shall send out a search party. You will find a lunch in this bag. We are going to 9 mile camp.'"

66. *Daily Telegraph* (31 January 1899; Glenbow Archives M-254). Barnard was acting for Lady Curtis.

67. "Sir Arthur Curtis—A Story That He did not Die on the Ashcroft Trail," *Montreal Star* (23 January 1899): 3, col. 8. Cole's opinion was repeated in *St. James's Gazette* on 13 February 1899 and in *Daily Graphic* on 14 February 1899 (Glenbow Archives M-254).

68. Quoted in Clark, "Into the Vast Wilds," 8.

69. Cecil A. Clark to Geoffrey A. Pocock, Victoria, British Columbia, 24 November 1979.

70. *Times* (London) (28 December 1899): 4, col. D.

71. "Toughest of Trips," *Daily World* (28 July 1898): 5.

72. "The Lost Englishmen" [*sic*], *Victoria Daily Colonist* 80, no. 42 (30 July 1898): 7, col. F. According to Sheppard, this story first appeared in the *Kamloops Inland Sentinel*. The *Daily Colonist* version was published in the *Daily World* in Vancouver on 1 August 1898, without credit to any other newspaper.

73. G.A. Sheppard, "The Lost Prospector: One of the Curtis Party Corrects a Published Story of the Fruitless Search," *Victoria Daily Colonist* 80, no. 66 (28 August 1898): 6, col. C.

74. Violet Butler to Geoffrey A. Pocock, Chieveley, Berkshire, n.d.

75. Cecil A. Clark to Geoffrey A. Pocock, Victoria, British Columbia, 24 November 1979.

76. Clark, "Into the Vast Wilds," 9.

77. Quoted in Cecil A. Clark to Geoffrey A. Pocock, Victoria, British Columbia, 24 November 1979.

78. Klondike Diary. Adamson, too, mentioned the loss but not its return. "Sheppard absentmindedly threw off his belt containing $1,000 one day, and it vanished like a snow-ball in a red hot fire" (T.M.B., "Sir Arthur Curtis' Bones").

79. "Was There Foul Play?: Grave Suspicion Entertained at Hazelton Regarding the Disappearance of Sir Arthur Curtis," *Victoria Daily Times* 27, no. 141 (22 August 1898): 1, col. F.

80. "Horrors of Starvation and Exposure on Ashcroft Trail Again Reported. Sir Arthur Curtis' Body Found by Indians Who Ask One Thousand Dollars," *Victoria Daily Colonist* 70, no. 89 (25 September 1898): 1, col. E; Glenbow Archives M-254; T.M.B., "Sir Arthur Curtis' Bones."

81. R. Pocock, *A Frontiersman*, 225.

82. *Buffalo Evening News*, 1898 (Glenbow Archives M-254).

83. "Suicide or Foul Play: Did Sir Arthur Curtis Take His Own Life?: Ambrose Attwood, an Ashcroft Pilgrim, Thinks the Unfortunate Nobleman Drowned Himself—The Rash Act Preceded by a Camp Quarrel—Another Phase in a Northern Tragedy," *The Province* (27 September 1898): 4, col. B. Suggestions that it was suicide also surfaced in the *Glasgow Herald*, the Toronto *Globe*, the Toronto *Mail*, the *Boston Herald*, the *Pontiac Advance* and the *Kamloops Inland Sentinel*. These clippings can be found in the Glenbow Archives, M-254.

84. R. Pocock, "A Drama of the Klondike Trail." The text owes much to Roger's *A Frontiersman* and "He Died in the Bush."

85. "A Captain's Secret of the Klondike: 'You Can Tell the World I Shot Sir Arthur Curtis,'" *News of the World* (19 April 1936): 12.

86. "A Captain's Secret of the Klondike" (parentheses in original).

87. R. Pocock, *A Frontiersman*, 211.

88. Roger Pocock to Frederick White, Swarthmore, Pennsylvania, 22 July 1898. Despite Roger's positive outlook here, Sheppard made it clear in his letter of 28 September 1898 that he did not agree with Roger's statement that the participants were "fully satisfied" or adequately provisioned (Glenbow Archives M-254).

6: THE GREAT RIDE TO MEXICO...

1. Roger Pocock to Charles Pocock, Philadelphia, 25 July 1898 (Glenbow Archives M-254).

2. "The Lost Baronet" and "Argonauts of the Klondike" both draw on Roger's Klondike experience. "Argonauts" reflects his residual pain and anger over the failure of his efforts. "A Tale of the Union Jack" uses the example of Jefferson Randolph "Soapy" Smith and William F. "Swiftwater Bill" Gates in Skagway to praise Mounted Police justice. Roger's other short pieces published after he returned to London include "Ishmael," which is set during the Mormon move west. In his "A Matter of Anarchists," the central character becomes a typist because he "wrote inferior fiction which would not sell," and thus becomes involved with Scotland Yard. "Piracy," about Lord Buntallow and his pirate ship *Sierpes*, is told with Roger's characteristic humour. In "The Priestess of the Tehuelche," a mate on the sealer *Rapscalion* is put ashore against his will at Punta Arenas, rides through a desert, is cursed and then saved by a Tehuelche

priestess, and marries her. In "What We May Live to See," Roger describes, among other things, how electricity will be transmitted via a system of balloons, office buildings "piled up twenty or thirty stories," special correspondents who take "a biogram and phonogram where anything happens which will be of public interest" and broadcast it "to the very ends of the world," and how a passion for flight replaces the passion for bicycles. In "Tragedy of the 'Smiling Fortune,'" Captain George St. Evrain seeks justice for his brother who was murdered over a gold claim named Smiling Fortune.

3. Roger, on 29 March 1899, paid £1 10s for grave B 75 V in All Saints Cemetery, Maidenhead, where his father was interred on 27 February 1899 (Pocock Scrapbook NMM; Linda Gardner, Admin Officer, Royal Borough of Windsor and Maidenhead, Maidenhead, Berkshire to Geoffrey A. Pocock, e-mail 6 June 2005).

4. R. Pocock, *A Frontiersman*, 227.

5. R. Pocock, *A Frontiersman*, 226–27; see also R. Pocock, *Horses*, 202–04. In Roger's *Captains of Adventure*, he described Carson's "famous ride…a total of four thousand, four hundred miles." Roger then added two components to the journey to arrive at "a total of five thousand, six hundred miles" (94–95). Roger also referred to "Carson who with one horse rode six hundred miles in six days" (ibid., 115). There were quite a number of books on the exploits of Christopher Houston Carson (popularly known as Kit, 1809–68) that might have inspired Roger. As for Peshkov (spelled *Peshkof* by Roger and *Paishkoff* by Thomas Stevens), Roger possibly read Thomas Stevens' *Through Russia on a Mustang* ([London & New York]: Cassell & Co., 1891). Stevens, a reporter for the New York *World*, described his own ride in 1890 from Moscow to the Black Sea. This trek in itself might have inspired Roger, but Stevens also enthusiastically described Peshkov's 1890 ride from Siberia to St. Petersburg (ibid., 23–29).

6. R. Pocock, *A Frontiersman*, 226–27. See also Roger's comments on Peshkov, Carson, and the great virtue of range horses, *Horses*, 202–04.

7. R. Pocock, *A Frontiersman*, 228.

8. R. Pocock, "Canada to Mexico: A Ride Across the Great American Desert: An Indian Festival." Roger used the same image later but included the word "homesick," so it reads, "when I reached the foot of the hill I looked back homesick" (R. Pocock, *A Frontiersman*, 228).

9. R. Pocock, "An Indian Festival."

10. R. Pocock, "An Indian Festival." The wording in the description of this scene is only slightly different in *A Frontiersman*, 229–30. Roger's admiration for the Blackfoot remained so strong that much later he wrote: "The daily bathing, winter and summer, in a very brisk climate, the sweat baths which preceded all religious rites, the freedom from vermin, the chastity of the women, the valour of the men, the purity and spirituality of their life, their wonderful psychic development, and hypnotic medical practice distinguished the Blackfeet even among the glorious tribes of that region" (*Horses*, 108).

11. R. Pocock, "An Indian Festival."

12. R. Pocock, "Canada to Mexico: A Ride Across the Great American Desert: Yellowstone Park—Tourists and Robbers." Roger also wrote about the Grand Canyon in "A Gap in the World."

13. R. Pocock, *A Frontiersman*, 234–35.

14. R. Pocock, "Yellowstone Park—Tourists and Robbers." Years later he wrote that these people "seemed *haunted*. These were the fiercest men I ever met, and withal gentlest, most trustworthy" (R. Pocock, *Search-Lights*, 58 [underscoring in original; Glenbow Archives M-981, box 1, file 4]).

15. Butch Cassidy, born Robert LeRoy Parker in 1866, has also been known as George Cassidy, among other names.

16. R. Pocock, "Yellowstone Park—Tourists and Robbers."

17. R. Pocock, "Canada to Mexico: A Ride Across the Great American Desert: Robbers in Hiding—The Trail of the Kids." The "Kids" were the mail riders.

18. Burroughs, *Where the Old West Stayed Young*, 130.

19. R. Pocock, "Robbers in Hiding"; R. Pocock, *A Frontiersman*, 240.

20. R. Pocock, "Robbers in Hiding"

21. Ibid.; R. Pocock, *A Frontiersman*, 242.

22. R. Pocock, *Horses*, 60–61; see also R. Pocock, *A Frontiersman*, 242.

23. R. Pocock, *A Frontiersman*, 243.

24. R. Pocock, "Robbers in Hiding." With only the slightest modification, this quotation appears in R. Pocock, *A Frontiersman*, 243–44.

25. R. Pocock, "Robbers in Hiding"; R. Pocock, *A Frontiersman*, 244.

26. Roger's photograph of Robbers' Roost was published in "A High-class and Colossal Liar."

27. R. Pocock, "Canada to Mexico: A Ride Across the Great American Desert: The Outlaw Strongholds." See also R. Pocock, *A Frontiersman*, 249–50, and R. Pocock, *Following the Frontier*, 289.

28. Redford, *Outlaw Trail*, 168.

29. R. Pocock, "Outlaw Strongholds."

30. R. Pocock, *A Frontiersman*, 246.

31. R. Pocock, "Outlaw Strongholds."

32. R. Pocock, "Outlaw Strongholds."; R. Pocock, *A Frontiersman*, 249.

33. R. Pocock, "Outlaw Strongholds"; see also R. Pocock, *A Frontiersman*, 247.

34. R. Pocock, "Outlaw Strongholds"; see also R. Pocock, *A Frontiersman*, 250.

35. Burroughs, *Where the Old West Stayed Young*, 124.

36. P.B. Baker, *Wild Bunch at Robbers Roost* (New York: Abelard-Schuman, 1971), 188.

37. R. Pocock, "Outlaw Strongholds"; Baker, *Wild Bunch*, 169, 171.

38. Kelly, *Outlaw Trail*, 3.

39. Horan, *Desperate Men: Revelations from the Sealed Pinkerton Files* (New York: G.P. Putnam's Sons, 1949), 384 (punctuation as in original). In an earlier book Horan titled a chapter "The Leader of the Wild Bunch: Butch Cassidy" (James D. Horan, *The Wild Bunch* [New York: Signet Books, 1958], 15–24). Later Horan wrote that "Cassidy and the Kid [Curry] shared leadership" (James D. Horan, *The Authentic Wild West: The Outlaws* [New York: Crown Publishers, 1977], 240).

40. Matt Warner, *Last of the Bandit Riders* (Caldwell, IN: Caxton, 1940), 306.

41. Prassel, *Great American Outlaw*, 308 (parentheses in original).

42. R. Pocock, "Outlaw Strongholds."

43. Baker, *Wild Bunch*, 169.

44. Baker, *Wild Bunch*, 97.

45. R. Pocock, *Horses*, 204. Earlier, however, he said that when he questioned "men whom I knew to be robbers…they lied cheerfully and at length to throw me off the scent" (R. Pocock, "Outlaw Strongholds").

46. Pointer, *In Search of Butch Cassidy*, 120–21.

47. R. Pocock, *A Frontiersman*, 247; R. Pocock, "Outlaw Strongholds." Roger is rather more definite about this method in the latter.

48. R. Pocock, *Curly*, 193. For his description of the heliograph see ibid., 182–83, and for covering trails see 268–69.

49. R. Pocock, "Canada to Mexico: A Ride Across the Great American Desert: The Outlaws' Stronghold" (italics in original). For a very slightly altered version, see R. Pocock, *A Frontiersman*, 254–55.

50. Burroughs, *Where the Old West Stayed Young*, 162.

51. Patterson, *Butch Cassidy*, 150; Horan, *Desperate Men*, 226. Charles Siringo later owned a copy of the *Frontiersmen's Pocket-book,* now in the possession of the author's son-in-law, Mr. Keith Strong.

52. R. Pocock, "Outlaw Strongholds"; R. Pocock, *A Frontiersman*, 251.

53. Kelly, *Outlaw Trail*, 249.

54. R. Pocock, *A Frontiersman*, 250; see also R. Pocock, "Outlaw Strongholds."

55. Kelly, *Outlaw Trail*, 308.

56. DeJournette and DeJournette, *One Hundred Years of Brown's Park*, 2, 313–14, 317, 453–64.

57. R. Pocock, *A Frontiersman*, 250; see also R. Pocock, "Outlaw Strongholds."

58. R. Pocock, "Outlaw Strongholds"; R. Pocock, *A Frontiersman*, 250.

59. R. Pocock, "Outlaw Strongholds." Roger went into more detail on the rustlers' "system of small sales and a quick turnover" involving travel and changing brands in *A Frontiersman*, 254–54.

60. R. Pocock, "Outlaw Strongholds."

61. R. Pocock, *Curly*, 176. Roger included some parts of this in *A Frontiersman* (254–57), but not his description of the people of Moab.

62. R. Pocock, "Outlaw Strongholds"; R. Pocock, *A Frontiersman*, 257.

63. R. Pocock, "Outlaw Strongholds." The only difference in Roger's autobiography is that the cowboys "explained that I was not armed" (R. Pocock, *A Frontiersman*, 257–58). Roger called the robber who was caught and hanged Parker. This was probably James Parker (aka Jim Parker and Fleming Parker, 1865–98), a northern Arizona cowboy and train robber.

64. R. Pocock, "Canada to Mexico: A Ride Across the Great American Desert: Wonders of the Desert."

65. R. Pocock, "Canada to Mexico: A Ride Across the Great American Desert: The Navajo Savages"; see also R. Pocock, *A Frontiersman*, 261.

66. R. Pocock, "Navajo Savages"; R. Pocock, *A Frontiersman*, 260–62.

67. R. Pocock, "Navajo Savages"; R. Pocock, *A Frontiersman*, 262–64.

68. R. Pocock, "Wonders of the Desert." For a slightly different version, see R. Pocock, *A Frontiersman*, 264.

69. R. Pocock, *A Frontiersman*, 265–66. For a somewhat different rendition, see R. Pocock, "Wonders of the Desert."

70. R. Pocock, "Wonders of the Desert." In *A Frontiersman* Roger wrote "on the face of a precipice" (266–67) instead of "on the Yaco of a mountain."

71. R. Pocock, *A Frontiersman*, 267–68; see also R. Pocock, "Canada to Mexico: A Ride Across the Great American Desert: Bloodstained Arizona."

72. R. Pocock, "Wonders of the Desert"; see also R. Pocock, *A Frontiersman*, 268.

73. R. Pocock, *A Frontiersman*, 268. For a slightly more subdued version, see R. Pocock, "Wonders of the Desert."

74. R. Pocock, "Wonders of the Desert"; see also R. Pocock, *A Frontiersman*, 269.

75. R. Pocock, "Wonders of the Desert"; R. Pocock, *A Frontiersman*, 270.

76. R. Pocock, *A Frontiersman*, 270–71.

77. R. Pocock, "Bloodstained Arizona."

78. R. Pocock, "Bloodstained Arizona."; see also R. Pocock, *A Frontiersman*, 275.

79. R. Pocock, "Canada to Mexico: A Ride Across the Great American Desert: Mexican Frontiersmen"; R. Pocock, *A Frontiersman*, 272–73.

80. R. Pocock, *A Frontiersman*, 274.

81. R. Pocock, *A Frontiersman*, 277. See also William Schell, Jr., "Lions, Bulls, and Baseball: Colonel R.C. Pate and Modern Sports Promotion in Mexico," *Journal of Sport History* 20, no. 3 (Winter 1993): 271n74.

82. R. Pocock, "Mexican Frontiersmen."

83. R. Pocock, "Mexican Frontiersmen"; see also R. Pocock, *A Frontiersman*, 274–75. Roger also caustically addressed guns for the range rider in his *Horses*, 174–76.

84. R. Pocock, "Mexican Frontiersmen." See also R. Pocock, *A Frontiersman* (279–80), where he focussed on branding at that ranch.

85. R. Pocock, "Canada to Mexico: A Ride Across the Great American Desert: Mexican Prisons." Years later Roger wrote, "I…hold the long-distance world-record from 1850, to 1930 when it was broken by Tschiffley [*sic*]" (Roger Pocock to Charles Palmer, Charterhouse, London, 10 April 1933 [Roger Pocock papers, Thomas Fisher Rare Book Library, University of Toronto, Ms. Coll. 417, box 1, folder 4]).

86. Casson and Adamson, *Riding the Outlaw Trail*, 7.

87. "Capt. Pocock, Pioneer, Dies: Was Founder of the Legion of Frontiersmen," *The Albertan* (14 November 1941): 2, col. H. The information in this obituary was largely, or perhaps exclusively, provided by Col. G.E. Sanders, one of Roger's old NWMP friends in Calgary. Many of the details are incorrect. An obituary for Schoof, who died aged seventy-five in 1942, mentions a great many adventures, including some in Mexico, but not a ride from Canada to Mexico ("Frtsm. [Major] G.H. Schoof Passes On," *The Canadian Frontiersmen* 12, no. 10 [October 1942]: [1]).

88. For example, Robert Redford's journey on parts of the Outlaw Trail involved both horses and vehicles (*Outlaw Trail*), while Eamonn O'Neill used only vehicles to explore the ground of his childhood fantasies (*Outlaws: A Quest for Butch and Sundance* [Edinburgh: Mainstream Publishing, 1997]). The Long Rider's Guild recognizes Roger's achievement.

89. Casson and Adamson, *Riding the Outlaw Trail*, 126. Casson and Adamson, two Englishmen, rode the Outlaw Trail from Sierra de Cristo Rey, Mexico, to the Canadian border (17 April–2

September 1999), with occasional support from vehicles and friendly ranchers, and the assistance of GPS. Barbara Whittome was part of the expedition from Mexico to Hole-in-the-Wall.

90. R. Pocock, *A Frontiersman* (1911), [ii]. Below this quotation from Cody, the publisher supplied fifteen lines of biography for Roger, of which four and a half describe Roger's ride from Fort Macleod to Mexico City.

91. "Dusty Files [Canada–Mexico ride]," *The Canadian Frontiersman* 37, no. 4 (July–August 1967): 9.

7: WAR; AND THE WANDERER WRITES...

1. Ashwell, *Myself a Player*, 119. For details on Lena's theatrical career, see Leask, "Lena Ashwell."
2. Ashwell, *Myself a Player*, 80.
3. Of these twenty-four articles on adventurers who spanned the globe and several centuries, only "Men Who Won Thrones," which served as an introduction to the series, and "The Laureate of Empire" on Rudyard Kipling, were omitted from Roger's *Captains of Adventure*. Generally there were only minor changes made to the text, including some to bring the essays up to date.
4. R. Pocock, *Chorus to Adventurers*, 55.
5. A good example is "The Guns for Cuba," the first chapter in *Adventures of Captain Kettle*.
6. R. Pocock, *A Frontiersman*, 289.
7. MacDonald, *Language of Empire*, 167.
8. R. Pocock, *A Frontiersman*, 289. "Sutler's" is a reference to a band of irregulars called the Butler's Scouts, which was part of Waldon's Scouts (sometimes written as Walden's or Waldron's). The only War Office file in which that group is mentioned describes it as National (Waldon's) Scouts (National Archives, WO 100/262).
9. R. Pocock, *A Frontiersman*, 290.
10. Dudley Collection.
11. R. Pocock, *A Frontiersman*, 297.
12. Thomas Pakenham, *The Boer War*, 1st ed. (New York: Random House, 1979), 605–06.
13. R. Pocock, *A Frontiersman*, 296.
14. R. Pocock, *A Frontiersman*, 302.
15. Leigh-Pink, "Adventure of the Legion," 6–7. That dinner was in 1901.
16. Leigh-Pink, "Adventure of the Legion," 7. Roger also told this part of the tale in *Chorus to Adventurers*, 74–75. Lubbock (1876–1944) earned the nickname "Klondike" from his 1897 trek up the Chilkoot Trail to the Klondike.
17. R. Pocock, *A Frontiersman*, 306. There is a Barkley listed in the National Scouts (National Archives, WO 100/262).
18. R. Pocock, *Horses*, particularly 223, 231–32.
19. R. Pocock, *A Frontiersman*, 306–07.
20. Roger Pocock to Rudyard Kipling, 1903 (Dudley Collection).
21. "Literature," *Lloyd's Weekly News* (26 July 1903): 3.
22. "A High-class and Colossal Liar."
23. Printed in *The Canadian Frontiersman* 22, no. 4 (October–December 1952): 3. The synopsis of the book appeared on p. 4. Earlier, Roger wrote in his diary that he "Sent off new edition of A Frontiersman to Bobbs Merrill, of Indianapolis" (10 May 1912), but nothing came of that, either.
24. *New York Times Saturday Review of Books and Art* (26 September 1903): 658.
25. Louis, Earl Mountbatten of Burma, to Geoffrey A. Pocock, 6 December 1978.
26. R. Pocock, *A Frontiersman* (1911), preliminary leaf of publisher's advertisements.
27. Wood, "Whines from the Wood."
28. R. Pocock, *Curly* (Boston, 1905), 295; cf. R. Pocock, "Outlaw Strongholds," 14, and R. Pocock, *A Frontiersman*, 249–50.
29. Burroughs, *Where the Old West Stayed Young*, 59.
30. R. Pocock, *Curly*, 176–77.
31. J.A. Sanderson, Foreign Office, to Viscount Mountmorres, London, 19 April 1904 (Dudley Collection). Mountmorres initially agreed to accompany Roger, but went instead to the Congo.

32. R. Pocock, "Most Northerly House on Earth." Five of Roger's photographs augmented his words.

33. R. Pocock, "Most Northerly House on Earth"; see also R. Pocock, *Chorus to Adventurers*, 104.

34. Sir Dighton Probyn to Roger Pocock (Dudley Collection); R. Pocock, *Chorus to Adventurers*, 104.

35. L, "Some Missionary," *Ottawa Evening Journal* (20 September 1921): 8, col. E.

36. Editor's introduction to R. Pocock, "Russia in War Time."

37. Editor's introduction to R. Pocock, "Russia in War Time."

38. R. Pocock, "Father Ivan—A Worker of Miracles"; R. Pocock, "Russian Peasant Who is Revolting"; and R. Pocock, "Tolstoi and Gorky—Prophets of Russia."

39. R. Pocock, *Chorus to Adventurers*, 15-16.

40. Legion of Frontiersmen, Canadian Division, *History of the Legion*, 145. For an earlier version, see R. Pocock, *Chorus to Adventurers*, 17-18, where he offers his explanation for having so many photographs: "My camera always liked to sit in a port hole and blink" (18).

41. R. Pocock, *Chorus to Adeventuers*, 17-18; see also Legion of Frontiersmen, *History of the Legion*, 16 and 145.

42. R. Pocock, *Chorus to Adeventuers*, 145.

43. *The Morning Post* (26 December 1904). Roger's letter was also published in some other British national newspapers.

44. [R. Pocock], "The Founding of the Legion."

45. R. Pocock, *Chorus to Adventurers*, 24

8: THE LISTING OF THE LEGION

1. Transcription of list in letter from Roger Pocock to New Zealand Command, Charterhouse, London, 18 February 1930 (collection of Geoffrey A. Pocock; hereinafter cited as Transcription of list, 1930).

2. Seton-Karr, *The Call to Arms 1900-1901: Or, A Review of the Imperial Yeomanry Movement and Some Subjects Connected Therewith* (London: Longmans, Green, & Co., 1902), 215.

3. Seton-Karr, *Call to Arms*, 219-20. The four lines form the first half of the third stanza of Rudyard Kipling's "A Song of the White Men" (1899).

4. Sutherland, *Yellow Earl*, 174.

5. Sutherland, *Yellow Earl*, 185, 170, 152 (italics in original).

6. "Legion of Frontiersmen: Inaugural Meeting of Suffolk Command," *East Anglian Daily Times* (10 February 1908): 3. This is a good example of how Roger travelled Britain recruiting for the Legion, often accompanied by Driscoll. Even that early on, the unnamed journalist described the uniform Roger wore as "picturesque."

7. In "A Forecast of the Legion of Frontiersmen," Roger gave an even longer list than usual of trades performed by frontiersmen, but his main point was that "Such a corps attached to the strength of the Army, is a weapon the like of which no people other than ours could offer to their King" (722).

8. Kerr, *Prince Louis of Battenberg*, 175-76.

9. Pocket Diary, 8 and 13 April 1905.

10. Roger Pocock to Frederick White, London, 15 April 1905 (Library and Archives Canada R 196-37-8-F).

11. "Lord Lonsdale and the Defence of the Empire: A Legion of Frontiersmen," *Penrith Observer* (18 April 1905), in Lord Lonsdale's press clippings book, Lowther Castle (copy in the collection of Geoffrey A. Pocock). While many important names were reported, support from Edward Marjoribanks, second Baron Tweedmouth (1849-1909), then first lord of the Admiralty and a highly respected political figure, would have been very helpful.

12. "Legion of Frontiersmen," *Daily Telegraph* (11 April 1905), in Lord Lonsdale's press clippings book.

13. Roger Pocock to Frederick White, London, 15 April 1905 (Library and Archives Canada R 196-37-8-F).

14. Frederick White to Roger Pocock, Ottawa, 1 May 1905 (Library and Archives Canada R 196-37-8-F).

15. Pocket Diary, 1 and 2 May 1905.

16. Pocket Diary, 8 May 1905 (capitalization as in original).

17. Pocket Diary, 15 May 1905 (capitalization as in original).

18. Pocket Diary, 13 and 19 June 1905. On 5 June Roger had written in his diary that "Biscoe comes on salary at £3 a week." On 12 July he wrote "Biscoe trouble renewed," and on 13 July, "Biscoe sacked." Roger never mentioned Biscoe's forename but once referred to him as "Commander Biscoe" (15 October 1908).

19. Pocket Diary, 28 July 1905. Lord Freddy is believed to be Lord Frederick Brudenell-Bruce. An account of that meeting was also published (*Times* (London) [31 July 1905]: 13, col. B).

20. Pocket Diary, 21 September 1905. On 29 September Roger noted he was "able to get up again."

21. Pocket Diary, 25 October and 13 November 1905. On 20 November he noted that "Lonsdale has signed the petition to War Office." The idea was to try to gain some official recognition for the Legion.

22. See entries on 14 December 1905, 19 December 1905, 20 December 1905.

23. The Barringtons were an influential couple who worked for the Legion behind the scenes. Lady Barrington was a close friend of Roger's sister Lena, and Lady Barrington's husband, Sir Eric, was in a position to be consulted by the most important men in Britain, and probably much of the Empire.

24. History of the Legion (as Obtainable from War Office Files), in National Archives, Kew, WO 32/10426.

25. R. Pocock, *Chorus to Adventurers*, 38.

26. E.W.D. Ward, War Office, to Secretary, Legion of Frontiersmen, London, 15 February 1906 (20/ General Number / 2605 [6.1]).

27. This claim was repeated countless times in Legion of Frontiersmen leaflets and publicity from 1906 until comparatively recently. Roger himself declared "The Legion received the approval of His Majesty's Government on February 15th, 1906" (R. Pocock, "Forecast of the Legion," 724).

28. Letters in the files of the Legion of Frontiersmen; see also, History of the Legion (as Obtainable from War Office Files), in National Archives, Kew, WO 32/10426.

29. *Times* (London) (27 April 1906): 4, col. C.

30. Lycett, *Rudyard Kipling*, 394.

31. Lycett, *Rudyard Kipling*, 395 (parentheses in original).

32. "Jungle Jim" Biddulph-Pinchard, conversation with Geoffrey A. Pocock, 1979. At a meeting of the Cumberland and Westmoreland Territorial Association at Penrith Town Hall on 26 July 1917 Lord Lonsdale made reference to a link between the Frontiersmen and the Boy Scouts. In fact, he claimed to have himself been the originator of the Boy Scouts: "I started the Boy Scouts. Roger Pocock told me of the idea of the Boy Scouts and the Legion of Frontiersmen, and I at once took it up and kept it going for some time. Then there were enormous difficulties and Lord Esher took it up. It required such an enormous amount of money and time that I could not stand it. Lord Esher saw the advantages of the movement and took it up, and then after a time it was passed on to General Baden Powell, but as a matter of fact I was the person who started it and I know we had no idea it was to be non-combatant." *Cumberland News* (28 July 1917): 3.

33. Stewart, *Sam Steele*, 264.

34. Jeal, *Baden-Powell*, 375.

35. Gilmour, *Long Recessional*, 238.

36. Lycett, *Rudyard Kipling*, 394. See also Gilmour, *Long Recessional*, 178–79.

37. Pocket Diary, 30 June, 1, 2, and 3 July 1907.

38. Pocket Diary, 27 February, 1, 6, 13, and 20 March 1907. The War Office had objected to de Hora's appointment from the beginning. Willard is believed to have been the bandmaster.

39. Pocket Diary, 28 September 1907.

40. *Times* (London) (12 July 1906): 13, col. D. Hill Rowan referred to this event (Rowan, "Legion of Frontiersmen").

41. *Times* (London) (21 January 1907): 4, col. E.

42. "Empire Day Entertainment," *The Legion of Frontiersmen Monthly Gazette: Northern Commands* 1, no. 4 (June 1907): 25.

43. *Times* (London) (4 September 1906): 8, col. B.

44. R. Pocock, *Chorus to Adventurers*, 31–32. Earlier Roger stated, "In proof of loyalty we shall not, in any Region, arm for service until we have the consent of the authorities" (R. Pocock, "Forecast of the Legion," 726).

45. Appendix A, History of the Legion (as Obtainable from War Office Files), in National Archives, Kew, WO 32/10426.

46. *Times* (London) (25 June 1907): 4, col. E. Onslow presided at the meeting since Lonsdale was "unable to attend." A long article was published two days before that meeting, which was essentially the text of the First Annual Report and Statement of Accounts (*Times* [22 June 1907]: 12, col. B).

9: GERMAN SPIES AND TROUBLES

1. Leigh-Pink said Roger told him in June 1931 that "Forbes ousted me as Commandant-General of the Legion in 1908 when German spies infiltrated our organization and worked to bring about my overthrow—oh, I served under him gladly, and without the slightest friction, we were the best of friends!" (Harry Leigh-Pink, "Great Men of Thet [*sic*] Legion of Frontiersmen: Heroes of the First Matabele War," *The Canadian Frontiersman* 32, no. 3 [July–September 1962]: 6).

2. R. Pocock, *Chorus to Adventurers*, 83. Forbes was in command of the column when Major Allan Wilson (1856–93) and his men were massacred on 4 December 1893.

3. In his diary for 1908, see 5 and 7 March, 21 and 26 April, 3 and 16 May, 6 and 7 June, 20, 22 and 23 July, 15 August, 2 and 17 September, and 7 November.

4. H.W. Koekkoek's drawings, with a little text, appeared as "A Saddle to Sail in: The Morgan Pack-saddle and Boat: The Legion of Frontiersmen Experimenting with the Morgan Pack-saddle," *Illustrated London News* (25 April 1908): 597.

5. "Secret Signs That May Save an Army: Cipher Messages by Scouts," *The Sketch* (23 September 1908): 348.

6. R. Pocock, *Chorus to Adventurers*, 288–89.

7. Pocket Diary, 21–22 September and 24 October 1908. Langton was a solicitor.

8. "Dusty Files [History of Legion of Frontiersmen]," *The Canadian Frontiersman* 37, no. 1 (January–February 1967): 7. Roger did not state who the woman was who spoke to the King, but perhaps the most likely person would be Muriel, Lady de la Warr. There is no clear mention of this incident in Roger's pocket diaries.

9. Henry Gray-Reid, "The Legion of Humbugs," *The Modern Man: A Weekly Journal of Masculine Interests* (16 January 1909): 2.

10. Editor, "In Defence of the Legion," *The Modern Man* (20 February 1909): 2.

11. R. Pocock, "Mr. Pocock's Challenge."

12. Henry Gray-Reid, "Mr. Pocock's Challenge Accepted," *The Modern Man* (27 February 1909): 1. In Roger's diary, the first mention of this interchange occurred before Gray-Reid's terms were published: "A contributor to the Modern Man challenges me to a duel with swords on Belgian coast. Considering reply" (13 February 1909). The next week he wrote: "Called on Modern Man refusing to reply to duel challenge" (16 February 1909).

13. D.P. Driscoll, letter to the editor, *The Modern Man* (17 April 1909): 8. The editor preceded Driscoll's letter with the statement that "This, so far as THE MODERN MAN is concerned, is the last of the Legion. I do not intend to refer to it again…" (capitalization as in original).

14. Roger noted in his diary that he read "proof Chariot of the Sun" (2 February 1910); "finished proofs, chariot of the sun" (24 February 1910); and received "Chariot Royalties [£]15.5.8" ("Cash Account—October," attributed to 6 October 1910).

15. R. Pocock, *Chorus to Adventurers*, 128–29.

16. Roger might also have read August Niemann, *Der Weltkrieg, deutsche Träume: Roman* (1904), translated as *The Coming Conquest of England* (1904). Niemann's story was "a highly optimistic and amateur attempt to rearrange the world to suit German pretensions. The book was immediately translated into English as a warning of what the Germans had in mind" (Clarke, *Voices Prophesying War*, 143). In *Chariot of the Sun*, Roger shared Niemann's idea that Russia, France, and Germany would unite against Britain.

17. Robert Baden-Powell, *Scouting for Boys: A Handbook for Instruction in Good Citizenship*, 3rd & enlarged ed. (London: C.A. Pearson, 1910), 97; see also Jeal, *Baden-Powell*, 375.

18. Roger Pocock to E.C. Wragge, London, 15 April 1909; Library and Archives Canada RG 18, vol. 371, file/dossier RCMP 1909, Nos. 186–195.

19. R. Pocock, comp. and ed., *Frontiersman's Pocket-book* (1911), vii.

20. R. Pocock, *Frontiersman's Pocket-Book*, 1.

21. For more on the role of Childers in the Legion see G.A. Pocock, *One Hundred Years of the Legion of Frontiersmen*, 33.

22. In 1915 Grogan "was still a central committee member" of the Legion (Paice, *Lost Lion of Empire*, 268).

23. Rt. Rev. Bishop H.H. Montgomery, "Morale: Introduction," in R. Pocock, comp. and ed., *Frontiersman's Pocket-book* (1911), 374.

24. *Times* (London) (10 May 1909): 7, col. C.

25. Lena Ashwell, letter to the editor, *Times* (London) (13 May 1909): 9, col. E. Roger noted both the subsidy suggestion and Lena's letter in his diary on 10 and 13 May 1909.

26. *Times* (London) (15 May 1909): 10, col. C.

27. Henry Seton-Karr, letter to the editor, *Times* (London) (15 May 1909): 10, col. C.

28. See the entries between 14 May and 25 May for an account of the affair.

29. See further the entries for 2 June, 7 June, 9 June, and 10 June.

30. Pocket Diary, 24 June, 27 June, and 7 July 1909.

31. Pocket Diary, memo space after 10 July 1909.

32. Clarke, *Voices Prophesying War*, 142.

33. Andrew, *Secret Service*, 45. For the context of the quotations within this quotation, see N. Sladen, *Real Le Queux*, vii.

34. Le Queux, *Things I Know*, 235. That claim is repeated by Sladen, although he gives the year as 1906 (N. Sladen, *Real Le Queux*, 181).

35. R. Pocock, *Chorus to Adventurers*, 64. Ironically, one writer's opinion is that this very enthusiasm backfired, for "by 1909 Pocock's behaviour was so odd that he became a victim of the mania he had sought to create, and was ousted because of suspicions that he himself was a German spy" (Judd, *Quest for C*, 162).

36. R.D. Blumenfeld, *In the Days of Bicycles and Bustles* ([New York]: Brewer and Warren, 1930), 223. This is part of his diary entry for 15 February 1908.

37. The note in Roger's pocket diary for 22 February 1908 is "See about Blumenfeld, qua article."

38. R. Pocock, *Chorus to Adventurers*, 65.

39. Morris, *Scaremongers*, 157.

40. Morris, *Scaremongers*, 156–57. Le Queux also bought spy "plans."

41. "Report and Proceedings of a Sub-Committee of the Committee of Imperial Defence" (National Archives, Kew, CAB 16/8, iii–iv). For the context see Andrew, *Secret Service*, 53–58.

42. Judd, *Quest for C*, 87.

43. R. Pocock, *Chorus to Adventurers*, 59–60.

44. R. Pocock, *Chorus to Adventurers*, 82.

45. Pocket Diary, memo page 1909.

46. R. Pocock, *Chorus to Adventurers*, 90. See also Pocket Diary, 30 and 31 August 1909.

47. "The Legion of Frontiersmen—Annual General Meeting, [Reproduced from the *United Service Gazette* by the kind permission of the Proprietors.]," *The Frontiersman: Official Organ of the London Command* no. 2 (November 1909): 4.

48. Roger Pocock to Sir William C.E. Serjeant, June 1909, quoted in ibid.

49. "Legion of Frontiersmen—Annual General Meeting," 5.

50. "Legion of Frontiersmen—Annual General Meeting," 6–7.

51. R. Pocock, *Chorus to Adventurers*, 89.

52. "Legion of Frontiersmen—Annual General Meeting," 6.

53. "Legion of Frontiersmen—Annual General Meeting," 7.

54. Roger Pocock to E.C. Wragge, London, 2 March 1910 (Library and Archives Canada RG 18, vol. 371, file/dossier RCMP 1909, Nos. 186–195).

55. Pocket Diary, 6 and 7 December 1909. Elsewhere Roger gave the sum as £200 (R. Pocock, *Chorus to Adventurers*, 91).

56. Lena's divorce from Arthur Playfair became final on 26 October 1908, and five days later she married Henry John Forbes Simson (later Sir Henry, 1872–1932) in a private registry office wedding. Simson had made his name in London society as a "woman's doctor." It is surprising that Simson was able to marry Lena Ashwell, whose social position as an actress and divorcee was not good, and yet later attended the Duchess of York at the births of the babies who became Queen Elizabeth II and Princess Margaret.

57. Pocket Diary, 9–10 December 1909.

58. See, for example, Pocket Diary, 22 December 1907; 4 February 1908; 1 November 1908; 4 September 1909; 22 May 1909; 1 January 1910; 22 February 1910; 9 March 1910; 8 and 21 April 1911; 15 and 28 September 1911; 1, 15, 16, and 25 January 1912; 4, 12, 18, and 25 March 1912; 1 April 1912; 29 March 1913; and 9 April 1914. The Ada Wright Roger knew is almost certainly not the suffragette Ada Cécile Wright.

59. Roger wrote this in a blank area above the space for 1 January. Despite that optimistic statement, on 24 January he wrote two mutually contradictory lines in his diary: "wound healed. it broke out again" (capitalization as in original).

60. *A Man in the Open*, directed by British-born Ernest C. Warde (1874–1923), was released 23 February 1919. It starred Dustin Farnum as Jesse, Lamar Johnstone as Bull Brookes, and Claire DuBrae as Polly. Roger complained that the story had been stolen from him, for the writing credit was given to Fred Myton (1885–1955), while his original book was given only the briefest of mentions (R. Pocock, *Chorus to Adventurers*, 289). Roger might have taken some comfort in the review in *Variety*, where his book is mentioned in the first paragraph (*Variety* [7 February 1919]: 61).

61. Hughes Massie to Roger Pocock, London, 12 December 1912 (Glenbow Archives M-981, box 1, file 2).

62. See the following entries in the Pocket Diary for *Jesse*: 7 May, 23 July, and 2 December 1910; 1 January, 26 February, 5 April, 19 April, 20 April, and 3 September 1911; 16 January 1912; and January 1914, cash page. *A Man in the Open* is mentioned on 18 January, 7 February, and 2 March 1912, as well as on 12 April 1913.

63. The quotation is from the *Standard* (London); ellipses in original (Glenbow Archives M-981, box 1, file 8).

64. Glenbow Archives M-981, box 1, file 8.

65. Simeon L. Sites to Roger Pocock, North McAlester, Oklahoma, 8 November 1912 (Glenbow Archives M-981, box 1, file 2).

66. The excision of fairy material began in the opening section, but is particularly striking in the only chapter that has a different heading: "The Minx" in *Jesse* (161–73) became "Billy O'Flynn" in *A Man in the Open* (203–09).

67. Thus, "foot swelled badly, fomentation" (8 April); "foot swelled evening" (11 April); "foot not so bad" (12 April); "had to rest foot" (17 April); and "Resting foot" (18 April).

68. Pocket Diary, 11 May 1910.

69. Pocket Diary, 20 July 1910.

70. H.G., "The Health Missionaries," *Daily Mail* (19 August 1910): 9; Pocket Diary, 24 August 1910. Henry Simson was a member of the executive council.

71. H.G., "Health Missionaries."

72. In 1909, in his diary, Roger recorded that he "pd £5.5 to dentist for set of teeth, swelling too big still" (3 March), and "got my new teeth" (16 April).

73. In one example of his fiscal relationship with Henry Simson, on 2 September 1910 he received £14.5.7 for *Sword and Dragon* and then paid to Simson that very sum (Pocket Diary, "Cash Account—September 1910"). *A Man in the Open* proved a great success in America, and on 12 April 1913 Roger was pleased to receive a royalty cheque for £342.2.1, but on 13 April he gave his brother-in-law a cheque for £344, with the notation "out of debt at last." It was not long before he was borrowing from Simson again.

74. Pocket Diary, 19 January 1911. He moved in on 25 January 1911.

75. "Notes for 1911" in Pocket Diary, 1910.

76. See pocket diary entries for 17 and 23 February 1910; and 11 and 23 August 1911.

77. Pocket Diary, 13, 19, and 23 March 1911.

78. The numerous small differences between the two editions start at the beginning; however, what is most striking is that *Splendid* has twenty-seven lines of text at the end of the last section that are altogether absent from *Cheerful*. Unlike *Cheerful*, which left the reader unsure whether either or neither of the two brothers were hanged, the addition in *Splendid* eliminates loose ends.

79. Steele, "Great Adventurer—Roger Pocock," 40.

80. R. Pocock *Splendid Blackguard*, 5; see also R. Pocock, *Cheerful Blackguard*, 6.

81. R. Pocock, *Wolf Trail*, 22; 18.

82. MacDonald, *Language of Empire*, 38.

83. MacDonald, *Language of Empire*, 37.

84. R. Pocock, *Splendid Blackguard*, 231; R. Pocock, *Cheerful Blackguard*, 286.

10: A CAPTAIN AT LAST

1. Pocket Diary, 14 April 1911; see also 31 March 1911 and 10 April 1911.

2. Pocket Diary, 14–15 and 26 April 1911 (parentheses in original).

3. Pocket Diary, 14 June 1911.

4. Pocket Diary, 2 March 1912 (underscoring in original).

5. Pocket Diary, 31 May and 6 June 1912.

6. Pocket Diary, 28 September and 3 October 1912.

7. Pocket Diary, 28–30 July 1912.

8. Pocket Diary, 11 August and 23 October 1912. On 24 October he noted in his diary: "Gilmer said book not ordered, all my own fault & I had to apologise for my letter[.]" On 28 April 1913 Roger noted "News that Bobbs Merrill nibble for the Annals of Great Adventure."

9. Pocket Diary, 1 and 30 November 1912. Gilmer had not been Roger's agent long: "Asked Gilmer to be my literary agent" (1 June 1912).

10. Pocket Diary, 1 and 3 January 1913.

11. R. Pocock, *Chorus to Adventurers*, 227–28.

12. [Roger Pocock], A Tonic in the North (Glenbow Archives M-981, box 1, file 7).

13. R. Pocock, *Chorus to Adventurers*, 109.

14. R. Pocock, *Chorus to Adventurers*, 109–10; Pocket Diary, 16 May 1913.

15. Rt. Rev. Lord Rupert Ernest William Cecil to Roger Pocock, 1913 (Dudley Collection, emphasis in the original).

16. R. Pocock, *Chorus to Adventurers*, 110.

17. This appears to be indicated in notes contained in the Dudley Collection.

18. R. Pocock, *Horses*, 55.

19. R. Pocock, *Chorus to Adventurers*, 120.

20. "Noted Novelist to Cross Rockies on Horseback: Roger Pocock, Former Mounted Policeman, will undertake Trip with Randal [*sic*] Cecil," *The Albertan* (18 June 1913).

21. R. Pocock, *Chorus to Adventurers*, 121.

22. R. Pocock, *Chorus to Adventurers*, 121.

23. This idea first shows up in his pocket diary on 21 February, and he again mentions meetings on movie ideas on 20, 23, 28, and 29 April 1914; Rudyard Kipling to Roger Pocock, Burwash, June 1914 (Dudley Collection).

24. Pocket Diary, 15, 19, 22, 23, 24, 26, 27, 30, and 31 July 1914.

25. R. Pocock, *Chorus to Adventurers*, 127.

26. Pocket Diary, 31 July and 1 August 1914.

27. Pocket Diary, undated, on page opposite 2–8 August 1914. Later Roger named another war correspondent, George Lynch, as his companion (R. Pocock, *Chorus to Adventurers*, 131).

28. L.S. Amery, *My Political Life*, 3 vols. (London: Hutchinson, 1953), 2:25–26.

29. Amery, *My Political Life*, 2:26.

30. Pocket Diary, 24 August, 2 and 3 September, 19 and 21 October 1914.

31. Pocket Diary, 20 and 21 January, 2 February 1915.

32. Pocket Diary, 10 February 1915.

33. Pocket Diary, 3 and 19 January 1916. By this time Roger had recruited Randle Cecil.

34. Major Commanding (1st Brigade, No. 8, R.H.A. [T.F.]) to Commandant (No. 8, R.H.A. [T.F.]), Training School, 15, Camp, Larkhill, March 1916 (War Office personal file on H.R.A. Pocock, National Archives, Kew, WO 339/69712).

35. Pocket Diary, 5 April 1915.

36. R. Pocock, *Chorus to Adventurers*, 144 (italics in original).

37. Pocket Diary, 3 and 4 April 1915.

38. Pocket Diary, 11–12 April 1915.

39. R. Pocock, *Chorus to Adventurers*, 144–45.

40. Major Commanding (1st Brigade, No. 8, R.H.A. [T.F.]) to Commandant (No. 8, R.H.A. [T.F.]), Training School, 15, Camp, Larkhill, March 1916 (National Archives, Kew, WO 339/69712).

41. "Secret Service Funds; Gun-running; Purchase of Presents; Payments to Agents [1909]" (National Archives, Kew, HD 3/139).

42. Pocket Diary, 10 May 1915.

43. R. Pocock, *Chorus to Adventurers*, 147. Both Jarvis and Jervis occur in Roger's diary and *Chorus to Adventurers*.

44. Pocket Diary, 30 October 1915.

45. Pocket Diary, 8 and 9 September 1915.

46. E. Bethune, Warwickshire Royal Horse Artillery, response to "Application recommended by the G.O.C-in-C, Southern Command for this Officer to be transferred to the Territorial Force Reserve" (National Archives, Kew, WO 339/69712).

47. Pocket Diary, 13 and 14 September 1915.

48. Roger's War Office file shows that they decided to wait and ask for another report in three months (National Archives, Kew, WO 339/69712). Based on internal evidence, between his 12 June and 23 October 1915 visits to Steele, Roger wrote "Canada's Fighting Troops."

49. Pocket Diary 10, 11, and 12 November 1915.

50. Pocket Diary, 25, 26, and 27 November 1915.

51. Pocket Diary, 14, 15, 17, and 30 January 1916.

52. Pocket Diary, 26 January and 3 February 1916.

53. Pocket Diary, 13 April 1916.

54. Pocket Diary, 19, 20, 21, and 24 May 1916; R. Pocock, *Chorus to Adventurers*, 149–51.

55. Pocket Diary, 29 and 30 May 1916. For 16 March 1916 he noted he "Took Miss Heatley to dinner & pictures."

56. Pocket Diary, 2, 6, and 13 June 1916.

57. Despite his consistent claims that his frontier ways of dealing with horses were frowned on in the Army, at least one of Roger's statements contradicts this: "Commandants inspection of stables, & Riding Master's riding test in afternoon. Both very successful" (17 December 1915).

58. Pocket Diary, 18, 20, and 24 June 1916; R. Pocock, *Chorus to Adventurers*, 151–52.

59. Major Commanding (1st Brigade, No. 8, R.H.A. [T.F.]) to Commandant (No. 8, R.H.A. [T.F.]), Training School, 15, Camp, Larkhill, March 1916 (National Archives, Kew, WO 339/69712).

60. Capt. H.R.A. Pocock, Warwickshire RHA, Larkhill, to Headquarters, 8 Artillery School, 25 May 1916 (National Archives, Kew, WO 339/69712).

61. R. Pocock, *Chorus to Adventurers*, 152. Roger repeated this claim in only slightly different words in two letters: Roger Pocock to Charles Palmer, Charterhouse, London, 10 April 1933 (Roger Pocock papers, Thomas Fisher Rare Book Library, University of Toronto, Ms. Coll. 417, box 1, folder 4); Roger Pocock to Frank Debenham, Charterhouse, London, 15 March 1933 (SPRI Archives 92 Pocock 1933/03/15).

62. Roger Pocock to Frank Debenham, Charterhouse, London, 15 March 1933 (SPRI Archives 92 Pocock 1933/03/15).

63. H.R.A. Pocock, Commanding 178 Labour Company to Headquarters, 57 Labour Group, 25 July 1917 (National Archives, Kew, WO 339/69712).

64. In 1916 Roger noted in his diary that he had "leave to write a Horse book" (5 February); "Laid up all week, busy with book" (6 March); and "Murrays agreement re Horse Book" (written above 9 July).

65. R. Pocock, *Horses*, vii–viii. In Roger's diary for 1916 he noted he was "Revising my Horse book from notes by Prof Cossar Ewart" (4 July); "Wrote to Prof Ewart for an Introduction to Horse

Book" (4 September); and "Sent Cossar Ewarts [*sic*] Introduction to Horse Book to Murray with the galley proofs corrected" (10 September).

66. R. Pocock, *Horses*, 1, 77, and 81.
67. R. Pocock, *Horses*, 83.
68. R. Pocock, *Horses*, 160.
69. In his diary for 1916 he noted that he "Started novel about Eric the Red & Leif Erickson" (6 July), and that he was "Working very hard on Eric the Red novel" (16 November).
70. Diary, 10–11 and 21 August 1916.
71. Diary, 11 September 1916.
72. Diary, 5, 6, 12, and 19 September 1916.
73. Diary, 21 and 22 September, 19 November 1916.
74. Diary, written above 16 February and 20 February 1917.
75. Diary, 21 and 28 February, 1 and 2 March 1917.
76. Diary, 10 and 11 March 1917.
77. Diary, 24 March 1917.
78. R. Pocock, *Chorus to Adventurers*, 158.
79. Legion of Frontiersmen, *History of the Legion of Frontiersmen*, 42.
80. Dudley Collection.
81. Pocket Diary, 5 April 1917. His version of events, and even the name of the camp—Toronto—is different in *Chorus to Adventurers* (158–59).
82. Pocket Diary, 9 and 20 April 1917.
83. Pocket Diary, 29 April 1917. For his later description see R. Pocock, *Chorus to Adventurers*, 161–63.
84. According to Roger's diary, on 21 May 1917 he "Met Gen Legge, & sent him copy of 'Horses,'" and on 23 May "Gen Legge called to thank me."
85. Diary, 20 and 22 May 1917.
86. Diary, 1 and 6 June 1917.
87. R. Pocock, *Chorus to Adventurers*, 164.
88. Pocket Diary, 8 and 9 June 1917.
89. R. Pocock, *Chorus to Adventurers*, 165.
90. Pocket Diary, 13 June 1917.
91. Pocket Diary, 16, 17, 18, and 22 June 1917.
92. Pocket Diary, 23 June 1917.
93. Pocket Diary, 10 and 11 July 1917.
94. Pocket Diary, 15 July 1917. Again the next day, he wrote "Group Commander 1 hour's torture, trying to drive me into a breach of discipline."
95. Pocket Diary, 18 and 19 July 1917. On 27 July Roger noted "Resignation & confidential Report provided by Group Commander."
96. Capt. H.R.A. Pocock, Commanding 178 Labour Company, to Headquarters, 57 Labour Group, 25 July 1917 (National Archives, Kew, WO 339/69712).
97. Lt. Col. Edward Kyme Cordeaux, Commanding 57th Labour Group, to DADL, XIX Corps, 27 July 1917 (ibid.).
98. Pocket Diary, 17 August 1917; see also R. Pocock, *Chorus to Adventurers*, 177.
99. Pocket Diary, 175. In his diary for 19 August he did not mention the premonition.
100. R. Pocock, *Chorus to Adventurers*, 175–76.
101. Pocket Diary, 20 August 1917. He noted "Report to War Office by letter" on 23 August. The official letter mentioned Roger's age and concluded, "I request that he may not be sent out to rejoin the Forces under my Command" (Field-Marshal, Commander-in-Chief, The British Armies in France, to The Secretary, War Office, 15 August 1917 [National Archives, Kew, WO 339/69712]).
102. Pocket Diary, 7–9 September 1917. Roger's involvement may antedate this official arrangement, for he noted in his diary that he "Wrote article for Pollard" (3 May 1917).
103. R. Pocock, *Chorus to Adventurers*, 184.
104. R. Pocock, *Chorus to Adventurers*, 188.

1. R. Pocock, *Chorus to Adventurers*, 197.
2. Pocket Diary, 15–31 July 1914.
3. R. Pocock, *Chorus to Adventurers*, 197–98.
4. R. Pocock, *Chorus to Adventurers*, 208.
5. R. Pocock, *Chorus to Adventurers*, 209.
6. R. Pocock, *Chorus to Adventurers*, 223.
7. R. Pocock, "Men Who Won Kingdoms." Roger deliberately did not deal with "big historic figures…found in hundreds of books" but rather addressed "the little adventurers who fought their way to small thrones" (751).
8. The copy inscribed to Stefansson is in the University of Alberta Library. The copy inscribed to Palmer is in the University of Toronto Library. Charles Lionel Palmer (b.1909) was the son of Lionel Hugo Palmer (1870–1914) and the grandson of Sir Charles Mark Palmer (1822–1907).
9. R. Pocock, *Chorus to Adventurers*, 114–15.
10. R. Pocock, *Wolf Trail*, 197. For the American edition the words "his loins" were excised (R.S. Pocock, *Wolf Trail*, 204). This book was published in the USA under the inaccurate author name of Roger S. Pocock.
11. R. Pocock, *Chorus to Adventurers*, 257.
12. R. Pocock, *Chorus to Adventurers*, 257–58.
13. See especially R. Pocock, *Chorus to Adventurers*, 175–76, 178–79.
14. R. Pocock, *Chorus to Adventurers*, 199.
15. The acknowledgement is to John Sebastian Marlow Ward, *A Subaltern in Spirit Land: A Sequel to "Gone West,"* 1st ed. (London: William Rider & Son, 1917).
16. *Spitsbergen Papers: Scientific Results of the First Oxford University Expedition to Spitsbergen (1921)* (London: Oxford University Press, 1925), vii.
17. R. Pocock, *Chorus to Adventurers*, 242.
18. For example, Anthony Huxley, son of Julian Sorell Huxley (1887–1975), wrote: "I have spoken to my Mother and she does dimly recollect that there was someone of that name who acted as Cook, because one of Father's letters referred to the quite good meals he was turning out whilst they were away. She does not however think that my Father and Pocock were particularly close friends, and certainly cannot recall any meeting between them after the expedition." (Anthony Huxley to Geoffrey A. Pocock, Surbiton, Surrey, 14 November 1979)
19. R. Pocock, *Chorus to Adventurers*, 243.
20. Julian Huxley, *Memories*, 2 vols. (London: George Allen and Unwin, 1970–73), 1:128; see generally, 1:128–34.
21. Derek Henry Strutt to Flora Macdonald Steele, quoted in Steele, "Great Adventurer—Roger Pocock," 38.
22. R. Pocock, *Chorus to Adventurers*, 244–45.
23. R. Pocock, *Chorus to Adventurers*, 263.
24. There are twenty of Roger's paintings of Spitsbergen in the archives at the Scott Polar Research Institute, in Case 34.
25. In his will Roger declared that "The manuscript book in three covers entitled 'The Great Design,' together with all my Arctic pictures to be placed at the disposal of Augustine Courtauld Esq[ui]re of Spensers, Great Yeldham, Essex." The date of the will was 8 April 1939. The "Arctic pictures" are probably the ones at the Scott Polar Research Institute.
26. R. Pocock, *Chorus to Adventurers*, 247.
27. See especially chapter 2, "Better and Flatter Earths," in Patrick Moore, *Can You Speak Venusian?: A Guide to the Independent Thinkers* (New York: W. W. Norton & Co., 1973).
28. Roger Pocock to Frank Debenham, Charterhouse, London, 30 September 1932 (SPRI Archives 92 Pocock 1932/09/30).
29. Roger Pocock to Frank Debenham, Charterhouse, London, 15 March 1933 (SPRI Archives 92 Pocock 1933/03/15).
30. Frank Debenham to Roger Pocock, Cambridge, 11 April 1933 (SPRI Archives 92 Pocock 1933/04/11).

31. Roger Pocock to Frank Debenham, Charterhouse, London, 13 April 1933 (SPRI Archives 92 Pocock 1933/04/13).

32. Roger Pocock to Frank Debenham, Charterhouse, London, 10 April 1937 (SPRI Archives 92 Pocock 1937/04/10).

33. Frank Debenham to Roger Pocock, Cambridge, 22 April 1937 (SPRI Archives 92 Pocock 1937/04/22).

34. Roger Pocock to Frank Debenham, Charterhouse, London, 7 January 1938 (SPRI Archives 92 Pocock 1938/01/07).

35. Roger Pocock to Flora Steele, Weston-Super-Mare, Somerset, 19 October 1941, quoted in Steele, "Great Adventurer—Roger Pocock," 41.

36. [Roger Pocock], "Commissioner's Notes," *The Legion of Frontiersmen Monthly Gazette: Northern Commands* 1, no. 2 (February 1907): 31.

37. Macmillan, *Freelance Pilot*, 119–20. The phrase "still be first" is a reference to the death of Sir Ross Smith on 13 April 1922.

38. Macmillan, *Freelance Pilot*, 124–25.

39. Macmillan, *Freelance Pilot*, 124–25; Blake, *Flying Round the World*, 12–13.

40. R. Pocock, *Chorus to Adventurers*, 263.

41. Macmillan, *Freelance Pilot*, 129. The chief sources of information on the 1922 flight are Macmillan, *Freelance Pilot*, 119–319, and Blake, *Flying Round the World*.

42. Macmillan, *Freelance Pilot*, 140.

43. Macmillan, *Freelance Pilot*, 279.

44. Macmillan, *Freelance Pilot*, 288.

45. Macmillan, *Freelance Pilot*, 308–10, 312, and 314–15. For an account with a very technical focus, see Norman Macmillan, "A Round-the-World Attempt," *The Aeroplane* (23 May 1952): 626–29.

46. Blake, *Flying Round the World*, 15.

47. Blake chose to include Macmillan's account from the *Daily News* in *Flying Round the World* (204–20).

48. Blake, *Flying Round the World*, 226–27.

49. G.H. Malins, "Major Blake and R.A.F. in India," *Times* (London) (5 March 1923): 8, col. E.

50. R. Pocock, *Chorus to Adventurers*, 266.

51. R. Pocock, *Chorus to Adventurers*, 266–67.

52. Although Roger was not personally involved in the initial breakaway of the Independent (later Imperial) Overseas Legion of Frontiersmen, in one of Roger's accounts of those events he wrote, "In 1921 I rejoined the Legion of Frontiersmen with my former rank as Commissioner (civil administrator).... My main purpose then was to promote for the Legion a British Flight round the world as the greatest patriotic service which could possibly be rendered" ("Army Organisation: Legion of Frontiersmen [Code 14(S)]: Charter of Incorporation" [National Archives, Kew, WO 32 10427]). That date is most probably an error of typography or memory.

53. "Rear-Admiral as Odd-Job Man: Roger Pocock's Own Story of the New World Argonauts," *World's Pictorial News* (23 June 1923; clipping in Heaton Scrapbook).

54. R. Pocock, *Chorus to Adventurers*, 267. Ransley, however, wrote that "Actually only 30 crew could be mustered" (Ransley, *Soldier, Sailor, Airman, Gaoler*, 26). Newspapers accounts set the numbers between 37 and 39.

55. Ransley, *Soldier, Sailor, Airman, Gaoler*, 25. I was able to have a long discussion with Ransley about the ill-fated voyage at his house when he was well into his eighties. I was honoured to be given a copy of his book and granted permission to quote from it.

56. Ransley, *Soldier, Sailor, Airman, Gaoler*, 26.

57. R. Pocock, *Chorus to Adventurers*, 269.

58. "Rear-Admiral as Odd-Job Man."

59. Undated clipping, almost certainly from the *Daily Telegraph*, in Heaton Scrapbook.

60. Ransley, *Soldier, Sailor, Airman, Gaoler*, 27.

61. Ransley, *Soldier, Sailor, Airman, Gaoler*, 26.

62. Major Kenneth Herbert, MBE (Guy Eardley-Wilmot's executor and friend), conversations with Geoffrey A. Pocock, July–November 1979; Clive Richardson (nephew), conversations with Geoffrey A. Pocock, March 1979–May 1980; John Eardley-Wilmot, conversations with Geoffrey A. Pocock, May 1980–July 1983.

63. "Rear-Admiral as Odd-Job Man."
64. Ransley, *Soldier, Sailor, Airman, Gaoler*, 26.
65. "Six Balloons over London To-day: To Make Atmospheric Tests for World Flight," *Daily Mirror* (8 June 1923 [newspaper name and date in ink]; clipping in Heaton Scrapbook).
66. "World Flight Plans: British Airmen's Second Attempt," *Times* (London) (5 June 1923): 11, col. C.
67. R. Pocock, *Chorus to Adventurers*, 270.
68. Heaton Album and Eardley-Wilmot Album.
69. *Daily Mirror* (9 June 1923; clipping in Heaton Scrapbook).
70. Frank Cecil Ransley, conversations with Geoffrey A. Pocock, summer 1980–winter 1982. See also Ransley, *Soldier, Sailor, Airman, Gaoler*, 27.
71. R. Pocock, *Chorus to Adventurers*, 270–71.
72. Ransley, *Soldier, Sailor, Airman, Gaoler*, 28.
73. Frank Cecil Ransley, conversations with Geoffrey A. Pocock, summer 1980–winter 1982.
74. Ransley, *Soldier, Sailor, Airman, Gaoler*, 29. Roger also mentioned the fate of the flying fish (R. Pocock, *Chorus to Adventurers*, 273).
75. Ransley, *Soldier, Sailor, Airman, Gaoler*, 29.
76. Ransley, *Soldier, Sailor, Airman, Gaoler*, 30. Roger simply wrote, "We went on to Manzanillo, where somebody stole our cash-box and left us penniless…" (R. Pocock, *Chorus to Adventurers*, 274). At least for public consumption, Macmillan had a different explanation for that sum: "In the ship's safe at the beginning of the voyage was £350. This was spent on the journey in food charges, Panama Canal dues, and other items…" ("Debt Ends an Adventure").
77. R. Pocock, *Chorus to Adventurers*, 274.
78. Ransley, *Soldier, Sailor, Airman, Gaoler*, 30–31.
79. Ransley, *Soldier, Sailor, Airman, Gaoler*, 32.
80. Ransley, *Soldier, Sailor, Airman, Gaoler*, 32.
81. Lady Agnew, "Memoire." Her son, Sir Crispin Hamlyn Agnew of Lochnaw, Bt, QC, supplied the relevant paragraphs. Menu in Eardley-Wilmot Album and Heaton Scrapbook.
82. Ransley, *Soldier, Sailor, Airman, Gaoler*, 32–33.
83. Ransley, *Soldier, Sailor, Airman, Gaoler*, 33.
84. Ransley, *Soldier, Sailor, Airman, Gaoler*, 33.
85. Ransley, *Soldier, Sailor, Airman, Gaoler*, 33–34.
86. "Raid and Seize British Yacht." Another article said "a Los Angeles shipbuilder claimed a debt against her of £50" ("British Yacht Seized").
87. "Adventure Ship: World-Flight Vessel Seized in U.S.," *Daily Mail* (14 September 1923 [name and date in ink above clipping]; in Heaton Scrapbook). The explanation by Malins also appeared in another newspaper ("British Yacht Seized").
88. Eardley-Wilmot Album and Heaton Album.
89. R. Pocock, *Chorus to Adventurers*, 278.
90. Eardley-Wilmot and Herbert Heaton, "The 'Frontiersman' Expedition."
91. R. Pocock, *Chorus to Adventurers*, 277.
92. Col. Tamplin to Arthur Burchardt-Ashton, London, 21 November 1923 (emphasis in original; Legion of Frontiersmen archives). At that time Burchardt-Ashton was treasurer of the Legion. The only "dinner of welcome" for which there is evidence is the one at Ince Studios.
93. This letter was also printed in *The Frontiersman* (June 1923).
94. *John Bull* (clipping undated but likely from December 1923; in Heaton Scrapbook).
95. Sefton Brancker to Guy Eardley-Wilmot, London, 28 November 1923 (Eardley-Wilmot Album).
96. Sefton Brancker to Guy Eardley-Wilmot, London, 30 November 1923 (Eardley-Wilmot Album).
97. Guy Eardley-Wilmot to Tom Pocock, King Edward VII Hospital, Midhurst, Sussex, 25 November and 3 December 1965 (double exclamation marks in original).
98. Macmillan was quoted as saying that "the ship has been sold for about £450" ("Debt Ends an Adventure"). Roger said that "The ship with all her contents was sold at about one hundred pounds…" (R. Pocock, *Chorus to Adventurers*, 279).

1. R. Pocock, *Chorus to Adventurers*, 283–84.
2. R. Pocock, *Chorus to Adventurers*, 289.
3. Dudley Collection. This address is also on a screenplay he wrote, "The Salvation Pirate: A Story of the Yokohama Pirates, by One of Them" (Glenbow Archives M-981, box 1, file 6).
4. R. Pocock, *Chorus to Adventurers*, 289–90.
5. R. Pocock, *Chorus to Adventurers*, 292. On his business card Roger claimed part authorship of two scripts for films named *Drifters* and *Reality*, but films of the right vintage do not show up in records under those titles.
6. "Brand of Cowardice," *Variety* (29 July 1925): 36.
7. Paul E. Mix, *The Life and Legend of Tom Mix* (South Brunswick NJ: A.S. Barnes & Co., 1972), 101.
8. Harry Leigh-Pink, "Brittanic-American Comradeship," *The Canadian Frontiersman* 29, no. 2 [April–June 1959]: 7). See Tom Mix, *The West of Yesterday*, comp. and ed. J.B.M. Clark (Los Angeles: Times-Mirror Press, 1923), [7–8]. That quotation is taken, with a little latitude, from R. Pocock, *Man in the Open*, 47–49.
9. Leask, "Lena Ashwell," appendix six: 19–20. It was also known as *Luck* and *The Claimants* (19). In 1936 Roger was still reworking *Celluloid Cat*: "I have just finished the rewriting of the Celluloid Cat, renamed The Claimants & have a copy for you. But I want to consult with you as to the cinema angle, & how to construct it as a Mounted Police story" (Roger Pocock to Charles Palmer, Charterhouse, London, 15 May 1936 [Roger Pocock papers, Thomas Fisher Rare Book Library, University of Toronto, Ms. Coll. 417, box 1, folder 12]). Roger used a very similar tale, setting, and group of characters in his unpublished manuscript, "Van Ymuiden Millions" (Glenbow Archives M-981, box 1, file 5).
10. *Middlesex County Times* (15 March 1924).
11. *The Era* (19 March 1924): 4.
12. Leask, "Lena Ashwell," 283, 321, 336–37, and appendix six: 19. See also Allardyce Nicoll, *English Drama, 1900–1930: The Beginnings of the Modern Period* (Cambridge: University Press, 1973), 485. The *Times* appears not to have reviewed *The Celluloid Cat*, but on Monday, 17 March 1924, there was a statement that "To-night a new play, *The Celluloid Cat*, the author of which is not yet announced, will be produced [at the Century]" (*Times* (London) [17 March 1924]: 10, col. C). That performance was also noted in *The Stage* (20 March 1924).
13. *The Frontiersman* (February 1926): 114.
14. *Times* (London) (8 February 1927): 12, col. C. Nicoll noted that the first licensed performance was this one at the Century (Nicoll, *English Drama*, 485).
15. *The Stage* (18 March 1927); *Times* (London) (29 March 1927): 12, col. D. See also Nicoll, *English Drama*, 485, and Leask, "Lena Ashwell," 349 and appendix six: 24.
16. Godfrey Kenton, telephone conversations with Geoffrey A. Pocock, 1979.
17. *The Stage* (4 August 1927). Manuscripts for both plays—*Crime and Punishment* and *Dr. Jekyll and Mr. Hyde*—are in the British Library.
18. Roger Pocock, "Search-Lights," chapter 1, [3] (Glenbow Archives M-981, box 1, file 4). For the complete poem by Gavriil Romanovich Derzhavin, in the translation by Sir John Bowring that Roger used, see Kenneth Sylvan Guthrie, ed., *Hymns to the Universal Divinity by Kleanthes, Derzhavin, Wordsworth, Symonds, and Others* (London: Luzac and Co., 1910).
19. R. Pocock, "Search-Lights," chapter 2, 27–28 (Glenbow Archives M-981, box 1, file 4).
20. Grace F. Wilson to Tom Pocock, Darlington, 26 November 1965. The cigarette case was presented to Roger by the pilots of Chattis Hill.
21. Guy Eardley-Wilmot wrote of Roger that "He used to be a Member of the Savage Club, where I first met him, & then when O'Dell [*sic*] died he took his place in that Charterhouse racket" (Guy Eardley-Wilmot to Tom Pocock, King Edward VII Hospital, Midhurst, Sussex, 3 December 1965).
22. Roger Pocock to Frank Pocock, London, 23 August 1928 (copy supplied to Geoffrey A. Pocock by Ken Pocock).
23. Harry Leigh-Pink, "Captain Pocock's Christmas Toast," *The Canadian Frontiersman* 28, no. 4 (October–December 1958): 9.

24. Roger Pocock to Doris Pocock, London, Christmas 1929 (photocopy supplied to Geoffrey A. Pocock by Ken Pocock). Frank never did return to England.

25. Roger Pocock to Capt. Hollis, quoted in the *British Imperial Frontier Man* (March 1931): 31.

26. In addition to the royalties, Leigh-Pink mentioned that he and Roger "spent many hours together preparing articles for the press and discussing syndication of his second book of memoirs" (Leigh-Pink, "Christmas with Roger Pocock," 6). He also wrote that in June 1931 "my firm [London General Press] was busy syndicating his memoirs to a dozen overseas newspapers" (Leigh-Pink, "Great Men of thet [*sic*] Legion of Frontiersmen, 6).

27. *Times* (London) (17 February 1931): 10, col. E. Legion calculations were that 9,000 Frontiersmen were killed out of a total membership of 14,000.

28. [J.H.W. Porter], "Captain Roger Pocock's Book: The Founder of the Legion Talks: 'Chorus to Adventurers,'" *British Imperial Frontier Man* (March 1931): 29.

29. R. Pocock, *Chorus to Adventurers*, 74; [Porter],"Captain Roger Pocock's Book," 30.

30. R. Pocock, *Chorus to Adventurers*, 29.

31. R. Pocock, *Chorus to Adventurers*, 31.

32. "Return of the Founder," *British Imperial Frontier Man* (September 1931): 101, see also 99. A month earlier he was listed as "Roger Pocock, Founder and Hon. Commissioner" (*The British Imperial Frontier Man* [August 1931]: 1). Roger was so keen that within a few months of his return to the Legion he tried to recruit the son of Lionel Palmer, in an otherwise social letter: "You're qualified & if you can face ten bob a year subscription you may like to join, in which case I'll send an application form. Packers are rare in the Legion now, & very much valued" (Roger Pocock to Charles Palmer, Charterhouse, London, 17 March 1932 [Roger Pocock papers, Thomas Fisher Rare Book Library, University of Toronto, Ms. Coll. 417, box 1, folder 1]).

33. This is set out in "Army Organisation: Legion of Frontiersmen (Code 14(S)): Charter of Incorporation" (National Archives, Kew, WO 32 10427). In that document, dated 1933, Roger is described as having "for the past two years been Commissioner of the Imperial Overseas Legion of Frontiersmen."

34. Dr. Cosmo Lang, Archbishop of Canterbury, to General Smuts, Lambeth Palace, London, 7 November 1934.

35. General Smuts to Dr. Cosmo Lang, Savoy Hotel, London, 10 November 1934.

36. Dr. Cosmo Lang to Lord Hanworth, Lambeth Palace, London, 12 November 1934.

37. Lord Hanworth to Dr. Cosmo Lang, London, 13 November 1934. Roger might have agreed with some of this concern for his health, since the year before he wrote, "I was exploring on foot all today, & found it rather too much for me, being lame & old" (Roger Pocock to Charles Palmer, Charterhouse, London, 28 March 1933 [Roger Pocock papers, Thomas Fisher Rare Book Library, University of Toronto, Ms. Coll. 417, box 1, folder 3]).

38. *The Frontiersman* (April 1935): 5.

39. *The Frontiersman* (September 1935): 3.

40. Roger Pocock, "A Fleeting Impression of My World Tour," *The Frontiersman* (January 1936): 2.

41. Roger Pocock to Frank Pocock, Charterhouse, London, Christmas 1935 (scan of photocopy supplied by Bruce Fuller, New Zealand Historian to the Legion of Frontiersmen). In an earlier letter, Roger wrote that on 30 August he "visited Motueka where I visited my father's house, my sister's grave and my Mother's maid, who cried her eyes out and enjoyed herself to the limit. Aged 86" (Roger Pocock to Commandant, Sydney, 18 September 1935 [scan supplied by courtesy of Bruce Fuller from original in Archives of New Zealand Division of Frontiersmen]).

42. R. Pocock, "A Fleeting Impression of My World Tour." In a letter Roger wrote, "One group came 165 miles by road from Napier, another 90 miles by road. This is the first unit I have ever seen on the actual frontier" (Roger Pocock to Commandant, Sydney, 18 September 1935). A version of this letter, Roger's detailed account of his time in New Zealand, was printed later; see *The Canadian Frontiersman* 39, no. 2 (March–April 1969): 18–19.

43. *The Frontiersman* (January 1936). Roger also "broadcasted for 20 minutes" on 4 September 1935 in Dunedin, New Zealand (Roger Pocock to Commandant, Sydney, 18 September 1935). Roger had been involved in radio a year earlier when he helped to compile a program for the BBC on episodes in Canada in which Legion members "took an active part many years ago" ("Broadcasting: Fourth Centenary of Canada," *Times* (London) [24 July 1934]: 12, col. D).

44. Legion of Frontiersmen, *History of the Legion of Frontiersmen*, 80–90, 215–16.

45. Quoted in *History of the Legion,* 108. No copy of the original letter has been found, and no date is attached to this quotation. Based on the Legion's knowledge of Roger and the problems associated with him over the years, it seems highly likely that this letter was also sent to other Commands around the world, although Roger's very close links with Canada would have made his Canadian visit the greatest source of concern to the Legion hierarchy.

46. "Frontiersmen Entertain Col. Roger Pocock: Legion's Founder Outlines Its History—17,500 Were Overseas," *The Province* (Vanvouver) (7 November 1935): 2, col. E.

47. "Frontiersmen Founder, Chief Visiting City: Colorful Ceremony as Commandant Roger Pocock Welcomed Friday," *Edmonton Bulletin* (9 November 1935): 15, col. E.

48. "Frontiersmen Founder, Chief Visiting City," col. F. Another Edmonton paper merely quoted Braithwaite as saying "Although his toes were lost, he still served with the force for a time" ("100 Honor Founder of Frontiersmen: Veteran, Soldier, Adventurers, Col. Roger Pocock, Banqueted," *Edmonton Journal* [9 November 1935]: 17, col. C).

49. "100 Honor Founder of Frontiersmen," col. C–D. Roger addressed famous members again some months later: "It gives us courage to know that great military leaders in the Dominions are ex-Frontiersmen, that some of the most famous men are sons of Frontiersmen, and that two ex-Prime Ministers of Dominions are serving with us" ([Roger Pocock], "Frontiersmen: The Legion's Outposts," *Times* (London) [16 May 1936]: 17, col. D). There he also referred to the Mounted Police, "which has always been revered as the mother regiment of the Legion."

50. One newspaper account noted, "The unveiling will be done by Capt. Commandant Roger Pocock…who has come here specially for the occasion" ("Frontiersmen to Unveil Memorial at Lake Sunday," *Edmonton Bulletin* [9 November 1935]: 15, col. F). The monument is registered in the National Inventory of Canadian Military Memorials.

51. "Pocock Tells Youth Always to Tackle Most Dangerous Thing," *The Province* (Vancouver) (27 November 1935): 4, col. F.

52. Roger Pocock to Frank Pocock, Charterhouse, London, Christmas 1935.

53. Steele, "Great Adventurer—Roger Pocock," 39.

54. Roger Pocock to Frank Pocock, Charterhouse, London, Christmas 1935.

55. *The Frontiersman* (January 1936): 4.

56. From *The Canadian Frontiersman* (October 1936), quoted in Legion of Frontiersmen, *History of the Legion of Frontiersmen*, 97.

57. Roger Pocock to "Units in the Home Commands…Organising Officers and Units Overseas," *The Frontiersman* (February 1936): 4.

58. [R. Pocock], "Frontiersmen: The Legion's Outposts."

59. Roger Pocock to "Units in the Home Commands."

60. *The Frontiersman* (February 1937): 1.

61. S.T. Wood, Commissioner RCMP, to Louis Scott, Commanding Officer Legion of Frontiersmen, Ottawa, 22 June 1939; reproduced in Legion of Frontiersmen, *History of the Legion of Frontiersmen*, 115.

62. For details of the dispute see G. Pocock, *One Hundred Years of the Legion of Frontiersmen*, 161–65, and Legion of Frontiersmen, *History of the Legion of Frontiersmen*, 118–36.

63. Legion of Frontiersmen, *History of the Legion of Frontiersmen*, 144.

64. *The Frontiersman* (November 1936): 9.

65. For example, in a letter Roger wrote he was busy with numerous nearby events but was relieved that Kaïd Belton was going to a particular event, because "I haven't enough money to pay the fare except for week-end rates" (Roger Pocock to Charles Palmer, Charterhouse, London, 11 March 1933 [Roger Pocock papers, Thomas Fisher Rare Book Library, University of Toronto, Ms. Coll. 417, box 1, folder 2]).

66. June Tobin and family, correspondence with Geoffrey A. Pocock, 1984–85.

67. Roger Pocock to "Units in the Home Commands." The oil painting is normally under the personal control of a senior officer of the Legion, since the Legion is temporarily without a British headquarters.

68. Steele, "Great Adventurer—Roger Pocock," 39.

69. Steele, "Great Adventurer—Roger Pocock," 40. Detailed inquiries have not unearthed any sign of the trophy.

70. "Horsemastership and Scouting: Empire Competition," *Times* (London) (12 May 1938): 11, col. D.

71. Roger Pocock to Frank Pocock, Charterhouse, London, 20 October 1936 (copy supplied to Geoffrey A. Pocock by Ken Pocock).

72. Lena (Lady Simson) was elected a Eugenics Society Fellow in 1932 (*Eugenics Review* 24, no. 2 [July 1932]: 130).

73. Hilda F. Pocock, "Sterilization in the Empire: An Account of the Working of the Alberta Act," *Eugenics Review* 24, no. 2 (July 1932): 127–30.

74. Roger Pocock to Frank Pocock, Charterhouse, London, 20 October 1936.

75. Roger Pocock to Mr. Simpson, Charterhouse, London, 28 April 1938 (Archives of New Zealand Division of Frontiersmen; scan in University of Alberta Pocock collection courtesy of Bruce Fuller).

76. [Porter], "Captain Roger Pocock's Book," 29; R. Pocock, *Chorus to Adventurers*, 253, quoted in [Porter], "Captain Roger Pocock's Book," 31.

77. [Porter], "Captain Roger Pocock's Book," 31.

78. R. Pocock, *Horses*, 192–93.

79. Pocket Diary, end notes on "Memoranda" pages, 1910 (asterisk in original).

80. Gilmour, *Long Recessional*, 164.

81. Ken Pocock to Geoffrey A. Pocock, Sparta, New Jersey, 30 April 1986.

82. "Memoranda by Lord Cobham and Colonel Golightly on the origins of the Local Defence Volunteers and Home Guard" (National Archives, Kew, CAB 106/1188).

83. Roger Pocock, "Describes Life in English Village: Inhabitants Ready for War; Fear Hitler Will 'Shirk Invasion,'" *Evening Star* (23 August 1940). The date-line for his contribution was "Charterhouse, London, E.C. 1, July 25."

84. Roger Pocock to Louis Scott, Weston-Super-Mare, England, 2 June 1941, quoted in Legion of Frontiersmen, *History of the Legion of Frontiersmen*, [145]. Roger's letter accompanied his "A Short History of the Legion" (ibid., [145–48]).

85. Roger Pocock to Colonel Stuart Taylor Wood, Weston-Super-Mare, England, 2 July 1941 (LAC 1107). Roger's continuing interest in the Mounted Police was not merely monetary. In 1931 he wrote to the comptroller asking for addresses of Mounted Police veterans in the United Kingdom to help "to form a Veteran's Association similar to those at Edmonton and Vancouver" (Roger Pocock to Comptroller, Royal Canadian Mounted Police, Charterhouse, London, 5 October 1931 [LAC 1107]). The "Coronation Dinner of 'Old Comrades' Association," was on 13 May 1937 in London. Roger is not in the published photograph but is listed as present (*Scarlet and Gold* 32 [1950]: 29).

86. Roger Pocock to Frank Pocock, Weston-Super-Mare, England, 30 June 1941 (copy supplied to Geoffrey A. Pocock by Ken Pocock).

87. Lady Simson to Flora MacDonald Steele, quoted in Steele, "Great Adventurer—Roger Pocock," 41. He was cremated at Arno's Vale, Bristol. His sister Lena lived until 1957, and Hilda until 1964.

88. "Funeral and Memorial Services: Captain R. Pocock," *Times* (London) (24 November 1941): 6, col. B. Capt. R.A. Smith was one of the men who had crammed into the little office at 6, Adam Street in the early days of the Legion, and one of the wise heads in the Legion during the problem days in the 1930s. In his will Roger left Smith "a gold-mounted cane." A Frontiersman who was present at the service wrote that Smith "referred to Pocock's imagination" and said "words to the effect that 'His wonderful imagination was bound to come in conflict with those who supposed they had common sense'—and one of the stepping stones to the attainment of this rare attribute is that you should read books" ("Bob" Darke, "The London Letter," *The Canadian Frontiersman: Official Gazette Canadian Division, The Legion of Frontiersmen* 12, no. 2 [February 1942]: 9).

89. "Captain R. Pocock: Founder of Legion of Frontiersmen," *Times* (London) (13 November 1941): 7, col. E. That issue of the *Times* also carried a very brief death statement (1, col. A) and obituary announcement (4, col. G).

90. *Times* (London) (15 November 1941): 6, col. F.

91. "Founder of the Legion of Frontiersmen dies at Weston," *Weston-Super-Mare Gazette* (15 November 1941): 1; "Town Talk: First of the Frontiersmen," *Weston-Super-Mare Gazette* (22 November 1941): 2.

92. "Captain R. Pocock," *Bristol Evening Post* (15 November 1941): 1.

93. Among them were "Noted Adventurer, Capt. Pocock Dies," *Edmonton Journal* (14 November 1941): 24, col. B; "Capt. Pocock Pioneer, Dies: Was Founder of the Legion of Frontiersmen," *The Albertan* (14 November 1941): 2, col. H; and "Reg. No. 1107, ex-Constable Henry Roger Ashwell Pocock," *R.C.M.P. Quarterly* 9, no. 3 (January 1942): 346–47. The obituary in the *R.C.M.P. Quarterly* is written with respect and is particularly full of detail, but unfortunately several details are inaccurate, though often quoted. Specifically, Roger was never a "missionary in Africa," nor did he sail "around the world in a tiny yacht" in 1908–10. In Roger's file in Ottawa (LAC 1107), there are quite a number of clippings of other obituaries from Canadian sources.

94. "Pocock Memorial Services," *R.C.M.P. Quarterly* 13, no. 1 (July 1947): 90–91. This article, which summarized Roger's activities, was reprinted, including the by then inaccurate phrase "two years ago," in *The Frontiersman* 1, no. 4 (December 1952): [17].

95. L., "Some Missionary," *Ottawa Evening Journal* (20 September 1921): 8, col. E.

INDEX

RP is an abbreviation for Roger Pocock.
Bold page numbers refer to photographs.

Attwood, Ambrose, 136–37
"A Useless Man," 38, 49, 53–54, 337n2
Australia, RP in
  RP in, 4–5, 308
  troops at Diamond Jubilee, 98–101

Baden-Powell, Robert S., 5, 95, 195–97,
  207–08, 214
Bain, Dr., 28
Baker, B. Granville, 233–34
Baker, Pearl, 150
Barnes, Gorrell, 130
Barrington, Sir Eric and Lady, 220, 354n23
Batoche, Saskatchewan, 23–24, 33
Battenberg, Prince Louis Alexander of, 2–3,
  181, 188, 192
Beaver (steamer), 63, 339n48
Bégin, J.V., 40–41
Belgium, 3, 245–48
Belton, Kaïd Andrew, 303, 366n65
Bent, Bill, 124
Bering Sea, 82
Biddulph-Pinchard, "Jungle Jim," 196,
  354n32
Big Bear, 23–24, 33–34
Biscoe, Commander, 354n18
"Black Box," 338n26
Blackfeet people
  in RP's fiction, 225–26, 256–57
  RP and, 75, 109, 141–42, 242, 349n10
Blackguard books, 31–32, 41, 75, 84–86, 99,
  224–26, 256
Blake, Wilfred Theodore, 268–71
Bluff, Utah, 154–15
Blumenfeld, R.D., 212–14
Boddam-Whetham, E.T., 120, 127
Boer War, RP in, 2, 166–70, 235, 306–07
Bottomley, Alfred, 218–19
Boundary Patrol, N W M P. *See* Thousand Mile
  Patrol, N W M P
Bowers, Fred, 183
Boy Scout movement, 5, 196–97, 207
  See also Baden-Powell, Robert S.
Brady, Robert M., 130–31, 136
Braithwaite, E.A., 26–28, 311
Brancker, Sir Sefton, 278–79, 290–91
Brand of Cowardice (film), 294
Brett, Reginald, 2nd Viscount Esher, 192–93,
  211–12, 216, 220
British Colonist (Victoria, B.C.), 62
British Columbia
  RP in Fraser River area, 113

RP in Kootenays, 69–70, 84, 88, 105
RP in Quesnel area, 128–29
RP in Skeena area, 2, 57–62, 67, 118–19,
  297, 338n42
RP in Vancouver, 309–10
RP in Victoria, 62–69
RP on Telegraph Trail, 119–23
British Empire
  RP's views of, 36–37, 102–03, 113–14, 185
British Imperial Frontier Man, 302
Brockville, Ontario, 10–12, 51, 54
Brodrick, St. John Fremantle, 167
Brokenshaw, Lt., 239
Broome, L.E., 268–69
Brotherton, Jack, 181
Brown's Hole (Park), Colorado, 145–46, 148,
  150
"Buck Stanton," 52, 53, 337n2
Burchardt-Ashton, Arthur, 300
Burgin, G.B., 92–93, 103
Burton, Percy, 184
Butler's (Sutler's) Scouts, 167–70, 352n8
"By My Own Hand," 165

Calgary, Alberta, 231–32, **315**
California, RP in, 4, 232, **284–85**, 284–89,
  293–96
Call to Arms (Seton-Karr), 184–85
Campbell, Annie, 80
Canada
  RP on Thousand Mile Patrol, 104–15, **109**,
    111, 344n88
  RP's early life in, 10–14
  RP's views on, 5, 34, 75, 184–85, 227, 314,
    328
  RP's world tour for Legion, 4–5, **307**,
    309–15, **315**
  RP with Cecil in, 230–32
  troops in WWI, 237
  See also Klondike expedition; North-
    West Mounted Police; North-West
    Rebellion of 1885; *and specific*
    provinces
Canada Life Assurance Company, 11
"Canada to Mexico," 161–62, 349n8, 349n12,
  351n85
Canadian Pacific Railway, 12, 15
Candler, Edmund, 184
Candless, Col., 236
Captains of Adventure, 165, 229, 349n5,
  352n3
Cariboo Mines, 121

Carr-Saunders, Alec, 260
Carson, Kit, 139–40, 163, 349n5–6
Carver, Will, 150, 153
Cassidy, Butch (Robert LeRoy Parker), 144, 150–54, 163, 349n15
Casson, Simon, 162, 351n89
Catling, Thomas, 103–04, 183, 344n88
Cecil, John, 243
Cecil, Randle, 230–32, 237–38
Cecil, Sir Rupert Ernest William, 230–31
Century Theatre, 274, 296
Chariot of the Sun, 207–08
Charterhouse, RP at, 298–300, 304, 320, 324–25
Cheerful Blackguard (Pocock), 86, 224–25, 256
Chevalier, Albert, 199
Chieveley, England, 325
Chilcotin trackers, 127, 129, 134–35, 346n52
Childers, Erskine, 209, 212
Chorus to Adventurers, 95, 99, 231, 301–03, 306, 320, 352n16
Christianity, RP and, 90–91, 250, 256, 319–20
cinema. *See* motion picture industry
Clark, Cecil A., 131, 134–35, 340n89, 346n52, 347n64
Clarke, Corporal, 237
Cobell, Louis, 109
Cody, Buffalo Bill, 163
Cody, Henry, 88
Coeur d'Alene, Idaho, 70–71
Cole, G.W., 130–31, 135–36
Colorado, RP in, 145–46, 148, 150
Cordeaux, Edward Kyme, 249–50
Cotton, S.M., 238
County of London (Royal Irish) Defence Corps, 4, 233–34
Courtauld, Augustine, 261–62
Crawshay, Miss, 212
Cree people, 171
Crime and Punishment, adaptation of, 296
Crime and Punishment (Dostoevsky), 296
Crowfoot, 23, 334n19
Crystal Palace, London, 253–54
Curly, 116, 151–52, 154–55, 159, 174–77, 221, 333n9
Currey, Ashwell, 11
Currey, Edward Hamilton, 185, 212, 215–16
Currey, Herbert and Frances Mary Pocock (father's sister), 115, 122, 217, 345n1
Currie, George, 153
Curry, Kid. *See* Logan, Harvey

Curtis, Lady Sarah J.
  life with Arthur, 120, 136
  reaction to Arthur's death, 128–30, 135–36, 347n59–60, 347n66
Curtis, Sir Arthur
  death of, impact on RP, 2, 5–6, 126–39, 204–05, 220, 227–28, 347n64–65
  death of, mystery of, 126–38
  life of, 120, 122–26
  See also Klondike expedition
Cutcliffe-Hyne, C.J., 85, 116, 166, 184, 199–200, 209, 341n27, 345n5
Cypress Hills, Alberta, 109–10

Daily Graphic, 82, 103
Daily Mail, 103, 189
Daily News, 103, 268
Daily Telegraph, 189
Dartford, England, 304
Davenport, Col., 247
"Death of Wakuzza," 337n2
Debenham, Frank, 261–66
de Hora, Manoel Herrera, 198–99
de la Mancha, José (fictional character), 84–86, 224–25, 342n31, 342n41
de la Mancha y O'Brien, José (fictional character), 224–25
de la Warr, Lady, 193–94, 355n8
de Reuter, Baron, 189
de Windt, Harry, 184
Diamond Jubilee celebrations, 98–102, 105
Dog Ranch, 144
Dolores Canyon, 146–47
Donkin, John G., 26–27, 333n2
Douglas-Scott, John W.E., 210
Downes, Andrew, 277, 286
Downie, Major, 62
Dr. Jekyll and Mr. Hyde, adaptation of, 296
Driscoll, Daniel Patrick, 3, 198, 212, 220, 249, 272, 303–04, 353n6
Driscoll's Tigers, 301
Duck Lake, Saskatchewan, 31
Dudley, Capt. Charles, ix, 344n116
Dullenty, Jim, 162
Duncan, Major, 235, 239
Durban, South Africa, 166

Eardley-Wilmot, Guy, 276, **278**, 279, 286, 289–91, 364n21
Edge, Selwyn F., 210, 251
Edinburgh, Scotland, 95–96
Edmonds, James, 213–14

Hanworth, Lord, 306
Harmsworth, Sir Alfred, 189
Hart, Pearl, 159, 176
Hastings Lake, Alberta, 309
Hawk, Sergeant-Major, 166–67
Hayter, Cecil G., 116
Hazzledine, G.D., 302
Heaton, G. Herbert "Bill" Heaton, 273–74, **278**, 289
"He Died in the Bush," 126, 128–29, 348n84
Herchmer, Lawrence W., 104–06
Hilton, Herbert Philip, 116, 120–22, 127, 137–38, 183
H.M.S. *Pheasant*, 67
Hogg, Mr., 83
Hole-in-the-Wall, 148, 149–50
Hollis, C.W., 302
Hollywood, California, 4, **284–85**, 284–89, 293–96
Hong Kong, 4–5
Hope, Anthony, 93
Hope, Graham, 199, 229
Hope, Linton, 229
Horseguards Parade, 304
Horses, 75, 163, 231, 240–43, 249, 297, 343n75, 359n64–65
Howland, H.H., 265
Hudson, Gerald C., 317
Hurst, Sgt., 246
Hutton, Alfred, 199
Huxley, Julian, 259–60, 361n18
Hyde, George Byron, 161

Idaho, RP in, 71–76
Illustrated London News, 204
Illustrated Mail, 2, 178–79
Imperial School of Colonial Instruction, 203–04
Independent (Imperial) Overseas Legion of Frontiersmen, 301, 303–04, 362n52
Ince Motion Picture Studios, 285–86, 361n92
Innes, Earls of, 7
"Into the Great Dominion," 113–15, 117, 140, 345n19
Inuit in Greenland, 177–78
Invasion of 1910 (Le Queux), 212–13
Irvine, Col. Acheson Gosford, 24, 33, 48, 334n41
"Ishmael," 348n2
Ivrea, Major, the Marquis of, 234–37

Jackson Hole, Wyoming, 144–45, 149–50
Japan, 4–5

Jarvis, Hal, 237
Jeffcock, Francis J.C., 120, 122, 127
Jerome, Jerome K., 93
Jesse of Cariboo, 208, 220–22, 333n9
    See also *A Man in the Open* (U.S. ed. of *Jesse of Cariboo*)
Johnson, Patrick Louis, 145, 152–53
Jones, Robert J., 102
Jourdain, Francis Charles R., 259–60
Journal of a Life in the Highlands (Queen Victoria), 15
Jukes, Dr. Augustus, 47–48, 333n1, 336n76–77

Kamalmuk (Gitksan), 57–58
Kamloops, B.C., 56–57
Keefer, Samuel and Rosalie Pocock (sister), 8–9, 12, 48, 51–55, 318, 325, 327, 332n25
Keenan, Harry, 41, 335n66
Kelly, Joe, 246
Kennedy, G.W., 82
Kenton, Godfrey, 296
Kettle, Capt. (fictional character), 116, 166, 345n5
Kilpatrick, Ben, 150, 153
Kipling, Rudyard
    National Service League and, 197, 322
    RP's interviews with, 68–69, 96–98
    RP's letters to, 170–71, 232, 321–22
    RP's writing style and Kipling's style, 85, 223
    works: "Lost Legion," 97, 166–67, 181, 322
Kirton, Walter, 184
Kitwangak (Gitwangak), B.C., 58–61
Klondike expedition
    RP's preparations for, 113, 115–20
    RP's role in, 2, 120–38, 340n67
    use of horses, 118–22, 124, 127, 129
    See also Curtis, Sir Arthur
Koekkoek, H.W., 204, 355n4
Koerner, Dutchy, 21
Kootenay Mountains, B.C., 69–70, 84, 88, 105

Lac Ste. Anne, Alberta, 231
Lang, Dr. Cosmo, 305–06
Lant, David, 145, 153
La Sal, Utah, 147
Lay, Elzy, 150, 153
Lee, Norman, 122–23
Leeds, William B., 286
Legge, General, 246

as soldier in Boer War, 2, 166–70, 235, 306–07

as soldier in National Reserve, 228–29, 233–34

as soldier in World War I, 4, 233–52, **241**

as traveller in Wales, 193

in motion picture industry in Hollywood, 288–89, 293–96

on ships, 81–83, 94–95, 191–92, 223, 229–30, 233, 253–55

on world tour for Legion, 4–5, 301, 304–14, **307, 315**

AS ARTIST AND PHOTOGRAPHER

artist and sculptor, 12, 299, 320, 324–25

on Norwegian expedition, **258–59**, 261, 361n18, 361n24

of NWMP, 37, **43–44**

photography in Canada, 15, 67–68, 112

photography in England, 204

photography in Russia, 2, 178–82

photography in USA, 70–72, 75, 82

AS JOURNALIST

in British Columbia, 57–59, 62–69, 137

in Russia, 2, 94–95, 178–82, 188

in Utah and Idaho, 1–2, 76

for *Lloyd's Weekly Newspaper*, 1–2, 83, 96, 103–06, **109**, 140–44, 163, 165–66, 183, 229, 344n88

NWMP newspaper, 21–22, 333n14

on Thousand Mile Patrol, 103–06, **109**, 344n88

for *Witness* (Montreal), 35–36, 57–59

AS WRITER

as "famous cowboy-novelist," **316**

autobiographical fiction and poetry, 54, 73–74, 86, 225

diaries, 10, 20–21, **43–44**, 81, 333n2, 333n13, 334n34, 341n17

dramatic scripts, 295–96, 339n62, 364n9, 364n12

film adaptation of *Jesse of Cariboo*, 220–21, 357n60

illustrations for works, 36, 84, 116, 175–76, **221**, 345n5

letters, 20–21, 35, 81–82, 333n2, 333n4, 333n8, 335n62, 341n17

list of major works, 329

names used by, 329, 336n84, 342n39

publishers and, 49–50, 92

songs and hymns, 21, 322

use of Morse code for privacy, 10, 32, 334n34, 337n1

use of personal experience, 20–23, 38–41, 45, 53–54, 83–85, 111–12, 175–76, 225, 255, 342n41

views of himself as a writer, 44–47, 82–83

views of press, 89–90

women in fiction, 225–26

writing style, 5–6, 207–08, 225–26, 296, 301–02, 333n4, 333n8, 335n70

FINANCIAL CHALLENGES

as lifelong challenge, 9, 13, 37, 45–46, 82, 103, 115, 133, 232, 293, 366n65

as organizer of World Flight Expedition, 273–78, 282–85, 291

earnings as artist and photographer, 37, 75

earnings as salesman, 37–38, 69, 72–73, 229–30

earnings as trip organizer, 230–31

earnings as writer, 35, 49, 62–63, 76–77, 82–84, 221, 224, 229, 298–99, 301, 306, 357n73

earnings from Legion, 182, 217–18

earnings in Klondike expedition, 120, 127, 347n55

pension from NWMP, 45–49, 233, 306, 324–25, 336n81

support from family, 37, 52, 83, 216, 223–24, 228–29, 235, 238–39, 274, 283, 304, 357n56, 357n70, 357n73

HORSEMANSHIP

in Boer War and WWI, 170, 235, 238–40, 359n57

in Kamloops, 56–57

on Klondike expedition, 118–22, 124, 127, 129

on Outlaw Trail (to Mexico), 139–42, **140–41**, 146–47, 151–52, 156, 160–63, 328

on Thousand Mile Patrol, 110–12, **111**

on trip from Calgary to California, 230–32

with NWMP, 20, 42–43

works on *(Horses)*, 75, 163, 231, 240–43, 249, 297, 343n75, 359n64–65

INTERESTS

in continental drift ("The Great Design," unfinished), 116, 251–52, 260–67